T0315913

The
Territories of the
Russian Federation
2003

The
Territories of the Russian Federation
2003

4th Edition

Routledge
Taylor & Francis Group

LONDON AND NEW YORK

First published 1999 by Europa Publications
Fourth Edition 2003

Published 2014
by Routledge
2 Park Square, Milton Park, Abingdon, Oxon OX14 4RN

and by Routledge
711 Third Avenue, New York, NY, 10017, USA

Routledge is an imprint of the Taylor & Francis Group, an informa business

ISBN 13: 978-1-85743-191-9 (hbk)

ISSN 1465-461X

Editor: Imogen Bell.
Technology Editor: Ian Preston.
Assistant Editors: Dominic Heaney, Priya Shah.

Typeset by MPG Dataworld

Foreword

This, the fourth edition of *The Territories of the Russian Federation*, aims to furnish a clear and comprehensive introduction to Russia's regions, without an understanding of which the world's largest country must remain opaque. Not only is Russia a federal state, but it is still emerging as a federal state; the balance of power between the centre and the federal subjects is not yet settled. Since the first edition of this book was published, Vladimir Putin has replaced Russia's first post-Soviet President, Boris Yeltsin, although the long-term consequences of Putin's efforts to consolidate the powers of regional governors and increase central dominance have still to be seen. Meanwhile, the diverging economic fortunes of the different territories present a further challenge to the structures of the state.

All the themes apparent in the Russian Federation overall are played out in its 89 constituent parts. Issues such as the balance of power between executive and legislative branches of government or the progress of economic and political reforms are alive in the territories as much as in the national capital, Moscow. The shifting tides of personal politics reveal the same conflicting and concurrent flows, of liberalism and conservatism, of socialism and nationalism, and the attempts to balance the need for powerful supporters and the drift towards corruption.

This book is divided into four parts. Part One is an Introduction, with an authoritative article, revised for this edition, providing a context for regional politics and a description of the place of the territories in the national economy. There is also a Chronology of Russian history and politics, some fully updated statistics, and information on the federal administration. The economic data clearly demonstrates the general trends of the economic situation, and that time has only consolidated the differences between the regions is often made clear in the text of the Territorial Surveys. This, Part Two, is the heart of the book, with individual chapters on each of the 89 federal units. The geographical and historical background, the current political situation and an economic outline are reinforced by the names and contact details of the main officials in every territory. Each chapter includes a map of the federal unit, and there are, in addition, five maps covering wider geographical areas. A Select Bibliography of books appears in Part Three. Finally, the Indexes of Part Four provide an alphabetic listing (including alternative or historical names) of the territories, and additional indexes group them according to their geographical location within the Federal Okrugs and Economic Areas into which Russia is divided.

December 2002

Acknowledgements

The editors gratefully acknowledge the co-operation, interest and advice of all who have contributed to this volume. We are also indebted to many organizations within the Russian Federation, such as the territorial administrations that responded to our enquiries, and, particularly, to the State Committee of Statistics.

Thanks are due to the authors of the introductory article, Professor Philip Hanson of the University of Birmingham and Professor Michael J. Bradshaw of the University of Leicester. We are also very grateful to Eugene Fleury, who originally prepared the maps included in this book.

Contents

PART THREE

Select Bibliography

PART FOUR

Indexes

List of Maps

Abbreviations

Acad.	Academician; Academy	Feb.	February
AD	anno domini	Fr	Father
Adm.	Admiral	Fri.	Friday
a/o	avtonomnyi okrug (autonomous okrug)	FSB	Federalnaya sluzhba bezopasnosti (Federal Security Service)
AOb	Autonomous Oblast	ft	foot (feet)
AOk	Autonomous Okrug		
ASSR	Autonomous Soviet Socialist Republic	g	gram(s)
		GDP	gross domestic product
Aug.	August	Gen.	General
		GNP	gross national product
BC	before Christ	Gov.	Governor
b/d	barrels per day	Govt	Government
Brig.	Brigadier	GRP	gross regional product
		ha	hectares
C	Centigrade	hl	hectolitre(s)
c.	circa		
Capt.	Captain	IBRD	International Bank for Reconstruction and Development (World Bank)
CIS	Commonwealth of Independent States		
cm	centimetre(s)	IMF	International Monetary Fund
CMEA	Council for Mutual Economic Assistance	in (ins)	inch (inches)
		Inc,	Incorporated
Co	Company; County	Incorp.,	
Col	Colonel	Incd	
Commdr	Commander	incl.	including
Commr	Commissioner	Is	Islands
Corpn	Corporation		
CP	Communist Party	Jan.	January
CPSU	Communist Party of the Soviet Union	Jr	Junior
		kg	kilogram(s)
cu	cubic	KGB	Komitet Gosudarstvennoi Bezopasnosti (Committee for State Security)
Dec.	December		
Dep.	Deputy	km	kilometre(s)
Dr	Doctor	kW	kilowatt(s)
		kWh	kilowatt hours
EBRD	European Bank for Reconstruction and Development	lb	pound(s)
EC	European Community	Lt, Lieut	Lieutenant
EEC	European Economic Community	Ltd	Limited
e.g.	exempli gratia (for example)	m	metre(s)
e-mail	electronic mail	m.	million
et al.	et alii (and others)	Maj.	Major
etc.	et cetera	mm	millimetre(s)
EU	European Union	MWh	megawatt hour(s)
excl.	excluding		
		n.a.	not available
F	Fahrenheit	nab.	naberezhnaya (embankment, quai)
fax	facsimile	NATO	North Atlantic Treaty Organization

NMP	net material product	sel.	seleniyi (settlement)
no.	number	Sept.	September
Nov.	November	sq	square (in measurements)
		SS	Saints
obl.	oblast (region)	SSR	Soviet Socialist Republic
Oct.	October	St	Saint
OECD	Organisation for Economic Co-operation and Development	Supt	Superintendent
Ok	Okrug (district)	tel.	telephone
p.	page	UK	United Kingdom
p.a.	per annum (yearly)	ul.	ulitsa (street)
per.	pereulok (lane, alley)	UN	United Nations
pl.	ploshchad (square)	UNDP	United Nations Development Programme
PLC	Public Limited Company		
POB	Post Office Box	UNEP	United Nations Environment Programme
pr.	prospekt (avenue)		
Prof.	Professor	USSR	Union of Soviet Socialist Republics
q.v.	quod vide (to which refer)		
		VAT	value-added tax
retd	retired	Ven.	Venerable
Rev.	Reverend	viz.	videlicet (namely)
RSFSR	Russian Soviet Federative Socialist Republic	vol.(s)	volume(s)
		yr	year

PART ONE
Introduction

The Territories and the Federation: An Economic Perspective

PHILIP HANSON AND MICHAEL J. BRADSHAW

It is customary in Russia to speak of the Russian Federation as consisting of 89 'federal subjects'. To convey something of the reality of Russia's administrative regions, however, one must begin by emphasizing that these are not 89 units of equal status, nor is there comparable information on all of them. The status of one, the Chechen Republic of Ichkeriya (Chechnya), is in dispute, and socio-economic data for the Republic are not reported by the State Committee of Statistics of the Russian Federation (Goskomstat). Of the remaining 88, the 10 autonomous okrugs (AOks) and one autonomous oblast (AOb) are, for most purposes, of lesser status than the 20 autonomous republics, 55 oblasts (regions) and krais (provinces), and two federal cities (Moscow and St Petersburg).

Nine of the autonomous okrugs (districts) officially form part of an oblast or krai. The Chukot AOk (Chukotka), in the far north-east of Russia, facing the US state of Alaska, is an anomaly: it was taken out of Magadan Oblast in July 1992 and left as a free-standing okrug (free-standing, that is, in a purely administrative sense—in every other sense it was collapsing, and the population declined by approximately one-half between 1985 and 1999; its fortunes improved, however, with the election of the oligarch Roman Abramovich as Governor in late 2000, although he subsequently made it clear that he would not seek re-election). The inappropriately named Jewish AOb, of which only 4.2% of the population was Jewish (according to the 1989 census), was separated from Khabarovsk Krai in 1991. This means that nine of the 11 'lesser autonomies', as they might be called, are parts of other regions (oblasts and krais). Many of the regional statistics available do not cover them separately.

In this chapter, we shall, therefore, refer mainly to the 79 territories (when Chechnya is excluded) that together cover the whole of Russia, whether they are autonomous republics, krais, oblasts, federal cities, an AOk (Chukot) or an AOb (the Jewish AOb). These 79 can, generically, be labelled as 'regions'. We shall not consider separately the nine AOks that form part of other regions. It should, however, be noted that of the nine sub-units, two are of considerable economic importance. They are the Khanty-Mansii and Yamal-Nenets AOks, both of which form part of Tyumen Oblast. They are two isolated, undeveloped and sparsely inhabited districts in West Siberia (although they form part of the Urals, rather than the Siberian, Federal Okrug), which happen to be floating on oceans of petroleum and natural gas. As might be expected, their local politicians are considerably more assertive than their counterparts in the other lesser autonomies, and they are also very closely linked to Russia's petroleum and gas companies. As a result, the nature of their administrative, electoral and fiscal relations with Tyumen Oblast is a matter of ongoing dispute and negotiation.

Following the election, in March 2000, of President Vladimir Putin, it was thought that he might simplify the federal structure by abolishing the autonomous okrugs and merging them with the regions to which they were subordinate—this might be welcomed by the poorer autonomous okrugs, which would benefit from greater budgetary support in a larger federal subject; however, rich regions, such as Khanty-Mansii and Yamal-Nenets, were bound to resist the loss of autonomy. In practice, the President proceeded cautiously. In late August 2002 he raised the possibility of absorbing the Taimyr (Dolgan-Nenets) and Evenk AOks into Krasnoyarsk Krai, thereby transforming three federal subjects into just one; however, he went on to state that any such change would depend on referendum results.

In May 2000 the territorial-administrative structure was modified. President Putin issued an edict (*ukaz*) establishing another layer of administration: seven Federal Okrugs covering the whole country and headed by centrally appointed presidential representatives. The creation of these seven okrugs (Central—based in the capital, Moscow; North-Western—based in St Petersburg; Volga—based in Nizhnii Novgorod; Southern—initially named North Caucasus and based in Rostov-on-Don; Urals—based in Yekaterinburg; Siberian—based in Novosibirsk; and Far Eastern—based in Khabarovsk) was part of a package of measures designed to curtail the autonomy of regional leaders. In September a new State Council was created to provide a means by which governors, who, together with the heads of regional parliaments, were gradually being removed from the upper house of the national legislature, the Federation Council, could advise the President on regional issues. The presidium of the State Council, which consists of the President and one governor from each of the seven Federal Okrugs, rotates every six months; the implications of this are considered below. In January 2002 a new session of the Federation Council opened, with a reformed composition, comprising the full-time appointees of both regional leaders and chairmen of regional legislative assemblies. Governors were no longer to be members *ex officio* and, in practice, regional representatives were not necessarily close allies of their territory's governor.

In the remainder of this essay we shall first describe the evolving status of the Russian federal territories and their relations with the central Government; then review the differences in the economic development levels and production structures they inherited from the Soviet past; next discuss the different economic trajectories that various regions have followed since 1991; then look at the differences in economic conditions among them and their greatly differing investment potential; and, finally, offer some thoughts about the likely longer-term evolution of these enormously different territorial economies.

THE FEDERALIZATION OF RUSSIA

In Soviet times Russia was a nominal federation within a nominal federation that was, in fact, a unitary state. The quaint patchwork of 15 Union Republics (Soviet Socialist Republics—SSRs), some of them sub-divided into autonomous republics and other administrative territories, was managed by the apparatus of the Communist Party of the Soviet Union (CPSU). The party's officials formed a clear hierarchy, with appointment from above; the territorial divisions were decorative. Part of that decoration consisted in assigning the names of particular national groups to areas historically associated with them. In general, this Soviet legacy has been preserved in the existing administrative divisions within the Russian Federation. The labels can, however, be grossly misleading. The Jewish AOb, as has already been noted, is one such oddity. Located on the Chinese border and containing very few people recorded as Jewish, it was more a message to Soviet Jewry than any sort of homeland. Many other 'ethnic' territories are more in the nature of heritage sites. Thus, Evenks constituted 14.0% of the population of the Evenk AOk, while Khants comprised 0.9% and Mansi 0.5% of the inhabitants of the Khanty-Mansii AOk. Even at the higher level of republics, ethnic Russians are often in the majority in what are nominally ethnic-minority territories: for example, they account for 73.6% of the population in Kareliya (Karelia), 57.7% in Komi, 60.8% in Mordoviya and 58.9% in Udmurt Republic (Udmurtiya), according to 1989 census figures.

The results of the census that took place in October 2002 were thought likely to demonstrate a change in the relative importance of the so-called titular nationalities in such regions. In many instances, the actions of republican governments had served to favour the titular group at the expense of others (both Russian and non-Russian), resulting in out-migration by non-titular groups. In addition, the Muslim population of many republics in the Volga-Urals region had continued to register high birth rates relative to the ethnic Russians in the region. However, there were concerns about the validity of the census results, and the census did not request information on religious affiliation, owing to historical reasons, as much as a desire to avoid causing offence.

When the USSR disintegrated into 15 states there was some discussion of reshaping Russia's internal administrative boundaries into units of comparable population size, without ethnic labels, but it came to naught. One consequence of this inheritance is that the 79 main territories or regions vary enormously in population size—from some 74,000 in Chukot to 8.5m. in Moscow City, at January 2002. They also vary enormously in levels of economic development, a matter that is dealt with in the next section.

Boundaries within independent Russia may have changed very little since the Soviet era, but the formal status of several territories has, however, been amended since 1991. While Russia was still part of the USSR, Boris Yeltsin (Russian leader from 1990 and President in 1991–99), notoriously advised the local leaderships throughout the USSR to 'grab as much sovereignty as you can'. He was engaged in doing just that for the Russian Federation, and the remark no doubt seemed a good idea at the time. The 1990–91 'parade of sovereignties', however, did not stop at the level of Russia and the other 14 SSRs. Autonomous republics (then known as Autonomous Soviet Socialist Republics—ASSRs) sought to become Union Republics and autonomous okrugs sought to become autonomous republics. At a later stage, in 1992–95, a number of the territorial regions (oblasts and krais) considered declaring themselves to be republics (within Russia), because the powers of republics were, in some ways, greater.

More precisely, it was members of the regions' political élite who initiated such claims. The extent of popular support for autonomist assertiveness varies greatly. In some republics, such as Tatarstan, it is strong, at any rate among ethnic Tatars. In others, a common attitude is that living in an autonomous republic merely means paying more to support a more elaborate and costly government—which is routinely assumed to be corrupt. On the whole, the most assertive republics have been those that are comparatively strong economically, such as Bashkortostan, Tatarstan and Sakha (Yakutiya).

Chechnya has been the main exception. Although a poor, mountainous region, its inhabitants fought Russian invaders throughout much of the 19th century and in the last decade of the 20th century they saw an opportunity to express their dissatisfaction once more. The first Chechen war (1994–96) ended, effectively, with a retreat by the federal authorities. The second, which commenced in late 1999, led to the central Government securing troubled and uncertain control over

Chechen territory north of the guerrillas' mountain strongholds. Official peace negotiations took place in November 2001, but international pressure on the Russian Government to halt what it presented as its 'anti-terrorism' activity in Chechnya declined substantially after the large-scale attacks on the US cities of New York and Washington, DC, on 11 September of that year, which the US attributed to the al-Qa'ida (Base) organization, led by the Islamist fundamentalist, Osama bin Laden. Putin made much of the fact that Russia and the USA had suffered at the hands of terrorists, in a reference to bombings in Moscow and elsewhere, which had been attributed to Chechen rebels. In late October 2002 a Chechen-led hostage crisis at a Moscow theatre only added to President Putin's determination to confront what he regarded as a terrorist threat, rather than a civil conflict, despite the Government's questionable handling of the incident (as a result of which, together with the kidnappers, over 100 hostages were killed by an incapacitating gas). At late 2002 fighting in Chechnya continued, at huge financial cost, and resulting in substantial human suffering.

Such jostling for autonomy, or even independence, became possible with the collapse of the communist monopoly on power. The regional élite was often little changed in personnel (one study in the mid-1990s found that about two-thirds of the regional political élite were former members of the communist-era regional *nomenklatura*). The chain of command from Moscow, however, had been broken as early as 1988, when Mikhail Gorbachev (the last Soviet leader, 1986–91) introduced the local election of regional leaders, in place of their appointment from above. This opened the way for the local party chiefs of the old order (or, often, their deputies) to transform their party positions into post-communist power.

From the beginning of the post-communist Russian state, therefore, there was a shifting struggle, between both the regions and the centre, and between the regions themselves, over who was to have power, and at how high a level. It was further complicated by a struggle between different branches of government, notably the executive and legislative branches. Friction over budgets and other matters is a part of everyday political life in any federation and, indeed, in any state with different levels of government. What was exceptional in 1990s Russia was that a new state was being constructed. The rules of the political game were still to be established in 1992, a situation that persisted, to some extent, even at 2002, when the new institutions created by Putin's reforms in 2000 were still becoming established. So far as the federal territories and the centre are concerned, the bargaining was described by some as a process of 'federalization', the making of a real federation from the smallest of bases. There are other Russians of influence, however, who do not even concede that Russia should be a federation, and who argue for the construction of a unitary state. This view is being re-asserted under the Putin presidency (which effectively began at the beginning of 2000).

In March 1992, three months after Russia's emergence as an independent state, three federal treaties (sometimes known collectively as the Federation Treaty) were signed between the federal leadership, on the one hand, and, on the other, separately, the republics, krais, oblasts and autonomous okrugs. Two republics refused to sign: Tatarstan on the middle Volga and what was then the Checheno-Ingush ASSR in the North Caucasus. (Later Ingushetiya was hived off as a separate republic and the cities of Moscow and St Petersburg were granted the status of federal units.) These treaties set out three areas of competence: those that were exclusively federal, those that were shared and those that were exclusively sub-federal.

The powers of the federal centre were predictable. They included: defence; weapons production; foreign policy; the adoption, amendment and enforcement of federal laws; the establishment of federal legislative, executive and judicial bodies; the determination of internal boundaries; citizenship issues; the operation of the federal budget, the central bank and the money supply; and energy, transport and communications policies. The list of shared powers was long, and the treaties contained little guidance about just how these powers would be distributed. Exclusively sub-national powers were merely whatever was left over. Relations between regional and sub-regional (local) government were left for later legislation and, in many ways, remain legally unclear. For instance, there are no clear rules governing budgetary relations between regions and municipalities or rural districts.

So far as federal-territorial relations were concerned, the federal treaties of March 1992 left three important unresolved problems: the non-participation of two republics; the large and ill-defined area of shared powers; and language that appeared (although contradicted elsewhere in the text) to give republics more control than other regions over natural resources on their territories. These problems were compounded by two other circumstances. There was very little to guarantee that devolved responsibilities would be supported by devolved tax-raising powers— that is, the powers to set tax rates and tax bases. Moreover, the judicial system, in practice, was unsuited to act as an arbiter between the centre and the regions when disagreement over the interpretation of these agreements occurred.

The new Russian Constitution approved in late 1993 superseded the federal treaties. This specified that where the federal treaties disagreed with the Constitution, the latter had priority. Moreover, the federal Constitution had precedence, in any conflicts, over sub-national constitutions or their equivalent. The new federal Constitution gave the President of the Russian Federation exceptionally strong powers. These were used to ensure that, for the next three years (approximately), regional governors were appointed and subject to dismissal by the President. That, however, did not apply to the republics, where presidents were, and are, locally elected. It was only in 1996–97 that the executive heads of all the territories became formally answerable to their electorates rather than to the federal President.

Meanwhile, the Federation negotiated a series of so-called power-sharing treaties with individual territories. This began in February 1994 with Tatarstan, and had extended to more than one-half of the regions by late 1998. At that time the First Deputy Head of the Presidential Administration, Oleg Sysoev, spoke publicly of plans to discontinue the practice and, eventually, to reorder uniformly federal-territorial relations. The power-sharing treaties were anomalous, often allowing conflicting provisions in the federal and regional Constitutions simply to co-exist. A number of the treaties also included special arrangements on the retention of larger-than-normal shares of taxes collected within the borders of the territory concerned. This applied to Bashkortostan, Kareliya, Sakha and Tatarstan—all republics and all comparatively strong economically (Sakha, for instance, accounted for almost all Russia's diamond-mining). Finally, these budget deals were, typically, not published.

'Asymmetric federalism' would be a generous description of the network of centre-territory relations that emerged. None the less, many observers concluded that, however shocking the arrangements may seem to constitutional lawyers, they probably helped as interim measures to hold Russia together. For much of the 1990s the centre was weak and divided, with the President and parliament often in conflict, and successive governments unable to implement key parts of their agendas (notably in tax collection). Consequently, all the territories, not just the favoured, strong republics, had considerable leeway. In practice, even in 1993–97, regional governors often defied the centre and acted as though they were more beholden to the local élite than to a President who could, in theory, dismiss them.

Thus, for example, Yevgenii Nazdratenko, in the Maritime (Primorskii) Krai on the Pacific coast, replaced a Yeltsin-nominated reformer. He subsequently ran a corrupt regime, while defying the centre's efforts to remove him, and was re-elected in December 1999 with a sizeable majority, largely owing to his ability to discredit the opposition and his control over the local media. Nazdratenko was eventually removed from the governorship in 2001, but the strength of such local power-bases was demonstrated by the fact that he was subsequently offered a federal post with ministerial status.

Until the 1998 Russian financial crisis four developments had tended to stabilize centre-territorial political relations. Firstly, the Russian invasion of Chechnya in December 1994, although ill-managed, costly in human life and unsuccessful in its immediate aim, acted as a deterrent to less determined and less advantageously located secessionists elsewhere. Secondly, the development of the Federation Council as a body representing the territories facilitated accommodation between the centre and the periphery. Thirdly, the eight associations of territories (based on the 11 Economic Areas) had, throughout 1997, begun to emerge as regular channels for informal policy consultation between the central Government and representatives of the regions, and had begun to supplement the Federation Council as an institutionalized communications channel. Finally, the Constitutional Court was beginning to act somewhat more independently and usefully in rulings over conflicts regarding the distribution of powers. The financial crisis undermined some of this progress. It brought to the fore an underlying problem: the centre's dwindling ability to provide economic help to weaker territories and to use economic levers to achieve some consistency in the implementation of economic policy across Russia. The crisis also revealed that many of Russia's poorest regions were simply being excluded from the country's new market economy, a fact that isolated them from the immediate impact of the crisis, but threatened the cohesion of Russia.

The measures introduced by Putin in May 2000 were designed to reclaim power from the regional governors by strengthening the central Government's control over its federal agencies in the regions and by ensuring regional compliance with federal legislation. By enforcing greater central control, Putin hoped to create a single economic space across Russia. Unlike his predecessor, Putin was prepared to move openly and boldly against concentrations of power that limited his own authority. With the advantage of a more compliant parliament and a background in the security service, he was prepared to attack determinedly both regional governors and business tycoons who attempted to influence politics at the federal level. Whereas Yeltsin had relied on negotiations that played region against region, Putin sought directly to limit regional political authority. He was assisted in this by the recovery of the Russian economy: the central Government was better resourced and, therefore, better able to fulfil its responsibilities. In the past, the poverty of the federal agencies often meant that they had to turn to regional presidents and governors for financial support, which made them pliable and more sympathetic to regional interests.

Putin's representatives in the seven Federal Okrugs come, for the most part, from a security or military background—in four cases directly from military or security posts. Their role is to oversee federal administrative work in the regions, monitoring the implementation of federal policies. They also monitor the legality of the actions of individual governors, and have appointed their own staff to help in this. Although they were not given direct authority over governors of regions or presidents of republics, it was intended that they would be able to assist the federal Government in removing difficult characters from office. In theory, a governor who enacts local legislation that contradicts federal law can now be dismissed.

Thus far, the presidential representatives have proved largely ineffective. They lack a clear mandate and the President appears unwilling to give them the necessary political power and financial resources to carry out the tasks that they have set themselves. Each representative faces a distinct set of problems and has approached the job somewhat differently. Some have received a hostile reception. The presidential representative in the Urals, Col-Gen. Petr Latyshev, encountered difficulties with the Governor of Sverdlovsk Oblast, Eduard Rossel. The circumstances surrounding the resignation of Maritime Governor Nazdratenko, following an extended energy crisis in the region, and the subsequent gubernatorial election, also proved a major embarrassment for the presidential representative in the Far East, Lt-Gen. Konstantin Pulikovskii. Pulikovskii (based, significantly, in Khabarovsk city, rather than Vladivostok, the capital of Maritime Krai) was unable to control Nazdratenko. The latter was subsequently eased out of the governorship, but only by means of what was, apparently, a negotiated deal with the centre (see above). Sergei Darkin (who was alleged to have connections with Nazdratenko) won the election to succeed him as governor, standing against a candidate supported by Pulikovskii. In general, the efforts by the presidential representatives to increase their powers and gain access to additional resources have been thwarted, not only by the resistance of the regional leaders, many of whom refused to take them seriously, but also by the power of federal ministries. Agencies of the federal Government report to the Prime Minister and not, in any direct sense, to the President. These agencies have resisted efforts by the presidential administration's territorial representatives to exercise control over regional branches of federal ministries. Moreover, the economic ministries have not established branches at the new, Federal Okrug level; the only agencies to have done so are concerned with law and order: the Ministry of Justice, the Ministry of Internal Affairs, the Procuracy and the Tax Police.

Russia is experiencing a re-centralization of power, but it is not necessarily the result of the creation of the Federal Okrugs and the appointment of presidential representatives. Changes in the tax law and a shift in the distribution of revenue between the centre and the regions, in favour of the federal authorities, mean that the central Government has increasing control over state expenditure (see below). The removal of governors from the Federation Council has reduced their influence in national politics and stripped them of their immunity from prosecution, and the centre has re-asserted its power to appoint regional heads of police and the Procuracy. Meanwhile, electricity-supply reform threatens the ability of governors to control electricity tariffs, and the re-investment of natural-resource-sector profits by Moscow-based, large-scale companies, for the acquisition of a wide range of other businesses, has, in several cases, disrupted what had been comfortable relationships between regional political leaders and regional entrepreneurs. By 2002 governors and presidents of republics were less frequently judged to be among the most influential people in Russia.

ECONOMIC DIFFERENTIATION

Russian regional inequality in Soviet times is impossible to assess, chiefly because such data as there were on rouble incomes and outputs concealed differences in availability that, in a geographically huge, shortage economy, were probably very large indeed. It was well-known that the biggest cities had priority in the allocation of consumer goods. Many everyday items that were widely available in Moscow were completely unobtainable in many lesser cities and small towns. Then, as now, barter and subsistence food production were predominant in rural areas, and were poorly accounted for in statistical reporting.

It is, nevertheless, clear that in 1992 the new Russian state had inherited an exceptionally uneven array of regional development levels. Underdeveloped, rural territories had little in common with the very big cities such as Moscow, St Petersburg, Yekaterinburg, Nizhnii Novgorod and Samara. In 1991 both Dagestan and Tyva, for example, had rural populations of more than 50% of the total, while, at the other end of the scale (omitting the far northern districts and cities with regional status), Kemerovo's rural population consisted of only 13% of the total and Samara's 19%. (The Russian average was 26%.) In a country where poverty was concentrated in rural areas, as it was in the USSR, these differences dictated large inequalities in average real incomes across the regions.

Later in the 1990s, as local food-price controls waned and the measurement of regional inequalities became a little less problematic, it was clear that differences in territorial, per-head, real output and personal incomes were very large indeed. They were also becoming larger over time. In 1998 per-head gross regional product (GRP—which approximates to regional gross domestic product—GDP) was 19 times higher in petroleum-rich Tyumen than in Ingushetiya. In mid-2002 the average money income in Moscow City, divided by the cost of the 'subsistence minimum' basket of goods at local prices, was more than eight times the equivalent measure for Tyva. This was substantially greater than the range from poorest to richest region in the European Union (EU), using the EU's second-tier definition of 'region' (in which the average population size happens to be very close to that for Russian regions—1.9m.). The Moscow–Tyva difference is probably overstated by this measure, because uncounted subsistence food production will play a larger role in Tyva. Nevertheless, even if one guesses at a 'true' ratio of 6:1, the range is still enormous.

A more comprehensive measure of dispersion among regional average real incomes, the co-efficient of variation, shows a clear, rapid increase throughout 1998. In 1992 it was 0.31. In 1998 it was 0.56, although the economic recovery that followed the rouble devaluation of that year seemed to lessen substantially this dispersion, bringing the indicator down to 0.40 by mid-1999, before edging up slightly, to 0.42, by mid-2002. It is clear that the regions' economic fortunes diverged rapidly from the end of communist rule. This suggests that there is a large capacity for inter-regional discord under the new economic order, and one that may, despite some fluctuation, increase in the long term. The growing concentration of state resources within the federal Government in Moscow makes it all the more important for the Government to create a mechanism to redistribute wealth from richer to poorer regions. The sum of federal transfers to sub-national budgets has indeed increased, but, at 2.5% of GDP in 2001, transfers remain below the size, relative to national income, of equivalent transfers in well-established federations such as Canada, Germany and the USA.

THE PROCESSES OF CHANGE AND THE ROLE OF THE CENTRE

So far as a territory's economic fortunes are concerned, the fundamental measure must be the standard of living of its inhabitants. The real-income measures that can be made for contemporary Russia are full of problems: neither the data on money incomes nor the data on regional price levels are of good quality, and one cannot assume that these defects produce a bias that is uniform across regions. Regions with particularly large informal economies, such as Kaliningrad, are probably doing better than the official figures suggest; casual observation certainly supports this so far as the Baltic oblast is concerned. Still, the regions that are doing particularly well or particularly badly are probably reasonably well identified by the official statistics. To put these differences in perspective, it should be said that post-communist economic adaptation in Russia as a whole has taken the form of collapse. In 2001 measured national income (GDP) was about 65% of the 1989 level. Only one region, Moscow City, has carried all the outward signs of economic success; and even in Moscow large parts of the population have been left behind. However, a small number of other regions have adapted comparatively well; typically, these were territories that began to show real growth in output in 1997, well above the marginal improvement of 0.8% recorded for Russian GDP as a whole.

Analyses of inter-regional differences in average real incomes suggest that two kinds of territory fared less badly than the Russian average: those with particularly strong reserves of exploitable petroleum, gas, metals and hydroelectric power (such as Tyumen Oblast, and Irkutsk Oblast in Eastern Siberia); and a handful of regions that contain emerging commercial and financial 'hubs' (Moscow, Nizhnii Novgorod, St Petersburg, Samara and Sverdlovsk). St Petersburg apart, maritime 'gateway' territories, such as Kaliningrad (on the Baltic), Krasnodar (Black Sea) and the Maritime Krai (Pacific), have fared far less well than might have been expected. The reasons for this are not clear, but each has had, for most of the post-communist period, a traditionalist, even xenophobic, leadership. In addition, the Maritime Krai has suffered for reasons common to the Russian Far East as a whole (on which, more below). A study by the Russian economy ministry confirmed this analysis. It suggested that the number of regions enjoying an 'above average' level of economic development increased from 20 in 1998 to 25 in 2000. Of these 25 regions, 17 were characterized as resource-processing, two (Moscow and St Petersburg) as financial-economic centres, and the remainder (including Samara, Moscow Oblast, Belgorod and Tatarstan) as industrial centres. This list reflected the regional consequences, post-1998, of high resource prices, which are of benefit to resource-exporting regions, and a devalued rouble, which increased the costs of imports and provided import-substitution benefits for the major industrial regions.

Those regions where economic adaptation has been more uniformly gloomy are, not to put too fine a point upon it, all the rest. They fall into two main categories: the strongly rural and agricultural regions; and what might be called 'typical Russian regions', mainly industrial, but without the particular attributes that have favoured the emerging hub regions or the industries that have been able to respond to domestic market opportunities post-1998. The former have suffered from a lack of farm restructuring and a massive deterioration in agricultural prices relative to all other prices; the latter have been victims of the lack of competitiveness of Russian industry and have failed to develop new activities on any scale. The natural-resource and the hub regions have in common an engagement with the outside world, either as generators of exports to the West or as magnets for foreign business and for trading in imports, or both. Throughout 1994 the per-head inflow of foreign currency into a region was a statistically significant, positive influence on per-head real incomes. This influence shows up less clearly thereafter, as currency markets within Russia become more integrated, but it probably provides a clue to early adaptation. If so, this is not surprising. The domestic economy was collapsing, but Western demand for Russian energy and materials was growing; also, Russians' appetite for imports was massive, and incomes from the domestic distribution of imports increased rapidly.

The reasons why these particular hub regions have emerged are harder to determine. Econometric studies suggest that small business, the development of which has been generally very weak, has grown rather better in regions with large populations and, therefore, large domestic markets, other things being equal. It also seems the case that those regions that have a positive attitude towards economic reform, in addition to a well-educated population, have the highest level of new-enterprise formation. It appears highly plausible that the development of financial and other services, stunted during the Soviet era, and of new lines of economic activity generally, would be easier in very large cities. In these very large communities a wide range of skills and lines of production are available. This must facilitate the recombining of capital and labour resources into new activities, as well as providing a large market for those activities.

The advantages of being a hub region look more durable than those of being a natural-resource region. Energy and raw-materials reserves become depleted and their prices fluctuate. The slide in petroleum and natural gas prices in 1996–99 and again, briefly, between late 2001 and early 2002, made a difference to the regional rankings. In addition, it is in petroleum, gas, gold, aluminium and diamonds that the Russian élite is most determined to maintain control of what it views as the serious earners. In many cases it is concerned simply to make private fortunes out of these assets, regardless of the long-term development of the business. Even where it does seem to be concerned with longer-term development, it has, hitherto, resisted any dilution of its control. The usual Russian stance is that Western money and Western technology are welcome, provided no Western control comes with them.

In 2001–02 there were indications that several leading Russian entrepreneurs, having secured their property rights as majority shareholders of major petroleum and metals companies, might be prepared to sell some of those companies to Western strategic investors, although this had not yet taken place on any significant scale. It is clear that Russia's current economic recovery (with GDP growth averaging 6% per year in 1999–2001 and slowing to around 4% in 2002) has been associated with some amelioration of inter-regional inequality, probably because the massive devaluation of the rouble enabled moribund industries like engineering, textiles and food-processing, which dominate many ordinary Russian regions, to revive as producers of import substitutes. However, the continuing real appreciation of the rouble may well undermine those gains and again lead to greater regional differentiation, as a relatively small number of regions enjoy sustained economic recovery, while the vast majority of the rest remain depressed. Russia's politicians are increasingly concerned about the development gap between Moscow and the rest of Russia, but outside Moscow there is also a huge gap between the winners in Russia's new economy and the losers from the old.

One other factor has been of great importance for the territories of Russia's Far North and Far East. This is the erosion of the enormous subsidies to transport, energy and food supplies that had supported their development in the Soviet era. Most of that development would not have occurred in a market economy; now that a market economy is being established, these regions have experienced an exceptionally severe decline. One reaction was substantial out-migration from those areas during the 1990s, and the Russian Government received financial assistance from the World Bank to support further out-migration from the Far North and the Far East. However, it is not the case that everyone wants to leave, since these regions are the homelands of indigenous ethnic groups, and there are also many ethnic Russians, mainly among the elderly, who consider these regions home. The net result is that the economically active are leaving behind a welfare-dependent population in regions that the federal Government is no longer inclined to support, a stark reminder of the human consequences of the collapse of Soviet socialism.

These, then, are (in very crude summary) the factors that lie behind the sharp divergence of regional fortunes. It is doubtful whether differences in policies among regional leaders have made much difference to the outcome. The economic structure inherited from the past, including population size and the presence or absence of major conurbations and natural-resource industries, seem to have been far more important, as have basic geographical characteristics, such as accessibility and remoteness. A few regional leaders, such as Boris Nemtsov in Nizhnii Novgorod (1991–97) and Mikhail Prusak in Novgorod, won reputations as serious reformers, but such cases are rare, and even they worked with the grain of their region's inheritance. Governors who were overtly hostile to foreign business activity and economic restructuring, as in Krasnodar and Maritime Krais, were probably capable of making matters worse, although they were usually at odds with the mayors of their major cities. The latter, like most governors, tended to be pragmatists who saw little personal benefit in making special efforts to block change.

By the end of the Yeltsin era an impasse had been reached. Regional politicians still looked to the centre and lobbied institutions in Moscow, but there was an element of inertia in this. In interviews, regional officials were apt to complain that the centre had become merely a source of trouble. Some regional policy-makers and administrators openly questioned the system of remittances of tax revenue to the centre and transfers back to the federal territories. There may have been little appetite for secession, but there was also little expectation that the central Government would do much to help a region deal with its most pressing problems. Meanwhile, the centre and regions competed to obtain revenue from the same sources (under tax-sharing arrangements), which led both to damagingly high nominal rates of tax and to collusion between regional governments and local businesses to conceal resources from the central budget—a process aided by the use of barter and money surrogates. At the same time, the centre had devolved some major responsibilities for public provision, notably welfare and housing, to sub-national levels, without making available the means to pay for them. It was estimated that in 1998 such 'unfunded mandates' amounted to at least 5% of GDP—an amount that should, in international accounting practice, have been added to the officially reported government deficit.

President Putin has changed things radically. He may not yet have succeeded in resolving the complex issue of centre-regional financial relations, but he is certainly prepared to attempt to tackle it directly. The Audit Chamber claimed that the regions received 60% of tax revenue in 1997, whereas they were to receive just 49% in 2001. This required the cancellation of the stipulation in the budget code that the regions receive at least 50% of such revenue. In 2002 the regions were initially expected to receive 38% of tax revenue, to be augmented by transfers from the centre. Thanks to the economic recovery, and the success of the new, uniform rate of income tax (of 13%), both of which replenished the coffers of the federal Government, the regions received a smaller proportion of a larger amount of funds. However, if the economy slowed and profits declined, then the regions would begin to come under financial pressure. By removing the influence of the governors from the federal policy-making process, and by increasing their reliance on funds channelled through the federal Government, President Putin was strengthening central control by stealth. If the Yeltsin era witnessed a shift in centre-regional relations that favoured the regions, the Putin presidency appeared to be heralding a reassertion of central influence. By 2002, at least, this had been achieved without open conflict, and most governors remained supportive of the President. However, other developments had an ambiguous effect on presidential power. The expansion of large, Moscow-based firms into the regions from 1999 both disrupted 'crony' relations between regional politicians and regional-level business magnates, and offered the possibility of new alliances. Many governors sought to build alliances with large-scale Russian enterprises, and in 2002 a World Bank study confirmed that the concentration of market power in a small number of firms was much greater at the regional than the national level. However, the relationship between the particular region and the dominant company varies. In the 2000–01 cycle of gubernatorial elections, large-scale businesses sought to ensure the election of governors who would promote their interests, as did the federal Government. In the gubernatorial election held in Krasnoyarsk Krai in September 2002 both leading candidates were supported by rival large firms. The most prominent cases of business executives becoming governors were those of the Chukot, Evenk and Taimyr AOks. In other regions there were close relationships between governors and corporations, for example, between the state-controlled gas monopoly, Gazprom, and Yurii Neyelov in Yamal-Nenets AOk. However, in a number of other regions businesses supported losing candidates. For example, in the Nenets AOk the petroleum company LUKoil tried, and failed, to oust the incumbent, Vladimir Butov. While governors are happy to receive the tax revenue that may be associated with having a high-placed corporate citizen located in their region, companies can benefit at the same time, by securing their own regional bases outside Moscow. Meanwhile, if governors are perceived to be interfering in the interests of businesses, the penalties can be severe, as was indicated by the murder of the Governor of Magadan Oblast in Moscow in October 2002.

INVESTMENT POTENTIAL

Throughout 1998 investment in Russia declined even more rapidly than output. The country's capital stock shrank, although the decline could not be measured with any confidence. Not surprisingly, while domestic investment was collapsing, foreign investment was small. A surge of foreign investment in 1996–97 was dominated by portfolio debt investment, mainly in government treasury bills

(GKOs). Foreign portfolio investment in Russia merely rearranged the liabilities. Domestic investment recovered, increasing strongly in 1999–2001, and profits from natural-resource exports at last began to be channelled in significant quantities into internal investment, rather than placed offshore. Although this investment was heavily concentrated in the natural-resource sectors, there was some expansion into other sectors. Domestic investment growth slowed sharply in early 2002, reflecting a decline in profits, associated with the weakening of petroleum prices after 11 September 2001, and also possibly in response to a change in rules on taxation, which reduced tax concessions on reinvested profits. However, growth was thought quite likely to resume.

Foreign direct investment (FDI) should also have helped to support production capacity, but it continued to languish. Accurate statistics on FDI are difficult to come by; estimates for the 1990s range from around US $17,000m., to almost $20,000m. by the end of 1999. In its *World Investment Report*, the United Nations Conference on Trade and Development estimated the value of FDI inward stock in Russia at the end of 2001 to be $18,579m., and the flow into Russia in 2001 to represent 0.35% of global FDI—compared with Russia's 2.6% share of global GDP. Despite its modest total, this FDI, establishing or expanding joint ventures and wholly foreign-owned firms, has a special role in channelling the flow of investment to different Russian regions. The regional distribution of FDI reflects the perceived economic potential of activities in each region, allowing for the barriers to foreigners gaining significant control in those activities. In turn, FDI influences regional outcomes: it must usually have beneficial effects on a region's output.

In practice, FDI has been heavily concentrated in Moscow City, although that dominance is dwindling quite significantly. During 2001 Moscow City accounted for 29% of total FDI in Russia, compared with 33.3% in 2000, a substantial decline from its peak level of 76.9% in 1997. Such a concentration on the capital city is not unusual for FDI in former communist countries. Some of it was recorded in Moscow only because head offices of large companies are often based there; in so far as the resource inflow goes through that head office to provincial production, the real concentration of FDI resources on the metropolis will be somewhat less. Despite the declining dominance of Moscow, there are still many Russian regions that have received little or no foreign investment. For what the official figures are worth, the 10 leading regions for foreign investment in 1995–2001 received, on average, over 80% of all inward FDI; of this, around one-half went to Moscow City and the rest was distributed in small amounts around an array of regions, which changed from year to year. Moscow Oblast (located around the City), St Petersburg, Tyumen and Samara feature with some regularity and prominence. It is clear, however, that, in a number of second-tier regions, a particular investment project in a particular year can push that region, a little fortuitously, into a leading ranking.

A notable exception is Sakhalin Oblast, home to two very large offshore petroleum and gas projects that are being developed under production-sharing agreements. In the period following the financial crisis of 1998 the regional pattern of foreign investment, measured both in terms of capital stock and number of enterprises with foreign involvement, moved away from the resource regions and favoured regions involved in import-substitution manufacturing. It is also noteworthy that, despite their political complexion, the major port regions—St Petersburg/

Leningrad, Krasnodar/Rostov and Primorskii, now figure consistently in the top 10. This pattern reflects the impact of rouble devaluation on the cost of imported consumer goods and the failure of the resource sector to capture substantial amounts of investment; the latter is partly the result of problems in reforming Russia's production-sharing legislation, and partly owing to the reluctance, thus far, of large-scale businesses to loosen their control over major hard-currency-earning assets.

Whether the pattern of foreign investment corresponds well to the potential of different Russian territories is not clear. Western investors can be assumed to know what they are doing, but one of the things they are forced to do is to take into account the obstacles placed in their way, often by regional administrations. There are, for instance, a number of natural-resource developments from which, as noted earlier, foreign business has been more or less excluded. There are also some regions, such as Archangel (Arkhangelsk) Oblast, where Russian interests, assisted by the local political élite, have served to exclude investors. Apart from direct investment, a number of research organizations have been evaluating the economies of Russia's territories. These organizations are mainly found in Russia itself. Indeed, the compilation of regional ratings is one of the few Russian growth industries. Typically, they consist of rankings of regions by investment potential and/or risk, on the basis of a collection of diverse indicators. Some of the major producers of regional ratings are *Ekspert* magazine, the (unrelated) Expert Institute of the Russian Union of Industrialists and Entrepreneurs, the Federal Fund for the Support of Small Business, Troika Dialog, and BankAustria (commissioning studies from the Institute for Advanced Studies in Vienna, Austria).

The purposes of these rankings are broadly similar: to assess the business climate, attractiveness for investment and risk levels associated with the various federal subjects. Their methods vary, but all perforce operate with official Russian statistics. The indicators used include a core of measures that are used by almost all of the ratings analysts: GRP, population size, per-head incomes (sometimes with adjustment for the still large differences in regional prices, some without), strength of the regional budget (deficit as a percentage of expenditure, for example), and volume of industrial output. Several try to incorporate measures of human capital, such as average years of education of the work-force, or infrastructural indicators, such as the number of telephones per 1,000 inhabitants. The weighting given to different indicators varies and is sometimes far from clear. We have taken three ratings that are very similar in purpose and devised a kind of 'poll of polls'. The three are the ratings of Troika Dialog (August 1997), BankAustria (1998) and *Ekspert* (1998–2000). They differ little in their selection of the most promising 10 territories; they differ rather more in their rankings within the 10, except that Moscow City comes out first in each of them. Combining the three (and assigning a ranking of 11th in the list in question to any region that is omitted from that particular list but does appear in the others), we get the following ranking of 10 (in descending order): Moscow City; St Petersburg; Tyumen Oblast; Sverdlovsk Oblast; Samara Oblast; Nizhnii Novgorod Oblast; Moscow Oblast; Krasnoyarsk Krai; Tatarstan; and Irkutsk Oblast.

This selection displays the mixture of emerging commercial hubs and natural-resource regions described earlier. They form the minority of Russian territories that have adapted less badly than most to the market, and they correspond fairly well to the rankings by inward FDI. However, the changing pattern of investment, away from the dominance of Moscow and the resource regions, and towards the port regions and market-orientated centres, suggests that post-1998 foreign investment is playing a much more constructive role in Russia's economic recovery.

PROSPECTS

Output in Russia declined between 1989 and 1998, with a brief halt in 1997. Thereafter, GDP recovered, rising by a total of about 24% in the four subsequent years. The Government hopes to attain growth averaging 5% per year in the first decade of the 2000s, although many analysts, including most leading Russian economists, are sceptical about this objective. They regard the massive devaluation of the rouble in 1998 and the unrelated subsequent strengthening of world petroleum prices as generating an upturn that can be sustained only if basic structural reforms are undertaken—not merely legislated, as was the case in 2001–02, but also implemented in everyday practice. Some continued growth, but at a slower rate (of, say, 3%–4% per year) seems more likely, while pervasive government intervention continues to hinder the competitive process. One factor in favour of effective reform was Russia's attempt to join the World Trade Organization (WTO). Members of the WTO were insisting on strong, further liberalization that would open up the Russian financial-services, telecommunications and energy sectors to Western business, introducing more competition to the system. Putin and a section of the Russian business élite had apparently chosen to pursue WTO membership on such terms.

Whatever the outcome for Russia in the medium term, the fortunes of individual regions will continue to differ enormously. Sustained convergence of regional living standards requires a strengthening of market institutions, to facilitate the establishment of new business in low-wage areas and the freer movement of people to high-wage areas. Even that, however, although desirable in itself, may not be sufficient to prevent inter-regional inequalities from increasing. Russia's regions differ so markedly in natural-resource endowments, infrastructure, location and human capital, that agglomeration in a number of comparatively successful places may well be stronger than the forces making for convergence.

Putin's evident desire to impose greater central control could help economic change. Regional governments have played a key role in blocking structural change by supporting favoured large enterprises and helping to generate barter and money-surrogate transactions. All other things being equal, the weakening of regional governments should aid economic adjustment. There are, however, two reasons for being cautious about this scenario. Firstly, the power of regional networks of politicians and businessmen may be such that the new federal okrugs and other measures, designed to give the centre more leverage, may turn out, in practice, to make very little difference. Secondly, even if regional power actually is reduced, there is no guarantee that a strengthened national centre will put an end to corrupt and ineffective government. Russia's problem may be not so much that regional government works poorly, but that all levels of government work poorly.

Chronology of Russia

c. 878: Kievan Rus, the first unified state of the Eastern Slavs, was founded, with Kiev (Kyiv) as its capital.

c. 988: Vladimir (Volodymyr) I ('the Great'), ruler of Kievan Rus, converted to Orthodox Christianity.

1237–40: The Russian principalities were invaded and conquered by the Mongol Tatars.

1462–1505: Reign of Ivan III of Muscovy (Moscow), who consolidated the independent Russian domains into a centralized state.

1480: Renunciation of Tatar suzerainty.

1533–84: Reign of Ivan IV ('the Terrible'), who began the eastern expansion of Russian territory.

1547: Ivan IV was crowned 'Tsar of Muscovy and all Russia'.

1552: Subjugation of the Khanate of Kazan.

1556: Subjugation of the Khanate of Astrakhan.

1581: Yermak Timofeyev, an adventurer, led an expedition to Siberia, pioneering Russian expansion beyond the Ural Mountains.

1645: A Russian settlement was established on the Sea of Okhotsk, on the coast of eastern Asia.

1654: Eastern Ukraine came under Russian rule as a result of the Treaty of Pereyaslavl.

1679: Russian pioneers reached the Kamchatka Peninsula and the Pacific Ocean.

1682–1725: Reign of Peter (Petr) I ('the Great'), who established Russia as a European Power, expanded its Empire, and modernized the civil and military institutions of the state.

1703: St Petersburg was founded at the mouth of the River Neva, in north-west Russia.

1721: Peter I, who was declared the 'Tsar of all the Russias', proclaimed the Russian Empire.

1728: The Treaty of Kyakhta with China secured the Russian annexation of Transbaikal.

1762–96: Reign of Catherine (Yekaterina) II ('the Great'—Princess Sophia of Anhaldt-Zerbst), who expanded the Empire in the south, after wars with the Ottoman Turks, and in the west, by the partition of Poland.

1774: As a result of the Treaty of Kuçuk Kainavci with the Turks, Russia gained a port on the Black Sea.

1783: Annexation of the Khanate ot Crimea (now in Ukraine).

1801–25: Reign of Alexander (Aleksandr) I.

1809: Finland became a possession of the Russian Crown.

1812: The French under Napoleon I invaded Russia.

1825: Accession of Nicholas (Nikolai) I, despite an unsuccessful coup attempt by a group of young officers known as the 'Decembrists'.

1853–56: The Crimean War was fought, in which the United Kingdom and France aided the Turks against Russia.

1855–81: Reign of Alexander II, who introduced economic and legal reforms.

1859: The conquest of the Caucasus was completed, following the surrender of rebel forces.

1860: Acquisition of provinces on the Sea of Japan from China and the establishment of Vladivostok.

1861: Emancipation of the serfs.

1864: Final defeat of the Circassian peoples and the confirmation of Russian hegemony in the Caucasus.

1867: The North American territory of Alaska was sold to the USA for US $7m.

1875: Acquisition of Sakhalin from Japan in exchange for the Kurile Islands.

1876: Subjugation of the last of the Central Asian khanates.

1881: Accession of Alexander III (upon the assassination of his father), who re-established autocratic principles of government.

1891: Construction of the Trans-Siberian Railway was begun.

1894–1917: Reign of Nicholas II, the last Tsar.

1898: The All-Russian Social Democratic Labour Party (RSDLP), a Marxist party, was founded, five years later dividing into 'Bolsheviks' (led by Lenin—Vladimir Ilych Ulyanov) and 'Mensheviks'.

1905: Russia's defeat in the Russo–Japanese War contributed to unrest, which eventually forced the Tsar to introduce limited political reforms, including the holding of elections to a Duma (parliament).

1912: Lenin formally established a separate party for the Bolsheviks.

1914: Russia entered the First World War against Austria-Hungary, Germany and the Ottoman Empire. St Petersburg was renamed Petrograd.

2 March (New Style: 15 March) 1917: Abdication of Tsar Nicholas II after demonstrations and strikes in Petrograd; a Provisional Government took power.

25 October (7 November) 1917: The Bolsheviks overthrew the Provisional Government; the Russian Soviet Federative Socialist Republic (RSFSR or Russian Federation) was proclaimed.

6 January (19 January) 1918: The Constituent Assembly (elected in November 1917) was dissolved by the Bolsheviks, who were now engaged in a civil war against various anti-communist leaders (the 'Whites').

14 February (Old Style: 1 February) 1918: First day upon which the Gregorian Calendar took effect in Russia.

3 March 1918: Treaty of Brest-Litovsk: the Bolsheviks ceded large areas of western territory to Germany and recognized the independence of Finland and Ukraine. The capital of Russia was moved to Moscow.

10 July 1918: The first Constitution of the RSFSR was adopted by the Fifth All-Russian Congress of Soviets.

18 July 1918: Tsar Nicholas II and his family were murdered in Yekaterinburg (Sverdlovsk, 1924–91) by Bolshevik troops.

11 November 1918: The Allied Armistice with Germany (which was denied its gains at Brest-Litovsk) ended the First World War.

March 1921: As the civil war ended, the harsh policy of 'War Communism' was replaced by the New Economic Policy (NEP), which allowed peasants and traders some economic freedom.

April 1922: Stalin (Iosif Vissarionovich Dzhugashvili) was elected General Secretary of the Bolshevik Russian Communist Party (RCP).

30 December 1922: The Union of Soviet Socialist Republics (USSR) was formed at the 10th All-Russian (first All-Union) Congress of Soviets by the RSFSR, Belarus, Transcaucasia, Ukraine and the Central Asian states of Khorezm and Bukhara.

21 January 1924: Death of Lenin; Stalin then consolidated his power.

31 January 1924: The first Constitution of the USSR was ratified. The RCP then became the Communist Party of the Soviet Union (CPSU).

1928: The NEP was abandoned; the forced collectivization of agriculture resulted in widespread famine.

5 December 1936: The second Constitution of the USSR (the 'Stalin' Constitution) was adopted—Kazakhstan was detached from the RSFSR, to become one of the 11 constituent Union Republics of the USSR. The decade was also dominated by a number of ruthless political purges.

1939: Following the Treaty of Non-Aggression with Germany (the Nazi-Soviet Pact), Soviet forces invaded eastern Poland and then Finland (the Baltic states and Bessarabia were annexed the following year).

22 June 1941: Germany invaded the USSR.

2 February 1943: German forces surrendered at Stalingrad (now Volgograd), marking the first reverse for the German Army. Soviet forces began to regain territory.

1944: In a consolidation of domestic authority, Stalin ordered a number of mass deportations of populations from the North Caucasus and Crimea. Tannu-Tuva (Tyva), a Russian protectorate from 1914, was formally incorporated into the USSR (as part of the RSFSR).

8 May 1945: The Red Army occupied the German capital, Berlin, and Germany subsequently capitulated; most of Eastern and Central Europe had come under Soviet control.

8 August 1945: The USSR declared war on Japan and occupied Sakhalin and the Kurile Islands.

25 January 1949: The Council for Mutual Economic Assistance (CMEA or Comecon) was established, as an economic alliance between the USSR and its Eastern European allies.

14 July 1949: The USSR exploded its first atomic bomb.

5 March 1953: Death of Stalin; he was replaced by a collective leadership.

September 1953: Nikita Khrushchev was elected First Secretary of the Central Committee of the CPSU.

14 May 1955: The Warsaw Treaty of Friendship, Co-operation and Mutual Assistance was signed by the USSR and its Eastern European satellites, establishing a military alliance known as the Warsaw Treaty Organization (or Warsaw Pact).

4 November 1956: Soviet forces invaded Hungary to overthrow Imre Nagy's reformist Government.

4 October 1957: The USSR placed the first man-made satellite (Sputnik I) in orbit around the earth.

August 1960: Soviet technicians were recalled from the People's Republic of China, as part of the growing dispute between the two communist countries.

18–28 October 1962: The discovery of Soviet nuclear missiles in Cuba by the USA led to the 'Cuban Missile Crisis'; tension eased when Khrushchev announced the withdrawal of the missiles, following a US blockade of the island.

13–14 October 1964: Khrushchev was deposed and replaced as First Secretary of the CPSU by Leonid Brezhnev.

20–21 August 1968: Soviet and other Warsaw Pact forces invaded Czechoslovakia to overthrow the reformist Government of Alexander Dubček.

May 1972: The US President, Richard Nixon, visited Moscow, thus marking a relaxation in US-Soviet relations, a process which came to be known as *détente*.

16 June 1977: Brezhnev became Chairman of the Presidium of the Supreme Soviet (titular head of state).

7 October 1977: The third Constitution of the USSR was adopted.

24 December 1979: Soviet forces invaded Afghanistan (all troops were withdrawn between July 1986 and February 1989).

10 November 1982: Death of Leonid Brezhnev; Yurii Andropov succeeded him as party leader.

9 February 1984: Death of Andropov; Konstantin Chernenko succeeded him as General Secretary.

10 March 1985: Death of Chernenko; he was succeeded as General Secretary of the CPSU by Mikhail Gorbachev.

24 February–6 March 1986: At the 27th Congress of the CPSU, Gorbachev proposed radical economic and political reforms and 'new thinking' in foreign policy; emergence of the policy of *glasnost* (openness).

26 April 1986: An explosion occurred at a nuclear reactor in Chernobyl (Chornobyl), Ukraine, which resulted in discharges of radioactive material.

October 1986: A summit took place in Reykjavík, Iceland, attended by Gorbachev and the US President, Ronald Reagan, at which the issue of nuclear disarmament was discussed.

January 1987: At a meeting of the CPSU Central Committee, Gorbachev proposed plans for the restructuring (*perestroika*) of the economy.

21 October 1987: Boris Yeltsin, who had been appointed First Secretary of the Moscow City Party Committee in 1985, resigned from the Politburo of the CPSU.

6 December 1988: With the pace of domestic reform quickening, in a speech at the UN Gorbachev outlined his 'new thinking' on foreign policy.

25 March 1989: Multi-party elections to the newly established legislature, the Congress of People's Deputies, took place.

4 March 1990: Elections took place to the local and republican legislatures of the Russian Federation; reformists made substantial gains in the larger cities (elections elsewhere in the USSR produced overtly nationalist majorities in the Baltic republics and Moldova).

15 March 1990: The all-Union legislature approved the establishment of the post of President of the USSR and elected Mikhail Gorbachev to that office.

29 May 1990: Boris Yeltsin was elected as Chairman of the Supreme Soviet of the Russian Federation. On 12 June, with a background of increasing restiveness in a number of other Union Republics, Congress adopted a declaration of sovereignty within the USSR.

17 March 1991: In an all-Union referendum on the issue of the future state of the USSR, some 75% of participants approved Gorbachev's concept of a 'renewed federation' (several Union Republics did not participate).

12 June 1991: Yeltsin was elected President of the Russian Federation in direct elections, with Aleksandr Rutskoi as Vice-President. Residents of Leningrad (as it had been known since 1924) voted to change the city's name back to St Petersburg.

1 July 1991: The USSR, together with the other member countries of the Warsaw Pact, signed a protocol that formalized the dissolution of the alliance.

18–21 August 1991: An attempted *coup d'état* was frustrated by popular and institutional opposition, with Yeltsin prominent in the successful campaign to reinstate Gorbachev.

6 September 1991: The newly formed State Council, which comprised the supreme officials of the Union Republics, recognized the independence of Estonia, Latvia and Lithuania.

8 December 1991: The leaders of the Russian Federation, Belarus and Ukraine resolved to form a Commonwealth of Independent States (CIS) to replace the USSR—the so-called Minsk Agreement.

21 December 1991: At a meeting in Almaty, Kazakhstan, the leaders of 11 former Union Republics of the USSR signed a protocol on the formation of the new CIS.

25 December 1991: Mikhail Gorbachev formally resigned as President of the USSR, thereby confirming the effective dissolution of the Union.

2 January 1992: A radical economic reform programme was introduced in Russia.

31 March 1992: President Yeltsin and the leaders of the country's administrative units signed three documents together known as the Federation Treaty; representatives from the Checheno-Ingush ASSR and Tatarstan did not participate.

June 1992: Yeltsin appointed Yegor Gaidar, an economist and supporter of radical market reform, as acting Prime Minister. Ingushetiya was recognized as a federal republic separate from Chechnya.

9 December 1992: The Russian legislature rejected Gaidar as Prime Minister; Viktor Chernomyrdin was subsequently appointed instead.

25 April 1993: In a referendum organized by President Yeltsin, in order to resolve the increasing conflict between the executive and the legislature, 57.4% of the electorate endorsed the President and 70.6% voted in favour of early parliamentary elections.

31 August 1993: A majority of territorial leaders approved President Yeltsin's proposal for the establishment of a Federation Council, which convened in mid-September.

21 September 1993: Yeltsin issued a decree On Gradual Constitutional Reform (Decree 1,400), which suspended the powers of the legislature with immediate effect. The defiance of the legislators, and Vice-President Rutskoi, eventually provoked a state of emergency to be declared in Moscow on 3 October.

4 October 1993: The White House, the seat of the legislature, was shelled by government forces and severely damaged by fire; the leaders of the parliamentary revolt surrendered.

12 December 1993: A proposed new Constitution was approved by 58.4% of participating voters in a referendum. On the same day elections to the State Duma, the lower house of a new Federal Assembly (the upper house was provided by the Federation Council) were held.

11 October 1994: The rouble collapsed, losing almost one-quarter of its value against the US dollar.

11 December 1994: Following the collapse of peace negotiations earlier in the month, Yeltsin ordered the invasion of Chechnya (which had ambitions to secede) by some 40,000 federal ground troops, who met with bitter resistance.

30 July 1995: Opposition to the continuing war in Chechnya prompted a military accord on the gradual disarmament of the Chechen rebels, in return for the partial withdrawal of federal troops from Chechnya; it remained in effect until October.

17 December 1995: At the general election the Communist Party of the Russian Federation (CPRF) achieved the greatest success, winning 22.7% of the votes cast; the radical nationalist Liberal Democratic Party of Russia (LDPR) won 11.2%, Our Home is Russia (a centre-right electoral bloc headed by Chernomyrdin) 10.1% and the liberal Yabloko 6.9%.

16 June 1996: Eleven candidates contested the presidential election; Yeltsin secured the greatest number of votes (35%), followed by the leader of the CPRF, Gennadii Zyuganov (32%); Lt-Gen. (retd) Aleksandr Lebed won an unexpectedly high level of support, with 15% of the votes cast, and was later appointed to the Government.

3 July 1996: Amid increasing speculation about his health, Boris Yeltsin won the second round of voting in the presidential election, with 53.8% of the votes cast. Yeltsin was inaugurated as President on 9 August.

31 August 1996: Lebed, who only survived in government until October, negotiated a cease-fire with the Chechen rebels; the so-called Khasavyurt Accords included postponing resolution of the issue of sovereignty until 2001.

27 March 1998: Following the dismissal, four days earlier, of Chernomyrdin and his Government, Sergei Kiriyenko, a reformist, but hitherto not a prominent minister, was nominated as premier. Kiriyenko was confirmed as Prime Minister by the State Duma on 24 April, having been rejected twice earlier in the month.

17 August 1998: Following an escalating financial crisis, and in a complete reversal of its monetary policies, the Government announced a series of emergency measures, which included the effective devaluation of the rouble.

23 August 1998: President Yeltsin dismissed Kiriyenko's administration and reappointed Chernomyrdin premier.

11 September 1998: Following the State Duma's second conclusive rejection of Chernomyrdin's nomination as Prime Minister, the foreign minister, Yevgenii Primakov, was confirmed as premier.

5 November 1998: The Constitutional Court ruled that Boris Yeltsin was ineligible to stand for a third presidential term.

24 March 1999: Russia condemned NATO airstrikes against Yugoslav targets, initiated in response to the repression of ethnic Albanians in the Serbian province of Kosovo and Metohija, and suspended relations with the Organization. The former Prime Minister and Russia's special envoy to the Balkans conflict, Chernomyrdin, helped to negotiate a peace settlement in June.

12 May 1999: The dismissal of Primakov and his Government was effected by Yeltsin, who appointed Sergei Stepashin, hitherto First Deputy Prime Minister and Minister of the Interior, as acting premier; he was approved by the State Duma one week later.

7 August 1999: Armed Chechen guerrillas invaded neighbouring Dagestan and seized control of two villages. Federal troops retaliated and claimed, by the end of the month, to have quelled the rebel action.

9 August 1999: Prime Minister Sergei Stepashin was dismissed by Yeltsin, and replaced by Vladimir Putin, hitherto the Secretary of the Security Council and head of the Federal Security Service (FSB).

9 and 13 September 1999: Two bomb attacks, which targeted apartment blocks in Moscow, killing almost 200 people, were attributed by the federal authorities to Chechen rebels. In August a bomb explosion at a Moscow shopping centre had injured more than 30 people, and further bombings in southern Russian, against both civilian and military targets, took place in mid-September.

23 September 1999: Russia initiated airstrikes against Chechnya, officially in retaliation for the bombings, and as part of a declared 'anti-terrorism' campaign. A full-scale invasion of Chechnya was initiated at the beginning of November, and in December a ground offensive commenced against the Republic's capital, Groznyi (Dzhokhar Gala).

19 December 1999: In elections to the State Duma, the CPRF secured the most seats, with 113. Unity, formed by 31 leaders of Russia's regions, obtained 72 seats, and the Fatherland—All Russia bloc obtained 67. The pro-market Union of Rightist Forces, led by Sergei Kiriyenko, obtained 29 seats, Yabloko took 21, and the Zhirinovskii bloc (contesting the election in place of the Liberal Democratic Party of Russia) won 17. The participation rate was 62%; the Chechen constituency remained vacant, owing to the continuing conflict.

31 December 1999: President Yeltsin unexpectedly resigned; he was succeeded, in an acting capacity, by Vladimir Putin.

26 March 2000: Fourteen candidates contested the presidential election. Putin achieved a clear victory in the first round, with 52.9% of the votes cast. He was inaugurated on 7 May, and subsequently formed a new Government, headed by the former First Deputy Prime Minister, Mikhail Kasyanov.

5 May 2000: Putin decreed that, henceforth, Chechnya was to come under direct federal, rather than direct presidential, rule.

13 May 2000: The President issued a decree dividing Russia's 89 constituent regions and republics between seven federal districts. Each district was to come under the control of a presidential envoy, who was to oversee local regions' compliance with federal legislation. Of the new presidential envoys, who were appointed a few days later, only two were civilians, the remainder being senior officers of the security services or the military.

31 May 2000: Three pieces of legislation, proposed by Putin to extend presidential powers and curtail those of the regional governors, were passed by the State Duma. The first proposed that regional governors should lose their seats in the Federation Council, and be replaced by representatives elected from regional legislatures;

following its ratification by the Federation Council in July, all existing Council members were to be replaced by the beginning of 2002. The second bill accorded the President the right to dismiss regional governors, and the third allowed governors to remove from office elected officials who were subordinate to them.

20 August 2000: Tsar Nicholas II and his family were canonized by the Patriarch of the Russian Orthodox Church, Aleksei II.

23 November 2000: The State Council, a body comprising the President and territorial governors and formed as part of the ongoing reform of the Federation Council, convened for the first time.

22 January 2001: Putin signed a decree transferring control of operations in Chechnya from the defence ministry to the FSB.

12 July 2001: New conditions for the registration of political parties were introduced, which were intended to facilitate the consolidation of national parties.

1 September 2001: Following condemnation by the Minister of Defence, Sergei Ivanov, of the reported appointment of the Islamist extremist, Osama bin Laden, as Commander-in-Chief of the defence forces of the Taliban leadership in Afghanistan, the military districts of Russia were reformed; the former Volga and Urals regions were combined in a new, strengthened Trans-Volga region, in response to the perceived heightened security threat from the Central Asian region.

16 January 2002: A new session of the Federation Council opened; for the first time, the Council comprised the full-time appointees of both regional governors and the chairmen of regional legislative assemblies. Sergei Mironov, an ally of Putin, had replaced Yegor Stroyev as Chairman of the Council in the previous month.

25 April 2002: Federal sources reported that the rebel Islamist leader, al-Khattab, who had led a faction in the war in Chechnya, had been killed, a report that was subsequently confirmed by rebel sources.

9 May 2002: During 'Victory Day' processions in Kaspiisk, Dagestan, 45 people were killed, and more than 130 others injured as the result of a bomb attack attributed to Chechen militants.

24 May 2002: President Putin and the US President, George W. Bush, signed an agreement, in accordance with which Russia and the USA were each to reduce their stocks of strategic nuclear warheads by more than one-half over a period of 10 years. This development followed an announcement by the USA in late 2001 that it was to withdraw from the Anti-Ballistic Missiles (ABM) Treaty, signed between the USA and the USSR in 1972, with effect from June 2002. On 13 June Russia withdrew from the START 2 Treaty, which had been superseded by the new nuclear arms reduction agreement.

28 May 2002: The new NATO-Russia Council, which made Russia a full partner of NATO in discussions on a number of issues, including counter-terrorism, non-proliferation and emergency planning, was inaugurated at a NATO conference in Rome, Italy.

19 August 2002: In the single largest loss of life since the re-commencement of military operations in Chechnya in 1999, some 118 federal troops were killed when rebels shot down a military helicopter.

23–26 October 2002: Over 40 heavily armed Chechen rebels took more than 800 people hostage in a Moscow theatre, demanding the immediate withdrawal of federal troops from Chechnya. Élite federal forces eventually stormed the theatre, killing the rebels in an operation that also resulted in the deaths of over 125 hostages. It rapidly emerged that the vast majority of these deaths had been caused by the use of an (initially unspecified) incapacitating gas by the federal troops.

7 November 2002: Putin appointed Stanislav Ilyasov, hitherto Chairman of the Republican Government (Prime Minister) of Chechnya, to the federal post of Minister for the Social and Economic Development of Chechnya. Ilyasov was replaced in his republican post by Capt. (retd) Mikhail Babich.

Statistics

MAJOR DEMOGRAPHIC AND ECONOMIC INDICATORS

	Area ('000 sq km)	Population at 1 Jan. 2001 ('000)	Population density, 2001 (per sq km)	Average annual change in population, 1991–2001 (%)	Life expectancy at birth, 2000
Autonomous Republics					
Adygeya	7.6	446	58.7	0.2	68.19
Altai	92.6	205	2.2	0.4	63.19
Bashkortostan . . .	143.6	4,102	28.6	0.3	66.76
Buryatiya	351.3	1,026	2.9	-0.3	63.16
Chechnya	n.a.	610	n.a.	-8.4*	n.a.
Chuvashiya	18.3	1,353	74.0	0.0	66.61
Dagestan	50.3	2,160	42.9	1.5	70.67
Ingushetiya	n.a.	460	n.a.	11.9*	74.01
Kabardino-Balkariya	12.5	784	62.7	0.2	68.06
Kalmykiya	76.1	314	4.1	-0.5	65.60
Karachayevo-Cherkessiya	14.1	431	30.5	0.1	68.47
Kareliya	172.4	761	4.4	-0.5	63.31
Khakasiya	61.9	578	9.3	0.1	63.81
Komi	415.9	1,126	2.7	-1.1	64.61
Marii-El	23.2	755	32.6	0.0	64.95
Mordoviya	26.2	918	35.1	-0.5	66.96
North Osetiya . . .	8.0	677	84.6	0.5	68.52
Sakha (Yakutiya) . .	3,103.2	986	0.3	-1.6	64.60
Tatarstan	68.0	3,777	55.5	0.2	67.54
Tyva	170.5	311	1.8	0.1	56.14
Udmurtiya	42.1	1,624	38.6	0.0	65.98
Krais					
Altai	169.1	2,643	15.6	0.0	66.59
Khabarovsk	788.6	1,496	1.9	-0.8	63.38
Krasnodar	76.0	4,999	65.8	0.7	66.75
Krasnoyarsk[1] . . .	2,339.7	3,032	1.3	-0.4	62.72
Maritime (Primorskii) .	165.9	2,155	13.0	-0.6	64.00
Stavropol	66.5	2,654	39.9	0.7	67.81

[1] Figures for Krasnoyarsk Krai include Evenk and Taimyr (Dolgan-Nenets) AOks.
* 1994–2001 figure.

Gross regional product (GRP), 1999 (m. roubles)	GRP per head, 1999 (roubles)	Rate of un-employment, mid-2000 (%)	Inflation rate, 2000 (%)†	Foreign investment, 2000 (US $m.)	
5,110.2	11,373.7	14.1	19.9	0.7	. . . . Adygeya
2,568.1	12,570.4	17.5	23.6	0.1	. . . . Altai
114,145.1	27,722.6	11.5	21.6	10.4	. . Bashkortostan
18,085.0	17,424.6	19.1	20.3	0.3	. . . Buryatiya
n.a.	n.a.	n.a.	n.a.	n.a.	. . . Chechnya
18,372.1	13,526.8	9.1	26.2	1.7	. . . Chuvashiya
13,043.6	6,110.3	25.6	12.2	0.1‡	. . . Dagestan
2,030.7	5,040.1	32.0	22.7	n.a.	. . . Ingushetiya
10,529.8	13,295.2	16.6	16.8	0.2	. Kabardino-Balkariya
2,127.1	6,733.3	20.1	16.9	1.6§	. . . Kalmykiya
4,317.5	9,916.2	20.7	13.4	0.1	Karachayevo-Cherkessiya
20,382.3	26,491.2	11.5	19.3	22.2	. . . Kareliya
14,317.1	24,591.3	12.3	25.0	0.0	. . . Khakasiya
50,914.3	44,587.4	12.1	19.8	54.0	. . . . Komi
10,467.7	13,771.5	11.3	21.7	0.1	. . . Marii-El
14,075.5	15,075.0	10.7	28.0	8.6	. . . Mordoviya
7,572.3	11,318.8	28.5	16.3	n.a.	. . North Osetiya
64,688.0	65,846.9	11.3	17.4	159.6	. Sakha (Yakutiya)
123,671.8	32,723.5	8.0	24.2	143.0	. . Tatarstan
2,616.3	8,404.4	22.9	22.2	0.4	. . . . Tyva
37,501.6	22,948.0	9.3	22.2	10.6	. . . Udmurtiya
34,837.7	13,103.8	11.5	22.6	6.5	. . . . Altai
49,534.8	32,467.0	11.6	19.9	27.2	. . . Khabarovsk
109,100.8	21,524.8	12.5	18.2	979.5	. . . Krasnodar
129,456.9	42,429.6	11.9	21.1	64.3	. . Krasnoyarsk[1]
54,791.9	25,070.7	11.9	19.0	78.1	Maritime (Primorskii)
43,440.1	16,148.1	13.8	18.8	34.2	. . . Stavropol

† Percentage change in the Consumer Price Index, Dec.–Dec.
‡ 1998 figure.
§ 1995 figure.

MAJOR DEMOGRAPHIC AND ECONOMIC INDICATORS (continued)

	Area ('000 sq km)	Population at 1 Jan. 2001 ('000)	Population density, 2001 (per sq km)	Average annual change in population, 1991–2001 (%)	Life expectancy at birth, 2000
Oblasts					
Amur	363.7	990	2.7	-0.7	63.12
Archangel[2] . . .	587.4	1,443	2.5	-0.9	63.59
Astrakhan	44.1	1,013	23.0	0.1	65.37
Belgorod	27.1	1,499	55.3	0.7	67.89
Bryansk.	34.9	1,425	40.8	-0.2	64.79
Chelyabinsk	87.9	3,651	41.5	-0.2	64.79
Chita[3]	431.5	1,247	2.9	-0.6	62.43
Irkutsk[4]	767.9	2,729	3.6	-0.3	61.92
Ivanovo.	21.8	1,205	55.3	-0.7	62.68
Kaliningrad	15.1	947	62.7	0.7	63.69
Kaluga	29.9	1,069	35.7	-0.1	64.14
Kamchatka[5]	472.3	384	0.8	-2.2	64.15
Kemerovo	95.5	2,962	31.0	-0.5	62.83
Kirov (Vyatka) . . .	120.8	1,576	13.0	-0.5	66.03
Kostroma	60.1	775	12.9	-0.4	64.04
Kurgan	71.0	1,087	15.3	-0.2	64.82
Kursk	29.8	1,299	43.6	-0.3	65.36
Leningrad[6]	85.3	1,659	19.4	0.0	62.89
Lipetsk	24.1	1,235	51.2	0.0	66.95
Magadan	461.4	234	0.5	-5.1	65.00
Moscow[7]	46.0	6,436	139.9	-0.4	65.23
Murmansk	144.9	989	6.8	-1.8	66.13
Nizhnii Novgorod . .	76.9	3,633	47.2	-0.4	65.06
Novgorod	55.3	719	13.0	-0.4	62.85
Novosibirsk	178.2	2,731	15.3	-0.1	66.49
Omsk	139.7	2,148	15.4	-0.1	66.43
Orel	24.7	891	36.1	-0.1	65.58
Orenburg	124.0	2,213	17.8	0.2	65.07
Penza	43.2	1,518	35.1	-0.2	66.29
Perm[8]	160.6	2,941	18.3	-0.3	63.74
Pskov	55.3	790	14.3	-0.7	61.92
Rostov	100.8	4,317	42.8	0.0	66.35
Ryazan	39.6	1,271	32.1	-0.6	64.97
Sakhalin	87.1	591	6.8	-2.0	63.94
Samara	53.6	3,279	61.2	0.1	64.48
Saratov	100.2	2,696	26.9	0.0	65.09
Smolensk	49.8	1,114	22.4	-0.4	63.50
Sverdlovsk	194.8	4,573	23.5	-0.4	63.94
Tambov.	34.3	1,257	36.6	-0.5	65.42
Tomsk	316.9	1,065	3.4	-0.2	65.03
Tula	25.7	1,716	66.8	-0.8	63.12
Tver	84.1	1,575	18.7	-0.6	62.81
Tyumen[9]	1,435.2	3,254	2.3	0.3	66.64
Ulyanovsk	37.3	1,453	39.0	0.2	66.10
Vladimir	29.0	1,589	54.8	-0.4	63.77
Volgograd	113.9	2,658	23.3	0.1	66.32
Vologda	145.7	1,311	9.0	-0.3	65.85
Voronezh	52.4	2,438	46.5	-0.1	63.77
Yaroslavl	36.4	1,401	38.5	-0.5	65.21

[2] Including Nenets AOk; [3] including Aga-Buryat AOk; [4] including Ust-Orda Buryat AOk;
[5] including Koryak AOk; [6] excluding St Petersburg; [7] excluding Moscow city;
[8] including Komi-Permyak AOk; [9] including Khanty-Mansii and Yamal-Nenets AOks.

Gross regional product (GRP), 1999 (m. roubles)	GRP per head, 1999 (roubles)	Rate of un-employment, mid-2000 (%)	Inflation rate, 2000 (%)†	Foreign investment, 2000 (US $m.)	
22,773.0	22,534.1	13.4	18.0	4.5	. . . . Amur
38,994.1	26,541.0	12.2	21.0	39.0	. . . Archangel[2]
18,942.9	18,479.1	11.5	16.6	0.4	. . . Astrakhan
34,526.3	23,097.6	5.8	20.9	35.4	. . . Belgorod
18,554.3	12,802.2	13.1	18.6	6.3	. . . . Bryansk
84,579.6	22,996.1	8.1	23.1	595.7	. . . Chelyabinsk
22,160.9	17,535.2	13.9	17.5	0.4	. . . . Chita[3]
85,889.1	31,163.3	11.4	21.8	82.3	. . . . Irkutsk[4]
12,760.9	10,382.3	10.1	16.6	3.3	. . . . Ivanovo
16,157.5	17,006.1	15.4	17.5	19.1	. . . Kaliningrad
17,300.8	15,935.1	8.2	18.6	80.7	. . . . Kaluga
15,462.2	39,984.9	16.0	24.3	29.4	. . . Kamchatka[5]
68,975.4	23,011.0	10.4	20.3	5.1	. . . Kemerovo
28,543.1	17,886.4	8.2	22.6	14.7	. . Kirov (Vyatka)
14,286.9	18,098.5	8.6	21.4	4.7	. . . Kostroma
15,424.2	14,016.9	13.2	19.3	0.6	. . . . Kurgan
25,351.6	19,182.5	10.4	19.1	7.5	. . . . Kursk
42,604.2	25,395.9	9.7	23.5	305.6	. . . Leningrad[6]
31,923.6	25,695.1	8.5	21.9	1.4	. . . . Lipetsk
11,328.6	47,941.5	10.8	18.3	27.7	. . . Magadan
160,034.6	24,509.9	7.4	21.8	290.6	. . . Moscow[7]
42,976.7	43,332.0	12.8	21.9	44.0	. . . Murmansk
83,456.2	22,741.4	7.5	21.7	64.3	. Nizhnii Novgorod
16,409.7	22,417.7	7.8	20.5	49.5	. . . Novgorod
58,301.8	21,217.6	13.4	22.7	157.2	. . . Novosibirsk
40,591.1	18,702.1	13.9	21.3	791.8	. . . . Omsk
17,928.2	19,884.8	8.5	19.0	42.8	. . . . Orel
56,583.4	25,411.3	11.8	18.7	78.8	. . . Orenburg
19,686.5	12,816.7	11.2	20.6	0.4	. . . . Penza
94,893.9	31,928.2	10.4	24.5	96.9	. . . . Perm[8]
11,548.8	14,312.6	12.6	18.6	1.1	. . . . Pskov
68,975.9	15,780.0	14.9	16.1	91.1	. . . . Rostov
22,789.8	17,666.5	9.5	18.1	1.3	. . . . Ryazan
28,329.3	46,980.5	13.0	15.6	250.6	. . . .Sakhalin
121,328.4	36,736.1	10.3	19.9	236.3	. . . Samara
48,595.4	17,888.3	9.5	19.0	5.5	. . . . Saratov
21,729.0	19,057.2	12.2	22.5	10.9	. . . Smolensk
123,408.9	26,674.9	10.0	23.9	163.1	. . . Sverdlovsk
17,878.8	14,016.0	8.2	20.3	9.5	. . . Tambov
31,166.3	29,135.5	12.2	19.2	25.1	. . . . Tomsk
30,286.0	17,232.4	9.7	21.7	81.6	. . . . Tula
27,887.7	17,307.6	9.4	21.9	7.9	. . . . Tver
356,139.0	110,475.2	10.3	20.8	1,842.6	. . . Tyumen[9]
26,050.1	17,693.5	6.4	23.5	1.5	. . . Ulyanovsk
25,577.0	15,828.3	12.2	18.1	21.3	. . . Vladimir
49,974.2	18,602.7	9.7	19.2	139.5	. . . Volgograd
47,279.0	35,591.0	8.0	19.7	19.9	. . . . Vologda
40,710.1	16,503.2	10.0	22.7	20.9	. . . Voronezh
37,749.3	26,580.3	7.3	20.1	7.7	. . . Yaroslavl

† Percentage change in the Consumer Price Index, Dec.–Dec.

31

MAJOR DEMOGRAPHIC AND ECONOMIC INDICATORS (continued)

	Area ('000 sq km)	Population at 1 Jan. 2001 ('000)	Population density, 2001 (per sq km)	Average annual change in population, 1991–2001 (%)	Life expectancy at birth, 2000
Federal Cities					
Moscow City . . .	1.0	8,546	8,546.0	-0.4	67.81
St Petersburg . . .	0.6	4,628	7,713.3	-0.8	66.03
Autonomous Oblast					
Jewish (Birobidzhan) .	36.0	196	5.4	-1.1	62.53
Autonomous Okrugs					
Aga-Buryat	19.0	79	4.2	0.1	64.59
Chukot	737.7	75	0.1	-7.9	66.90
Evenk	767.6	19	0.0	-3.3	61.15
Khanty-Mansii . . .	523.1	1,402	2.7	0.5	67.92
Komi-Permyak . . .	32.9	149	4.5	-0.7	61.28
Koryak	301.5	29	0.1	-3.3	60.17
Nenets	176.7	45	0.3	-1.8	63.66
Taimyr (Dolgan-Nenets)	862.1	44	0.1	-2.1	63.07
Ust-Orda Buryat . .	22.4	143	6.4	0.4	61.74
Yamal-Nenets . . .	750.3	505	0.7	0.1	69.35
Russian Federation. .	17,075.4	144,819	8.5	-0.2	65.27

Source: Goskomstat, *The Regions of Russia*, 2 vols (in Russian). Moscow, 2001.

Gross regional product (GRP), 1999 (m. roubles)	GRP per head, 1999 (roubles)	Rate of un- employment, mid-2000 (%)	Inflation rate, 2000 (%)†	Foreign investment, 2000 (US $m.)	
677,372.2	78,487.7	3.8	22.1	4,037.1	. . Moscow City
161,748.5	34,333.5	6.3	23.5	1,159.9	. . St Petersburg
2,443.5	12,156.7	15.2	16.9	0.1	Jewish (Birobidzhan)
n.a.	n.a.	25.6	19.9	n.a.	. . . Aga-Buryat
3,212.1	43,173.5	10.0	19.7	n.a.	. . . . Chukot
n.a.	n.a.	3.2	18.1	n.a.	. . . . Evenk
n.a.	n.a.	11.2	21.3	61.3	. . Khanty-Mansii
n.a.	n.a.	8.0	19.9	n.a.	. . Komi-Permyak
n.a.	n.a.	12.5	31.3	0.3	. . . . Koryak
n.a.	n.a.	10.9	25.1	346.0‡	. . . . Nenets
n.a.	n.a.	5.7	22.0	n.a.	Taimyr (Dolgan-Nenets)
n.a.	n.a.	8.9	18.7	0.0	. . Ust-Orda Buryat
n.a.	n.a.	7.9	18.7	102.9	. . Yamal-Nenets
4,157,278.9	28,546.9	10.5	20.2	10,958.3	. **Russian Federation**

† Percentage change in the Consumer Price Index, Dec.–Dec.
‡ 1999 figure.

RUSSIAN CURRENCY AND EXCHANGE RATES

Monetary Units
    100 kopeks = 1 Russian rouble (rubl or ruble).

Sterling, Dollar and Euro Equivalents (30 September 2002)
    £1 = 49.469 roubles;
    US $1 = 31.636 roubles;
    €1 = 31.193 roubles;
    1,000 roubles = £20.21 = $31.61 = €32.06.

Average Exchange Rates (roubles per US dollar)
1999	24.6199
2000	28.1292
2001	29.1685

On 1 January 1998 the new rouble, equivalent to 1,000 of the former units, was introduced. Figures in this book are expressed in terms of new roubles unless otherwise indicated.

RUSSIAN INFLATION

The annual increase in consumer prices in the Russian Federation as a whole, according to official figures, for the year to December was:
1999	36.5%
2000	20.2%
2001	18.6%

For the same years the IMF cites average annual inflation rates of 85.7% in 1999, 20.8% in 2000 and 21.5% in 2001.

The Government of the Russian Federation

(December 2002)

According to the Constitution of December 1993, the Russian Federation is a democratic, federative, multi-ethnic republic, in which state power is divided between the executive, the legislature and the judiciary, which are independent of one another. The President of the Russian Federation is Head of State and Commander-in-Chief of the Armed Forces. The President, who wields considerable executive authority, is elected for a term of four years by universal direct suffrage. The President appoints the Chairman (Prime Minister) of the Government, but the cabinet must be approved by the legislature. Supreme legislative power is vested in a bicameral Federal Assembly.

There are 89 members (federal territorial units) of the Russian Federation. The recognized territories consist of 21 autonomous republics, six krais (provinces), 49 oblasts (regions), two cities of federal status, one autonomous oblast and 10 autonomous okrugs (districts). Largely based on the old Soviet divisions, their status as constituent members of the Federation began to be regularized by the so-called Federation Treaty of 31 March 1992. These three documents provided for a union of 20 republics (16 of which had been Autonomous Soviet Socialist Republics—ASSRs under the old regime, and four of which were autonomous oblasts), six krais and one autonomous oblast. The 10 autonomous okrugs remained under the jurisdiction of the krai or oblast within which they were located (a situation which largely continued thereafter) but, as federal units, were raised to the same status as oblasts and krais. The former republic of Chechno-Ingushetiya was divided into two republics in June 1992, by the formal recognition of a republic of Ingushetiya. Moscow and St Petersburg subsequently assumed the status of federal cities.

Under the terms of the 1992 treaties, republics were granted far wider-reaching powers than the other federal units, specifically over the use of natural resources and land. They consequently represent autonomous states within the Russian Federation, as opposed to being merely administrative units of a unitary state. The exact delimitation of powers remained controversial and, often, modified by bilateral treaty between a territory and the central authorities. This process began in 1995 with treaties with seven republics and one oblast, but by the end of 1998 more than one-half of all the territories had signed such agreements. In March 1996 the precise terms of the delimitation of jurisdiction and powers between federal and regional authorities was decreed; no treaty could change the status of a federal unit, threaten the territorial integrity of the Russian Federation or violate the terms of the federal Constitution.

Autonomous republics, autonomous okrugs and the autonomous oblast are ethnically defined, while krais and oblasts are defined on territorial grounds. One of Vladimir Putin's earliest actions after his election as federal President in March 2000 was to group the federal subjects into seven large Federal Okrugs (see the index of territories by okrug in Part Four). These seven districts, broadly similar to the organizational units of the Federation's armed forces in existence at that time, are the Central Federal Okrug (based in the capital, Moscow), the North-Western Federal Okrug (St Petersburg), the Southern (initially named North Caucasus) Federal Okrug (Rostov-on-Don), the Volga Federal Okrug (Nizhnii Novgorod), the Urals Federal Okrug (Yekaterinburg), the Siberian Federal Okrug (Novosibirsk) and the Far Eastern Federal Okrug (Khabarovsk). Additionally, each of the federal units is grouped into one of 11 economic areas (see the index of territories by area in Part Four). These are the Central Economic Area, the Central Chernozem (Black Earth) Economic Area, the East Siberian Economic Area, the Far Eastern (sometimes known as the Pacific) Economic Area, the North Caucasus Economic Area, the North-Western Economic Area, the Northern Economic Area, the Urals Economic Area, the Volga Economic Area, the Volga-Vyatka Economic Area and the West Siberian Economic Area.

Of the 89 members of the Russian Federation, the 21 republics are each administered by a president and/or prime minister. The republics each have their own governments and ministries. The remaining federal units are governed by a local administration, the head (governor) of which is the highest official in the territory, and a representative assembly (usually known as a soviet or duma). Governors are able to veto regional legislation, although their vetoes may be overridden by a two-thirds' parliamentary majority. The federal legislature, which created the post of governor in August 1991, intended that the official be elected by popular vote. The federal President, Boris Yeltsin, however, secured an agreement that the governors be appointed. In many regions conflict subsequently arose between the executive and legislative bodies, as the presidential appointees encountered much resistance from the communist-dominated assemblies. In those cases where a vote of 'no confidence' was passed in the governor, elections were permitted. (This occurred in seven oblasts and one krai in December 1992.) Following President Yeltsin's dissolution of the Russian legislature in September 1993, and parliament's violent resistance, it was announced that all heads of local administrations would, henceforth, be appointed and dismissed by presidential decree. In response to increasing pressure, however, this ruling was relaxed in December 1995, when gubernatorial elections were held in one krai and 11 oblasts. From the late 1990s elected governors became the norm in all federal subjects.

Presidential Representative in the Central Federal Okrug: Lt-Gen. GEORGII S. POLTAVCHENKO; 103132 Moscow, Nikolskii per. 6; tel. (095) 206-12-76; e-mail malakhov_dm@gov.ru; internet www.cfo-regions.ru.

Presidential Representative in the North-Western Federal Okrug: Col-Gen. VIKTOR V. CHERKESOV; 193015 St Petersburg, ul. Shpalernaya 47; tel. (812) 326-69-84; fax (812) 326-64-84.

Presidential Representative in the Southern Federal Okrug: Col-Gen. VIKTOR G. KAZANTSEV; 344006 Rostov-on-Don, ul. B. Sadovaya 73; tel. (8632) 44-16-16; fax (8632) 40-39-40; e-mail polpred@polpred-ug.donpac.ru.

Presidential Representative in the Volga Federal Okrug: SERGEI V. KIRIYENKO; 620031 Sverdlovsk obl., Yekaterinburg, pl. Oktyabrskaya 3; tel. (3432) 77-18-96; e-mail info@kirienko.ru; internet www.pfo.ru.

Presidential Representative in the Urals Federal Okrug: Col-Gen. PETR M. LATYSHEV; 603082 Nizhnii Novgorod, Kreml, kor. 1; tel. (8312) 31-46-07; fax (8312) 31-47-51; e-mail support@uralfo.ru; internet www.uralfo.ru.

Presidential Representative in the Siberian Federal Okrug: LEONID V. DRACHEVSKII; 630091 Novosibirsk, ul. Derzhavina 18/120; tel. (3832) 20-17-56; fax (3832) 20-13-90; e-mail sibokrug@online.sinor.ru; internet www.sfo.nsk.su.

Presidential Representative in the Far Eastern Federal Okrug: Lt-Gen. KONSTANTIN B. PULIKOVSKII; 680030 Khabarovsk, ul. Sheronova 22; tel. (4212) 31-30-44.

Head of State

President of the Russian Federation: VLADIMIR V. PUTIN (elected President 26 March 2000; inaugurated 7 May).

PRESIDENTIAL ADMINISTRATION

Office of the President: 103073 Moscow, Kremlin; tel. (095) 925-35-81; fax (095) 206-51-73; e-mail president@gov.ru; internet president.kremlin.ru.

The Government

Chairman (Prime Minister): MIKHAIL M. KASYANOV.

Deputy Chairman and Minister of Agriculture and Foodstuffs: ALEKSEI V. GORDEYEV.

Deputy Chairman and Minister of Finance: ALEKSEI L. KUDRIN.

Deputy Chairmen: VIKTOR B. KHRISTENKO, VALENTINA I. MATVIYENKO.

Minister for Antimonopoly Policy and Support for Entrepreneurship: ILYA A. YUZHANOV.

Minister for the Social and Economic Development of Chechnya: STANISLAV ILYASOV.

Minister of Civil Defence, Emergencies and Clean-up Operations: Lt-Gen. SERGEI K. SHOIGU.

Minister of Communications and Information Technology: LEONID D. REYMAN.

Minister of Culture: MIKHAIL YE. SHVYDKOI.

Minister of Defence: SERGEI B. IVANOV.

Minister of Economic Development and Trade: GERMAN O. GREF.

Minister of Education and Vocational Training: VLADIMIR M. FILIPPOV.

Minister of Energy: IGOR KH. YUSUFOV.

Minister of Foreign Affairs: IGOR S. IVANOV.

Minister of Health: YURII L. SHEVCHENKO.

Minister of Industry, Science and Technology: ILYA I. KLEBANOV.

Minister of Internal Affairs: BORIS V. GRYZLOV.

Minister of Justice: YURII YA. CHAIKA.

Minister of Labour and Social Development: ALEKSANDR P. POCHINOK.

Minister of Natural Resources: VITALII G. ARTYUKHOV.

Minister of Nuclear Energy: ALEKSANDR YU. RUMYANTSEV.

Minister of the Press, Broadcasting and Mass Media: MIKHAIL YU. LESIN.

Minister of Railways: GENNADII M. FADEYEV.

Minister of State Property: FARIT R. GAZIZULLIN.

Minister of Transport: SERGEI O. FRANK.

Minister of Taxes and Levies: GENNADII I. BUKAYEV.

Head of the Presidential Administration and Minister without Portfolio: IGOR I. SHUVALOV.

Minister without Portfolio, with responsibility for Nationalities Policy: VLADIMIR YU. ZORIN.

MINISTRIES

Office of the President: 103073 Moscow, Kremlin; tel. (095) 925-35-81; fax (095) 206-51-73; e-mail president@gov.ru; internet president.kremlin.ru.

Office of the Government: 103274 Moscow, Krasnopresnenskaya nab. 2; tel. (095) 205-57-35; fax (095) 205-42-19; internet www.pravitelstvo.gov.ru.

Ministry of Agriculture and Foodstuffs: 107139 Moscow, Orlikov per. 1/11; tel. (095) 207-83-62; fax (095) 207-80-00; e-mail info@aris.ru; internet www.aris.ru.

Ministry for Antimonopoly Policy and Support for Entrepreneurship: 123995 Moscow, ul. Sadovaya-Kudrinskaya 11; tel. (095) 254-74-00; fax (095) 254-75-21; e-mail gak1@infpres.ru; internet www.maprus.ru.

Ministry of Civil Defence, Emergencies and Clean-up Operations: 103012 Moscow, Teatralnyi proyezd 3; tel. (095) 926-39-01; fax (095) 924-19-46; e-mail pressa@emercom.gov.ru; internet www.emercom.gov.ru.

Ministry of Communications and Information Technology: 103375 Moscow, ul. Tverskaya 7; tel. (095) 292-71-44; fax (095) 292-74-55; internet www.minsvyaz.ru.

Ministry of Culture: 103074 Moscow, Kitaigorodskii proyezd 7; tel. (095) 925-11-95; fax (095) 928-17-91; e-mail root@mincult.isf.ru; internet www.mincult.isf.ru.

Ministry of Defence: 103160 Moscow, ul. Znamenka 19; tel. (095) 296-84-37; fax (095) 296-84-36; internet www.mil.ru.

Ministry of Economic Development and Trade: 125993 Moscow, ul. Tverskaya-Yamskaya 1/3, POB A-47; tel. (095) 200-03-53; e-mail presscenter@economy.gov.ru; internet www.economy.gov.ru.

Ministry of Education and Vocational Training: 113833 Moscow, ul. Lyusinovskaya 51; tel. (095) 237-76-75; fax (095) 237-83-81; e-mail mail@ministry.ru; internet www.ed.gov.ru.

Ministry of Energy: 103074 Moscow, Kitaigorodskii proyezd 7/191; tel. (095) 220-42-88; fax (095) 220-56-56; e-mail abs@cdu.oilnet.ru; internet www.mte.gov.ru.

Ministry of Finance: 103097 Moscow, ul. Ilinka 9; tel. (095) 298-91-01; fax (095) 925-08-89; internet www.minfin.ru.

Ministry of Foreign Affairs: 121200 Moscow, Smolenskaya-Sennaya pl. 32/34; tel. (095) 244-16-06; fax (095) 230-21-30; e-mail ministry@mid.ru; internet www.mid.ru.

Ministry of Health: 101431 Moscow, Rakhmanovskii per. 3; tel. (095) 927-28-48; fax (095) 928-58-15; e-mail minzdrav@cnt.ru; internet www.minzdrav-rf.ru.

Ministry of Industry, Science and Technology: 125889 Moscow, Miusskaya pl. 3, POB A-47; tel. (095) 229-11-92; fax (095) 229-55-49; e-mail info@mpnt.gov.ru; internet www.minprom.ru.

Ministry of Internal Affairs: 117049 Moscow, ul. Zhitnaya 16; tel. (095) 239-74-26; fax (095) 293-59-98; e-mail uimvd@mvdinform.ru; internet www.mvdinform.ru.

Ministry of Justice: 109830 Moscow, ul. Vorontsovo Pole 4A; tel. (095) 206-05-54; fax (095) 916-29-03; internet www.minjust.ru.

Ministry of Labour and Social Development: 103706 Moscow, Birzhevaya pl. 1; tel. (095) 928-06-83; fax (095) 230-24-07; e-mail press_mt@zanas.ru; internet www.mintrud.ru.

Ministry of Natural Resources: 123812 Moscow, ul. B. Gruzinskaya 4/6; tel. (095) 254-48-00; fax (095) 254-43-10; e-mail admin@mnr.gov.ru; internet www.mnr.gov.ru.

Ministry of Nuclear Energy: 101000 Moscow, ul. B. Ordynka 24/26; tel. (095) 239-45-45; fax (095) 230-24-20; e-mail info@minatom.ru; internet www.minatom.ru.

Ministry of the Press, Broadcasting and Mass Media: 127994 Moscow, Strastnoi bulv. 5/51, POB 1; tel. (095) 950-64-97; fax (095) 200-22-81; internet www.mptr.ru.

Ministry of Railways: 107174 Moscow, ul. Novobasmannaya 2; tel. (095) 262-10-02; e-mail info@mps.ru; internet www.mps.ru.

Ministry of State Property: 103685 Moscow, Nikolskii per. 9; tel. (095) 298-75-62; fax (095) 206-11-19; e-mail mgi1@ftcenter.ru; internet www.mgi.ru.

Ministry of Taxes and Levies: 103381 Moscow, ul. Neglinnaya 23; tel. (095) 200-38-48; fax (095) 200-11-78; e-mail mns@nalog.ru; internet www.nalog.ru.

Ministry of Transport: 101433 Moscow, ul. Sadovaya-Samotechnaya 10; tel. (095) 200-08-09; fax (095) 200-33-56; e-mail mcc@morflot.ru; internet www.mintrans.ru.

Federal Assembly

The Federal Assembly of the Russian Federation is the bicameral national parliament. Its upper chamber, the Federation Council, comprises 178 deputies, two appointed from each of the federal units, representing the executive and legislative branches of power in each territory. The lower chamber is the State Duma, with 450 deputies elected for a four-year term (the last general election was held on 19 December 1999).

Chairman of the Federation Council: SERGEI M. MIRONOV; 103426 Moscow, ul. B. Dmitrovka 26; tel. (095) 203-90-74; fax (095) 203-46-17; e-mail post_sf@gov.ru; internet www.council.gov.ru.

Chairman of the State Duma: GENNADII N. SELEZNEV; 103265 Moscow, Okhotnyi ryad 1; tel. (095) 292-83-10; fax (095) 292-94-64; internet www.duma.ru.

State Council

The State Council is a consultative body, established in September 2000, and intended to improve co-ordination between federal and regional government, and to strengthen federal control in the regions. The membership of the Council comprises the leaders of the 89 federal subjects and the President of the Russian Federation, who chairs the Council. The President appoints a presidium, comprising seven members of the Council, who serve for a period of six months.

PART TWO
Territorial Surveys

Republics
Adygeya (9)
Altai Republic (71)
Bashkortostan (24)
Chechnya (2)
Chuvashiya (26)
Dagestan (1)
Ingushetiya (3)
Kabardino-Balkariya (6)
Kalmykiya (8)
Karachayevo-Cherkessiya (7)
Kareliya (58)
Komi Republic (48)
Marii-El (37)
Mordoviya (27)
North Osetiya (4)
Tatarstan (25)
Udmurtiya (38)

Krais (Provinces)
Altai (70)
Krasnodar (10)
Stavropol (5)

Oblasts (Regions)
Archangel (60)
Astrakhan (11)
Belgorod (17)
Bryansk (31)
Chelyabinsk (43)
Ivanovo (35)
Kaliningrad (57)
Kaluga (32)
Kemerovo (69)
Kirov (39)
Kostroma (50)
Kurgan (44)
Kursk (18)
Leningrad (56)
Lipetsk (19)
Moscow (33)

Murmansk (59)
Nizhnii Novgorod (36)
Novgorod (55)
Novosibirsk (67)
Omsk (66)
Orel (30)
Orenburg (15)
Penza (21)
Perm (40)
Pskov (54)
Rostov (12)
Ryazan (28)
Samara (23)
Saratov (14)
Smolensk (53)
Sverdlovsk (42)
Tambov (20)
Tomsk (68)

Tula (29)
Tver (52)
Tyumen (45)
Ulyanovsk (22)
Vladimir (34)
Volgograd (13)
Vologda (49)
Voronezh (16)
Yaroslavl (51)

Cities of Oblast Status
Moscow
St Petersburg

Autonomous Okrugs (Districts)
Khanty-Mansii (46)
Komi-Permyak (41)
Nenets (61)
Yamal-Nenets (47)

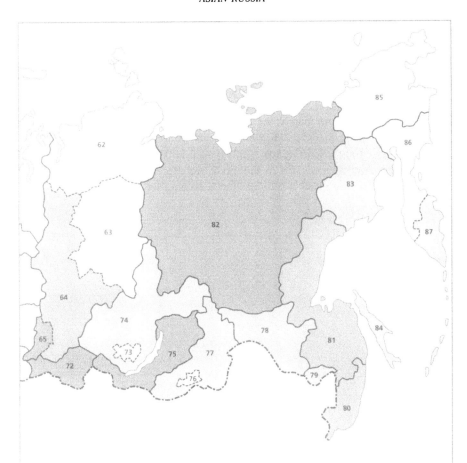

Republics
Buryatiya (75)
Khakasiya (65)
Tyva (72)
Republic of Sakha (82)
(Yakutiya)

Krais (Provinces)
Khabarovsk (81)
Krasnoyarsk (64)
Maritime (Primorskii) (80)

Oblasts (Regions)
Amur (78)
Chita (77)
Irkutsk (74)
Kamchatka (87)
Magadan (83)
Sakhalin (84)

Autonomous Oblast
Jewish Autonomous Oblast (79)

**Autonomous
Okrugs (Districts)**
Aga-Buryat (76)
Chukot (85)
Evenk (63)
Koryak (86)
Taimyr (Dolgan-Nenets) (62)
Ust-Orda Buryat (73)

Notes

The maps distinguish between international borders (dots and dashes), borders between separate federal units (bold unbroken line) and borders of units that are formally part of another territory. Maps of European and Asian Russia are included on the two preceding pages. For Krasnoyarsk Krai, Archangel Oblast and Tyumen Oblast, the map at the beginning of the chapter illustrates the 'core' region only—for the territory as a whole, see the extra maps at the end of Part Two.

On 1 January 1998 a new rouble, equivalent to 1,000 of the former units, was introduced. Any figures cited in this book are expressed in terms of the new rouble, unless otherwise indicated.

AUTONOMOUS REPUBLICS

Republic of Adygeya

The Republic of Adygeya (Adygheya) is situated in the foothills of the Greater Caucasus, a land-locked region in the basin of the Kuban river, within Krasnodar Krai. The Republic is in the Southern Federal Okrug and the North Caucasus Economic Area. The territory of the Republic, of which some two-fifths is forested, is characterized by open grassland, fertile soil and numerous rivers. The Republic has an area of 7,600 sq km (2,930 sq miles) and is comprised of seven administrative districts and two cities. At 1 January 2002 it was estimated to have 444,900 inhabitants, giving a population density per sq km of 58.5. In January 2001 54.0% of the population of the Republic were urban. In 1989 of the total republican population some 68% were ethnic Russian and 22% Adyges (Lower Circassians or Kiakhs). Of the Adyge population, an estimated 95% speak the national tongue, Adyge—part of the Abkhazo-Adyge group of Caucasian languages—as their native language, although some 82% are also fluent in Russian. The dominant religion in the Republic, owing to the preponderance of Russian inhabitants, is Orthodox Christianity, but the traditional religion of the Adyges is Islam. The administrative centre of Adygeya is the only large city, Maikop, which had a total of 167,000 inhabitants at 1 January 2001.

History
The Adyges were traditionally renowned for their unrivalled horsemanship and marksmanship. They emerged as a distinct ethnic group among the Circassians in

the 13th century, when they inhabited much of the area between the Don river and the Caucasus, and the Black Sea and the Stavropol plateau. They were' conquered by the Mongol Empire in the 13th century. In the 1550s the Adyges entered into an alliance with the Russian Empire, as protection against the Tatar Khanate of Crimea and against Turkic groups such as the Karachai, the Kumyks and the Nogai, which had retreated into the Caucasus from the Mongol forces of Temujin (Chinghiz or Ghengis Khan). Russian settlers subsequently moved into the Don and Kuban regions, causing unrest among the Adyges and other Circassian peoples, many of whom supported the Ottoman Empire against Russia in the Crimean War of 1853–56. The Circassians were finally defeated by the Russians in 1864. Most were forced either to emigrate or to move to the plains that were under Russian control. A Kuban-Black Sea Soviet Republic was established in 1918, but the region was soon occupied by anti-communist forces ('Whites'). The Adygeya Autonomous Oblast was established on 27 July 1922. From 24 August 1922 until 13 August 1928 it was known as the Adygeya (Circassian) Autonomous Oblast. The Oblast subsequently formed part of Stavropol Krai, which was constituted in 1937.

Following the emergence of the policy of *glasnost* (openness) in the USSR, under Mikhail Gorbachev, the Adyge-Khase Movement was formed. This group, which demanded the formation of a national legislative council or khase, began to raise the issues of nationalism and independence in the Autonomous Oblast. Adygeya officially declared its sovereignty on 28 June 1991 and was recognized as an autonomous republic, separate from the surrounding Krai, at the signing of the Federation Treaty in March 1992. Its Constitution was adopted on 10 March 1995. The Communist Party remained the most popular (winning 41% of the votes cast in the Republic at the Russian State Duma elections of December), while suspicion of the reformists and the federal Government was widespread. From the mid-1990s the Republic developed close links with the other Circassian Republics (Kabardino-Balkariya and Karachayevo-Cherkessiya). In May 1998, at the second session of an interparliamentary council, a programme was adopted on the co-ordination of legislative, economic, environmental and legal activities. The Adyge President, Aslan Aliyevich Dzharimov, was among those instrumental in forming the parliamentary bloc 'All Russia' in 1999. In an election held on 13 January 2002 Dzharimov was conclusively defeated, receiving only around 10% of the votes cast; he was succeeded by Khazrat Sovmen, the owner of a gold-mining co-operative.

Economy

Agriculture is, traditionally, the principal economic activity of Adygeya. In 1999 the territory's gross regional product was 5,110.2m. roubles, or 11,373.7 roubles per head. The territory's major industrial centres are at the cities of Maikop and Kamennomostskii. At 2000 there were 148 km (92 miles) of railway track on its territory, and 1,537 km of paved roads.

Agricultural production consists mainly of grain, sunflowers, sugar beet, tobacco and vegetables, cucurbit (gourds and melons) cultivation and viniculture. The Republic produced over 17% of the Federation's output of grape wine in the first half of 2000. The entire sector employed some 22.1% of the working population in 2000. The decline in overall agricultural production in the Republic slowed during the mid-1990s, although animal husbandry decreased to less than one-half of its 1991 level by 1998. By 2000 the value of agricultural output was 2,240m. roubles, compared with 995m. roubles in 1998. There is some extraction of natural gas. In industry, food-processing is particularly important, accounting for almost one-half of industrial production. Timber-processing, mechanical engineering and metal-working are also significant. Adygeya lies along the route of the 'Blue Stream' pipeline, which was to deliver gas to Turkey, and planned petroleum pipelines from the Transcaucasus and Dagestan to the Black Sea ports of Novorossiisk and Tuapse. Some 18.5% of the working population were engaged in industry in 2000. Industrial production declined during the early 1990s, but it stabilized in the second half of the decade, and began to increase from 1999. In 2000 the value of industrial production was 2,795m. roubles, compared with 1,018m. roubles in 1998.

In 2000 the economically active population in Adygeya amounted to 200,200, and some 14.1% of the labour force were unemployed, one of the highest rates in the Federation at that time. The average monthly wage was 2,625.9 roubles in mid-2002. In 2000 there was a budgetary deficit of 84.9m. roubles. In that year the Republic's external trade amounted to a value of US $10.4m., of which $7.9m. was accounted for by imports and $2.5m. by exports. Adygeya's main trading partners, in the mid-1990s, in terms of exports, were Belarus, France, Kazakhstan, Poland, Turkey and Ukraine. Exports consisted mainly of food products, machine-tools and petroleum and chemical products. There was relatively little foreign investment in the Republic: in 2000 it amounted to just $719,000. At 31 December 2000 there were 2,200 small businesses registered on Adygeya's territory.

Directory

President: KHAZRAT M. SOVMEN; 385000 Adygeya, Maikop, ul. Zhukovskogo 22; tel. (87722) 2-19-00; fax (87722) 2-59-58.

Prime Minister: NIKOLAI V. DEMCHUK; 385000 Adygeya, Maikop, ul. Zhukovskogo 22; tel. (87722) 2-22-22.

Chairman of the Khase (State Council): ANATOLII G. IVANOV; 385000 Adygeya, Maikop, ul. Zhukovskogo 22; tel. (87722) 2-19-02; e-mail apparat@parlament .adygheya.ru; internet www.parlament.adygheya.ru.

Chief Representative of the Republic of Adygeya in the Russian Federation: RUSLAN YU. GUSARUK; 115184 Moscow, per. Staryi Tolmachevskii 6; tel. (095) 230-34-01; fax (095) 230-07-48.

Head of Maikop City Administration: MIKHAIL N. CHERNICHENKO; 352700 Adygeya, Maikop, ul. Krasnooktyabrskaya 21; tel. (87722) 2-17-08; internet www.maykop.ru.

Republic of Altai

The Republic of Altai (Gornyi Altai—Mountainous Altai) is situated in the Altai Mountains, in the basin of the Ob river. The Republic forms part of the Siberian Federal Okrug and the West Siberian Economic Area. It has international borders with Kazakhstan in the south-west, a short border with the People's Republic of China to the south, and with Mongolia to the south-east. Kemerovo Oblast lies to the north, the Republics of Khakasiya and Tyva to the east, and the Altai Krai, of which the Republic formerly constituted a part, to the north-west. The Republic includes the highest peak in Siberia, Belukha, at 4,506 m (14,783 feet), and about one-quarter of its territory is forested. Its major rivers are the Katyn and the Biya, and it has one lake, Teletskoye. It contains one of Russia's major national parks, Altai State National Park, covering an area of some 9,000 sq km (3,475 sq miles). The Republic occupies 92,600 sq km and comprises 10 administrative districts and one city. Its climate is continental, with short summers and long, cold winters. At 1 January 2002 it was estimated to have a population of 204,900 and a population density, therefore, of only 2.2 per sq km. Of its inhabitants, 25.7% resided in urban areas in January 2001. The census of 1989 put the number of Russians at some 60% of the total and of ethnic Altai at 31%, while some 5.6% of the population were Kazakh. The Altai people can be divided into two distinct groups: the Northern Altai, or Chernnevye Tatars, consisting of the Tubalars, the Chelkans or Leberdin and the Kumandins; and the Southern Altai, comprising the Altai Kizhi, the Telengit, the Telesy and the Teleut. The language spoken by both groups is from the Turkish branch of the Uralo-Altaic family: that of the Northern Altais is from the Old Uigur group, while the language of the Southern Altais is close to the Kyrgyz language and is part of the Kipchak group. Over 84% of Altais speak one or other language as their native tongue, and some 62% of the Altai population is fluent in Russian. Although the traditional religion of the Altai was animist, many were converted to Christianity, so the dominant religion in the Republic is Russian Orthodoxy. The Republic's administrative centre is at Gorno-Altaisk, which had a population of 52,700 at 1 January 2001.

History

From the 11th century the Altai peoples inhabited Dzungaria (Sungaria—now mainly in the north-west of the People's Republic of China). The region was under Mongol control until 1389, when it was conquered by the Tatar forces of Tamerlane (Tamberlane or Timur 'the Lame'); it subsequently became a Kalmyk confederation. In the first half of the 18th century many Altais moved westwards, invading Kazakh territory and progressing almost as far as the Urals. In 1758, however, most of Dzungaria was incorporated into Xinjiang (Sinkiang), a province of the Chinese Empire. China embarked on a war aimed at exterminating the Altai peoples. Only a few thousand survived, finding refuge in the Altai Mountains. In the 19th century Russia began to assert its control over the region and the Altai territory was finally annexed in 1866. In the early 1900s Burkhanism or White Faith, a strong nationalist religious movement, emerged. The movement was led by Oirot Khan, who claimed to be a descendant of Chinghiz (Genghis) Khan and promised to liberate the Altais from Russian control. However, in February 1918 it was a secular nationalist leader, B. I. Anuchin, who convened a Constituent Congress of the High Altai and demanded the establishment of an Oirot Republic—to include the Altai, the Khakassians and the Tyvans. In partial recognition of such demands, on 1 July 1922 the Soviet Government established an Oirot Autonomous Oblast in Altai Krai. Nationalist feeling remained strong in the region, however, and in 1933 many members of the local Communist Party were purged. On 7 January 1948 the region was renamed the Gorno-Altai Autonomous Oblast, in an effort to suppress nationalist sentiment.

In the late 1980s nationalism re-emerged in response to Mikhail Gorbachev's policy of *glasnost* (openness). Renamed the Altai Republic, the region became an autonomous republic, independent of Altai Krai, at the signing of the Russian Federation Treaty in March 1992, having adopted its State Sovereignty Declaration on 25 October 1990. A resolution adopted on 14 October 1993 provided for the establishment of a State Assembly (El Kurultai), which comprised 27 deputies and represented the highest body of power in the Republic. Following the blockade by public-sector workers of the State Assembly in mid-1998, in protest at payment arrears, the legislature obtained urgent federal transfers of 100m. roubles. The Altai Republic was one of only four subjects of the Russian Federation to award the communist candidate, Yevgenii Zyuganov, a higher proportion of the votes than Vladimir Putin in the presidential election of 26 March 2000. In June the Russian Constitutional Court demanded that several articles of the Altai Republic's Constitution be amended in order to conform with the fundamental laws of the Russian Federation. Several amendments to this end were approved by the republican parliament in February 2001, including the removal of a provision that had forbidden persons of the same nationality from simultaneously occupying the posts of chairman of the republican government and parliamentary speaker. Following an inconclusive first round of voting in the election to the post of chairman of the government held in the Republic on 16 December, the incumbent, Semen Zubakin, and Agrarian Party of Russia leader Mikhail Lapshin progressed to a second round, held on 20 January 2002. On that occasion Lapshin decisively defeated Zubakin, receiving

68% of the votes cast, according to preliminary results. Notably, Lapshin received the support of the pro-Government Unity and Fatherland-United Russia party in the second round, in addition to that of the Communist Party of the Russian Federation. Legislative elections were held in the Republic in December.

Economy

The Republic of Altai is predominantly an agricultural region. Its gross regional product amounted to 2,568.1m. roubles in 1999, or 12,570.4 roubles per head. The main industrial centre in the Republic is at its capital, Gorno-Altaisk. Owing to its mountainous terrain, in 2000 it contained just 2,774 km (1,724 miles) of paved roads, including a section of the major Novorossiisk–Biisk–Tashanta highway. There are no railways or airports. In March 1996 the Russian Government allocated some 1,800m. old roubles to alleviate the effects in the Republic of the nuclear tests conducted at Semipalatinsk, Kazakhstan, in 1949–62. However, in the early 2000s further concern was expressed about the negative effect of frequent rocket launches from the Baikonaur Cosmodrome in Kazakhstan on both the health of the residents of the Republic and the surrounding environment.

Agriculture in the Republic of Altai, which employed 31.4% of the working population in 2000, consists mainly of livestock-breeding (largely horses, deer, sheep and goats, amounting to 60% of agricultural activity in the late 1990s), bee-keeping, grain production and hunting. The export of the antlers of Siberian maral and sika deer, primarily to South-East Asia, is an important source of convertible ('hard') currency to the Republic. In 2000 the total value of agricultural output was 1,479m. roubles. The Republic's mountainous terrain often prevents the easy extraction or transport of minerals, but there are important reserves of manganese, iron, silver, lead and wolfram (tungsten), as well as timber. Stone, lime, salt, sandstone, gold, mercury and non-ferrous metals are also produced. There are food-processing, light, chemicals, metal-working and machine-tool industries, as well as factories assembling tractors, automobiles, radios, televisions, engines, boilers and electrical appliances. Industry employed just 8.2% of the working population in 2000, and the value of industrial production amounted to 361m. roubles.

In 2000 a total of 91,000 of the Republic's inhabitants were economically active, and some 17.5% of the labour force were unemployed. The average monthly wage was 3,160.6 roubles in mid-2002. The territory suffered severe financial difficulties in the late 1990s, and there was a budgetary deficit of 47.9m. roubles in 2000. In that year the value of the Republic's exports was US $51.8m., and its imports were equivalent to around $68.5m. The level of foreign investment was very low, amounting to just $99,000 in 2000. At December 2000 there were approximately 1,400 small businesses registered in the Republic.

Directory

Chairman of the Government: MIKHAIL I. LAPSHIN; 659700 Altai Republic, Gorno-Altaisk, ul. Kirova 16; tel. (38822) 2-26-30; e-mail root@apra.gorny.ru; internet www.altai-republic.com.

Chairman of the El Kurultai (State Assembly): IGOR E. YAIMOV; 659700 Altai Republic, Gorno-Altaisk, ul. Erkemena Palkina 1; tel. (38822) 2-26-18; fax (38822) 9-51-65; e-mail postmaster@altek.gorny.ru.

Chief Representative of the Altai Republic in the Russian Federation: SERGEI D. KONCHAKOVSKII; 103795 Moscow, ul. M. Dmitrovka 3/221; tel. (095) 299-41-94; fax (095) 299-81-97.

Head of Gorno-Altaisk City Administration: VIKTOR A. OBLOGIN; 659700 Altai Republic, Gorno-Altaisk, pr. Kommunisticheskii 18; tel. (38822) 2-07-31.

Republic of Bashkortostan

The Republic of Bashkortostan (Bashkiriya) is situated on the slopes of the Southern Urals. It forms part of the Volga Federal Okrug and the Urals Economic Area. Orenburg Oblast lies to the south and south-west of Bashkortostan, and the Republics of Tatarstan and Udmurtiya lie to the north and north-west, respectively. There are borders with Perm and Sverdlovsk Oblasts to the north and Chelyabinsk to the east. The north of the Republic (more than one-third of its land area) is forested, while the southern part is steppe. The Republic occupies an area of 143,600 sq km (55,440 sq miles) and comprises 54 administrative districts and 21 cities. At 1 January 2002 Bashkortostan had an estimated population of 4,090,600, giving a population density of 28.5 per sq km. In January 2001 some 65.3% of the Republic's population inhabited urban areas. The most numerous ethnic group was Russian (39% in 1989). Tatars made up 28% of the population, while Bashkirs only constituted 22%. Of the ethnic Bashkir inhabitants, some 72% spoke Bashkir as their native tongue. Bashkir is a Kipchak language closely related to that spoken by the Tatars. There are two distinct Bashkir dialects: Kuvakan is spoken in the north of the Republic, while Yurmatin (Yurmatyn) is current in the south. The majority of Bashkirs and Tatars are Sunni Muslims of the Hanafi school, although some Bashkirs, the Nagaibak (Noghaibaq or Nogaibak), were converted to Orthodox Christianity. The Republic's administrative centre is at Ufa, which had a population of 1,088,800 in 2001. Its other major cities, with populations in excess of 100,000, are Sterlitamak, Salavat, Neftekamsk and Oktyabrskii.

History

The Bashkirs were thought to have originated as a distinct ethnic group during the 16th century, out of the Tatar, Mongol, Volga, Bulgar, Oguz, Pecheneg and Kipchak peoples. They were traditionally a pastoral people renowned for their bee-keeping abilities. The territory of Bashkiriya was annexed by Russia in 1557, during the reign of Ivan IV, and many Bashkirs subsequently lost their land and wealth and were forced into servitude. Rebellions against Russian control, most notably by Salavat Yulai in 1773, were unsuccessful, and the identity and survival of the Bashkir community came under increasing threat. A large migration of ethnic Russians to the region in the late 19th century resulted in their outnumbering the Bashkir population. Formal recognition of the Bashkirs as an ethnic group occurred on 23 March 1919, when the Bashkir ASSR was created. The Soviet Government remained intolerant of unrest and Bashkir resistance to the collectivization policy of Stalin (Iosif V. Dzhugashvili) caused many to be relocated to other regions in the USSR. It was this, combined with losses during the civil wars of the revolutionary period, which resulted in the Bashkirs becoming outnumbered by the Tatar population in the Republic.

The Bashkir Autonomous Republic declared its sovereignty on 11 October 1990. On 12 December 1993, the same day that Murtaza Rakhimov was elected to the new post of President, a republican majority voted against acceptance of the Russian Constitution, which was approved in the Federation as a whole. On 24 December the republican Supreme Soviet (State Assembly) adopted a new Constitution, which stated that its own laws had supremacy over federal laws. The name of Bashkortostan was adopted. The Republic's constitutional position was regularized and further autonomy granted under a treaty signed on 3 August 1994. By this, the federal authorities granted Bashkortostan, which had one of the strongest sovereignty movements of any of the ethnic republics, greater independence in economic and legislative matters, including that of the right to levy taxes. A further bilateral treaty was signed in 1995. Bashkortostan enjoyed close relations with the Republic of Tatarstan: on 28 August 1997 the Presidents of the two territories signed a treaty on co-operation. The Republic's administration was traditionally centralized and conservative, but keen to attract foreign investment. A presidential election, held on 14 June 1998, returned Rakhimov to office, with 73% of the votes cast, his candidacy having been endorsed publicly by the Russian President, Boris Yeltsin. In the federal parliamentary elections of December 1999, the candidates of Rakhimov's favoured grouping, Fatherland—All Russia, were successful in the Republic; prior to the election Rakhimov was rebuked by the federal Prime Minister, Vladimir Putin, for blocking the transmission of two television channels opposed to the grouping. Commentators also observed the absence of any opposition press in Bashkortostan, and the removal from electoral lists of most of Rakhimov's opponents, owing to alleged electoral violations. In the federal presidential election of 26 March 2000, Bashkortostan returned 62% of votes in favour of Vladimir Putin, well above the national average, reflecting Rakhimov's support for Putin during the election campaign. None the less, two months later Putin ordered that Bashkortostan's Constitution be altered to conform with Russia's basic law. A new republican Constitution was introduced in November, although several articles continued to contradict federal norms. In January 2001 one of the most significant contradictions, the statement that republican legislation should take precedence over federal law, was rescinded, and several powers formerly attributed to the republican prime minister were transferred to the republican president. In March Rakhimov was appointed by President Putin to serve on the presidium of the State Council for a period of six months; in this position he established himself as a leading critic of proposed reforms that sought to increase the powers of the federal authorities. In June 2002 the federal Supreme Court ruled that some 37 articles of Bashkortostan's Constitution failed to comply with federal law, and in early December another Constitution was adopted, which, notably, combined the posts of President and Prime Minister.

Economy

Bashkortostan's economy is dominated by its fuel and energy and agro-industrial complexes. The Republic is one of Russia's key petroleum-producing areas and the centre of its petroleum-refining industry. It produced 4% of Russia's total petroleum output in the first six months of 2000 and accounted for around 15% of its petroleum refining. However, the quantity of petroleum both produced and refined in the Republic declined significantly during the 1990s. In 1999 the territory's gross regional product stood at 114,145.1m. roubles, or 27,722.6 roubles per head. Amid concerns that the federal Government was seeking to gain increased control over the natural resources of the Republic, at the expense of the republican authorities, Governor Rakhimov announced, in August 2002, that several of the republican petroleum companies were to be transferred to private ownership. Bashkortostan's major industrial centres are at Ufa (at which the Republic's petroleum refineries are based), Sterlitamak, Salavat and Ishimbai. In 2000 there were 1,475 km (917 miles) of railways on its territory, and 21,869 km of paved roads. Bashkir Airlines (BAL) operates air services between Ufa and major centres within Russia and elsewhere within the Commonwealth of Independent States from the Republic's international airport.

Bashkortostan's agricultural production, the value of which amounted to 27,918m. roubles in 2000, ranks among the highest in the Russian Federation. Its main agricultural activities are grain, sugar beet, sunflower and vegetable production, animal husbandry, poultry-farming and bee-keeping. Some 19.8% of the Republic's work-force were employed in agriculture in 2000. As well as its petroleum resources (of which the deposits amount to 400m. metric tons), Bashkortostan contains deposits of natural gas (55m. tons), brown coal—lignite (250m. tons), iron ore, copper, gold (with reserves amounting to 32 tons in 1997, sufficient for 19 years of production), zinc, aluminium, chromium, salt (2,270m. tons), manganese, gypsum and limestone. The Republic's other industries include processing of agricultural and forestry products, mechanical engineering, metal-working, metallurgy, electricity generation, production of mining and petroleum-exploration equipment, automobiles, geophysical instruments, cables and electrical equipment and building materials. In 2000 industry employed 24.1% of the Republic's working population. Total industrial output was worth 141,792m. roubles in that year.

In 2000 the economically active population in the Republic amounted to 1,928,000, and 11.5% of the labour force were unemployed. The average monthly wage was 3,780.0 roubles in mid-2002. In 2000 there was a budgetary surplus of 1,425.7m. roubles. In the same year the Republic's external trade totalled

US \$2,910m., of which exports, largely comprising petroleum products and petrochemical goods, accounted for \$2,668.6m. Bashkortostan's principal trading partner is Germany. Foreign investment in the Republic in 2000 amounted to some \$10.4m. At the end of the year there were 14,300 small businesses registered on the Republic's territory.

Directory

President and Prime Minister: MURTAZA G. RAKHIMOV; 450101 Bashkortostan, Ufa, ul. Tukayeva 46; tel. (3472) 50-27-24; fax (3472) 50-02-81; e-mail aprb_webmaster@kmrb.bashnet.ru; internet president.bashkortostan.ru.

Chairman of the State Assembly (Kurultai): KONSTANTIN B. TOLKACHEV; 450101 Bashkortostan, Ufa, ul. Tukayeva 46; tel. (3472) 50-19-15; fax (3472) 50-08-86.

Chief Representative of the Republic of Bashkortostan in the Russian Federation: IREK YU. ABLAYEV; 103045 Moscow, Sretenskii bulv. 9/2; tel. (095) 208-46-62; fax (095) 208-39-25.

Head of Ufa City Administration (Mayor): RAUF S. NUGUMANOV; 450098 Bashkortostan, Ufa, pr. Oktyabrya 120; tel. (3472) 79-05-79; fax (3472) 33-18-73; e-mail cityadmin@ufacity.info; internet www.ufacity.info.

Republic of Buryatiya

The Republic of Buryatiya is situated in the Eastern Sayan Mountains of southern Siberia and forms part of the Siberian Federal Okrug and the East Siberian Economic Area. It lies mainly in the Transbaikal region to the east of Lake Baikal, although it also extends westwards along the international boundary with Mongolia in the south, to create a short border with the Russian federal territory of Tyva in the extreme south-west. Irkutsk Oblast lies to the north and west, and Chita Oblast to the east. Buryatiya's rivers mainly drain into Lake Baikal, the largest being the Selenga, the Barguzin and the upper Angara, but some, such as the Vitim, flow northwards into the Siberian plains. The Republic's one lake, Baikal, forms part of the western border of the Republic. Baikal is the oldest and deepest lake in the world, possessing over 80% of Russia's freshwater resources and 20% of the world's total. Considered holy by the Buryats, until the 1950s it was famed for the purity of its waters and its unique ecosystem. Intensive industrialization along its shores threatened Baikal's environment, and only in the 1990s were serious efforts made to safeguard the lake. Some 70% of Buryatiya's territory, including its low mountains, is forested, and its valleys are open steppe. The Republic's territory covers 351,300 sq km (135,640 sq miles) and comprises a total of 21 administrative districts and six cities. The winter is protracted but sees little snow, with the average temperature in January falling to –27.1°C; the average temperature in July is 16.0°C. Buryatiya is sparsely populated: it had an estimated population of 1,019,400 at 1 January 2002, and a population density of 2.9 per sq km. Around 59.9% of the population inhabited urban areas in January 2001. In 1989 some 70% of the inhabitants were ethnic Russians and 24% Buryats. The industrial areas of the Republic are mainly inhabited by ethnic Russians. The Buryats are a native Siberian people of Mongol descent. The majority of those inhabiting the Republic are Transbaikal Buryats, as distinct from the Irkutsk Buryats, who live west of Lake Baikal. The Buryats' native tongue is a Mongol dialect. Some Buryats are Orthodox Christians, but others still practise Lamaism (Tibetan Buddhism), which has been syncretized with the region's traditional animistic shamanism. The Khambo Lama, the spiritual leader of Russia's Buddhists, resides in Buryatiya's capital, Ulan-Ude, which had a population of 368,900 in January 2001 and is paired, for the purpose of commercial, cultural and social exchanges, with Taipei in Taiwan.

History

Buryatiya was regarded as strategically important from the earliest years of the Muscovite Russian state, as it lay on the Mongol border. Russian influence reached the region in the 17th century and Transbaikal was formally incorporated into the Russian Empire by the Treaties of Nerchinsk and Kyakhta in 1689 and 1728, respectively. The latter agreement ended a dispute over the territory between the Russian and the Chinese Manzhou (Manchu) Empires. Many ethnic Russians subsequently settled in the region, often inhabiting land confiscated from the Buryats, many of whom were 'russified'. Other Buryats, however, strove to protect their culture, and there was a resurgence of nationalist feeling in the 19th century. Jamtsarano, a prominent nationalist, following a series of congresses in 1905 demanding Buryat self-government and the use of the Buryat language in schools, led a movement that recognized the affinity of Buryat culture to that of the Mongolians. Russia's fears about the Buryats' growing allegiance to its eastern neighbour were allayed, however, after a formal treaty signed with Japan in 1912 recognized Outer Mongolia (Mongolia) as a Russian sphere of influence.

With the dissolution of the Far Eastern Republic (based at Chita), a Buryat-Mongol ASSR was established on 30 May 1923. In the early 1930s, following Stalin—Iosif V. Dzhugashvili's policy of collectivization, many Buryats fled the country or were found guilty of treason and executed. In 1937 the Soviet Government considerably reduced the territory of the Republic, transferring the eastern section to Chita Oblast and a westerly region to Irkutsk Oblast. Furthermore, the Buryat language's Mongolian script was replaced with a Cyrillic one. In 1958 the Buryat-Mongol ASSR was renamed the Buryat ASSR, amid suspicions of increasing co-operation between the Mongolian People's Republic (Mongolia) and the People's Republic of China. The territory declared its sovereignty on 10 October 1990, and was renamed the Republic of Buryatiya in 1992. In March 1994 the republican legislature, the Supreme Soviet, adopted a Constitution, providing for an executive presidency. The hitherto Chairman of the Supreme Soviet, Leonid Potapov, became the Republic's first President, and the legislature was redesignated the People's Khural. A bilateral treaty on the division of powers was signed with the Federation Government in 1995. On 21 June 1998 presidential and legislative elections were held in the Republic: Potapov was re-elected President, with 63% of the votes cast. In October 2000 the People's Khural approved several amendments to Buryatiya's Constitution, in order that it conform more closely with federal norms. However, the Khural rejected the implementation of several proposed amendments required by federal legislation, including, notably, the abolition of the requirement that presidential candidates know both state languages, Russian and Buryat. However, the People's Khural proposed that a special commission be created in order to establish mechanisms for the future co-ordination of regional and federal legislation. In early 2002 Potapov resigned from the Communist Party of the Russian Federation. In April he threatened to dissolve the Khural if it opposed the cancellation of the declaration of sovereignty issued in 1990; the declaration of sovereignty was consequently rescinded. On 23 June Potapov was re-elected for a third term as President of the Republic, receiving 68% of the votes cast. The pro-Government Unity and Fatherland-United Russia party (UF-UR) chose to support Potapov, in preference to his closest electoral opponent, Bato Semenov, a representative of the UF-UR in the State Duma. Notably, in the period preceding the election, three of the four independent radio stations in Ulan-Ude had their operations suspended by the republican State Communications Inspectorate. Following his re-election, Potapov announced the dismissal of the republican Government, as part of a programme of proposed executive reform.

Economy

In 1999 Buryatiya's gross regional product amounted to 18,085.0m. roubles, equivalent to 17,424.6 roubles per head. Its major industrial centre is at Ulan-Ude, which is on the route of the Trans-Siberian Railway. In 2000 there were 1,199 km (745 miles) of railways on Buryatiya's territory, and 6,226 km of paved roads.

The Republic's agriculture, which employed around 14.3% of the work-force in 2000, consists mainly of animal husbandry (livestock and fur-animal breeding), grain production and hunting. Total agricultural production in 2000 was worth 4,829m. roubles. The Republic is rich in mineral resources, including gold, uranium, coal, wolfram (tungsten), molybdenum, brown coal, graphite and apatites. Its main gold-mining enterprise, Buryatzoloto, operates two mines near Lake Baikal. In 1996 its reserves were estimated at 3.2m. troy ounces (almost 100 metric tons). Apart from ore-mining and the extraction of minerals, its main industries are mechanical engineering, metal-working, food-processing, timber production and wood-working. The Republic is also a major producer of electrical energy. The industrial sector employed 19.1% of the Republic's work-force in 2000, and its total output in that year was worth 11,570m. roubles. The services sector with the most potential is tourism, owing to the attractions of Lake Baikal.

Buryatiya's economically active population totalled 491,000 in 2000, and some 19.1% of the Republic's labour force were unemployed. The average monthly wage in the Republic was 4.088.4 roubles in mid-2002. In 2000 there was a budgetary deficit of 1,151.7m. roubles. Foreign trade in that year comprised US $116.5m. in exports and $29.7m. in imports; the Republic had over 50 trading partners, although in 1999 over one-half of its international trade was with the People's Republic of China. Foreign investment in Buryatiya amounted to just $291,000 in 2000. At 31 December 2000 there were 4,100 small businesses registered in the Republic.

Directory

President and Chairman of the Government: LEONID V. POTAPOV; 670001 Buryatiya, Ulan-Ude, Dom Pravitelstva; tel. (3012) 21-46-52; fax (3012) 21-25-55; e-mail president@buryatia.ru; internet www.buryatia.ru.

Chairman of the People's Khural: MIKHAIL I. SEMENOV; 670001 Buratiya, Ulan-Ude, ul. Sukhe-Batora 9; tel. (3012) 21-35-40; fax (3012) 21-49-61; e-mail meconomy@icm.buryatiya.ru.

Chief Representative of the Republic of Buryatiya in the Russian Federation: INNOKENTII N. YEGOROV; 107108 Moscow, ul. Myasnitskaya 43/2; tel. (095) 925-95-00; fax (095) 923-60-46.

Head of Ulan-Ude City Administration (Mayor): GENNADII A. AYDAYEV; 670000 Buryatiya, Ulan-Ude, ul. Lenina 54; tel. (3012) 21-57-05; fax (3012) 26-32-44; internet www.ulan-ude.ru.

Chechen Republic of Ichkeriya (Chechnya)

The territory of Chechnya is located on the northern slopes of the Caucasus. It forms part of the Southern Federal Okrug and the North Caucasus Economic Area. To the east, Chechnya abuts into the Republic of Dagestan. Stavropol Krai lies to the north-west and the Republics of North Osetiya—Alaniya (Ossetia) and Ingushetiya to the west. There is an international boundary with Georgia (South Osetiya) to the south-west. The exact delimitation of the western boundary remained uncertain in 2002, awaiting final agreement between Chechnya and Ingushetiya on the division of the territory of the former Chechen-Ingush ASSR. The region consists of lowlands along the principal waterway, the River Terek, and around the capital, Groznyi (also known as Dzhokhar Gala), in the north; mixed fields, pastures and forests in the Chechen plain; and high mountains and glaciers in the south. The former Checheno-Ingush ASSR had an area of some 19,300 sq km (7,450 sq miles), most of which was allotted to the Chechens. At 1 January 2002 the Republic had an estimated population of 624,600, compared with an estimated population of 780,500 in January 1999. Some 26.0% of the total population lived in urban areas in 2001. The Chechens, who refer to themselves as Nokchi, are closely related to the Ingush (both of whom are known collectively as Vainakhs). They are Sunni Muslims, and their language is one of the Nakh dialects of the Caucasian linguistic family. Founded as Groznyi in 1818, the capital had a population of 405,000 in 1989, but an estimated 182,700 inhabitants in 1995. The Republic's other major towns are Urus-Martan, Gudermes (the oldest town in the territory, founded in the mid-18th century), Shali and Argun.

History

In the 18th century the Russian, Ottoman and Persian (Iranian) Empires fought for control of the Caucasus region. The Chechens violently resisted the Russian forces with the uprising of Sheikh Mansur in 1785 and throughout the Caucasian War of 1817–64. Chechnya was finally conquered by Russia in 1858 after the resistance led by Imam Shamil ended. Many Chechens were exiled to the Ottoman Empire in 1865. Subsequently, ethnic Russians began to settle in the lowlands, particularly after petroleum reserves were discovered around Groznyi in 1893. Upon the dissolution of the Mountain (Gorskaya) People's Soviet Republic in 1922, Chechen and Ingush Autonomous Oblasts were established; they merged in 1934 and became the Checheno-Ingush ASSR two years later. This was dissolved in 1944, when both peoples were deported en masse to Central Asia and Siberia, in retaliation for their alleged collaboration with Germany in the Second World War. On 9 January 1957 the ASSR was reconstituted, but with limited provisions made for the restoration of property to the dispossessed Chechens (and Ingush).

During 1991 an All-National Congress of the Chechen People seized effective power in the Checheno-Ingush ASSR and agreed the division of the territory with Ingush leaders. Exact borders were to be decided by future negotiation, but by far the largest proportion of the territory was to constitute a Chechen Republic. Elections to the presidency of this new polity, Chechnya, which claimed independence from Russia, were held on 27 October, and were won by Gen. Dzhokhar Dudayev. The Chechen Republic under Dudayev, although unrecognized internationally, continued to insist on its independence. In 1993 the territory refused to participate in the Russian general election and rejected the new federal Constitution. Dudayev's policies provoked the Chechen opposition into violent conflict from August 1994. In December federal troops entered Chechnya and, by January 1995, had taken control of the city, including the presidential palace, although fierce resistance continued throughout the Republic. In an effort to end hostilities, the federal President, Boris Yeltsin, signed an accord with the Chechen premier granting the Republic special status, including its own consulate and foreign-trade missions. A peace agreement was not signed, however, until late May 1996, one month after the death of Dudayev in a Russian missile attack. (Dudayev was succeeded by Zemlikhan Yandarbiyev.) However, the truce ended following Yeltsin's re-election to the Russian presidency in July. In August Chechen rebel forces led a successful assault on Groznyi, prompting the negotiation of a cease-fire by Lt-Gen. Aleksandr Lebed (newly appointed Secretary of the federal Security Council). This agreement, the Khasavyurt Accords, was signed in Dagestan on 31 August. A proposed peace settlement incorporated a moratorium on discussion of Chechnya's status for five years, until 2001. An agreement on the withdrawal of the last Russian troops by January 1997 was signed in November 1996, signalling the end of a war that had claimed up to 100,000 lives. A formal Treaty of Peace and Principles of Relations was signed on 12 May 1997 and ratified by the Chechen Parliament the following day.

On 1 January 1997 a presidential election was held in the Republic, at which Khalid 'Aslan' Maskhadov, a former Chechen rebel chief of staff, obtained 64.8% of the votes cast, defeating another rebel leader, Shamil Basayev. On 25 March 1998 the republican Parliament unilaterally renamed the capital Dzhokhar Gala, after the late Gen. Dudayev, and changed the territory's name to the Chechen Republic of Ichkeriya. The main issues to dominate politics were the increasing lawlessness in the Republic and the growth of Islamist groupings. During 1998 two particularly dramatic incidents drew attention to the disorderly state of Chechen society: Valentin Vlasov, the federal presidential representative in Chechnya, was kidnapped in May and held for six months; later in the year international attention was focused on the Republic following the capture and murder of four engineers from the United Kingdom and New Zealand. By the end of the year the capital was no longer secure for the Government and Maskhadov was mainly based on the outskirts of the city.

The resurgence of nationalism in the 1990s was accompanied by a renaissance for Islam. Even after the 1996 peace agreement the Chechen leadership remained committed to complete independence from Russia, reinforcing this intent with the 1997 decision to introduce Islamic *Shari'a* law over a three-year period from 1999, in contravention of federal norms. Hostilities between armed groupings in Gudermes in July 1998 resulted in the outlawing of oppositionist Islamist groups, which the authorities, apparently erroneously, described as representative of 'Wahhabism'. The process of transition to an Islamist state was also fraught with difficulties and engendered instability.

In August 1999 Chechen Islamist factions associated with Basayev launched a series of attacks on Dagestan. The incursions continued, and a series of bomb explosions, including several which destroyed entire apartment blocks, officially attributed to Chechen separatists, killed almost 300 people across Russia in August–September, prompting the redeployment of federal armed forces in the Republic from late September; the recently inaugurated premier, Vladimir Putin, presented the campaign as necessary to quell incipient terrorism. The federal regime declined requests from Maskhadov for the negotiation of a settlement, stating that it recognized only the Moscow-based State Council of the Chechen Republic, which had been recently formed by former members of the republican legislature.

In February 2000 federal forces took control of Groznyi and proceeded to destroy much of the city; many republican and federal administrative bodies were relocated to Gudermes. However, Maskhadov stated that the rebels' withdrawal from Groznyi was tactical, and the federal army's victory remained largely symbolic. In May 2000 Putin, by this time the elected President of the Russian Federation, decreed that Chechnya would, henceforth, be ruled federally. Akhmad haji Kadyrov was inaugurated as President of the Republic on 20 June. Kadyrov, a former ally of Maskhadov, was directly responsible to the federal presidential administration.

By 2000 Maskhadov's authority over the Chechen rebels was believed to be growing, as the Islamist politics of Basayev, and al-Khattab, another commander, thought to be of Saudi Arabian or Jordanian origin, and reputedly a supporter of Afghanistan-based Islamist dissident Osama bin Laden, reportedly failed to secure widespread popular support. In September the elected speaker of the Chechen Parliament, Ruslan Alikhadzhiyev, who had been imprisoned in Moscow for three months, died; Chechen rebels imputed the death to torture. In October it was announced that all Chechen ministries and government departments were to be relocated from Gudermes to Groznyi, with effect from November. In January 2001 Putin signed a decree transferring control of operations in Chechnya from the Ministry of Defence to the Federal Security Service (FSB). The majority of troops in the region were to be withdrawn, leaving a 15,000-strong infantry division and 7,000 interior ministry troops. The FSB was to strengthen its presence in Chechnya, however, in order to combat insurgency. The local administration in Chechnya was restructured to allow it greater autonomy, and Stanislav Ilyasov, a former Governor of Stavropol Krai, was appointed as Chechen premier.

Despite claims that the military phase of the 'anti-terrorist operation' had ended, guerrilla attacks showed no sign of abating, and concern escalated among international human rights organizations about reportedly widespread detention, torture and extortion by federal troops and, in particular, the discovery of a mass grave, containing severely mutilated corpses, prompted outrage. In late August 2001 Kadyrov criticized the federal defence forces for abusing the human rights of civilians while conducting so-called 'cleansing' operations, in which entire towns or areas were searched for rebels. Although hostilities in Chechnya intensified in mid-September, as rebels staged a co-ordinated series of attacks in Gudermes and Argun, on the outskirts of Groznyi, proposals for a political solution to the conflict arose. In late September Putin urged rebels to 'halt all contacts with international terrorists' (with particular reference to bin Laden's al-Qa'ida—Base organization, which had carried out large-scale attacks against the USA earlier than month) and to establish contact with the federal authorities, citing a 72-hour period during which arms could be surrendered without charge; however, only a negligible quantity of weapons was surrendered during the amnesty. None the less, on 18 November the first official, direct negotiations to take place since the renewal of hostilities in 1999 commenced in Moscow, between Col-Gen. Viktor Kazantsev and Akhmed Zakayev, a representative of Maskhadov, although the meetings reached no substantive agreement, and no further high-level meetings were planned. In mid-October 2001 federal losses during the campaign were officially announced at 3,438 dead and 11,661 wounded, although Chechen estimates were considerably higher. (It was also estimated that some 11,000 rebel fighters had been killed by that time.) Also in mid-October, Kadyrov reformed the Chechen administration; although Ilyasov (who remained resident in Stavropol) was maintained as republican Prime Minister, a new, more senior position, the Chief of Staff of the Chechen Administration, was assigned to Lt-Gen. Yan Sergunin, hitherto responsible for the judicial system in Chechnya. In mid-November the trial of Salman Raduyev, the only prominent Chechen rebel leader to have been captured by federal forces, began in Makhachkala, Dagestan, on 10 charges, including murder, terrorism and hostage-taking. In December Raduyev was sentenced to life imprisonment (he died in December 2002).

In late December 2001 Maskhadov, whose five-year mandate as President of Chechnya was to expire in late January 2002, announced the extension of his presidency for an additional year. (None the less, Maskhadov, who was believed to be in hiding in the mountainous regions of southern Chechnya, remained unable to exercise any presidential prerogatives.) In March further progress towards a negotiated settlement of the conflict was reported. A newly established 'Chechen Consultative Council', comprising both Chechens supportive of, and opposed to, the independence of the Republic held its first meeting in the building of the Federal Assembly in Moscow. At the end of March the federal authorities announced new measures intended to ensure greater respect for human rights in the conduct of military actions in Chechnya. Human rights activists largely dismissed the efficacy of these measures, and it was suggested that an attack on Kadyrov's convoy by federal troops, in early April, was a deliberate attempt to discredit the republican administration in light of the new regulations. Although Putin again announced that the military stage of the conflict in Chechnya had ended, rebel activity appeared to increase markedly during April. In late April it was reported, and subsequently confirmed by Zakayev, that al-Khattab had been killed by federal forces. In late July the UN announced, for the second time in one year, the suspension of its humanitarian operations in Chechnya, following the kidnapping of an aid worker in the Republic. In mid-August federal forces experienced their single largest loss of life since the commencement of operations in 1999, when a military helicopter was shot down by rebels in Groznyi, killing 118 troops; at the end of the month a second federal helicopter was attacked, killing its two crew members, and a third helicopter was shot down in late October.

On 23–26 October 2002 over 40 heavily armed rebels, led by Movsar Barayev, the cousin of a Chechen rebel leader who had been killed by federal troops in 2001, held captive more than 800 people in a Moscow theatre, and demanded the withdrawal of federal troops from the Republic. The rebels described themselves as members of a 'suicide batallion' and, notably, included several women, armed with explosive devices. The siege ended when élite federal forces stormed the theatre, having initially filled the building with an (unidentified) incapacitating gas. The rebels were killed, and it subsequently emerged that some 129 hostages had also died, in almost all cases owing to the toxic effects of the gas. Maskhadov issued a statement condemning the rebels' use of terrorist methods, but, despite denials by the Chechen authorities of their involvement in the incident, Akhmed Zakayev was arrested on 29 October, on the orders of the federal Government, while attending a World Chechen Congress in Copenhagen, Denmark. In early December Denmark formally rejected demands for Zakayev's extradition, and he was released. However, he was subsequently detained on arrival in the United Kingdom, as a result of new charges by the Russian Government, before being released on bail.

In mid-November 2002 Capt. (retd) Mikhail Babich, who had previously held the post of First Deputy Governor of Ivanovo Oblast, was inaugurated as the Republic's new Prime Minister, replacing Stanislav Ilyasov, who had been appointed federal Minister for the Social and Economic Development of Chechnya earlier in the month; the new appointment followed persistent reports of conflict between Ilyasov and Akhmed haji Kadyrov. In December President Putin decreed that preparations be made for a referendum on a new, draft Chechen constitution.

Economy

Prior to the outbreak of armed hostilities in the region in 1994–95 Groznyi was the principal industrial centre in Chechnya. In 2000 there were 304 km (189 miles) of railways and 3,057 km of paved roads on the Republic's territory. Its agriculture consisted mainly of horticulture, production of grain and sugar beet and animal husbandry. Its main industrial activities were production of petroleum and petro-chemicals, petroleum refining, power engineering, manufacture of machinery and the processing of forestry and agricultural products. Conflict in 1994–96, and again from 1999, seriously damaged the economic infrastructure and disrupted both agricultural and industrial activity. At April 1998 around four-fifths of the Republic's population were unemployed, and the 1998 budget showed a deficit of 68m. roubles. However, future developments depended on greater stability in the territory. Another asset that could be sabotaged by, or displaced because of, violence was one of Russia's major petroleum pipelines that crossed Chechnya (transit fees from Caspian hydrocarbons could be a major source of revenue). In mid-1999 the

Chechen section of a petroleum pipeline from Baku, Azerbaijan, to Novorossiisk, was closed, owing to the lack of security in the region. However, attempts were being made to restore industry in the Republic, and a sugar refinery and a brickworks were in operation there in 2001. A new polypropylene-fabric factory was constructed in Groznyi in 2002. In November 2002 it was reported that the federal budget for 2003 was to allocate some 3,500m. roubles to the Republic, under a programme that aimed to promote economic and social recovery.

Directory

President and Head of the Republic: Gen. KHALID ('ASLAN') A. MASKHADOV.

Governor and Head of the Administration: AKHMED haji KADYROV; 364000 Chechnya, Groznyi, ul. Garazhnaya 10A; tel. and fax (095) 777-92-28.

Chief of Staff of the Chechen Administration: Lt-Gen. YAN SERGUNIN.

Chairman of the Republican Government (Prime Minister and First Deputy Head of the Administration): Capt. (retd) MIKHAIL V. BABICH; 364000 Chechnya, Groznyi, ul. Garazhnaya 10A; tel. (095) 777-92-14.

Chief Representative of the Chechen Republic of Ichkeriya (Chechnya) in the Russian Federation: ADLAN MAGOMADOV; 127025 Moscow, ul. Novyi Arbat 19; tel. (095) 203-91-45; fax (095) 203-63-52.

Head of Groznyi (Dzhokhar Gala) City Administration (Mayor): OLEG ZHIDKOV; tel. (8712) 22-01-42.

Chuvash Republic (Chuvashiya)

The Chuvash Republic is situated in the north-west of European Russia. It forms part of the Volga Federal Okrug and the Volga-Vyatka Economic Area. The Republic lies on the Eastern European Plain on the middle reaches of the Volga. Ulyanovsk Oblast neighbours it to the south, the Republic of Mordoviya to the south-west, Nizhnii Novgorod Oblast to the west and the Republics of Marii-El and Tatarstan to the north and the east, respectively. The Republic's major rivers are the Volga and the Sura, and one-third of its territory is covered by forest. It occupies 18,300 sq km (7,070 sq miles) and comprises 21 administrative districts and nine cities. The territory measures 190 km (118 miles) from south to north and 160 km from west to east. At 1 January 2002 the Republic had an estimated total population of 1,346,300 and a relatively high population density of 73.6 per sq km. Some 61.2% of the population lived in towns in January 2001. In contrast to the native peoples in the majority of autonomous republics, the Chuvash outnumber ethnic Russians in Chuvashiya: at the census of 1989, 67.8% of inhabitants were Chuvash and 26.7% Russian. The native tongue of the Republic is Chuvash, which has its origins in the Bulgar group of the Western Hunnic group of Turkic languages and is related to ancient Bulgar and Khazar. It is spoken as a first language by an estimated 76.5% of Chuvash. The dominant religions in Chuvashiya are Islam and Orthodox Christianity. Chuvashiya's capital is at Cheboksary (Shupashkar—with a population of 461,200 in 2001). Its other major town is Novocheboksarsk, with 124,200 inhabitants.

History

The Chuvash, traditionally a semi-nomadic people, were conquered by the Mongol-Tatars in the 13th century. Their territory subsequently became part of the dominion of the Golden Horde and many were converted to Islam. From the late 1430s the Chuvash were ruled by the Kazan Khanate. In 1551 Chuvashiya became a part of the Russian Empire and Kazan itself was subjugated by Ivan IV in 1552. The Chuvash nation had been formed by the end of the 15th century, with a syncretized culture of Suvar-Bulgar and Finno-Ugric components. Despite intense Christianization and 'russification' on the part of the Russian state, the Chuvash acquired their own national and cultural identity. The Chuvash capital was founded at Cheboksary in 1551, at the site of a settlement first mentioned in Russian chronicles in 1469. The construction of other towns and forts, intended to encourage migration into the area, followed. After 1917 the Chuvash people made vociferous demands for autonomy to the Soviet Government. A Chuvash Autonomous Oblast was established on 24 June 1920, which was upgraded to the status of an ASSR on 21 April 1925.

Chuvash nationalism re-emerged in the early 1990s: the Chuvash ASSR declared its sovereignty on 27 October 1990. It adopted the name of the Chuvash (Chavash) Republic in March 1992. In December 1993 the Republic voted against acceptance of the federal Constitution. In May 1996 the Chuvash Government signed a treaty with the Russian President, Boris Yeltsin, on the delimitation of powers. It granted the Republic greater freedom to determine policy in political, economic and social areas. Elections to the 87-seat State Council were held on 13 July 1998, with further elections for 23 unfilled seats on 1 November. Compliant voting habits, however, did not mean a passive population—particularly during 1998, the territory experienced a notable volume of litigation, encouraged by the media, over arrears in pension payments and the lack of discounts on utility bills for veterans (in accordance with federal law). Wage arrears continued to rank among the most serious in the Russian Federation into 2000. In October 2001 the Chairman of the republican Council of Ministers, Enver Ablyakimov, resigned; republican President Nikolai Fedorov appointed himself to the position, announcing that combining the roles of republican president and prime minister would increase the Government's accountability. Fedorov was re-elected, with some 41% of the votes, in the presidential election held in Chuvashiya on 16 December. However, immediately following his re-election as Governor, Fedorov announced that he was to rescind his position as Chairman of the Council of Ministers (Prime Minister); Nataliya Partasova assumed this position, initially in an acting capacity.

Economy

In 1999 the Republic's gross regional product amounted to 18,372.1m. roubles, equivalent to 13,526.8 roubles per head. Chuvashiya's major industrial centres are at Cheboksary, Novocheboksarsk, Kanash and Alatyr. In 2000 there were 396 km of railways and 4,474 km of paved roads on the Republic's territory.

Its agriculture, which employed 25.3% of the work-force in 2000, consists mainly of grain, potato, vegetable, hop, hemp and makhorka-tobacco production, horticulture and animal husbandry. The value of total agricultural output in that year amounted to 8,563m. roubles. The Republic contains deposits of peat, sand, limestone and dolomite. Its main industries are mechanical engineering, metal-working, electricity generation, production of chemicals, light industry, wood-working, manufacture of building materials and food-processing. The industrial sector employed 24.4% of the working population in 2000 and generated 19,531m. roubles in income.

The economically active population in Chuvashiya amounted to 686,000 in 2000; 9.1% of the Republic's labour force were unemployed, one of the lowest levels in the Federation. The average monthly wage in the territory was 2,435.3 roubles in mid-2002. In 2000 there was a budgetary surplus of 35.7m. roubles. In that year exports from the Republic amounted to US $62.0m., and imports to the Republic to $55.7m. Chuvashiya's major trading partners are the People's Republic of China, Finland, Germany, Italy, the Netherlands, Poland, Ukraine and the USA. Foreign investment in 2000 was worth $1.7m. At 31 December 2000 there were 4,000 small businesses operating in Chuvashiya.

Directory

President: NIKOLAI V. FEDOROV; 428004 Chuvashiya, Cheboksary, pl. Respubliki 1; tel. (8352) 62-46-87; fax (095) 973-22-38; e-mail president@cap.ru; internet www.cap.ru.

Chairman of the Cabinet of Ministers (Prime Minister): NATALIYA YU. PARTA-SOVA; 428004 Chuvashiya, Cheboksary, pl. Respubliki 1; tel. (8352) 62-01-76; fax (8352) 62-31-84; e-mail partasova@chuvashia.com.

Chairman of the State Council (Parliament): MIKHAIL A. MIKHAILOVSKII; 428004 Chuvashiya, Cheboksary, pl. Respubliki 1; tel. (8352) 62-22-72; e-mail respublika@cap.ru; internet www.gs.chuvashia.com.

Chief Representative of the Chuvash Republic in the Russian Federation: GENNADII S. FEDOROV; 119017 Moscow, ul. B. Ordynka 46/1; tel. and fax (095) 953-21-59.

Head of Cheboksary City Administration: ANATOLII A. IGUMNOV; 428004 Chuvashiya, Cheboksary, ul. K. Marksa 36; tel. (8352) 22-35-76; e-mail gcheb@chuvashia.com; internet www.cheboksary.chuvashia.com.

Republic of Dagestan

The Republic of Dagestan (Daghestan) is situated in the North Caucasus on the Caspian Sea. Dagestan forms part of the Southern Federal Okrug and the North Caucasus Economic Area. It has international borders with Azerbaijan to the south and Georgia to the south-west. The Republic of Chechnya and Stavropol Krai lie to the west and the Republic of Kalmykiya to the north. Its largest rivers are the Terek, the Sulak and the Samur. It occupies an area of 50,300 sq km (19,420 sq miles) and measures some 400 km (250 miles) from south to north. Its Caspian Sea coastline, to the east, is 530 km long. The north of the Republic is flat, while in the south are the foothills and peaks of the Greater Caucasus. The Republic's lowest-lying area is the Caspian lowlands, at 28 m (92 feet) below sea level, while its highest peak is over 4,000 m high. Dagestan is made up of 41 administrative districts and 10 cities. The climate in its mountainous areas is continental and dry, while in coastal areas it is subtropical, with strong winds. Dagestan had an estimated population of 2,179,500 at 1 January 2002, giving a population density of 43.3 per sq km. In January 2001 some 39.9% of the Republic's population inhabited urban areas. In 1989, according to the census, some 27.5% of the population of Dagestan were Avars, 15.6% Dargins, 12.9% Kumyks, 11.3% Lezgis, 5.1% Laks, 4.3% Tabasarans, 1.6% Nogai, 0.8% Rutuls, 0.8% Aguls and 0.3% Tsakhurs, while ethnic Russians formed the fifth-largest nationality, accounting for 9.2%. Dagestan's capital is at Makhachkala, which had 327,600 inhabitants in 2001. The city lies on the Caspian Sea and is the Republic's main port. Other major cities are Derbent (93,200), Khasavyurt (85,300), Kaspiisk (69,500) and Buinaksk (55,400).

History

Dagestan formally came under Russian rule in 1723, when the various Muslim khanates on its territory were annexed from Persia (now Iran). The Dagestani peoples conducted a series of rebellions against Russian control, including the Murid Uprising of 1828–59, before Russian control could be established. A Dagestan ASSR was established on 20 January 1920.

The Republic of Dagestan acceded to the Federation Treaty in March 1992 and officially declared its sovereignty in May 1993. The Republic voted against the new Russian Constitution in December and adopted its own on 26 July 1994. On 21 March 1996 the powers of the Dagestani State Council, the supreme executive body, were prolonged by a further two years. When this extra term had elapsed, the republican legislature convened as a Constituent Assembly and, on 26 June 1998, confirmed Magomedali Magomedov as the Chairman of the State Council. Parliamentary elections, for a new People's Assembly, were held on 7 March 1999, at the same time as a referendum to decide whether to institute an executive presidency in Dagestan; the proposal was rejected for a third time. The republican Government was widely regarded as the federal Government's closest ally, and the most active supporter of Russian territorial integrity, among the North Caucasian republics. Consequently, it was a focus of opprobrium for rebel groups from neighbouring Chechnya, which sought to destabilize the regime or initiate political unity between the two republics. Wider inter-ethnic tensions in the North Caucasus area further destabilized the republic, although until the mid-1990s it was felt that the continuing dominance of the Communist Party had largely prevented ethnic concerns rising to the fore among the extremely diverse ethnic communities of Dagestan itself. In the second half of the decade, however, particularly strong demands for greater autonomy came from the Lezgin and Avar communities, ethnic groups represented on both sides of the Azerbaijani–Dagestani border. A constitutional change of March 1998, which permitted Magomedov to serve a second term, also removed the nationality requirements for senior republican positions; this was thought to further unsettle the fragile balance of power between the different ethnic groups in the Republic.

In January 1996 Chechen rebels seized some 2,000 hostages in the town of Kizlyar, and fighting ensued between Chechen groups and Russian federal troops at Pervomaiskoye. (The Chechen field commander, Salman Raduyev, accused of co-ordinating the incident, was sentenced to life imprisonment in December 2001, and died one year later.) Between the two wars in Chechnya (November 1994–August 1996, and from September 1999), insurgency and hostage-taking took place in Dagestan and, indeed, formed a major factor in the federal Government's decision to recommence armed conflict in Chechnya. In 1998 alone, over 100 hostages were reported in the Republic, with the actual figure considered to be probably twice that number. At that time political unrest in the Republic was led by Nadirshakh Khachilayev, the leader of the republican parliamentary faction, Union of Russian Muslims, and the brother of the head of the ethnic Lak community in Dagestan. In May 1998 a group of 200–300 fighters belonging to the Union of Russian Muslims, a political party represented in the republican parliament, occupied a government building in Makhachkala; simultaneously, 2,000 demonstrators gathered in the main city square to demand the resignation of the republican Government. Fears of increasing religious fundamentalism in the region were heightened in 1999. In August Islamist militants, described by the authorities as proponents of Wahhabism, seized several villages in Buinaksk district as 'a separate Islamic territory', while later in the same month a self-styled 'Islamic Parliament of Dagestan' was established under Siradjin Ramazanov; this Parliament was defended by an armed guard and called for a *jihad* or holy war in the North Caucasus. Although the captured villages were returned to federal control, incursions by Chechen guerrillas became more common, with Chechen Islamists, believed to be linked to the rebel commander Shamil Basayev, seeking to form a single Islamist state. A dissident campaign continued in Dagestan once armed conflict had returned to Chechnya; in September an explosion in Buinaksk, outside accommodation used by Russian troops, killed about 60 people; a larger bomb nearby was defused. Conversely, in August 2000 an Islamist group from Dagestan was thought to be responsible for ambushing and killing an élite unit of Russian paratroopers in Chechnya five months earlier. In the second half of 2001 and early 2002 a number of explosions in Dagestan, some of which targeted infrastructure, including a gas pipeline and railway line, were attributed to dissident groups linked to Chechen separatists. The republican Minister of National Policy, Information and Foreign Affairs, Magomedsalikh Gusayev, escaped an assassination attempt in Makhachkala in early June 2001, and seven federal troops were killed in an explosion in Makhachkala in January 2002. On 9 May, during celebrations in Kaspiisk to mark 'Victory Day', some 45 people were killed and more than 130 injured in an explosion, which the federal authorities attributed to Chechen rebels; following this attack, influential members of the republican State Council urged the reinstatement of capital punishment, in particular for those convicted of direct involvement in 'terrorist acts'. On 25 June the Constitutional Assembly voted by an overwhelming majority for Magomedov to serve for a third term as Chairman of the State Council. In mid-August there was renewed concern about lawlessness in the Republic when a Dutch medical worker was abducted from the suburbs of Makhachkala.

Economy

In 1999 gross regional product in the Republic of Dagestan amounted to 13,043.6m. roubles, or 6,110.3 roubles per head—one of the lowest figures among the federal units. The economic situation in the Republic suffered greatly from the wars in Chechnya, mainly as a result of the transport blockade, the energy shortage and the influx of refugees. The Republic's major industrial centres are at Makhachkala, Derbent, Kaspiisk, Izberbash, Khasavyurt, Kizlyar, Kizilyurt and Buinaksk. In 2000 there were 516 km railways and 4,474 km of paved roads in the Republic. There are fishing and trading ports in Makhachkala, which is a major junction for trading routes by rail, land and sea. The major railway line between Rostov-on-Don and Baku, Azerbaijan, runs across the territory, as does the federal Caucasus highway and the petroleum pipeline between Groznyi (Dzhokhar Gala) and Baku. There is an airport some 15 km from Makhachkala. In September 1997 the federal Government announced that a new section of the petroleum pipeline from Baku would traverse the southern part of Dagestan, rather than run through Chechnya.

The construction of the section was expected to take up to two years. However, the section was closed indefinitely in June 1999, following an explosion, caused by insurgents.

Owing to its mountainous terrain, Dagestan's economy is largely based on animal husbandry, particularly sheep-breeding. Its agriculture also consists of grain production, viniculture, horticulture and fishing. The agricultural sector employed around 33.6% of the Republic's work-force in 2000 (when just 14.3% worked in industry) and total output in that year amounted to a value of 8,199m. roubles. Its main industries are petroleum and natural gas production, electricity generation, mechanical engineering, metal-working, food-processing, the production of building materials, and handicrafts (especially chiselling and carpet-making). Industrial production in 2000 was worth 5,715m. roubles. The Republic's large defence-sector enterprises, such as the Dagdizel Caspian Plant, the Mogomed Gadzhiyev Plant, Aviagregat and the Dagestan Plant of Electrothermal Equipment, were operating below capacity by the mid-1990s.

Dagestan's economically active population comprised 830,000 inhabitants in 2000. In that year over one-quarter of the Republic's labour force (25.6%) were unemployed. In mid-2002 the average monthly wage was 2,188.6 roubles, the lowest in the Federation. There was a budgetary surplus of 307.3m. roubles in 2000. Foreign investment in the territory was minimal (amounting to just US $53,000 in 1998), owing to Dagestan's proximity to Chechnya and its own incidences of insurgency and unrest. In August 1999 the federal Government approved funds of 100m. roubles in reconstruction assistance and a further 12m. roubles to aid displaced persons. There were 2,000 small businesses in Dagestan at the end of 2000.

Directory

Chairman of the State Council (Head of the Republic): MAGOMEDALI M. MAGOMEDOV; 367000 Dagestan, Makhachkala, pl. Lenina 1; tel. and fax (8722) 67-30-60.

Chairman of the Government: KHIZRI I. SHIKHSAIDOV; 367005 Dagestan, Makhachkala, pl. Lenina; tel. (8722) 67-20-17.

Chairman of the People's Assembly: MUKHU G. ALIYEV; 367065 Dagestan, Makhachkala, pl. Lenina; tel. (8722) 67-30-55; fax (8722) 67-3066.

Chief Representative of the Republic of Dagestan in the Russian Federation: Gadzhi MAGOMED K. GAMZAYEV; 105062 Moscow, ul. Pokrovka 28; tel. (095) 916-15-36; fax (095) 928-41-12.

Head of Makhachkala City Administration: SAID DZ. AMIROV; 367025 Dagestan, Makhachkala, pl. Lenina 2; tel. (8722) 67-21-57; internet www .makhachkala.dgu.ru.

Republic of Ingushetiya

The Republic of Ingushetiya (formerly the Ingush Republic and prior to that part of the Checheno-Ingush ASSR) is situated on the northern slopes of the Greater Caucasus, in the centre of the Northern Caucasus mountain ridge. It forms part of the Southern Federal Okrug and the North Caucasus Economic Area. The Republic of Chechnya borders Ingushetiya on its eastern and northern sides and the Republic of North Osetiya—Alaniya (Ossetia) lies to the west. In the southern mountains there is an international border with Georgia. The Terek, which forms part of the northern border of Ingushetiya, the Assa and the Sunzha are the territory's main rivers. The Republic is extremely mountainous, with some peaks over 3,000 m high. The territory of the Republic occupies about 3,600 sq km (1,400 sq miles) and includes four cities. However, the border with Chechnya is not exactly determined, and the Ingush were also in dispute with the Osetians. There were thought to be around 35,000 displaced persons from the Prigorodnyi raion of North Osetiya—Alaniya in the Republic. The number of refugees from Chechnya has fluctuated with the conflict; estimated figures in October 1999, in the early stages of the 'Second Chechen War', were in the region of 155,000, but one year later the establishment of large-scale refugee camps in the Republic brought the total to around 210,000. (However, in late 2002 there were reports that such refugee camps were to be closed by the end of the year.) At 1 January 2002 the estimated population of the Republic had increased to 466,300, giving a population density of some 129.5 per sq km. In 2001 some 42.2% of the population lived in urban areas. The Ingush are a Muslim people closely related to the Chechens (collectively they are known as Vainakhs). They are indigenous to the Caucasus Mountains and have been known historically as Galgai, Lamur, Mountaineers and Kist. With the Chechens, the Ingush are the only people of the North Caucasus to have had no aristocracy. Like the Chechen language, their native tongue is a dialect of the Nakh group of the Caucasian language family. Ingushetiya's administrative centre is at Magas, a new city, opened officially in October 1998, which was named after the medieval Alanic capital believed to have been situated thereabouts. Initially the city consisted solely of a gold-domed presidential palace and government buildings, and by January 2001 its population was only about 100. The former capital of Nazran, approximately 15 miles from Magas, remained the largest city in the Republic, with a population of 113,400 at January 2001. Its other principal cities are Malgobek (53,100) and Karabulak (27,700).

History

The Ingush are descended from the western Nakh people, whose different reaction to Russian colonization of the Caucasus region in the 1860s distinguished them from their eastern counterparts (subsequently known as the Chechens). The Chechens resisted the invaders violently and were driven into the mountains, while the Ingush reacted more passively and settled on the plains. Despite this, the Ingush suffered severely under Soviet rule. In 1920 their territory was temporarily integrated into the Mountain (Gorskaya) People's Republic, but became the Ingush Autonomous Oblast on 7 July 1924. In 1934 the region was joined to the Checheno-Ingush Autonomous Oblast, which was upgraded to the status of a Republic in 1936. At this time, many leading Ingush intellectuals became victims of 'purges' and the Ingush literary language was banned. In February 1944 the entire Ingush population (74,000, according to the 1939 census) was deported to Soviet Central Asia, owing to its alleged collaboration with Nazi Germany. The territory was subsequently handed over to the Osetians. On their return after rehabilitation in 1957 the Ingush were forced to purchase the property from Osetian settlers.

Their treatment at the hands of the Government encouraged anti-Russian sentiment among the Ingush, who began to seek more autonomy and independence from their Chechen neighbours (who had also been deported). With the ascendancy in the ASSR of the All-National Congress of the Chechen People in 1991, a *de facto* separation was achieved. In June 1992 the Supreme Soviet of the Russian Federation formalized Ingushetiya's existence as an autonomous republic within Russia. The exact borders within the former ASSR were not delineated, but the Ingush dominated the western territories. In addition, the new Republic claimed the eastern regions of North Osetiya and part of the Osetian capital, Vladikavkaz; the city had been a shared capital until the 1930s. The raion of Prigorodnyi, with a majority of Ingush inhabitants, was at the centre of the dispute. (A federal law passed in April 1991 established the right for deported peoples to repossess their territory.) Armed hostilities between the two Republics ensued from October 1992, until a peace agreement was signed in 1994, although subsequent relations remained strained, particularly over the issue of the return and resettlement of refugees; protests at the failure of both the regional and federal Government to facilitate rehabilitation arrangements continued in 2001. The successful implementation of a settlement between Ingushetiya and North Osetiya, signed in March, according to which the Ingush could return to their former homes in Prigorodnyi and Vladikavkaz, was inhibited by logistical difficulties and protests by Osetiyans. In October 2002 Ingushetia and North Osetiya signed an 'Agreement on the Development of Co-operation and Good Neighbourly Relations', which committed both sides to adopting measures to resolve their remaining differences.

On 27 February 1994, alongside simultaneous parliamentary and presidential elections in the Republic, 97% of the electorate voted in favour of a draft republican constitution, which took immediate effect. The population of Ingushetiya remained generally supportive of the regime of the federal President, but strongly opposed the war in Chechnya. This apparent inconsistency was reflected in the outcome of the federal presidential election of 26 March 2000; despite his leading role in recommencing armed hostilities in Chechnya, Ingushetiya awarded Vladimir Putin the largest proportion of the votes (85.4%) cast for any candidate in any federal subject. At the republican presidential election, held on 1 March 1998, Ruslan Aushev was re-elected. Against a background of continuing extremist violence in the Republic, Aushev declared his intention to pursue a policy of further stabilization in the Caucasus. His popular mandate, however, emboldened him to seek to amend federal law to conform more closely to what he termed 'national traditions', but which also incorporated aspects *Shari'a*, or Islamic law. Following a declaration by President Boris Yeltsin that a planned referendum, which sought, in particular, to pardon those charged with crimes such as revenge killings, was unconstitutional, in February 1999 Aushev signed a power-sharing agreement with the federal Government. In July Aushev issued a decree, permitting men up to four wives, in breach of the Russian Federation's family code. Aushev was critical of the federal Government's actions in Chechnya, stating in June 2001 that the conflict in the Republic could not be resolved by the use of military force; in 2000 Aushev had been stripped of the rank of lieutenant-general by President Putin, and sources suggested this was in response to his criticism of federal policy in Chechnya. In November 2001 the People's Assembly voted to shorten the presidential term by one year, to four years, and scheduled presidential elections for March 2002. However, in December 2001 the republican Supreme Court declared these measures to be unconstitutional. In late December Aushev resigned as republican President, having announced that he would not seek re-election; in January 2002 he was appointed as Ingushetiya's representative in the Federation Council, the upper chamber of the Russian Federal Assembly. (However, Aushev resigned from this position in April, protesting at the apparent powerlessness of the Assembly, and at alleged interference by the federal authorities in the republican electoral process, following the disqualification of Khamzat Gutseriyev, Aushev's preferred candidate for the republican presidency.) After an inconclusive first round of voting on 7 April, Murat Zyazikov, the Deputy Presidential Representative in the Southern Federal Okrug (and a general in the Federal Security Service—FSB), and Alikhan Amirkhanov, a State Duma deputy supported by Aushev, progressed to a second round. On 28 April Zyazikov was elected President, receiving 53% of the votes cast. In late September up to 70 deaths were reported near the village of Galashki, as Chechen rebels clashed with Russian federal forces; notably, rebels shot down a helicopter gunship, killing two people.

Economy

In 1999 the gross regional product of the Republic totalled 2,030.7m. roubles, or just 5,040.1 roubles per head. Essentially agricultural, Ingushetiya had hoped to benefit from the transit of Caspian hydrocarbons from the beginning of the 2000s, although continuing instability in neighbouring Chechnya and Dagestan appeared to reduce its prospects in the short term. In 2000 there were 39 km (24 miles) of railways and 804 km of paved roads in the Republic.

In the early 1990s Ingushetiya's economy was largely agricultural (the sector employed only 6.6% of the Republic's work-force in 2000, compared with 28.5% in 1995), its primary activity being cattle-breeding. The serious decline in agricultural production led to intervention by the republican Government; unprofitable collective farms were converted into private enterprises and joint-stock companies. By 1 January 1997 there were over 1,000 private farms and 20 joint-stock companies in the Republic. In 2000 the value of its agricultural output was 826m. roubles. Ingushetiya's industry, which employed just 8.1% of the working population in 2000, consists of electricity production, petroleum-refining and food-processing. The major petroleum company, LUKoil, was a participant in the construction of the Caspian pipeline running through the territory. Total industrial production amounted to a value of 895m. roubles in 2000. From the mid-1990s the services sector had also made a contribution to the economy, with the local economy receiving substantial benefits from registration fees paid by companies operating in the so-called 'offshore' tax haven that was in operation in 1994–97. At that time, the resources of this zone accounted for some 70% of the Republic's capital investments, but it was terminated following criticism by the IMF. In 2000 the economic sectors providing the largest share of employment in Ingushetiya were trade and commerce (19.4% of the total) and construction (17.2%).

In 2000 the economically active population of Ingushetiya numbered 112,000, and in that year some 32.0% of the Republic's labour force were unemployed, by far the highest level of any federal subject (excluding Chechnya, for which no figures were available). None the less, this represented a considerable improvement compared with preceding years; in 1997 as many as 58.2% of Ingushetiya's labour force were out of work, and the rate of unemployment remained in excess of 50% in 1998 and 1999. In 2002 the average monthly wage in the Republic was 3,518.8 roubles. In 2000 the regional budget showed a surplus of 25.7m. roubles. In that year the value of the Republic's foreign trade amounted to US $72.6m. in exports and $91.6m. in imports. In 2000 there were approximately 300 small businesses in the Republic.

Directory

President: MURAT M. ZYAZIKOV; 366720 Ingushetiya, Magas, Dom Pravitelstva; tel. and fax (87345) 5-11-55; e-mail murad@ingushetia.ru; internet ingushetia.ru.

Chairman of the Government (Prime Minister): VIKTOR A. ALEKSENTSEV (acting); 366720 Ingushetiya, Magas, Dom Pravitelstva; tel. (87134) 2-33-06.

Chairman of the People's Assembly: RUSLAN S. PLIYEV; 366720 Ingushetiya, Magas, Narodnoye Sobraniye; tel. (87322) 2-61-81.

Chief Representative of the Republic of Ingushetiya in the Russian Federation: KHAMZAT M. BELKHAROYEV; 109044 Moscow, ul. Vorontsovskaya 22/2; tel. (095) 912-93-09; fax (095) 912-92-75.

Head of Magas City Administration: ILEZ M. MIZIYEV; tel. (87322) 6-10-81.

Kabardino-Balkar Republic (Kabardino-Balkariya)

The Kabardino-Balkar Republic is situated on the northern slopes of the Greater Caucasus and on the Kabardin Flatlands. It forms part of the Southern Federal Okrug and the North Caucasus Economic Area. The Republic of North Osetiya—Alaniya (Ossetia) lies to the east and there is an international border with Georgia in the south-west. Stavropol Krai lies to the north, with the Republic of Karachayevo-Cherkessiya to the west. Kabardino-Balkariya's major rivers are the Terek, the Malka and the Baskan. The territory of the Republic occupies an area of 12,500 sq km (4,800 sq miles), of which one-half is mountainous. The highest peak in Europe, twin-peaked Elbrus, at a height of 5,642 m (18,517 feet), is situated in Kabardino-Balkariya. The Republic consists of nine administrative districts and eight cities. At 1 January 2002 the estimated population of the Republic was 782,000, giving a population density of 62.6 per sq km, one of the highest in the Russian Federation. In January 2001 57.0% of the Republic's population lived in urban areas. Figures from the census of 1989 indicate that at that time some 48.2% of inhabitants were Kabardins, 9.4% were Balkars and 32.0% were Russian. Both the Kabardins and the Balkars are Sunni Muslims. The Kabardins' native language belongs to the Abkhazo-Adyge group of Caucasian languages. The Balkars speak a language closely related to Karachai, part of the Kipchak group of the Turkic branch of the Uralo-Altaic family. Both peoples almost exclusively speak their native tongue as a first language, but many are fluent in the official language, Russian. The capital of the Republic is at Nalchik, which had a population of 228,400 at 1 January 2001. Its other major city, Prokhladnyi, had around 59,000 inhabitants at that time.

History

The Turkic Kabardins, a Muslim people of the North Caucasus, are believed to be descended from the Adyges. They settled on the banks of the Terek river, mixed with the local Alan people, and became a distinct ethnic group in the 15th century. The Kabardins were converted to Islam by the Tatar Khanate of Crimea in the early 16th century, but in 1561 appealed to Tsar Ivan IV for protection against Tatar rule. The Ottoman Turks and the Persians (Iranians) also had interests in the region and in 1739 Kabardiya was established as a neutral state between the Ottoman and Russian Empires. In 1774, however, the region once again became Russian territory under the terms of the Treaty of Kuçuk Kainavci. Although the Kabardins were never openly hostile to the Russian authorities, in the 1860s many of them migrated to the Ottoman Empire. The Balkars were pastoral nomads until the mid-18th century, when they were forced by threats from marauding tribes to retreat further into the Northern Caucasus Mountains and settle there as farmers and livestock breeders. They were converted to Islam by Crimean Tatars, followed by the Nogai from the Kuban basin, although their faith retained strong elements of their animist traditions. Balkariya came under Russian control in 1827, when it was dominated by the Kabardins. Many ethnic Russians migrated to the region during the 19th century. In 1921 Balkar District was created as part of the Mountain (Gorskaya) People's Republic (which also included present-day Chechnya, Ingushetiya, Karachayevo-Cherkessiya and North Osetiya), but was integrated into the Kabardino-Balkar Autonomous Province the following year. The Kabardino-Balkar ASSR was established on 5 December 1936. In 1943 the Balkars were deported to Kazakhstan and Central Asia and the Balkar administrative district within the Republic was disbanded. The Balkars were not recognized as a people until 1956, when they were allowed to return to the Caucasus region.

Thus, although greatly outnumbered by Kabardins and Russians, the Balkars had developed a strong sense of ethnic identity. In 1991 they joined the Assembly of Turkic Peoples and on 18 November the first congress of the National Council of the Balkar People declared the sovereignty of Balkariya and the formation of a 'Republic of Balkariya' within the Russian Federation. Kabardino-Balkariya declared its sovereignty on 31 December 1991, and signed a bilateral treaty with the federal authorities during 1995. The Republic also developed links with its neighbours: on 21 February 1996 its President, Valerii Kokov, declared that Kabardino-Balkariya would not abide by the Commonwealth of Independent States' decision to impose sanctions on Abkhazia, Georgia, as that would run counter to a treaty between the two polities. In May 1998, at the second session of an interparliamentary council with the Republics of Adygeya and Karachayevo-Cherkessiya, a programme was adopted on the co-ordination of legislative, economic, environmental and legal activities.

Kabardino-Balkariya has an executive presidency and a bicameral Legislative Assembly or Parliament, consisting of an upper chamber known as the Soviet of the Republic and a lower chamber known as the Soviet of Representatives. The old *nomenklatura* class remained firmly in control, although its allegiance was divided between the federal Government and the Communist Party. The republican leadership took a pragmatic approach to reform and encouraged foreign investment. A new republican Constitution was adopted in July 2001, which prevented the Republic from existing independently of the Russian Federation. In August it was reported that an attempt to stage a *coup d'état* in the Republic, and in neighbouring Karachayevo-Cherkessiya, had been prevented, and that the alleged leader of the plot, Khysyr Sallagarov, had been arrested, along with his accomplices. On 13 January 2002 the incumbent republican President, Valerii Kokov, was elected to serve a third term of office, receiving 87% of the votes cast. Revisions to the republican Constitution, implemented in mid-2002, appeared to have the effect of increasing the protection of political and civil rights in the Republic; henceforth, the ability of the republican authorities to prohibit public demonstrations, rallies and meetings was to be significantly reduced.

Economy

Gross regional product in Kabardino-Balkariya amounted to 10,529.8m. roubles in 1999, equivalent to 13,295.2 roubles per head. The Republic's main industrial centres are at Nalchik, Tyrnyauz and Prokhladnyi. In 2000 there were 133 km (83 miles) of railways and 2,887 km of roads in the Republic. Prokhladnyi is an important junction on the North Caucasus Railway. There is an international airport at Nalchik, from which there are regular flights to the Middle East, as well as to other cities within the Russian Federation.

Karbardino-Balkariya's main agricultural products are maize and sunflowers. Animal husbandry, horticulture and viniculture are also important. By 1997 there were over 600 private agricultural enterprises in the Republic, covering some 5,500 ha. In 2000 around 26.6% of the Republic's work-force was engaged in the agricultural sector, the output of which was worth a total of 8,110m. roubles. Like the rest of the North Caucasus region, the Republic is rich in minerals, with reserves of petroleum, natural gas, gold, iron ore, garnet, talc and barytes. The Republic's main industries, which employed some 23.1% of the work-force in 2000, are mechanical engineering, metal-working, non-ferrous metallurgy, food-processing and light industry, the production of electricity, manufacture of building materials and the production and processing of tungsten-molybdenum ores. Total industrial output in 2000 was worth 6,033m. roubles.

In 2000 the economically active population of Kabardino-Balkariya numbered 353,000, and some 16.6% of the Republic's labour force were unemployed. In mid-2002 those in employment were earning an average of 2,375.0 roubles per month. In 2000 there was a budgetary deficit of 211.2m. roubles. External trade is minimal, amounting to only US $23.2m. in 2000. Most of the Republic's exports (of which raw materials comprise some 70%) are to Finland, Germany, the Netherlands, Turkey and the USA. Some four-fifths of its imports are from Europe. Foreign investment in the Republic in 2000 amounted to just $244,000. At 31 December 2000 there was a total of 2,200 small businesses in operation.

Directory

President: VALERII M. KOKOV; 360028 Kabardino-Balkariya, Nalchik, pr. Lenina 27; tel. (86622) 2-21-52; fax (86622) 7-61-74.

Prime Minister: KHUSEIN DZ. CHECHENOV; 360028 Kabardino-Balkariya, Nalchik, pr. Lenina 27; tel. (86622) 2-21-26; fax (86622) 7-61-83.

Chairman of the Council of the Republic of the Legislative Assembly (Parliament): ZAURBI A. NAKHUSHEV; 360028 Kabardino-Balkariya, Nalchik, pr. Lenina 55; tel. (86622) 7-13-74; fax (86622) 7-27-13.

Chairman of the Council of Representatives in the Legislative Assembly: LYUDMILA M. FEDCHENKO; 360028 Kabardino-Balkariya, Nalchik, pr. Lenina 55; tel. (86622) 40-55-79; fax (86622) 76-27-13.

Chief Representative of the Kabardino-Balkar Republic in the Russian Federa-

tion: ANATOLII M. CHERKESOV; 109004 Moscow, ul. B. Kommunisticheskaya 4; tel. (095) 911-18-52; fax (095) 912-40-53.

Head of Nalchik City Administration: MUKHAMED M. SHOGENOV; 360000 Kabardino-Balkariya, Nalchik, ul. Sovetskaya 70; tel. (86622) 2-20-04.

Republic of Kalmykiya

The Republic of Kalmykiya (known as the Republic of Kalmykiya-Khalmg Tangch in 1992–96) is situated in the north-western part of the Caspian Sea lowlands. It forms part of the Southern Federal Okrug and the Volga Economic Area. The south-eastern part of the Republic lies on the Caspian Sea. It has a southern border with the Republic of Dagestan and a south-western border with Stavropol Krai, while Rostov, Volgograd and Astrakhan Oblasts lie to the west, north-west and north-east, respectively. The Republic occupies an area of 75,900 sq km (29,300 sq miles), one-half of which is desert, and comprises 13 administrative districts and three cities. At 1 January 2002 it had an estimated population of 305,600, giving a population density of 4.0 per sq km. In January 2001 42.3% of the Republic's population lived in urban areas. In 1989, according to the census, some 45.4% of the total population were Kalmyks and 37.7% Russians. Unusually for Europe, the dominant religion among the Kalmyks is Lamaism (Tibetan Buddhism). Their native language is from the Mongol division of the Uralo-Altaic family and is spoken as a first language by some 90% of the indigenous population. The capital of Kalmykiya is at Elista, which had 107,800 inhabitants at 1 January 2001.

History

The Kalmyks (also known as the Kalmuks, Kalmucks, and Khalmgs) originated in Eastern Turkestan (Central Asia—Dzungaria or Sungaria, mostly now part of

81

the province of Xinjiang, People's Republic of China) and were a semi-nomadic Mongol-speaking people. Displaced by the Han Chinese, some 100,000 Kalmyks migrated westwards, in 1608 reaching the Volga basin, an area between the Don and Ural rivers, which had been under Russian control since the subjugation of the Astrakhan Khanate in 1556. The region, extending from Stavropol in the west to Astrakhan in the east, became the Kalmyk Khanate, which was dissolved by Russia in 1771. By this time the Kalmyk community was severely depleted, the majority having been slaughtered during a mass migration eastwards to protect the Oirots from persecution by the Chinese. Those that remained were dispersed: some settled along the Ural, Terek and Kuma rivers, some were moved to Siberia, while others became Don Cossacks. Many ethnic Russians and Germans invited by Catherine (Yekaterina) II (the 'Great') settled in Kalmykiya during the 18th century. In 1806 the Kalmyks' pasture lands were greatly reduced by the tsarist Government, forcing many to abandon their nomadic lifestyle and find work as fishermen and salt miners. A Kalmyk Autonomous Oblast was established by the Soviet Government on 4 November 1920 and the Kalmyks living in other regions of Russia were resettled there. Its status was upgraded to that of an ASSR in 1935. In 1943 the Republic was dissolved as retribution for the Kalmyks' alleged collaboration with German forces. The Kalmyks were deported to Central Asia, where they lived until their *de facto* rehabilitation in 1956. A Kalmyk Autonomous Oblast was reconstituted in 1957 and an ASSR in 1958. However, in the late 1990s territorial disputes between Kalmykiya and Astrakhan Oblast over a particularly fertile area known as the 'Black Lands' resurfaced, with Kalmykiya claiming three districts that had been part of the pre-1943 Kalmyk Republic. These territories were of particular significance, because they stood on the route of a pipeline being constructed from Tengiz, Kazakhstan, to Novorossiisk, in Krasnodar Krai.

During the late 1980s a growing Kalmyk nationalist movement began protesting against the treatment of the Kalmyks under Stalin (Iosif V. Dzhugashvili) and demanding local control of the region's mineral resources. A declaration of sovereignty by the Republic was adopted on 18 October 1990. On 28 December 1993 the Kalmyks were formally rehabilitated by the federal President. On 11 March 1994 the President of Kalmykiya, Kirsan Ilyumzhinov, abrogated the republican Constitution and decreed that from 25 March only the Russian basic law would be valid in the Republic. However, a new republican Constitution, known as the Steppe Legislation, was adopted on 5 April 1994.

In 1995 Ilyumzhinov was the sole, unopposed candidate in the presidential election, in contravention of federal legislation. There was little serious challenge to his rule in the second half of the decade, although he attracted an increasing degree of controversy. On 16 February 1998 he issued a decree abolishing the republican Government, in order to reduce public spending and bureaucracy. Of particular concern, however, was the arrest of one of the President's former aides in connection with the alleged murder, on 6 June, of Larisa Yudina, editor of the sole opposition newspaper (printed by necessity outside the Republic, in Volgograd). The controversy surrounding Yudina's death added to outside interest in the 1998 Chess Olympiad, held in September in Elista. The event, promoted by Ilyumzhinov (head of the International Chess Federation—FIDE), was allegedly funded by government funds intended for social security and investment in agriculture and industry. There were repeated reports of financial irregularities on the part of the republican authorities—the federal legislature instructed the Audit Chamber to investigate the legitimacy of federal budget spending in 1996–98. Subsequently, Ilyumzhinov became regarded as one of the founders of the pro-Government Unity bloc prior to the federal parliamentary election of December 1999. Reforms to the republican Constitution, approved in mid-2002 as part of a federal programme to ensure the harmonization of federal and republican legislation, appeared to place greater restrictions upon the Kalmyk authorities than had hitherto existed; notably, elected local councils were to be established, and heads of local and city administrations to be re-instated. Ilyumzhinov was re-elected as President on 27 October, securing some 57% of the votes cast.

Economy

The Republic's gross regional product amounted to 2,127.1m. roubles, or 6,733.3 roubles per head in 1999. Kalmykiya is primarily an agricultural territory. In the 1990s much of its agricultural land suffered from desertification, a consequence of its irresponsible exploitation by the Soviet authorities during the 1950s, when the fragile black topsoil on the steppe was ploughed up or grazed all year round by sheep and cattle. Kalmykiya's major industrial centres are at Elista and Kaspiisk. In 2000 there were 154 km (96 miles) of railway lines and 2,367 km of paved roads in the Republic; 65% of the road network was paved in 1998. The Republic is intersected by the Astrakhan–Kizlyar railway line. The Republic has serious problems with its water supply, with a deficit of fresh water affecting almost all regions.

Kalmykiya's agriculture consists mainly of grain production and animal husbandry. Although agricultural output declined sharply, in real terms, throughout much of the 1990s, by 2000 the sector continued to employ 28.4% of the Republic's work-force, and it generated 1,281m. roubles in that year, compared with 465m. roubles in 1998. The Republic's industry, which engaged just 7.9% of the working population in 2000, consists mainly of electricity production, the manufacture of building materials, food-processing and the production of petroleum and natural gas. In 2000 industrial output was equivalent to 1,546m. roubles. The Republic has major hydrocarbons reserves, the more efficient exploitation of which was named a primary objective of Aleksandr Dordzhdeyev, the premier appointed in August 1999, who aimed to increase petroleum output in the Republic to between 1.5m. and 2.0m. metric tons each year. In August 1995, Kalmykiya began negotiations with several foreign countries to build a petroleum refinery in Elista with an annual capacity of 500,000 tons of petroleum products. The Oman Oil Company and LUKoil (a Russian company) showed interest in exploiting the Republic's petroleum and natural gas deposits, as part of a wider programme of exploitation across the Northern Caspian region. In September 2000 discussions began on the establishment of a Kalmyk-Belarusian joint venture to extract and process crude petroleum. Despite its potential, Kalmykiya is a net importer of energy.

The economically active population in the Republic amounted to 145,000 in 2000, when some 20.1% of the Republic's labour force were unemployed. The average monthly wage in mid-2002 was 2,564.4 roubles. There was a budgetary deficit of 26.0m. roubles in 2000. In 1995 there was some US $1.64m. of foreign investment in the Republic. At the end of 2000 the Republic had 900 small businesses.

Directory

President: KIRSAN N. ILYUMZHINOV; 358000 Kalmykiya, Elista, pl. Lenina, Dom Pravitelstva; tel. (84722) 6-13-88; fax (84722) 6-28-80; e-mail aris_rk@cityline.ru; internet kirsan.kalmykia.ru.

Chairman of the Government: ALEKSANDR V. DORZHDEYEV; 358000 Kalmykiya, Elista, pl. Lenina, Dom Pravitelstva; tel. (84722) 5-27-14.

Chairman of the People's Khural (Parliament): VYACHESLAV A. BEMBETOV; 358000 Kalmykiya, Elista, pl. Lenina, Dom Pravitelstva; tel. (84722) 5-27-32; fax (84722) 5-03-02.

Chief Representative of the Republic of Kalmykiya in the Russian Federation: ALEKSEI M. ORLOV; 121170 Moscow, ul. Poklonnaya 12/2; tel. (095) 249-87-30; fax (095) 249-87-41; e-mail kalmykia@data.ru; internet www.kalmykembassy.ru.

Head of Elista City Administration (Mayor and Representative of the President): VYACHESLAV M. SHAMAYEV; 358000 Kalmykiya, Elista, pl. Lenina; tel. (84722) 5-35-81; fax (84722) 2-55-35.

Republic of Karachayevo-Cherkessiya

The Republic of Karachayevo-Cherkessiya (formerly an Autonomous Oblast within Stavropol Krai) is situated on the northern slopes of the Greater Caucasus. It forms part of the Southern Federal Okrug and the North Caucasus Economic Area. Krasnodar Krai borders it to the north-west, Stavropol Krai to the north-east and the Republic of Kabardino-Balkariya to the east. There is an international boundary with Georgia (mainly with Abkhazia) to the south. Its major river is the Kuban. The total area of the Republic occupies some 14,100 sq km (5,440 sq miles). The territory measures 140 km (87 miles) from north to south and 160 km from west to east. Karachayevo-Cherkessiya consists of eight administrative districts and four cities. It had an estimated population of 428,600 at 1 January 2002, giving a population density of 30.4 per sq km. In 2001 some 44.1% of the Republic's population inhabited urban areas and the capital city, Cherkessk, had a population of 120,700. Figures from the 1989 census showed that the Karachai accounted for 31.2% of the Republic's population, the Cherkess (Circassians) for 9.7% and ethnic Russians for 42.4%. Both the Karachai and the Cherkess are Sunni Muslims of the Hanafi school. The Cherkess speak a language close to Kabardin, from the Abkhazo-Adyge group of Caucasian languages, while the Karachais' native tongue, from the Kipchak group, is the same as that of the Balkars.

History

The Karachais, a transhumant group descended from Kipchak tribes, were driven into the highlands of the North Caucasus by marauding Mongol tribes in the 13th century. Their territory was annexed by the Russian Empire in 1828, although, like their neighbouring North Caucasian peoples, they continued to resist Russian rule throughout the 19th century. In the 1860s and 1870s many Karachai migrated to the Ottoman Empire to escape oppression by the tsarist regime. Many of the Cherkess, a Circassian people descended from the Adyges who inhabited the region between the lower Don and Kuban rivers, also fled across the Russo–Turkish border at this time. They had come under Russian control in the 1550s, having sought protection from the Crimean Tatars and some Turkic tribes, including the Karachai. Relations between the Cherkess and Russia deteriorated as many Russians began to settle in Cherkess territory. Following the Treaty of Adrianople in 1829, by which the Ottomans abandoned their claim to the Caucasus region, a series of rebellions by the Circassians and reprisals by the Russian authorities occurred. In 1864 Russia completed its conquest of the region and many Cherkess fled.

The Cherkess Autonomous Oblast was established in 1928 and was subsequently merged with the Karachai Autonomous Oblast to form the Karachayevo-Cherkess Autonomous Oblast. This represented part of Stalin—Iosif V. Dzhugashvili's policy of 'divide and conquer', by which administrative units were formed from ethnically unrelated groups (the same applied to the Kabardino-Balkar ASSR). The Karachai were deported to Central Asia in late 1943, but the Cherkess remained in the region, which was renamed the Cherkess Autonomous Oblast, until the Karachai were rehabilitated and permitted to return in 1957. Ethnic separatism in the territory, which was upgraded to republican status, and separated from Stavropol Krai, under the terms of the 1992 Federation Treaty, was, however, relatively minimal. On 6 March 1996 a new constitutional system was adopted in the Republic, based on the results of a referendum on a republican presidency. The Republic had already, in the previous year, agreed on a division of responsibilities by treaty with the Russian Federation. The Communist Party remained the predominant party, winning 40% of the republican vote in federal parliamentary elections in late 1995. In May 1998, at the second session of an interparliamentary council with the Republics of Adygeya and Kabardino-Balkariya, a programme was adopted on the co-ordination of the Republics' legislative, economic, environmental and legal activities. In September enabling legislation providing for direct elections to the republican presidency was enacted. However, the Republic's first presidential election provoked violence and ethnic unrest, when a second round of voting, in May 1999, reversed the positions achieved by the 'run-off' candidates, Stanislav Derev, an ethnic Cherkess (who secured 40% of the votes in the first round and 12% in the second), and Gen. Vladimir Semonov, an ethnic Karachai and a former Commander-in-Chief of the Russian Ground Troops (who secured 18% of the votes in the first round and 85% in the second). Semonov was confirmed as the winning candidate in August and sworn in on 14 September. Derev's supporters continued to protest at the decision, and in mid-September a congress of the Republic's Cherkess and Abazin groups voted to pursue reintegration into the former Cherkess Autonomous Oblast in neighbouring Stavropol Krai. The Republic also contained sympathizers of the secessionist regime of fellow Circassians in Abkhazia, Georgia. In August 2001 it was reported that an attempt to stage a *coup d'état* in the Republic, and in neighbouring Kabardino-Balkariya, had been prevented, and that the alleged leader of the plot, Khysyr Sallagarov, and his accomplices, had been arrested. Strong concern was subsequently expressed in the Republic at the rising levels of crime, which included the murder of both police-officers and politicians.

Economy

In 1999 gross regional product in Karachayevo-Cherkessiya totalled 4,317.5m. roubles, or 9,916.2 roubles per head. The predominant sector within the economy, in terms of volume of output and number of employees, is industry. The Republic's major industrial centres are at Cherkessk, Karachayevsk and Zelenchukskaya. In

2000 it contained 51 km of railway track and 1,887 km of paved roads, including the Stavropol–Sukhumi (Georgia) highway.

Karachayevo-Cherkessiya's agriculture, which employed some 19.0% of the working population in 2000, consists mainly of animal husbandry. At 1 January 1999 there were some 133,000 cattle, 11,700 pigs and 362,800 sheep and goats in the Republic. The production of grain, sunflower seeds, sugar beet and vegetables is also important. In 2000 total agricultural production amounted to a value of 3,106m. roubles. The Republic's main industries are petrochemicals, chemicals, mechanical engineering and metal-working, although the manufacture of building materials, food-processing and coal production are also important. In 2000 the total output of the industrial sector was equivalent to 2,834m. roubles, and it employed around 19.5% of the work-force.

In 2000 the economically active population of the Republic numbered 145,000, and 20.7% of the Republic's labour force were unemployed. The average wage was 2,596.6 roubles per month in mid-2002. In 2000 there was a budgetary surplus of 31.0m. roubles. International trade was minimal in comparison with other areas in the Federation, amounting to only US $9.6m. in 2000, and foreign investment in the Republic in that year amounted to just $65,000. At the end of that year there were 1,800 small businesses registered in the Republic.

Directory

President and Head of the Republic: VLADIMIR M. SEMENOV; 357100 Karachayevo-Cherkessiya, Cherkessk, ul. Lenina; tel. (87822) 5-88-37; fax (87822) 5-29-80.

Chairman of the Government: ALIK KH. KARDANOV; 357100 Karachayevo-Cherkessiya, Cherkess, ul. Komsomolskaya 23; tel. (87822) 5-40-08; fax (87822) 5-29-80.

Chairman of the People's Assembly: DZHANIBEK YU. SUYUNOV; 357100 Karachayevo-Cherkessiya, Cherkess, ul. Krasnoarmeiskaya 54; tel. (87822) 5-10-26; fax (87822) 5-26-47.

Chief Representative of the Republic of Karachayevo-Cherkessiya in the Russian Federation: GENNADII B. LOPATIN; Moscow; tel. (095) 959-55-15.

Head of Cherkessk City Administration (Mayor): STANISLAV E. DEREV; 357100 Karachayevo-Cherkessiya, Cherkessk, pr. Lenina 54A; tel. (87822) 5-37-23; fax (87822) 5-78-43.

Republic of Kareliya

The Republic of Kareliya (Karelia) is situated in the north-west of Russia, on the edge of the Eastern European Plain. The Republic forms part of the North-Western Federal Okrug and the Northern Economic Area. It is bordered by Finland to the west. The White Sea lies to the north-east, Murmansk Oblast to the north and Vologda and Archangel Oblasts to the south. It contains some 83,000 km (51,540 miles) of waterways, including its major rivers, the Kem and the Vyg, and its numerous lakes (the Ladoga, Ladozhskoye, and the Onega, Onezhskoye, being the largest and second largest lakes in Europe). A canal system 225 km long, the Belomorkanal (White Sea Canal), connects the Kareliyan port of Belomorsk to St Petersburg. One-half of its territory is forested and much of the area on the White Sea coast is marshland. It lies, on average, 300 m–400 m above sea level. Kareliya measures some 600 km south–north and 400 km west–east and occupies an area of 172,400 sq km (66,560 sq miles). It comprises 16 administrative districts and 13 cities. At 1 January 2002 it had an estimated population of 756,400, giving a population density of 4.4 per sq km. In January 2001 some 74.0% of the Republic's population inhabited urban areas. In 1989 some 10.0% of the population were Kareliyans (Finnish—also known as Karjala or Karyala, Korela and Karya-lainen) and 73.6% Russians. The dominant religion among Kareliyans, and in the

Republic as a whole, is Orthodox Christianity. The Kareliyan language consists of three dialects of Finnish (Livvi, Karjala and Lyydiki), which are all strongly influenced by Russian. In 1989, however, more than one-half of the ethnically Kareliyan population spoke Russian as their first language. The capital of Kareliya is at Petrozavodsk, with a population of 282,900 at 1 January 2001. Other major cities are Kondopoga (36,600) and Segezha (33,800).

History

Kareliya was an independent, Finnish-dominated state in medieval times. In common with much of present-day Finland, in the 16th century the area came under Swedish hegemony, before being annexed by Russia in 1721. A Kareliyan Labour Commune was formed on 8 June 1920 and became an autonomous republic in July 1923. A Karelo-Finnish SSR, including territory annexed from Finland, was created in 1940 as a Union Republic of the USSR. However, part of its territory was ceded to the Russian Federation in 1946 and Kareliya subsequently resumed the status of an ASSR within the Russian Federation. The Republic declared sovereignty on 9 August 1990, and was renamed the Republic of Kareliya in November 1991: a republican Constitution was adopted in January 1994. In April elections took place to a new bicameral legislature, the Legislative Assembly (consisting of a Chamber of the Republic and a Chamber of Representatives). The premier, Viktor Stepanov, who was vested with a quasi-presidential status as the republican head, was prominent in urging greater decentralization in the Russian Federation. On 17 May 1998 Stepanov was narrowly defeated in the second round of direct elections to the premiership by the former Mayor of Petrozavodsk, Sergei Katanandov. In December 2001 Stepanov (who had hitherto been widely regarded as the most popular potential challenger to the incumbent President in the forthcoming elections) was appointed as the Republic's representative to the Federation Council, the upper chamber of the Russian Federal Assembly. Katanandov was re-elected for a third term of office on 28 April 2002, receiving 54% of the votes cast.

Economy

The economy of Kareliya is largely based on its timber industry. In 1999 its gross regional product was 20,382.3m. roubles, equivalent to 26,491.2 roubles per head. Its major industrial centres include those at Petrozavodsk, Sortavala and Kem. In 2000 there were 2,105 km of railway lines and 6,567 km of paved roads in the Republic. In the mid-1990s Russia's first privately operated railway was constructed on Kareliya's territory. The Republic is at an important strategic point on Russia's roadways, linking the industrially developed regions of Russia with the major northern port of Murmansk. Its main port is at Petrozavodsk.

Kareliya's agriculture, which employed just 6.1% of the work-force in 2000, consists mainly of animal husbandry, fur farming and fishing. In that year total production within the sector was equivalent to a value of 1,705m. roubles. The Republic has important mineral reserves, and ranks among the leading producers of rosin and turpentine in the Russian Federation. An important agreement with the city of Moscow, which had need for construction materials, promised an increase in natural-stone production from some 3,000 cu m in 1998 to 20,000 cu m by 2002. Kareliya's main industries, apart from the processing of forestry products, are mechanical engineering, metallurgy and the extraction of iron ore and muscovite (mica). Industry engaged some 25.5% of the Republic's labour force in 2000, when total output within the sector was worth 25,305m. roubles. The Republic's major enterprise, Segezhabumprom, is one of the world's largest pulp and paper manufacturers; it was reorganized as a joint-stock company in 1999. In the first quarter of 2000, Kareliya produced over 50% of the paper bags, over 30% of newsprint, and over 22% of all paper in the Russian Federation. It was suggested that new duties on forestry products, introduced in December 1999, might threaten the fulfilment of existing contracts with Western customers.

The economically active population amounted to 394,000 in 2000, when 11.5% of the labour force were unemployed. The average monthly wage in the Republic was 4,613.8 roubles in mid-2002. The republican budget showed a surplus of 185.6m. roubles in 2000. In that year international exports from the Republic were worth US $538.8m., and the value of imports from abroad was $157.8m. Foreign investment in Kareliya at that time amounted to $22.2m. There were 79 foreign joint enterprises in Kareliya in 2000, of which 39 had Finnish partners. At 31 December 2000 there were some 4,000 small businesses operating in the Republic.

Directory

Chairman of the Government (Head of the Republic): SERGEI L. KATANANDOV; 185028 Kareliya, Petrozavodsk, pr. Lenina 19; tel. (8142) 76-41-41; fax (8142) 77-41-48; e-mail government@karelia.ru; internet www.gov.karelia.ru.

Legislative Assembly: 185610 Kareliya, Petrozavodsk, ul. Kuibysheva 5; tel. (8142) 77-27-48; fax (8142) 78-28-27; e-mail root@parl.karelia.ru; internet www.gov.karelia.ru/LA.

Chairman of the Chamber of the Republic: VLADIMIR V. SHILNIKOV.

Chairman of the Chamber of Representatives: NIKOLAI I. LEVIN.

Chief Representative of the Republic of Kareliya in the Russian Federation: ANATOLII A. MARKOV; 101934 Moscow, per. Arkhangelskii 1; tel. (095) 207-87-24; fax (095) 208-03-18.

Head of Petrozavodsk City Administration: VIKTOR N. MASLYAKOV; 185630 Kareliya, Petrozavodsk, pr. Lenina 2/501; tel. (8142) 78-35-70; fax (8142) 78-47-53; e-mail admcity@karelia.ru; internet admpetrozavodsk.karelia.ru.

Republic of Khakasiya

The Republic of Khakasiya is situated in the western area of the Minusinsk hollow, on the left bank of the River Yenisei, which flows northwards towards, ultimately, the Arctic Ocean. In the heart of Eurasia, it lies on the eastern slopes of the Kuznetsk Alatau and the northern slopes of the Western Sayan Mountains. It comprises part of the Siberian Federal Okrug and the East Siberian Economic Area. The Republic of Tyva lies to the south-east and the Republic of Altai to the south-west. To the west is Kemerovo Oblast, while Krasnoyarsk Krai lies to the north and east. Its major rivers are the Yenisei and the Abakan. Khakasiya occupies 61,900 sq km (23,900 sq miles) and comprises eight administrative regions and five cities. At 1 January 2002 it had an estimated population of 575,400 and a population density, therefore, of 9.3 per sq km. In 2001 some 71.0% of the population lived in urban areas. In 1989 ethnic Khakasiyans were found to number 11.1% of the population, and Russians 79.5%. However, at that time over 76% of the Khakass spoke the national language, primarily derived from the Uigur group of Eastern Hunnic languages of the Turkic family, as their native tongue. Khakasiya's capital is at Abakan, with 167,900 inhabitants in 2001.

History
The Khakasiyans were traditionally known as the Minusinsk (Minusa), the Turki, the Yenisei Tatars or the Abakan Tatars. They were semi-nomadic hunters, fishermen

and livestock-breeders. Khakasiya was a powerful state in Siberia, owing to its trading links with Central Asia and the Chinese Empire. Russian settlers began to arrive in the region in the 17th century and their presence was perceived as valuable protection against Mongol invasion. The annexation of Khakasiyan territory by the Russians was eventually completed during the reign of Peter (Petr) I ('the Great'), with the construction of a fort on the River Abakan. The Russians subsequently imposed heavy taxes, seized the best land and imposed Orthodox Christianity on the Khakasiyans. After the construction of the Trans-Siberian Railway in the 1890s the Khakasiyans were heavily outnumbered. Following the Revolution in Russia the Khakass National Okrug was established in 1923, becoming the Khakass Autonomous Oblast on 20 October 1930, as part of Krasnoyarsk Krai. In 1992 it was upgraded to the status of an Autonomous Republic under the terms of the Federation Treaty, having declared its sovereignty on 3 July 1991.

The Communist Party remained the most popular political grouping in the Republic in the early 1990s, and the nationalist ideas of Vladimir Zhirinovskii (leader of the Liberal Democratic Party of Russia) also enjoyed significant support. On 25 May 1995 the Republic adopted its Constitution. Aleksei Lebed, an independent candidate and younger brother of the politician and former general, Aleksandr Lebed (Governor of Krasnoyarsk Krai from May 1998 until his death in 2002), was elected to the presidency of the Republic in December 1996, when elections were also held for a new republican legislature. A former representative of the Republic in the State Duma, Aleksei Lebed had based his electoral campaign on the issues of administrative, budgetary, social and economic reform. There were reports in mid-1998 that the Khakass Government was considering re-union with Krasnoyarsk Krai and withholding transfers to the federal budget, but neither came to pass once Aleksei Lebed's Government convinced the federal authorities to increase financial transfers to the Republic for 1999. Lebed was re-elected as Chairman of the Government, receiving 72% of the votes cast, in December 2000.

Economy

Khakasiya's gross regional product amounted to 14,317.2m. roubles in 1999, or 24,591.3 roubles per head. Khakasiya's major industrial centres are at Abakan, Sorsk, Sayanogorsk, Chernogorsk and Balyksa. In 2000 there were 642 km (399 miles) of railway lines and 2,485 km of paved roads in the Republic.

The Republic's agriculture, which employed around 12.1% of the working population in 2000, consists mainly of grain production and animal husbandry. Total agricultural production in 2000 was worth 3,377m. roubles. The Republic's main industries are ore-mining, electricity production, light manufacturing, mechanical engineering, non-ferrous metallurgy and the processing of agricultural products. A major element of industrial activity was the processing of natural resources. In 1997 Khakasiya was estimated to have reserves of 36,000m. metric tons of coal and 1,500m. tons of iron ore. Other mineral reserves included molybdenum, lead, zinc, barytes, aluminium and clay. There was also the potential for extraction of petroleum and natural gas. In 2000 the Republic's industrial output amounted to a value of 14,114m. roubles, and the industrial sector employed 24.6% of the work-force.

The Republic's economically active population numbered 267,000 in 2000, when 12.3% of the labour force were unemployed. The average monthly wage stood at 4,146.5 roubles in mid-2002. The republican budget for 2000 showed a deficit of

30.7m. roubles. Foreign investment in Khakasiya was minimal. Throughout the 1990s the highest level recorded was US $2.3m., in 1996, and such investment totalled just $24,000 in 2000. However, external trade was been somewhat more substantial; in 2000 exports amounted to a value of $380.0m., of which some 91% were with countries outside the Commonwealth of Independent States, and imports amounted to $187.2m. At 31 December 2000 there were 1,500 small businesses registered in the Republic.

Directory

Chairman of the Government: ALEKSEI I. LEBED; 662619 Khakasiya, Abakan, pr. Lenina 67; tel. (39022) 9-91-02; fax (39022) 6-50-96; e-mail pressa@khakasnet.ru; internet www.gov.khakassia.ru.

Chairman of the Supreme Council: VLADIMIR N. SHTYGASHEV; 662619 Khakasiya, pr. Lenina 67; tel. (39022) 6-74-00; fax (39022) 6-50-96.

Chief Representative of the Republic of Khakasiya in the Russian Federation: VIKTOR K. BABAKHIN; 127025 Moscow, ul. Novyi Arbat 19/830; tel. (095) 203-83-41; fax (095) 203-83-45.

Head of Abakan City Administration: NIKOLAI G. BULAKIN; 662600 Khakasiya, Abakan, ul. Shchetinkina 10A/6, POB 6; tel. and fax (39022) 6-37-91; internet meria.abakan.ru.

Republic of Komi

The Republic of Komi is situated in the north-east of European Russia. Its northern border lies some 50 km within the Arctic Circle. It forms part of the North-Western Federal Okrug and the Northern Economic Area. Mountains of the Northern, Circumpolar and Polar Urals occupy the eastern part of the Republic. Its major rivers are the Pechora, the Vychegda and the Mezen. Komi is bordered to the west by Archangel Oblast, to the north by the Nenets Autonomous Okrug, and to the east by the Tyumen Oblast (both the Oblast proper and the two Autonomous Okrugs, Khanty-Mansii and Yamal-Nenets). To the south Komi borders Kirov Oblast, Perm Oblast (including the Komi-Permyak Autonomous Okrug) and Sverdlovsk Oblast. Some 90% of its territory is taiga (forested marshland), while the extreme north-east of the Republic lies within the Arctic tundra zone. The Republic occupies an area of 415,900 sq km (160,580 sq miles). It comprises 12 administrative districts and 10 cities and had an estimated population of 1,117,200 at 1 January 2002, and a population density, therefore, of 2.7 per sq km. In 2001 some 74.2% of the population lived in urban areas. In 1989 some 23.3% of the Republic's inhabitants were Komi and 57.7% were ethnic Russians. The predominant religion in the region is Orthodox Christianity, although among the Komi this faith is combined with strong animist traditions. Their language, spoken as a native tongue by some 74% of the Komi population, belongs to the Finnic branch of the Uralo-Altaic family. Komi's capital is at Syktyvkar, which had a population of 227,700 in 2001. The Republic's other major cities are Ukhta (98,700), Vorkuta (87,400) and Pechora (58,800).

History

The Komi (known historically as the Zyryans or the Permyaks) are descended from inhabitants of the river basins of the Volga, the Kama, the Pechora and the Vychegda. From the 12th century Russian settlers began to inhabit territory along the Vychegda, and later the Vym, rivers. The Vym subsequently acquired a strategic significance as the main route along which Russian colonists advanced to Siberia, and Ust-Sysolsk (now Syktyvar), the territory's oldest city, was founded in 1586. The number of Slavs increased after the territory was annexed by Russia in 1478. The region soon acquired importance as the centre of mining and metallurgy, following the discovery of copper and silver ores in 1491. In 1697 petroleum was discovered in the territory; the first refinery was built by F. Pryadunov in 1745. The Komi were renowned as shrewd commercial traders and exploited important trade routes between Archangel and Siberia, via the Vyatka-Kama basin. Trade in fish, furs and game animals developed in the 17th century, while coal, timber, iron ore and paper became significant in the years prior to the Russian Revolution. The Komi Autonomous Oblast was established on 22 August 1921 and became an ASSR in 1931.

The Komi Republic declared its sovereignty on 30 August 1990. A new republican Constitution was adopted on 17 February 1994, establishing a quasi-presidential premier at the head of government and a State Council as the legislature; the territory became known as the Republic of Komi. In March 1996 the republican and federal Governments signed a power-sharing treaty, which included agreements on foreign relations, energy, education, natural resources and employment. In mid-1998 the republican Government came under pressure from local miners, who were owed more than 400m. roubles in wage arrears, and in November the Government retained federal revenues in order to pay pensioners. The Republic repudiated its declaration of sovereignty in September 2001, following a ruling of the federal Supreme Court, which stated that over one-half of the provision's declarations were in contravention of federal law. The republican presidential election, held on 16 December, was won by Vladimir Torlopov, hitherto Chairman of the Republic's State Council, who received 40% of the votes cast, while the incumbent, Yurii Spiridonov, received 35%. Torlopov received the support of the liberal Yabloko party, whereas Spiridonov's supporters included the pro-Government Unity and Fatherland-United Russia party. In May 2002 Torlopov signed an agreement with federal President Vladimir Putin, annulling the power-sharing treaty signed with Komi in 1996.

Economy

The Republic of Komi is Russia's second largest fuel and energy base. Apart from a wealth of natural resources, it is strategically placed close to many of Russia's major industrial centres and has a well-developed transport network. It also contains Europe's largest area of virgin forest—approximately one-third of its massive forest stock (amounting to 2,800m. cu m) has never been cut. In the 1990s Komi had a high ranking within the Federation in terms of gross domestic product per head and it possessed a wealth of natural resources. However, in order to fulfil its economic potential the Republic needed to improve its export performance and diversify its economy into higher value-added activities. In 1999 gross regional product in the Republic amounted to 50,914m. roubles, equivalent to 44,587.4 roubles per head—one of the highest figures in Russia. Komi's major industrial centres are at Syktyvkar, Ukhta and Sosnogorsk. In 2000 the Republic contained 1,692 km (1,051 miles) of railway lines and 5,253 km of paved roads.

Komi's agriculture, which employed 4.8% of the work-force in 2000, consists mainly of animal husbandry, especially reindeer-breeding. Total production within the sector amounted to a value of 2,715m. roubles in 2000. Ore-mining was developing from the mid-1990s: the Republic contained the country's largest reserves of bauxite, titanium, manganese and chromium ore. It also accounted for around one-half of northern Europe's petroleum stock and one-third of its natural gas reserves. Total output from industry, which was based on the processing of forestry products, the production of coal and the production and processing of petroleum and natural gas, was worth 53,362m. roubles in 2000, when the sector employed 24.3% of the work-force.

In 2000 the economically active population numbered 594,000, and 12.1% of the labour force were unemployed. In mid-2002 the average monthly wage in the Republic was relatively high, at 6,274.0 roubles. In 2000 there was a budgetary surplus of 149.5m. roubles. Foreign trade was encouraged, with, for example, an agreement being reached with Iran in December 1998. In 2000 exports from the Republic amounted to US $1,121.5m., compared with $73.3m. of imports to the Republic. Foreign investment in Komi was substantial in the late 1990s, amounting to $218.1m. in 1998, although the level of investment had declined, to $54.0m., by 2000. In the mid-1990s a number of joint ventures were established in Komi, with investment from France, the United Kingdom and the USA. These included Komi Arctic Oil, Sever TEK and Northern Lights. At 31 December 2000 there were 4,000 small businesses in operation.

Directory

Chairman of the Government (Head of the Republic): VLADIMIR A. TORLOPOV; 167010 Komi, Syktyvkar, ul. Kommunisticheskaya 9; tel. (8212) 28-51-05; fax (8212) 28-52-52; internet www.rkomi.ru.

Chairman of the State Council: YEVGENII N. BORISOV; 167010 Komi, Syktyvkar, ul. Kommunisticheskaya 9; tel. (8212) 28-55-08; fax (8212) 42-44-90.

Chief Representative of the Republic of Komi in the Russian Federation: NIKOLAI N. KOCHURIN; 125367 Moscow, Volokolamskoye shosse 62; tel. and fax (095) 490-10-80.

Head of Syktyvkar City Administration: YEVGENII N. BORISOV; 167000 Komi, Syktyvkar, ul. Babushkina 22; tel. (8212) 42-41-20.

Republic of Marii-El

The Republic of Marii-El is situated in the east of the Eastern European Plain in the middle reaches of the River Volga. It forms part of the Volga Federal Okrug and the Volga-Vyatka Economic Area. Tatarstan and Chuvashiya neighbour it to the south-east and to the south, respectively. Nizhnii Novgorod Oblast lies to the west and Kirov Oblast to the north and north-east. Its major rivers are the Volga and the Vetluga and about one-half of its territory is forested. Marii-El measures 150 km (over 90 miles) from south to north and 275 km from west to east. It occupies an area of 23,200 sq km (9,000 sq miles) and consists of 14 administrative districts and four cities. At 1 January 2002 the estimated population was 750,300, and the population density approximately 32.3 per sq km. In 2001 some 61.6% of the population inhabited urban areas. In 1989 some 43.3% of the Republic's inhabitants were Mari (also known as Cheremiss) and 47.5% ethnic Russians. Orthodox Christianity is the predominant religion in Marii-El, although many Mari have remained faithful to aspects of their traditional animistic religion. Their native language belongs to the Finnic branch of the Uralo-Altaic family. The capital of the Republic is at Ioshkar-Ola, with a population of 248,500 at 1 January 2001. The Republic's other major cities are Volzhsk (61,400) and Kozmodemyansk (24,100).

History
The Mari emerged as a distinct ethnic group in the sixth century. In the eighth century they came under the influence of the Khazar empire, but from the mid-ninth to the mid-12th century they were ruled by the Volga Bulgars. In the 1230s Mari territory was conquered by the Mongol Tatars and remained under the control of the Khazar Khanate until its annexation by Russia in 1552. Nationalist feeling on the part of the Mari did not become evident until the 1870s, when a religious movement, the Kugu Sorta (Great Candle), attacked the authority of the Orthodox Church in the region. A Mari Autonomous Oblast was established in 1920. On 5 December 1936 the territory became the Mari ASSR.

The Republic declared its sovereignty on 22 October 1990. A presidential election was held on 14 December 1991. In December 1993 elections were held to a new 300-seat parliament, the State Assembly, which was dominated by the Communist Party. The new legislature adopted the republican Constitution in June 1995, when the territory became known as the Republic of Marii-El. Republican legislative elections in October 1996 saw 18 of the 67 seats won by mayors and executive branch officials, despite this being in breach of federal law; consequently the Russian Supreme Court ruled these elections illegal on 23 October. A power-sharing agreement between the Republic and the federal Government was signed in May 1998. At parliamentary elections held in the Republic in October 2000, left-wing and communist candidates again secured the highest proportion of the votes cast. At gubernatorial elections in December the incumbent, Vyacheslav Kislitsyn, was defeated by Leonid Markelov, who represented the nationalist Liberal Democratic Party of Vladimir Zhirinovskii.

Economy

In 1999 the Republic's gross regional product amounted to 10,467.7m. roubles, equivalent to 13,771.5 roubles per head. Its major industrial centres are at Ioshkar-Ola and Volzhsk. In 2000 there were 204 km of railway lines and 3,233 km of paved roads on the Republic's territory.

Marii-El's agriculture, which in 2000 employed 20.0% of the work-force, consists mainly of animal husbandry and flax and grain production. Total agricultural output in 2000 was worth 5,847m. roubles. The Republic's main industries are mechanical engineering, metal-working, electricity production and the processing of forestry and food products. The total value of production within the industrial sector (which employed 24.4% of the work-force) was 8,585m. roubles in 2000.

In 2000 the economically active population in the Republic numbered 370,000, and 11.3% of the labour force were unemployed; in mid-2002 those in employment earned an average of 2,358.6 roubles per month. In 2000 there was a budgetary deficit of 36.2m. roubles. In that year the value of external trade with the Republic amounted to just US $45.2m. (of which exports accounted for $32.6m.). Exports primarily comprised raw materials (peat), machine parts and medical supplies, and its major trading partners were Belarus, Finland, France, Germany, Ireland, Italy, Kazakhstan, the Netherlands, Ukraine, the United Kingdom and the USA. Foreign investment in Marii-El was minimal, amounting to just $140,000 in 2000. At 31 December 2000 there were 4,100 small businesses registered in the Republic.

Directory

President and Head of the Government: LEONID I. MARKELOV; 424001 Marii-El, Ioshkar-Ola, Leninskii pr. 29; tel. (8362) 64-15-25; fax (8362) 64-19-21; e-mail president@gov.mari.ru; internet gov.mari.ru.

Chairman of the State Assembly: YURII A. MINAKOV; 424001 Marii-El, Ioshkar-Ola, Leninskii pr. 29; tel. (8362) 64-14-13; e-mail parliament@gov.mari.ru; internet parliament.mari.ru.

Chief Representative of the Republic of Marii-El in the Russian Federation: VIKTOR P. RASSONOV; 119019 Moscow, ul. Novyi Arbat 21; tel. (095) 291-48-38; fax (095) 291-46-32.

Head of Ioshkar-Ola City Administration (Mayor): VENIAMIN V. KOZLOV; 424001 Marii-El, Ioshkar-Ola, Leninskii pr. 27; tel. (8362) 55-64-01; fax (8362) 55-64-22; internet capital.mari-el.ru:8101.

Republic of Mordoviya

The Republic of Mordoviya is situated in the Eastern European Plain, in the Volga river basin. The north-west of the Republic occupies a section of the Oka-Don plain and the south-east lies in the Volga Highlands. The region forms part of the Volga Federal Okrug and the Volga-Vyatka Economic Area. The Republic of Chuvashiya lies to the north-east of Mordoviya. The neighbouring oblasts are Ulyanovsk to the east, Penza to the south, Ryazan to the west and Nizhnii Novgorod to the north. The major rivers in Mordoviya are the Moksha, the Sura and the Insar; one-quarter of its land area is forested. The territory of Mordoviya straddles the two major natural regions in Russia, forest and steppe, and occupies an area of 26,200 sq km (10,110 sq miles). The Republic consists of 22 administrative districts and seven cities. Its climate is continental, but with unpredictable levels of precipitation. At 1 January 2002 the Republic had a population of 910,000 and a population density, therefore, of approximately 34.7 per sq km. In 2001 some 59.8% of the Republic's population inhabited urban areas. In 1989 some 32.5% of the total population were Mordovians and 60.8% Russians. The majority of Mordovians inhabited the agricultural regions of the west and north-east. The capital, Saransk, is a major rail junction and the Moscow–Samara highway passes through the south-west of the Republic. The dominant religion among the Republic's inhabitants is Orthodox Christianity. The native tongue of the Mordovians belongs to the Finnic group of the Uralo-Altaic family, although this is spoken as a first language by less than two-thirds of the ethnic group. Mordoviya's capital is at Saransk, which lies on the River Insar and had a population of 313,200 at 1 January 2001.

History

The Mordovians (Mordvinians) first appear in historical records of the sixth century, when they inhabited the area between the Oka and the middle Volga rivers. Their territory's capital was, possibly, on the site of Nizhnii Novgorod, before it was conquered by the Russians in 1172. In the late 12th and early 13th centuries a feudal society began to form in Mordoviya. One of its most famous fiefdoms was Purgasov Volost, headed by Prince Purgas, which was recorded in the Russian chronicles. The Mordovians came under the control of the Mongols and Tatars between the 13th and the 15th centuries and, at the fall of the Khanate of Kazan in 1552, they were voluntarily incorporated into the Russian state. Many thousands of Mordovians fled Russian rule in the late 16th and early 17th centuries to settle in the Ural Mountains and in southern Siberia, while those that remained were outnumbered by ethnic Russian settlers. The region was predominantly agricultural until the completion of the Moscow–Kazan railway in the 1890s, when it became more commercial and its industry developed.

Mordovians became increasingly assimilated into Russian life from the end of the 19th century, although in 1919 a Mordovian section was established in the People's Commissariat for Nationalities. The Mordovian Autonomous Okrug was created in 1928, which was upgraded to an Autonomous Oblast in 1930, and to an ASSR in 1934. It declared its sovereignty on 8 December 1990. A conservative region, the territory was only renamed the Republic of Mordoviya (dispensing with the words Soviet and Socialist from the title) in January 1994. Its Constitution was adopted on 21 September 1995, establishing an executive presidency and a State Assembly as the legislature. In February 1998 President Nikolai Merkushkin was re-elected, with 96.6% of the votes cast, owing to a legislative device that disqualified all opponents other than the director of a local pasta factory, who had frequently announced his support for Merkushkin's policies. Merkushkin had also increased his popularity by paying pension and salary arrears in the months preceding the election.

Economy

In 1999 the gross regional product of Mordoviya was 14,075.5m. roubles, or 15,075.0 roubles per head. The territory's major industrial centres are at Saransk and Ruzayevka. In 2000 there were 546 km (339 miles) of railway lines and 4,205 km of paved roads on the Republic's territory.

The principal crops in Mordoviya are grain, sugar beet, potatoes and vegetables. Animal husbandry (especially cattle) and bee-keeping are also important. Agriculture employed 18.1% of the working population in 2000, when total agricultural production was worth 8,688m. roubles. Industry is the dominant sector of the economy, with output amounting to a value of 14,977m. roubles in 2000. The main industries are mechanical engineering and metal-working. There is also some production of electricity, production of chemicals and construction materials, and food-processing. Total employment in industry was equal to 24.4% of the Republic's work-force in 2000. Mordoviya is the centre of the Russian lighting-equipment industry and contains the Rossiiskii Svet (Russian Light) association. In December 1995 the federal Government approved a programme for the economic and social development of Mordoviya, to be implemented in 1996–2000 at a cost of around US $10,000m. The regional President, Nikolai Merkushkin, established close links and trading relationships with Moscow City under Mayor Yurii Luzhkov; the capital purchased over one-half of the Republic's output.

In 2000 the economically active population was 445,000, and 10.7% of the labour force were unemployed. The average monthly wage in the Republic was

2,346.6 roubles in mid-2002 (one of the lowest wages in the Federation). In 2000 there was a budgetary deficit of 38.7m. roubles. External trade was relatively low, earning US $19.7m. in exports and $25.8m. in imports in that year. In 2000 foreign investment in the Republic amounted to $8.6m. At 31 December 2000 there were some 2,300 small businesses in the Republic.

Directory

President: NIKOLAI I. MERKUSHKIN; 430002 Mordoviya, Saransk, ul. Sovetskaya 35; tel. and fax (8342) 17-45-26; e-mail radm@whrm.moris.ru; internet whrm .moris.ru.

Chairman of the Government (Prime Minister): VLADIMIR D. VOLKOV; 430002 Mordoviya, Saransk, ul. Sovetskaya 35; tel. (8342) 32-74-69; fax (8342) 17-36-28; e-mail pred@whrm.moris.ru.

Chairman of the State Assembly: VALERII A. KECHKIN; 430002 Mordoviya, Saransk, ul. Sovetskaya 26; tel. and fax (8342) 17-04-95; e-mail gsprot@whrm .moris.ru.

Chief Representative of the Republic of Mordoviya in the Russian Federation: VIKTOR I. CHINDYASKIN; 127018 Moscow, ul. Obraztsova 29; tel. (095) 219-40-49; fax (095) 218-01-42.

Head of Saransk City Administration: IVAN YA. NENYUKOV; 430002 Mordoviya, Saransk, ul. Sovetskaya 34; tel. (8342) 17-64-16; fax (8342) 17-67-70; e-mail saransk@moris.ru.

Republic of North Osetiya—Alaniya

The Republic of North Osetiya (Severnaya Osetiya), Alaniya, is situated on the northern slopes of the Greater Caucasus and forms part of the Southern Federal Okrug and the North Caucasus Economic Area. Of the other federal subjects, Kabardino-Balkariya lies to the west, Stavropol Krai to the north and Ingushetiya to the east. There is an international boundary with Georgia (South Osetiya or Ossetia) in the south. Its major river is the Terek. In the north of the Republic are the steppelands of the Mozdok and Osetian Plains, while further south in the foothills are mixed pasture and beechwood forest (about one-fifth of the territory of the Republic is forested). Narrow river valleys lie in the southernmost, mountainous region. The territory of North Osetiya covers a total of 8,000 sq km (3,090 sq miles) and comprises eight administrative districts and six cities. It had an estimated population of 678,200 at 1 January 2002, giving a population density of 84.8 per sq km. In 2001 some 67.1% of the Republic's population inhabited urban areas. In 1989 some 53.0% of the population were Osetians and 29.9% ethnic Russians, although around one-quarter of Russians were thought to have left North Osetiya between 1989 and 1999, largely owing to the decline of the military-industrial complex in the Republic, which had been their major employer. The Osetians speak an Indo-European language of the Persian (Iranian) group. In January 2001 310,600 of the region's inhabitants lived in the capital, Vladikavkaz (Ordzhonikidze 1932–90), situated in the east of the Republic. At the end of 1999 there were approximately 37,000 registered refugees from the armed hostilities between South Osetian and Georgian government forces, although around 1,500 others had returned

to Georgia from 1997, as conditions there improved and the economy of North
Osetiya deteriorated further. By the end of 1999 about 35,000 Ingush had been
displaced from the Prigorodnyi raion of North Osetiya, most of whom were living
in Ingushetiya.

History

The Osetians (Ossetins, Oselty) are descended from the Alans, a tribe of the
Samartian people. The Alans were driven into the foothills of the Caucasus by
the Huns in the fourth century and their descendants (Ossetes) were forced further
into the mountains by Tatar and Mongol invaders. Although the Osetians had been
converted to Orthodox Christianity in the 12th and 13th centuries by the Georgians,
a sub-group, the Digors, adopted Islam from the neighbouring Kabardins in the
17th and 18th centuries. Perpetual conflict with the Kabardins forced the Osetians
to seek the protection of the Russian Empire, and their territory was eventually
ceded to Russia by the Ottoman Turks at the Treaty of Kuçuk Kainavci in 1774
and confirmed by the Treaty of Iaşi (Jassy) in 1792. (Transcaucasian Osetiya, or
South Osetiya—Ossetia, subsequently became part of Georgia.) The Russians
fostered good relations with the Osetians, as they represented the only Christian
group among the hostile Muslim peoples of the North Caucasus. Furthermore,
both ends of the strategic Darial pass were situated in the region. The completion
of the Georgian Military Road in 1799 facilitated the Russian conquest of Georgia
(Kartli-Kakheti) in 1801.

After the Russian Revolution, and having briefly been part of the Mountain
(Gorskaya) People's Autonomous Republic, North Osetiya was established as an
Autonomous Oblast on 7 July 1924. It became an ASSR in 1936. The Osetians
were rewarded for their loyalty to the Soviet Government during the Second World
War: in 1944 their territory was expanded by the inclusion of former Ingush
territories to the east and of part of Stavropol Krai to the north. Furthermore, for
10 years the capital, renamed Ordzhonikidze in 1932, was known as Dzaudzikau,
the Osetian pronunciation of Vladikavkaz. The Digors, however, were deported
to Central Asia, along with other Muslim peoples, in 1944.

The Republic declared sovereignty in mid-1990. From 1991 there was considerable debate about some form of unification with South Osetiya. This resulted in
armed hostilities between the South Osetiyans and Georgian troops, during which
thousands of refugees fled to North Osetiya. Meanwhile, the Republic's administration refused to recognize claims by the Ingush to the territory they were deprived
of in 1944 (the Prigorodnyi raion), which led to the onset of violence in October
1992 and the imposition of a state of emergency in the affected areas (see
Ingushetiya). Despite a peace settlement in 1994, the region remained unstable.
Under the terms of its Constitution, adopted on 7 December 1994, the Republic's
name reverted to Alaniya. A power-sharing agreement was signed with the federal
authorities the following year. The territory was a redoubt of the Communist
Party, as proved by federal parliamentary elections of 1995 and 1999, republican
parliamentary elections in 1999 and the Russian presidential election of 1996;
however, in the presidential election of 2000 Vladimir Putin defeated his communist
opponent, Gennadii Zyuganov, in this region. In January 1998 Aleksandr Dzasokhov,
a former member of the Communist Party of the Soviet Union Politburo, and a
subsequent member of the State Duma and the Chairman of the Russian delegation
to the Parliamentary Assembly of the Council of Europe, was elected the President

of North Osetiya—Alaniya, with 75% of the votes cast. His election was initially welcomed by the President of Ingushetiya, Ruslan Aushev, who had dispatched several thousand displaced eligible voters from that Republic. However, relations between the two Republics remained strained, and Aushev subsequently suggested that the administration of the Prigorodnyi raion be appointed by the Government of Ingushetiya. On 30 July 1999 Aushev announced the suspension of all negotiations with North Osetiya and proposed that direct federal rule be imposed on Prigorodnyi, owing to an influx of Osetian Ingush into Ingushetiya; in March 2000, however, Putin rejected the proposal as unconstitutional. Instability in North Osetiya, as elsewhere in the North Caucasus, increased during 1999, as insurgency became increasingly widespread. A bomb exploded in Vladikavkaz in March, killing 42, and three further bombs exploded in military residences in May. In March 2001 three simultaneous explosions, which killed over 20, were attributed to Chechen separatists. On 27 January 2002 Dzasokhov was re-elected as President, receiving 57% of the votes cast, according to preliminary results. Notably, 10 days before the election the republican Supreme Court had invalidated the candidacy of the former republican Chairman of the Government, Sergei Khetagurov; this decision was subsequently confirmed by the Federal Supreme Court. In late April eight people were killed, and more than 30 others injured, after a bomb was detonated at a market in Vladikavkaz. As concern about incipient terrorism in the North Caucasus region heightened, in May the North Osetiyan Parliament announced its support for proposals by the State Council of Dagestan for the reintroduction of capital punishment for those convicted of terrorist-related offences. In September the power-sharing agreement of 1995 was dissolved. In the following month North Osetiya and Ingushetiya signed an 'Agreement on the Development of Co-operation and Good Neighbourly Relations', which committed both sides to adopting measures to resolve their remaining differences.

Economy

In 1999 gross regional product in North Osetiya—Alaniya totalled 7,572.3m. roubles, equivalent to 11,318.8 roubles per head. Its major industrial centres are at Vladikavkaz, Mozdok and Beslan. In 2000 the Republic contained 144 km (89 miles) of railway track, including a section of the North Caucasus Railway. There were 2,309 km of paved roads, and the only direct road route from Russia to the Transcaucasus. There is an international airport at Vladikavkaz.

Agriculture in North Osetiya, which employed 14.5% of the labour force in 2000, consists mainly of vegetable and grain production, horticulture, viniculture and animal husbandry. The rate of reform in agriculture during the 1990s was slow. In 2000 agricultural production amounted to a value of 2,803m. roubles. In the same year industrial output was worth 4,466m. roubles, and the sector employed 17.1% of the working population. The Republic's main industries are radio-electronics (until the 1990s largely used for defence purposes), non-ferrous metal-lurgy, mechanical engineering, wood-working, light industry, chemicals, glass-making and food-processing. There are also five hydroelectric power-stations, with an average capacity of around 80 MWh. By the mid-1990s some 70% of industrial production within the defence sector had been converted to civilian use.

The economically active population totalled 328,000 in 2000, when some 28.5% of the labour force were unemployed. Those in employment earned an average wage of 2,522.4 roubles per month in mid-2002. The republican budget showed a surplus of 16.5m. roubles in 2000. In 2000 export trade amounted to US $67.1m., and imports to $67.4m. Foreign investment remained deterred by the instability endemic to much of the North Caucasus region. At 31 December 2000 there were some 3,700 small businesses in operation in North Osetiya.

Directory

President of the Republic: ALEKSANDR S. DZASOKHOV; 362038 North Osetiya—Alaniya, Vladikavkaz, pl. Svobody 1, Dom Pravitelstva; tel. (8672) 53-35-24.

Chairman of the Government: MIKHAIL M. SHATALOV; 362038 North Osetiya—Alaniya, Vladikavkaz, pl. Svobody 1, Dom Pravitelstva; tel. (8672) 53-30-71.

Chairman of the Parliament: TAIMURAZ DZ. MAMSUROV; 362038 North Osetiya—Alaniya, Vladikavkaz, pl. Svobody, Dom Pravitelstva; tel. (8672) 33-34-22; fax (8672) 75-24-72.

Chief Representative of the Republic of North Osetiya—Alaniya in the Russian Federation: ERIK R. BUGULOV; 109028 Moscow, per. Durasovskii 1/9; tel. (095) 916-21-47; fax (095) 916-25-22.

Head of Vladikavkaz City Administration (Mayor): MIKHAIL M. SHATALOV; 362040 North Osetiya—Alaniya, Vladikavkaz, pl. Shtyba 1; fax (8672) 75-34-35.

Republic of Sakha (Yakutiya)

The Republic of Sakha (Yakutiya) is situated in eastern Siberia on the Laptev and Eastern Siberian Seas. Some two-fifths of the Republic's territory lies within the Arctic Circle. It forms part of the Far Eastern Federal Okrug and the Far Eastern Economic Area. To the west it borders Krasnoyarsk Krai (the Taimyr and Evenk AOks), while Irkutsk and Chita Oblasts lie in the south-west, Amur Oblast to the south and Khabarovsk Krai and Magadan Oblast in the south-east. In the north-eastern corner of the territory there is a border with the Chukchi AOk. Its main river is the Lena, which drains into the Laptev Sea via a large swampy delta; other important rivers are the Lena's tributaries, the Aldan, the Viliyuy, the Olenek, the Yana, the Indigirka and the Kolyma. Apart from the Central Yakut Plain, the region's territory is mountainous and four-fifths is taiga (forested marshland). Yakutiya is the largest federal unit in Russia, occupying an area of 3,103,200 sq km (1,198,150 sq miles), making it larger than Kazakhstan, itself the second largest country, after Russia, in Europe or the former USSR. The Republic consists of 33 administrative districts and 13 cities. Its climate, owing to its size, is varied: the north lies within the arctic zone whereas the south has a more temperate climate. The average temperature in January is as low as −35.6°C, and the average temperature in July is around 13.3°C. At 1 January 2002 the Republic had an estimated population of just 982,900, and a population density, therefore, of 0.3 per sq km. Some 64.3% of the population inhabited urban areas in 2001. In the late 1990s and early 2000s there was a continuous outflow of population from the Republic. In 1989 33.4% of the total population were the indigenous Yakuts (who represent the largest ethnic group in Siberia, apart from Russians) and 50.3% Russians. Orthodox Christianity is the dominant religion in the region. The Yakuts' native tongue, spoken as a first language by over 93% of the indigenous population, is part of the North-Eastern branch of the Turkic family, although it is considerably influenced by Mongolian. The capital is at Yakutsk, which had a population of 197,800 at 1 January 2001. The Republic's other major cities are Neryungri (74,300) and Mirnyi (37,000).

History

The Yakuts (Iakuts), also known as the Sakha (Saka), were historically known as the Tungus, Jekos and the Urangkhai Sakha. They are believed to be descended from various peoples from the Lake Baikal area, Turkish tribes from the steppe and the Altai Mountains, and indigenous Siberian peoples, including the Evenks. They were traditionally a semi-nomadic people, with those in the north of the region occupied with hunting, fishing and reindeer-breeding, while those in the south were pastoralists who bred horses and cattle and were also skilled blacksmiths. Their territory, briefly united by the toion (chief), Tygyn, came under Russian rule in the 1620s and a fur tax was introduced. This led to violent opposition from the Yakuts between 1634 and 1642, although all rebellions were crushed. Increasing numbers of Russians began to settle in the region as Yakutiya became a link between eastern and western Siberia. The completion of the mail route also increased the Russian population, as did the construction of camps for political opponents to the tsars and the discovery of gold in 1846. The territory became commercialized after the construction of the Trans-Siberian Railway in the 1880s and 1890s and the development of commercial shipping on the River Lena. The economic resources of the territory enabled the Yakut to secure a measure of autonomy as an ASSR in 1922 (its first leader was the Yakut poet, Platon Oyunskii). Collectivization and the purges of the 1930s greatly reduced the Yakut population during the Soviet era, and the region was rapidly industrialized, largely involving the extraction of gold, coal and timber.

Nationalist feeling re-emerged during the period of *glasnost* (openness) in the late 1980s. Cultural, ecological and economic concerns led to the proclamation of a Yakut-Sakha SSR on 27 April 1990. The Yakut Republic was officially declared by the Supreme Soviet on 15 August 1991, which demanded local control over the Republic's reserves of gold, diamonds, timber, coal, petroleum and tin. On 22 December elections for an executive presidency were held, and were won by the former Chairman of the Supreme Soviet, Mikhail Nikolayev. The Republic was renamed the Republic of Sakha (Yakutiya) in March 1992 and a new Constitution was promulgated on 27 April. On 12 October 1993 the Supreme Soviet dissolved itself and set elections to a 60-seat bicameral legislature for 12 December. On 26 January 1994 the new parliament named itself the State Assembly; it consisted of an upper Chamber of the Republic and a lower Chamber of Representatives. Although communist support was relatively high in Sakha, the federal Government's willingness to concede a significant degree of local control over natural resources ensured that it too enjoyed some confidence. Native languages were designated official in certain areas and attempts to protect traditional lifestyles even involved the restoration of land. Thus, a Yeven-Bytantai Okrug was established on traditional Yeven territory in the mid-1990s. In June 1997 the Republic was honoured at a UN special session on the environment held in New York, the USA, for its commitment to preserving its natural heritage (around one-quarter of its territory had been set aside as protected areas). Meanwhile, in December 1996 Nikolayev was re-elected President by an overwhelming majority and continued his efforts to win greater autonomy from the centre, including the maintenance (in breach of federal law) of gold and hard-currency reserves and, from August 1998, a ban on the sale of gold outside the republican government. A power-sharing agreement with the federal Government in June 1995 was followed, in March 1998, by a framework agreement on co-operation for five years, which provided for collaboration on a series of mining and energy projects. In May 2001 over 5,000 people were adversely affected by particularly severe flooding in the Republic. In December the federal Audit Chamber announced that an investigation was to take place into the alleged misspending by the republican Government of funds allocated for restoration work. In the same month Nikolayev withdrew his candidacy from the forthcoming gubernatorial election, and urged voters to transfer their support to Vyacheslav Shtyrov, the President of the local diamond-producing joint-stock company, Almazy Rossii-Sakha—Alrosa, who was the candidate of the pro-presidential Unity and Fatherland-United Russia party. (It was reported that Nikolayev had withdrawn his candidacy as the result of pressure from the federal Government.) In the first round of voting, held on 23 December, Shtyrov received 45% of the votes cast, more than any other candidate, but fewer than the 50% required to secure an outright victory. Shtyrov subsequently received 59% of the votes in the second round, held on 13 January 2002, defeating businessman Fedot Tumusov. The election, in particular the second round, was characterized by widespread allegations of malpractice, including offers to voters of discounts on utility bills and free lottery tickets. After the election, Nikolayev was appointed as the Republic's representative in the Federation Council, the upper chamber of the Federal Assembly. Meanwhile, controversy ensued with regard to discrepancies between the republican and federal Constitutions; in March the approval by the republican legislature of amendments to 11 articles of Sakha's Constitution was reportedly regarded as insufficiently rigorous by the federal authorities, and it was reported that the Republic's Chief Prosecutor was to recommend that President Shtyrov dissolve the legislature.

Economy

Owing to the Republic's wealth of mineral reserves, its gross regional product in 1999 was 64,688.0m. roubles, equivalent to 65,846.9 roubles per head, the second highest figure in the Russian Federation, after the city of Moscow. The Republic's major industrial centres are at Yakutsk, Mirnyi, Neryungra, Aldan and Lensk. Its main port is Tiksi. In 2000 there were 165 km (103 miles) of railways in the Republic, and during the 1990s the extent of paved roads increased over two-fold, to reach some 7,292 km by 2000.

Sakha (Yakutiya)'s agriculture, in which 10.3% of the working population was engaged in 2000, consists mainly of animal husbandry (livestock- and reindeer-breeding), hunting and fishing. Grain and vegetable production tends to be on a small scale. Total agricultural output in 2000 was worth 5,793m. roubles (compared with a figure of 64,898m. roubles for the industrial sector). Industry employed 16.2% of the Republic's working population in 2000: its main industries are ore-mining (gold—Sakha produced approximately 25% of the Russian Federation's output in the first half of the 1990s, diamonds—of which Sakha is the second largest producer and exporter in the world, tin, muscovite—mica, antimony and coal), the production of electricity, food-processing and natural gas production. Both industrial output and foreign trade in Sakha (Yakutiya) increased throughout the 1990s. In September 1997, following a decree passed by federal President Boris Yeltsin, Alrosa signed a preliminary one-year trade accord with the South African diamond producer, De Beers. The accord was subsequently extended until 2001, and De Beers was to purchase US $550m. worth of raw diamonds during this period. Alrosa also diversified its operations into polishing and selling its gems. A new, five-year agreement was signed with De Beers in December 2001.

The economically active population of the Republic amounted to 497,000 in 2000, and some 11.3% of the labour force were unemployed. The social situation in Yakutiya from the mid-1990s was typical of the northern regions of the Russian Federation. Growth in the cost of goods and services was compounded by a weak economic structure, poorly developed social services and inappropriate conditions for people to grow their own food. In 1999, in terms of a 'consumer basket', the Republic was one of the most expensive regions in the country. The average monthly wage was 8,357.8 roubles in mid-2002 (considerably higher than the national average, but offset by the high cost of living). During the late 1990s the Republic maintained consistently large budgetary deficits; in 1998 the deficit amounted to 2,238m. roubles. However, in 2000 the republican budget recorded a surplus of 649.7m. roubles. In the same year the value of export trade amounted to some US $1,089.5m., compared with imports of $39.0m. Foreign investment in Sakha (Yakutiya) amounted to $159.6m in 2000. At 31 December 2000 there were 2,700 small businesses registered on its territory.

Directory

President: VYACHESLAV A. SHTYROV; 677012 Sakha (Yakutiya), Yakutsk, ul. Kirova 11; tel. (4112) 43-50-50; fax (4112) 24-06-24; internet www.sakha.ru.

Chairman of the Government: SEMEN N. NAZAROV; 677000 Sakha (Yakutiya), Yakutsk, ul. Kirova 11; tel. (4112) 43-55-55; internet www.sakha.ru/sakha/gov/html/il2men.htm.

State Assembly (Il Tumen): 677000 Sakha (Yakutiya), Yakutsk, ul. Kirova 11.

Chairman of the Chamber of the Republic: VASILII V. FILIPPOV; tel. (4112) 43-53-04.

Chairman of the Chamber of Representatives: NIKOLAI I. SOLOMOV; tel. (4112) 43-52-03.

Chief Representative of the Republic of Sakha (Yakutiya) in the Russian Federation: ANDREI V. KRIVOSHAPKIN; 107078 Moscow, Myasnitskii pr. 3/26; tel. (095) 925-52-81; fax (095) 928-42-21.

Head of Yakutsk City Administration (Mayor): ILYA F. MIKHALCHUK; 677000 Sakha (Yakutiya), Yakutsk, ul. Kirova 11; tel. (4112) 42-30-20; fax (4112) 42-48-80; e-mail erb@yacc.yakutia.su.

Republic of Tatarstan

The Republic of Tatarstan is situated in the east of European Russia and forms part of the Volga Federal Okrug and the Volga Economic Area. It neighbours several other Republics: Bashkortostan to the east; Udmurtiya to the north; Marii-El to the north-west; and Chuvashiya to the west. The Oblasts of Ulyanovsk, Samara and Orenburg lie to the south, and that of Kirov to the north. Its major rivers are the Volga and the Kama, and one-fifth of its total territory of 67,836 sq km (26,260 sq miles) is forested. It measures 290 km (180 miles) from south to north and 460 km from west to east. The Republic is divided into 43 administrative districts and 20 cities. At 1 January 2002 it had an estimated population of 3,768,200 and, therefore, a population density of 55.4 per sq km. In 2001 some 73.9% of the Republic's population inhabited urban areas. In 1989 some 48.5% of the total population were Tatars and 43.3% ethnic Russians. Tatarstan's capital is Kazan, which lies on the River Volga and had a population of 1,090,200 in 2001. Other major cities include Naberezhnye Chelny (formerly Brezhnev—with a population of 518,300), Nizhnekamsk (226,100), Almetevsk (141,600) and Zeleno-dolsk (100,500).

History

After the dissolution of the Mongol Empire the region became the Khanate of Kazan, the territory of the Golden Horde. It was conquered by Russia in 1552. Some of the Muslim Tatars succumbed to Russian pressures to convert to Orthodox Christianity (the Staro-Kryashens—'Old-Baptized' still exist, using Tatar as their spoken and liturgical tongue), but most did not. A modernist school of thought in Islam, Jadidism, originated among the Volga Tatars, who attained an exceptionally

111

high cultural level in the 19th-century Russian Empire. A Tatar ASSR was established on 27 May 1920.

On 31 August 1990 the Chairman of the republican Supreme Soviet, Mintimer Shamiyev (elected President of the Republic in 1991), declared Tatarstan a sovereign republic. As President, Shamiyev continued to strive for the Republic's independence from the Federation Government, and a combination of harmony and tension between the regional and federal regimes characterized post-Soviet politics in Tatarstan. Apart from secessionist Chechnya, Tatarstan was the only Republic to reject the Federation Treaty, adopting its own Constitution in November 1992, which provided for a presidential republic with a legislative, bicameral State Council. In February 1994 Shamiyev won important concessions from Russia's central Government by signing a treaty that ceded extensive powers to Tatarstan, including full ownership rights over its petroleum reserves and industrial companies, the right to retain most of its tax revenue and the right to pursue its own foreign-trade policy. This was the first agreement of its kind in the Federation and, despite significant contradictions and weaknesses, it became a model for other federal subjects seeking to determine their relations with the federal centre. The division of responsibilities was confirmed by treaty with the Federation in 1995.

In a republican presidential election, held on 24 March 1996, Shamiyev was re-elected, winning some 93% of the votes cast: hitherto his Government had adapted the reforms of *perestroika* (restructuring) to the conditions of the region, thereby averting the negative consequences of excessively rapid privatization and social upheaval. In August 1997 the Presidents of the Republics of Tatarstan and Bashkortostan signed a treaty on co-operation at the second World Congress of Tatars, held in Kazan. The Congress adopted a resolution praising the development of Tatarstan into a 'new kind of sovereign state'. During 1999 Shamiyev was one of the regional governors most active in the creation of the new All Russia political bloc. Republican parliamentary by-elections in March gave the President's supporters a clear majority in the legislature. The moderate nationalism adopted by the regime was reflected in a decision, to be implemented over 10 years from August 2000, to revert to the use of the Latin (as opposed to the Cyrillic) script for the Tatar language. In 1999 the Tatar authorities had suspended conscription to the Russian army following a number of deaths of Tatar draftees in Dagestan, also reflecting Shamiyev's previously stated support for Chechen President Khalid 'Aslan' Maskhadov. In 2000 federal President Vladimir Putin had offered Shamiyev the post of presidential envoy to the new Volga Federal Okrug, which he declined, amid constitutional uncertainty regarding the legitimacy of Shamiyev's intention to contest a third term of office as Governor. In the event, Shamiyev was permitted to compete in the election in March 2001, when he obtained some 80% of the votes cast, thereby becoming the first Governor of any federal subject in the Russian Federation to have been elected three times to that post. In May the Russian Supreme Court declared that some 42 articles of the Republic's Constitution were at variance with federal law (a ruling by the republican Supreme Court confirmed these findings in October). Despite federal government demands that the inconsistencies be removed, in July Shamiyev signed an agreement with the Presidential Representative to the Volga Federal Okrug, Sergei Kiriyenko, which permitted the continued operation of various practices that contradicted federal practice; in particular, a highly centralized system of local governance was to be retained in Tatarstan. Revisions to the Constitution, intended to bring it into compliance with federal law, were approved by the republican State Council in late February 2002. None the less, the revised document continued to declare the sovereignty of the Republic and preserved the notion of Tatar citizenship, and renewed concern was expressed that the republican Constitution continued to contravene federal legislation. In early April Tatarstan's legislature approved a constitutional amendment, which required any change to the Republic's status to be approved by referendum.

Economy

In 1999 the Republic's gross regional product stood at 123,671.8m. roubles, or 32,723.5 roubles per head. The territory is one of the most developed economic regions of the Russian Federation and has vast agricultural and industrial potential. Its main industrial centres are Kazan, Naberezhnye Chelny, Zelenodolsk, Nizhnekamsk, Almetyevsk, Chistopol and Bugulma. Kazan is the most important port on the Volga and a junction in the national rail, road and air transport systems. Russia's second primary petroleum export pipeline to Europe starts in Almetyevsk. In 2000 there were 878 km of railway lines and 12,508 km of paved roads on the Republic's territory.

Tatarstan's agriculture, in which some 14.9% of the work-force were engaged in 2000, consists mainly of grain production, animal husbandry, horticulture and bee-keeping. Total output in this sector amounted to a value of 31,049m. roubles in 2000. Mineral natural resources are more important, and the Republic has significant reserves of hydrocarbons reserves. The region is an important industrial centre (industry accounted for 25.3% of employment in 2000): its capital, Kazan, and the neighbouring towns of Zelendolsk and Vasilyevo are centres for light industry, the manufacture of petrochemicals and building materials, and mechanical engineering. The automobile and petroleum industries are major employers in the region. Kazanorgsintez, a petrochemicals giant, is the largest polyethylene producer in Russia. Industries connected with the extraction, processing and use of petroleum represent around one-half of the Republic's total industrial production, which was worth 191,300m. roubles in 2000. In the mid-1990s the US automobile company, General Motors, signed a contract to manufacture 50,000 automobiles per year at the Yelabuga plant, which later became the centre of a zone offering special tax incentives. In April 1996 a programme, drafted with French and US assistance, which envisaged the transformation of Tatarstan's economy from a military to a socially orientated system, was adopted by the Council of Ministers.

The economically active population in the Republic amounted to 1,845,000 in 2000, when 8.0% of the labour force were unemployed, one of the lowest levels in the Russian Federation. The average monthly wage was 3,866.4 roubles in mid-2002. The 2000 budget recorded a surplus of 914.5m. roubles. Tatarstan also fared well in terms of trade; the value of exports amounted to US $2,990.2m. in 2000, and imports to $363.1m. In the same year foreign investment in the Republic amounted to $143.0m. In 2000 there were 93 foreign joint-stock enterprises in Tatarstan, 20 of which received financing from the USA, while 13 received financing from Germany, 10 from the United Kingdom and seven from Cyprus. By the beginning of 1997 over 1,000 large and medium-sized enterprises in Tatarstan had been privatized; at 1 December 2000 there were some 16,100 small businesses.

Directory

President: MINTIMER SH. SHAIMIYEV; 420014 Tatarstan, Kazan, Kreml; tel. (8432) 92-74-66; fax (8432) 92-70-88; e-mail secretariat@tatar.ru; internet www.tatar.ru.

Prime Minister: RUSTAM N. MINNIKHANOV; 420060 Tatarstan, Kazan, pl. Svobody 1; tel. (8432) 32-79-03; fax (8432) 36-28-24.

Chairman of the State Council: FARID KH. MUKHAMETSHIN; 420060 Tatarstan, Kazan, pl. Svobody 1; tel. (8432) 92-14-02; fax (8432) 64-10-95; e-mail gossov@kabmin.tatarstan.ru; internet www.gossov.tatarstan.ru.

Chief Representative of the Republic of Tatarstan in the Russian Federation: NAZIF M. MIRIKHANOV; 115172 Moscow, per. 3-i Kotelnicheskii 13–15/1; tel. (095) 915-05-02; fax (095) 915-06-10.

Head of Kazan City Administration: KAMIL SH. ISKHAKOV; 420014 Tatarstan, Kazan, ul. Kremlevskaya 1; tel. (8432) 92-38-38; fax (8432) 92-76-72; e-mail kanc@kazan.gov.tatarstan.ru; internet www.kazan.org.ru.

Republic of Tyva

The Republic of Tyva (Tuva) is situated in the south of eastern Siberia in the Sayan Mountains. It forms part of the Siberian Federal Okrug and the East Siberian Economic Area. Tyva has an international border with Mongolia to the south. The Republic of Altai lies to the west, the Republic of Khakasiya to the north-west and Krasnoyarsk Krai to the north, Irkutsk Oblast lies to the north-east and the Republic of Buryatiya forms part of the eastern border. Its major river is the Yenisei, which rises in the Eastern Sayan mountain range. The territory of the Republic consists of a series of high mountain valleys. One-half of its area is forested. The Republic has numerous waterways, including over 12,000 rivers and 8,400 freshwater lakes. Tyva occupies 170,500 sq km (65,830 sq miles) and consists of 16 administrative districts and five cities. At 1 January 2002 it had an estimated population of 310,300 and a population density of only 1.8 per sq km. Some 48.4% of the population lived in urban areas in 2001. In 1989 some 64.3% of inhabitants were Tyvans (Tuvinians) and 32.0% Russians. Lamaism (Tibetan Buddhism) is the predominant religion in the Republic. The Tyvan language belongs to the Old Uigur group of the Turkic branch of the Uralo-Altaic linguistic family. The capital of Tyva is at Kyzyl, which had a population of 101,500 at 1 January 2001.

History

The Tyvans (known at various times as Soyons, Soyots and Uriankhais) emerged as an identifiable ethnic group in the early 18th century. The territory of what is now Tyva was occupied in turn between the sixth and the ninth centuries by the Turkish Khanate, the Chinese, the Uigurs and the Yenisei Kyrgyz. The Mongols controlled the region from 1207 to 1368. In the second half of the 17th century the Dzungarians (Sungarians) seized the area from the Altyn Khans. In 1758 the Manzhous (Manchus) annexed Dzungaria and the territory thus became part of the Chinese Empire. Russian influence dates from the Treaty of Peking (Beijing) of 1860, after which trade links were developed and a number of Russians settled there. One year after the Chinese Revolution of 1911 Tyva declared its independence.

In 1914, however, Russia established a protectorate over the territory, which became the Tannu-Tuva People's Republic. This was a nominally independent state until October 1944, when it was incorporated into the USSR as the Tuvinian Autonomous Oblast. It became an ASSR on 10 October 1961, within the Russian Federation.

The Republic declared sovereignty on 11 December 1990 and renamed itself the Republic of Tuva in August 1991. On 21 October 1993 the Tyvan Supreme Soviet resolved that the Republic's name was Tyva (as opposed to the russified Tuva) and adopted a new Constitution. The Constitution provided for a legislature, the Supreme Khural, and a supreme constitutional body, the Grand Khural. The new parliament was elected on 12 December. On the same day the new Constitution was approved by 62.2% of registered voters in Tyva. Only 32.7%, however, voted in favour of the Russian Constitution. The victory of a nationalist Liberal Democratic candidate, Aleksandr Kashin, in the April 1998 mayoral elections in Kyzyl was, perhaps, a sign of intolerance with the reformism of the federal Government (particularly among the predominantly ethnic Russian population of the city). Apathy was also a likely cause, as a low rate of participation in the general election of the same month meant that only 21 of the 38 seats in the Supreme Khural were filled. Further rounds later in the year failed to resolve the situation and, indeed, for two months in 1998–99 the parliament was rendered inquorate by the death of a deputy. In 2000 the Grand Khural was obliged to make 26 amendments to the republican Constitution, in order to comply with the All-Russian Constitution. A new Constitution, which removed Tyva's right to self-determination and to secede from the Federation, was approved by referendum in May 2001; in early March 2002 various amendments to this Constitution were approved, in order to bring it more closely into compliance with federal norms. On 17 March the incumbent President, Sherig-ool Oorzhak, was elected to serve a third term of office, receiving 53% of the votes cast.

Economy

Tyva's economy is largely agriculture-based. In 1999 its gross regional product stood at 2,616.3m. roubles, or 8,404.4 roubles per head. The Republic's main industrial centres are at Kyzyl and Ak-Dovurak. There are road and rail links with other regions, although the distance from Kyzyl to the nearest railway station is over 400 km (250 miles). In 2000 there were 2,473 km of paved roads in the Republic.

The Republic's agriculture, which employed 16.1% of the work-force in 2000, consists mainly of animal husbandry, although forestry and hunting are also important. Total agricultural production in 2000 amounted to a value of 1,285m. roubles. At 1 January 1999 there were some 670,400 sheep and goats, 140,100 cattle and 19,200 pigs in the Republic. Gold extraction was developed from the mid-1990s: in 1996 it amounted to almost one metric ton. Tyva's main industries were ore-mining (asbestos, coal, cobalt and mercury), production of electricity, the processing of agricultural and forestry products, light manufacturing, manufacture of building materials and metal-working. In 2000 industry employed 8.6% of the working population and total production within the sector was worth just 692m. roubles.

The economically active population of Tyva totalled 115,000 in 2000, when 22.9% of the labour force were unemployed. In mid-2002 the average monthly wage in the Republic was 3,870.5 roubles, somewhat lower than the national average. However, in the late 1990s the Republic was one of the areas of the Russian Federation worst affected by wage arrears and most dependent on federal transfers. In September 2000 the federal Government arranged to pay wage arrears amounting to 216.7m. roubles in Tyva, in addition to providing for improvements to educational and medical services in the Republic. The 2000 budget showed a surplus of 100.9m. roubles. Foreign investment in the Republic was minimal, and amounted to just US $381,000 in 2000. At 31 December 2000 a total of 700 small businesses were registered in the Republic.

Directory

President (Chairman of the Government): SHERIG-OOL D. OORZHAK; 667000 Tyva, Kyzyl, ul. Chulduma 18, Dom Pravitelstva; tel. (39422) 1-12-77; fax (39422) 3-74-59; e-mail tuva@tuva.ru; internet www.tuva.ru/tuva.

Chairman of the Supreme Khural: SHOLBAN V. KARA-OOL; 667000 Tyva, Kyzyl, ul. Lenina 32; tel. (39422) 3-66-30; fax (39422) 3-33-71; e-mail parliament@tuva.ru; internet www.tuva.ru/tuva/gosvo/verhohur.htm.

Chief Representative of the Republic of Tyva in the Russian Federation: ORLAN O. CHOLBENEI; 119049 Moscow, ul. Donskaya 8/2; tel. (095) 236-48-01; fax (095) 236-45-53.

Head of Kyzyl City Administration (Mayor): ALEKSANDR Y. KASHIN; 667000 Tyva, Kyzyl, ul. Lenina 32; tel. (39422) 3-50-55.

Udmurt Republic (Udmurtiya)

The Udmurt Republic occupies part of the Upper Kama Highlands. It forms part of the Volga Federal Okrug and the Urals Economic Area. Tatarstan lies to the south, Bashkortostan to the south-east, Perm to the east and Kirov to the north and west. Its major river is the Kama, dominating the southern and eastern borderlands, while the Vyatka skirts the territory in the west. About one-half of its territory is forested. Its total area covers some 42,100 sq km (16,250 sq miles). The Republic consists of 25 administrative districts and six cities. At 1 January 2002 Udmurtiya had an estimated population of 1,616,200, and a population density, therefore, of 38.4 per sq km. In 2001 some 69.4% of the population inhabited urban areas. In 1989 some 30.9% of the total population were Udmurts and 58.9% ethnic Russians. The dominant religion in the Republic is Orthodox Christianity. The 1989 census showed that some 70% of Udmurts spoke their native tongue, from the Permian group of the Finnic branch of the Uralo-Altaic family, as their first language. The capital of Udmurtiya is at Izhevsk (known as Ustinov for much of the Soviet period), which had a population of 650,300 in 2001. Other major towns in the region are Glazov (106,800), Sarapul (104,200) and Votkinsk (101,700).

History

The first appearance of the Votyaks (the former name for Udmurts) as a distinct ethnic group occurred in the sixth century. The territories inhabited by Votyaks were conquered by the Khazars in the eighth century, although Khazar influence gave way to that of the Volga Bulgars in the mid-ninth century. In the 13th century the Mongol Tatars occupied the region, but were gradually displaced by the Russians from the mid-15th century. By 1558 all Votyaks were under Russian rule. A Votyak Autonomous Oblast was established on 4 November 1920. On 1 January 1932 it was renamed the Udmurt Autonomous Oblast, which became an ASSR on 28 December 1934.

The Republic declared sovereignty on 21 September 1990, although a new republican Constitution was not adopted until 7 December 1994. The Chairman of the legislature, the State Council, remained head of the Republic, and a premier chaired the Government. In 1996 the Udmurt parliament was accused of having virtually eliminated local government in the Republic, in contravention of federal law. Measures to introduce a presidential system of regional government in Udmurtiya, in common with most other Republics within the Russian Federation, were endorsed by a referendum held on 26 March 2000. In June the Udmurt State Council adopted a number of draft laws transferring the Republic to presidential rule. Aleksandr Volkov, hitherto the parliamentary speaker, was elected President on 15 October. The Republic's Prime Minister, Nikolai Ganza, who was supported by the Unity party, was the third-placed candidate; he resigned three days later. From the 1990s the disposal of chemical weapons on the territory of Udmurtiya proved to be a serious social and ecological problem—the Republic was thought to contain around one-quarter of Russia's entire arsenal of such weapons.

Economy

in 1999 the Republic's gross regional product amounted to 37,501.6m. roubles, equivalent to 22,948.0 roubles per head. Udmurtiya possesses significant hydrocarbons reserves and is an important arms-producing region. Its major industrial centres are at Izhevsk, Sarapul and Glazov. Its main river-ports are at Sarapul and Kambarka. In 2000 there were 768 km (477 miles) of railway track and 5,487 km of paved roads on its territory. In 1998 there were 178 km of navigable waterways. Twelve major gas pipelines and two petroleum pipelines pass through the Udmurt Republic.

Udmurtiya's agriculture employed 15.4% of the working population in 2000 and consists mainly of livestock-breeding, grain production and flax-growing. Total agricultural production in 2000 was worth 10,100m. roubles. There are substantial reserves of coal and of petroleum (prospected resources are estimated at 379,543m. metric tons), which in the late 1990s the Republic hoped to exploit with the aid of foreign investment. In 2000 some 27.8% of its working population was engaged in industry. The main industries in Udmurtiya, apart from the manufacture of weapons, are mechanical engineering (in the first half of 2000 the Republic produced some 89% of all the motorcycles manufactured in Russia), metal-working, metallurgy, processing of forestry and agricultural products, petroleum production, glass-making and the production of peat. Total industrial output in 2000 amounted to a value of 54,804m. roubles.

In 2000 the economically active population amounted to 820,000, and 9.3% of the labour force were unemployed; in mid-2002 those in employment earned an average monthly wage of 3,475.8 roubles. The republican budget recorded a surplus of 334.5m. roubles in 2000, when there was US $10.6m. of foreign investment in the Republic. External trade in 2000 amounted to $1,037.2m., of which exports accounted for $959.6m. The principal exports are metallurgical products, engines and machinery, and rifles. In the late 1990s the Republic had particularly active trade links with Germany. At 31 December 2000 there were approximately 8,000 small businesses registered in the Republic.

Directory

President: ALEKSANDR A. VOLKOV; 426074 Udmurtiya, Izhevsk, pl. 50 let Oktyabrya 15; tel. (3412) 75-48-01; fax (3412) 25-50-17; e-mail president@ udmurt.ru.

Chairman of the Government: YURII S. PITKEYVICH; 426007 Udmurtiya, Izhevsk, ul. Pushkinskaya. 214, Dom Pravitelstva; tel. (3412) 25-45-67; fax (3412) 25-50-17; e-mail premier@udmurt.ru.

Chief Representative of the Udmurt Republic in the Russian Federation: ANDREI V. SAKOVICH; 127025 Moscow, ul. Novyi Arbat 19; tel. (095) 203-53-52; fax (095) 203-91-47.

Head of Izhevsk City Administration (Mayor): ANATOLII I. SALTYKOV; 426070 Udmurtiya, Izhevsk, ul. Pushkinskaya 276; tel. (3412) 22-38-62; fax (3412) 22-84-94; e-mail izhersk@izh.ru; internet www.izh.ru.

KRAIS (PROVINCES)

Altai Krai

Most of Altai Krai lies within the Western Siberian Plain. Part of the Siberian Federal Okrug and the West Siberian Economic Area, it has international boundaries to the south with Kazakhstan, the People's Republic of China and Mongolia. To the north lie the federal subjects of Novosibirsk Oblast, Kemerovo Oblast and the Republic of Khakasiya, while the Republic of Altai (see above—formerly the Gorno-Altai Autonomous Oblast, then a constituent part of the Krai) and the Republic of Tyva lie to the east. Its major river is the Ob, which has numerous tributaries (there are altogether some 17,000 rivers within the territory). It has one main lake, the Teletskoye, although there are a total of 13,000 lakes, one-half of which are fresh water. About one-third of its total area is forested. In the east of the Krai are mountains, in the west steppe. The Krai occupies an area of 169,100 sq km (65,290 sq miles). It is divided into 60 administrative districts and 12 cities. It had an estimated population of 2,621,000 at 1 January 2002, giving a population density of 15.5 per sq km. In 2001 some 52.3% of the population lived in urban areas. In 1996 ethnic Russians comprised an estimated 90.3% of the population, Germans 4.8%, Ukrainians 2.4% and Altais just 0.1%. The Krai's administrative centre is at Barnaul, which had a population of 573,300 at 1 January 2001. Other major cities are Biisk (223,500) and Rubtsovsk (161,800).

History

The territory of Altai Krai was annexed by Russia in 1738. The region was heavily industrialized during the Soviet period, particularly in 1926–40. Altai Krai was formed on 28 September 1937. On 13 March 1994, in accordance with a federal presidential decree of October 1993, a new provincial legislature, the Legislative Assembly, was elected, in place of the Provincial Soviet. The new legislature was bicameral, comprising a lower chamber of 25 deputies and an upper chamber of 72 deputies (one from each district in the Krai). The Legislative Assembly speaker, Aleksandr Surikov, a communist, defeated the incumbent Governor, Lev Korshunov, in the gubernatorial election of November 1996. Surikov retained his post in the election of 26 March 2000, obtaining 77% of the votes cast.

Economy

Altai Krai's gross regional product in 1999 totalled 34,837.7m. roubles, equivalent to 13,103.8 roubles per head. Its main industrial centres are at Barnaul, Biisk, Rubtsovsk, Novoaltaisk and Slavgorod. There are major river-ports at Barnaul and Biisk. It has well-developed transport networks—1,803 km (1,067 miles) of railway lines in 2000, and 14,441 km of paved roads. About one-quarter of its territory is served by water transport, which operates along a network of some 1,000 km of navigable waterways. There are five airports, including an international airport at Barnaul, with a service to Düsseldorf, Germany. The Krai is bisected by the main natural gas pipeline running from Tyumen to Barnaul via Novosibirsk.

The Krai's principal crops are grain, flax, sunflowers and sugar beet. Horticulture, animal husbandry and fur-animal breeding are also important. In 2000 some 25.7% of its work-force was engaged in agriculture, while total production in the sector amounted to 24,428m. roubles. The Krai contains substantial mineral resources, including salt, iron ore, soda and precious stones, most of which are not industrially exploited. Its main industries are mechanical engineering (including tractor-manufacturing, primarily by the Rubtsovsk tractor plant), food-processing (the Krai's agro-industrial complex is one of the largest in the country), electricity production, metallurgy, chemicals and petrochemicals, and the manufacture of building materials. In addition, Barnaul contains one of the largest textiles enterprises in Russia, producing cotton fibre and yarn for cloth. Industry employed 20.0% of the population in 2000, when total production in the sector amounted to a value of 30,357m. roubles.

In 2000 the economically active population in Altai Krai totalled 1,260,000, and 11.5% of the Krai's labour force were unemployed. The average monthly wage was 2,558.8 roubles in mid-2002. In 2000 the local budget showed a deficit of 121.5m. roubles. External trade amounted to a value of US $206.6m. in exports and $114.0m. in imports; the majority of trade was conducted with other member countries of the Commonwealth of Independent States. Foreign investment in the territory in 2000 totalled $6.5m. At 31 December 2000 there were 12,100 small businesses registered in the Krai.

Directory

Head of the Provincial Administration (Governor): ALEKSANDR A. SURIKOV; 656035 Altai Krai, Barnaul, pr. Lenina 59; tel. (3852) 35-69-35; e-mail glava@ alregn.ru; internet www.altairegion.ru.

Chairman of the Provincial Council of People's Deputies: ALEKSANDR G. NAZARCHUK; 656035 Altai Krai, Barnaul, pr. Lenina 59; tel. (3852) 35-69-86; fax (3852) 22-85-42; e-mail press@alregn.ru.

Chief Representative of Altai Krai in the Russian Federation: TEIMURAZ S. BABLUMYAN; 109017 Moscow, per. B. Tolmachevskii 5/9; tel. (095) 953-36-83; fax (095) 953-01-84.

Head of Barnaul City Administration: VLADIMIR N. BAVARIN; 656099 Altai Krai, Barnaul, pr. Lenina 18; tel. (3852) 39-37-72.

Khabarovsk Krai

Khabarovsk Krai is situated in the Far East, on the Sea of Okhotsk and the Tatar Strait. The region forms part of the Far Eastern Federal Okrug and the Far Eastern Economic Area. Maritime Krai lies to the south, the Jewish Autonomous Oblast (Birobidzhan—part of the Krai until 1991) is to the south-west, Amur Oblast lies to the west, the Republic of Sakha (Yakutiya) to the north-west and, in the north of the province, Magadan Oblast lies to the east. The island of Sakhalin (part of Sakhalin Oblast) lies offshore to the east, across the Tatar Strait. There is a short international border with the People's Republic of China in the south-west. Its main river is the Amur, which rises near the Russo–Chinese border and flows into the Tatar Strait at the town of Nikolayevsk-on-Amur (Nikolayevsk-na-Amure). More than one-half of the Krai's total area of 788,600 sq km (304,400 sq miles) is forested and almost three-quarters comprises mountains or plateaux. The territory, one of the largest in the Federation, measures 1,780 km (1,105 miles) south to north and 7,000 km west to east. Its coastline is 2,500 km long. It is divided into 17 administrative districts and seven cities. The climate is monsoon-like in character, with hot, humid summers. Annual average precipitation in mountain areas can be as much as 1,000 mm (40 inches), while in the north it averages 500 mm. The total population in Khabarovsk Krai at 1 January 2002 was an estimated 1,485,800; the population density was 1.9 per sq km. In 2001 80.8% of the population lived in urban areas. Khabarovsk Krai's administrative centre is at Khabarovsk, which had a population of 603,500 in 2001. The Krais' second largest city is Komsomolsk-on-Amur (Komsomolsk-na-Amure—289,500).

History

Khabarovsk city was established as a military outpost in 1858. It was named after Yerofei Khabarov, a Cossack, who in 1650 led an expedition to the junction of the Amur and Ussuri rivers, the approximate location of Khabarovsk. The region prospered significantly with the construction of the Trans-Siberian Railway, which reached Khabarovsk in 1905. The Krai was formally created on 20 September 1938. The area was industrialized in 1946–80. Following the dissolution of the Provincial Soviet in late 1993, elections to a new, provincial legislative body, the Duma, were held in March 1994. In April 1996 the Russian President, Boris Yeltsin, and the head of the provincial administration, Viktor Ishayev, signed an agreement on the division of powers between the provincial and federal governments. Ishayev also headed the Far East-Transbaikal Association of Economic Interaction, which sought to promote a coherent programme of economic development across the Russian Far East. Ishayev was re-elected as Governor on 10 December 2000, obtaining 88% of the votes cast.

Economy

The Krai's principal land use is forestry. In 1999 its gross regional product totalled 49,534.8m. roubles, or 32,467.0 roubles per head. Its main industrial centres are at Khabarovsk, Komsomolsk-on-Amur, Sovetskaya Gavan, Nikolayevsk-on-Amur and Amursk. Its principal ports are Vanino (the port of Sovetskaya Gavan), Okhotsk and Nikolayevsk-on-Amur. It is traversed by two major railways, the Trans-Siberian and the Far Eastern (Baikal–Amur). In 2000 there were 2,307 km of railway lines and 4,492 km of paved roads in the territory. A ferry service runs between the Krai and Sakhalin Oblast. The Krai is the most important Far Eastern territory in terms of its national and international air services, which connect Moscow and other European cities with Japan.

Agriculture, which employed just 4.0% of the working population in 2000 and generated 3,841m. roubles, consists mainly of grain production, animal husbandry, bee-keeping, fishing and hunting. Hunting is practised on about 97.5% of the Krai's territory. The Krai's main industries are mechanical engineering, electricity production, metal-working, non-ferrous and ferrous metallurgy, food-processing, the processing of forestry products, extraction of coal (2.0m. metric tons of which were mined in 2000), ores and non-ferrous metals, shipbuilding (including oil rigs) and petroleum-refining. Some 21.6% of the territory's work-force was engaged in industry in 2000, when total industrial output amounted to a value of 59,898m. roubles.

Khabarovsk Krai's economically active population was 792,000 in 2000, when 11.6% of the labour force were unemployed. In mid-2002 the average monthly wage was some 5,639.5 roubles. In 2000 the provincial administration recorded a budgetary deficit of 868.1m. roubles. A lack of funds to convert former military enterprises to civilian production, and the liquidation of both the only steel mill in the Russian Far East and a major paper and pulp producer counterbalanced the effects of considerable foreign trade and investment. In the 1990s the territory began to develop its trade links with 'Pacific Rim' nations apart from Japan (with which it had a long trading history), such as Canada, the People's Republic of China, the Democratic People's Republic of Korea (North Korea) and the Republic of Korea (South Korea), Australia, New Zealand, Singapore and the USA. Its exports largely consisted of raw materials (timber, petroleum products, fish and metals). External trade amounted to a value of some US $1,308.2m. in exports and $122.2m. in imports in 2000, when 99.3% of such trade was conducted with countries outside the Commonwealth of Independent States. In 2000 total foreign investment amounted to $27.2m. According to the regional foreign investment promotion agency, in January 2000 731 joint ventures were registered in the territory. At 31 December there were 8,300 small businesses in operation.

Directory

Head of the Provincial Administration (Governor): VIKTOR I. ISHAYEV; 680000 Khabarovsk, ul. K. Marksa 56; tel. (4212) 33-55-40; fax (4212) 33-87-56; internet www.adm.khv.ru.

Chairman of the Provincial Legislative Duma: YURII I. ONOPRIYENKO; 680002 Khabarovsk, ul. Muravyeva-Amurskogo 19; tel. (4212) 32-50-27; e-mail serge@duma.khv.ru; internet www.duma.khv.ru.

Chief Representative of Khabarovsk Krai in the Russian Federation: ANDREI B. CHIRKIN; 127025 Moscow, ul. Novyi Arbat 19; tel. (095) 203-41-28; fax (095) 203-83-25; e-mail khab.rep@g23.relcom.ru; internet www.khabrep.ru.

Head of Khabarovsk City Administration (Mayor): ALEKSANDR N. SOKOLOV; 680000 Khabarovsk, ul. K. Marksa 66; tel. (4212) 23-58-67; fax (4212) 33-53-46; internet www.khabarovsk.kht.ru.

Krasnodar Krai

Krasnodar Krai, often known as the Kuban, is situated in the south of European Russia, in the north-western region of the Greater Caucasus and Kuban-Azov lowlands. The Krai forms part of the Southern Federal Okrug and the North Caucasus Economic Area. It has a short international border with Georgia in the south, while Karachayevo-Cherkessiya and Stavropol Krai lie to the east and Rostov Oblast to the north-east. The Krai's territory encloses the Republic of Adygeya, which became an Autonomous Republic, independent of the jurisdiction of Krasnodar Krai, in 1992. The Krai lies on the Black Sea (on the shores of which is sited the famous resort town of Sochi) in the south-west and on the Sea of Azov in the north-west. The narrow Kerch Gulf, in places only 10 km (six miles) wide, separates the western tip of the province from the Crimean Peninsula (Ukraine). Its major river is the Kuban. The territory of Krasnodar Krai covers 76,000 sq km (29,340 sq miles) and measures 372 km south to north and 380 km west to east. The region is divided into 38 administrative districts and 26 cities. It had an estimated population of 4,987,600 at 1 January 2002. Its population density at that time was 65.6 per sq km, a considerably higher figure than the national average. In 2001 some 53.0% of the population lived in urban areas. Krasnodar, the Krai's administrative centre, had a population of 634,700 in 2001.

History

Krasnodar city (known as Yekaterinodar until 1920) was founded as a military base in 1793, during the campaign of Catherine (Yekaterina) II ('the Great') to win control of the Black Sea region for the Russian Empire, which was eventually achieved in 1796. Dominated by the 'Whites' in the civil wars that followed the collapse of the tsarist regime, by the end of the Soviet period the area's innate conservatism was confirmed by its support for the communists in independent Russia. The Krai had been formed on 13 September 1937. On 22 September 1993 the Krasnodar Provincial Soviet condemned President Boris Yeltsin's Decree 1,400, which dissolved the federal legislature. The following month the Soviet refused to dissolve itself, but announced that elections would be held to a new, 32-member, provincial legislative assembly in March 1994, although this poll was subsequently postponed. Communist leadership of the new Provincial Soviet was not seriously challenged by other forces, and the communists also fared well in federal parliamentary and presidential elections in 1995–96.

During 1996 the incumbent Governor, Nikolai Yegorov, attempted to use the regional courts to postpone the gubernatorial election scheduled for December. He failed, however, and Nikolai Kondratenko, a communist, and the former Chairman of the Provincial Soviet, was elected Governor by a large majority. The communists and other supporters of Kondratenko retained control of the provincial legislative assembly at elections held in November 1998. Kondratenko consistently attracted national notoriety by making overtly anti-Semitic remarks and promoting the notion that the Krai should be protected from an 'invasion of foreigners', defined largely as Meshketian Turks—who had largely been exiled to the region from Georgia under Stalin (Iosif V. Dzhugashvili), although others sought refuge in the Krai following the outbreak of inter-ethnic violence in the Fergana valley (a region that comprises parts of Kyrgyzstan, Tajikistan and Uzbekistan) in 1989—Jews, and Armenians. Kondratenko was aided in this latter point by the establishment of a voluntary Cossack militia in the region, which was accused of persecuting minority groups. (Notably, however, more than 100,000 migrants from other regions of Russia arrived in the Krai in 1995–2000.) Following a gubernatorial election, held on 3 December 2000, Kondratenko was replaced as Governor by Aleksandr Tkachev, who obtained 82% of the votes cast. Kondratenko did not stand as a candidate in the election, citing ill health. Tkachev, in common with his predecessor, became noted for his xenophobic remarks, on occasion urging various groups of non-ethnic Russians to leave the region. Tkachev was also a vocal opponent of land-reform measures supported by federal President Vladimir Putin in 2001. In March 2002, in violation of federal law, the Krai authorities declared the implementation of a 5-km 'border zone' between the Krai and Georgia, with special permits required for those wishing to enter, leave, reside or work in the zone. In May Tkachev and Putin signed an agreement annulling a power-sharing treaty agreed between the federal and provincial authorities in 1996. In June it was announced that the Armenian Government was to open a consulate in the Krai, as part of measures that were intended to combat anti-Armenian feeling in the region. At a legislative election, held in the Krai on 24 November 2002, former Governor Kondratenko's left-wing movement, which had held over 75% of the seats in the previous legislature, obtained only around 15% of the votes cast, according to preliminary reports. The rate of participation by the electorate was low, at some 29%.

Economy

In 1999 gross regional product in Krasnodar Krai amounted to 109,100.8m. roubles, or 21,524.8 roubles per head. Krasnodar is one of the Krai's main industrial centres, as are Armavir, Novorossiisk, Kropotkin, Tikhoretsk and Yeisk. Novorossiisk, Tuapse, Yeisk, Temryuk and Port Kavkaz are important sea-ports. In 2000 the Krai had 2,174 km of railway track and 10,397 km of paved roads.

The Krai's principal crops are grain, sugar beet, rice, tobacco, essential-oil plants, tea and hemp. Horticulture, viniculture and animal husbandry are also important. Agricultural output was worth 48,056m. roubles in 2000, when some 23.9% of the working population was engaged in agriculture. There are important reserves of petroleum and natural gas in Krasnodar Krai. In 2000 around 1.7m. metric tons of petroleum were extracted, and 4.3m. tons were refined on the Krai's territory in 1996. Its main industries are food-processing (which comprised 42.8% of industrial output in 2000), electricity generation, fuel extraction, mechanical engineering and building materials. Total production in the sector (which employed 16.4% of the work-force) amounted to a value of 57,293m. roubles in 2000. The tourism sector is also important: the Kuban region's climate, scenery and mineral and mud springs attracted around 6m. visitors annually in the mid-1990s, when some 400,000 people were employed in tourism. The Krai contains the resort towns of Sochi, Anapa and Tuapse. In 1997 there were over 50 commercial banks operating in Krasnodar Krai. The transportation and refinery of Caspian Sea hydrocarbons reserves (particularly in Novorossiisk, the terminus of a major petroleum pipeline from Baku, Azerbaijan) brought economic benefits to the region from the late 1990s.

In 2000 the economically active population numbered 2,335,000, and 12.5% of the labour force were unemployed. The average monthly wage was 3,483.8 roubles in mid-2002. In 2000 there was a budgetary surplus of 287.7m. roubles. In that year international trade comprised exports amounting to US $995.7m., and imports of $571.7m. Foreign investment amounted to $979.5m., more than 60 times greater than the figure recorded in 1997. At 31 December 2000 there were 20,500 small businesses in operation in the Krai.

Directory

Head of the Provincial Administration: ALEKSANDR N. TKACHEV; 350014 Krasnodar, ul. Krasnaya 35; tel. (8612) 62-57-16; fax (8612) 68-45-38.

Chairman of the Legislative Assembly: (vacant); tel. (8612) 52-50-07; fax (8612) 52-88-80.

Representation of Krasnodar Krai in the Russian Federation: 119180 Moscow, per. 2-i Kazachii 6; tel. (095) 238-20-28.

Head of Krasnodar City Administration (Mayor): NIKOLAI V. PRIZ; 350000 Krasnodar, ul. Krasnaya 122; tel. (8612) 55-43-48; fax (8612) 55-01-56; e-mail post@krd.ru; internet www.krd.ru.

Krasnoyarsk Krai

Krasnoyarsk Krai occupies the central part of Siberia and extends from the Arctic Ocean coast in the north to the western Sayan Mountains in the south. The Krai forms part of the Siberian Federal Okrug and the East Siberian Economic Area. It is bordered by the Republic of Sakha (Yakutiya) and Irkutsk Oblast to the east and the Republic of Tyva to the south. To the west lie the Republic of Khakasiya, the Oblasts of Kemerovo and Tomsk, as well as Tyumen Oblast's Khanty-Mansii and Yamal-Nenets AOks. Its major river is the Yenisei, one of the longest in Russia, measuring 4,102 km (2,549 miles). Most of its area is covered by taiga (forested marshland). The Krai, including its two autonomous okrugs (Evenk and Taimyr—Dolgan-Nenets), covers a total area of 2,339,000 sq km (902,850 sq miles), the second largest federal unit in Russia, or 710,000 sq km (274,133 sq miles) when they are excluded. Krasnoyarsk Krai measures almost 3,000 km from south to north. In the Krai proper there are 42 administrative districts and 24 cities. The Krai lies within three climatic zones—arctic, sub-arctic and continental. It had an estimated total population of 3,015,300 at 1 January 2002, and a population density of 1.3 per sq km. Some 74.6% of the population inhabited urban areas in 2001. The Krai's administrative centre is at Krasnoyarsk, which had a population of 758,700 in 2001. Other major cities include Norilsk (143,100), Achinsk (120,400), Kansk (108,100) and Zheleznogorsk (95,300).

130

History

The city of Krasnoyarsk was founded in 1628 by Cossack forces as an ostrog (military transit camp) during the period of Russian expansion across Siberia (1582–1639). The region gained importance after the discovery of gold, and with the construction of the Trans-Siberian Railway. The Krai was formed on 7 December 1934. During the Soviet era the region was closed to foreigners, owing to its nuclear-reactor and defence establishments.

A gubernatorial election in December 1992 was won by Valerii Zubov (the incumbent, a supporter of federal President Boris Yeltsin), and elections to a new parliament, the Legislative Assembly, were held on 6 March 1994. In the mid-1990s Zubov's regime proved to be increasingly ineffectual—in 1997 the provincial administration collected less than one-half of the taxes it was owed and had one of the worst records on wage arrears in the country. This largely contributed to the victory in the 1998 gubernatorial election of Aleksandr Lebed, who was perceived by many as a suitably strong leader capable of defending the interests of the territory against the federal Government. Lebed defeated Zubov in the second round of elections, held on 17 May, with 57.3% of the votes cast. Lebed died in a helicopter crash on 28 April 2002. An election to appoint a successor, held on 8 September, proved inconclusive, and the two leading contenders in this first round, the Chairman of the regional Legislative Assembly, Aleksandr Uss, and the Governor of Taimyr AOk, Aleksandr Khlopanin, proceeded to a second round, held on 22 September. In the 'run-off' election Khlopanin was the first-placed candidate, winning 48.1% of the votes cast, compared with the 41.8% of the votes received by Uss. Although Khlopanin emphasized that he did not intend to transfer officials from the AOk administration to the Krai, his success appeared to heighten speculation that the two federal subjects (and potentially the third constituent part of the Krai, the Evenk AOk) would eventually merge to form a single unit. However, at the end of the month the Krai's electoral commission annulled the results of the election, citing irregularities, and announced that new polls were to be held. Khlopanin declared that he was to appeal against the commission's decision; in the mean time, the First Deputy Governor of the Krai, Nikolai Ashlapov, was to serve as Governor, in an acting capacity, as he had done, effectively, since Lebed's death. In early October, however, federal President Vladimir Putin announced that Ashlapov had resigned his post, and appointed Khlopanin to serve as acting Governor. Subsequently, in mid-October the central electoral commission confirmed Khlopanin's election as Governor, and he was inaugurated shortly afterwards. The Supreme Court confirmed the validity of the election results in November.

Economy

Krasnoyarsk Krai is potentially one of Russia's richest regions, containing vast deposits of minerals, gold and petroleum, although, particularly since the late 1990s, it has experienced serious economic problems, many of them typical of northern regions. All of the figures included in this survey include figures for the two autonomous okrugs, which are also considered separately. In 1999 the Krai's gross regional product amounted to 129,456.9m. roubles, equivalent to 42,429.6 roubles per head. The Krai's major industrial centres are at Krasnoyarsk, Norilsk,

Achinsk, Kansk and Minusinsk. In 2000 there were 2,068 km of railway track and 12,842 km of paved roads on the Krai's territory.

The principal crops are grain, flax, and hemp. Animal husbandry, fur farming and hunting are also important. The agricultural sector employed 10.2% of the working population in 2000, when total output within the sector was worth 20,347m. roubles. The Krai's main industries are non-ferrous metallurgy, electricity production, mechanical engineering, metal-working, ore-mining (particularly bauxite, for aluminium), chemicals, forestry and food-processing. Industry employed 25.1% of the work-force in 2000, when the industrial output of Krasnoyarsk Krai amounted to a value of 199,618m. roubles. The Krai contains the world's second largest aluminium smelter, Krasnoyarsk Aluminium, which in 1998 was 20%-owned by the British-based company, Trans-World and which forms part of the Krasnoyarsk Metallurgical Plant (KraMZ).

In 2000 the territory's economically active population totalled 1,556,000, and 11.9% of the Krai's labour force were unemployed. The average monthly wage in the Krai was 5,971.7 roubles in mid-2002, somewhat in excess of the national average. In 2000 the local budget showed a surplus of 1,118.2m. roubles. In that year export trade amounted to US $3,632.9m., and imports to $649.6m. Foreign investment totalled $64.3m. in 2000. At the end of the year there were 14,000 small businesses in Krasnoyarsk Krai.

Directory

Head of the Provincial Administration (Governor): ALEKSANDR G. KHLO-PANIN; 660009 Krasnoyarsk, pr. Mira 110; tel. (3912) 22-22-63; fax (3912) 22-11-78; e-mail klimik@krskstate.ru; internet www.krskstate.ru.

Chairman of the Legislative Assembly: ALEKSANDR V. USS; 660009 Krasnoyarsk, pr. Mira 110; tel. (3912) 23-28-10.

Representation of Krasnoyarsk Krai in the Russian Federation: 107996 Moscow, ul. Gilyarovskogo 31/2; tel. (095) 284-86-56; fax (095) 284-82-41.

Head of Krasnoyarsk City Administration (Mayor): PETR I. PIMASHKOV; 660049 Krasnoyarsk, ul. K. Marksa 93; tel. (3912) 22-22-31; fax (3912) 22-25-12; e-mail webmaster@admkrsk.ru; internet www.admkrsk.ru.

Maritime (Primorskii) Krai

Maritime (Primorskii) Krai—Primorye is situated in the extreme south-east of Russia, on the Tatar Strait and the Sea of Japan. The province is part of the Far Eastern Federal Okrug and the Far Eastern Economic Area. Its only border with another federal subject is with Khabarovsk Krai to the north. There is an international border with the People's Republic of China to the west and a short border with the Democratic People's Republic of Korea (North Korea) in the south-west. Its major river is the Ussuri. The territory occupies 165,900 sq km (64,060 sq miles), more than two-thirds of which is forested. It is divided into 24 administrative districts and 12 cities. At 1 January 2002 the total number of inhabitants in the territory was estimated at 2,124,700 and the population density was, therefore, 12.8 per sq km. In 2001 some 78.1% of the population lived in urban areas. Maritime Krai's administrative centre is at Vladivostok, which had 598,600 inhabitants. Other major cities are Ussuriisk (formerly Voroshilov—156,600) and Nakhodka (155,600).

History

The territories of the Maritime Krai were recognized as Chinese possessions by Russia in the Treaty of Nerchinsk in 1687. They became part of the Russian Empire in 1860, however, being ceded by China under the terms of the Treaty of Peking (Beijing), and the port of Vladivostok was founded. Along with other Transbaikal and Pacific regions of the former Russian Empire, the territory was part of the Far Eastern Republic until its reintegration into Russia under Soviet rule in 1922. Maritime Krai was created on 20 October 1938.

The territory declared itself a republic in mid-1993, but was not recognized as such by the federal authorities. On 28 October 1993 the provincial Governor disbanded the Soviet, as it had failed to muster a quorum. Elections for a provincial

133

Governor were set for October 1994, but were cancelled by presidential decree, after alleged improprieties by the incumbent, Yevgenii Nazdratenko, during his election campaign. Nazdratenko was elected, however, in December 1995, with 76% of the votes cast, and was re-elected by a similar majority in December 1999. His populist and nationalistic style of government, development of a 'cult of personality', and control of the local media reinforced his position.

The Governor's disputes with the central Government, particularly with President Boris Yeltsin's reformist chief of staff, Anatolii Chubais, continued after his election—in October 1996 Chubais publicly blamed Nazdratenko for the serious energy crisis in the region, citing his failure to introduce market reforms. An ongoing energy crisis in the region, owing to non-payment of bills, finally forced the resignation of Nazdratenko (officially on health grounds), in February 2001, following reports that President Vladimir Putin had accused the Governor of incompetence. In gubernatorial elections held in May–June, Sergei Darkin, a local businessman, was elected Governor in the second round of voting, with some 40% of the votes cast, defeating Gennadii Apanasenko, the deputy presidential representative to the region, who secured 24% of the votes; the rate of voter participation was just 36%. Viktor Cherepkov, the former Mayor of Vladivostok (and a long-standing opponent of Nazdratenko), who had taken second place in the first round of voting, behind Darkin, was barred from standing as a candidate in the second round of the elections by the regional court, which cited irregularities in his campaign. Following his exclusion from the electoral process, Cherepkov encouraged his supporters to vote against all candidates, and 34% of voters did so. (Cherepkov subsequently founded his own party, Freedom and Peoples' Power, which was registered in June 2002.) Regional legislative elections, held in December 2001, were declared invalid in 20 of the 36 constituencies, as the rate of voter participation was lower than the 25% required to legitimize the results; residents in Vladivostok, Nakhodka and Ussuriisk failed to elect a single candidate. Repeat elections, in which the majority of votes were cast by supporters of Nazdratenko, were held in June 2002; although the rate of participation by the electorate was just 18%, the elections were declared valid, as the 25% threshold had been abolished.

Economy

Maritime Krai's gross regional product totalled 54,791.9m. roubles in 1999, equivalent to 25,070.7 roubles per head. Its major industrial centres are at Vladivostok, the terminus of the Trans-Siberian Railway, Ussuriisk, Nakhodka, Dalnegorsk and Lesozavodsk. The Krai's most important ports are at Vladivostok, Nakhodka and Vostochnyi (formerly Vrangel). Vessels based in these ports comprise around four-fifths of maritime transport services in the Far East. Maritime Krai has rail links with Khabarovsk Krai and, hence, other regions, as well as international transport links with North Korea and the Republic of Korea (South Korea). In 2000 there were 1,553 km (965 miles) of railway lines and 7,057 km of paved roads on the Krai's territory.

The Krai's agricultural sector, which employed 9.0% of the labour force in 2000, consists mainly of grain and soya production, animal husbandry, fur farming, bee-keeping and fishing. Total agricultural output in 2000 amounted to a value of 5,317m. roubles. Illicit agricultural activities were also thought to include the cultivation of marijuana, particularly in the Khankai district. The Krai contains some 1,200m. metric tons of coal reserves. The hydroelectric-energy potential of the region's rivers is estimated at 25,000m. kWh, and timber reserves are estimated at 1,500m.–1,800m. cu m. Its main industries are food-processing (which accounted for 46.7% of industrial production in 2000), fuel and electrical energy production, non-ferrous metallurgy, ore-mining, the processing of fish and forestry products, mechanical engineering and ship repairs, metal-working, building materials and chemicals. Total industrial production was worth 40,618m. roubles in 2000, when the sector employed 21.1% of the working population. Energy production in the Krai was hindered by political mismanagement from the mid-1990s. Dalenergo, its electricity-generation monopoly, was notorious as one of the worst-performing utilities in the country, unable to collect accounts, service debts or pay for fuel, which led to fuel shortages and frequent strikes by its workers. The territory is ideally placed, in terms of its proximity to the Pacific nations, for international trade, although the perception of widespread corruption restrained its development. A new railway crossing into the People's Republic of China at Makhalino-Hunchun, which was expected to carry 3m. tons of cargo annually by 2002, opened in August 1998. The construction of a cross-border trade and economic centre, uniting the city of Pogranichnyi, in the Krai, with Suifenhe, in China, was expected to commence in late 2002, and was due for completion in 2005.

The economically active population of Maritime Krai numbered 1,166,000 in 2000, when 11.9% of the labour force were unemployed. The average monthly wage was 4,573.2 roubles in mid-2002. In 2000 there was a budgetary deficit of 639.7m. roubles. External export trade amounted to US $612.4m. in that year, when imports totalled $329.3m. According to the European Bank for Reconstruction and Development, the Krai had huge investment potential; foreign investment totalled $78.1m. in 2000. In August 1997 Hyundai (of South Korea), opened a $100m. hotel and business centre in Vladivostok. South Korea also planned to create an industrial park for high-technology industries over an 11-year period in the free economic zone of Nakhodka, although some analysts doubted the practicality of the project. At 31 December 2000 there were 16,100 small businesses registered in the territory.

Directory

Head of the Provincial Administration (Governor): SERGEI M. DARKIN; 690110 Maritime Krai, Vladivostok, ul. Svetlanskaya 22; tel. (4232) 22-38-00; fax (4232) 22-50-10; e-mail gubernator@primorsky.ru; internet www.primorsky.ru.

Chairman of the Provincial Duma: SERGEI A. SOPCHUK; 690110 Maritime Krai, 690110 Vladivostok, ul. Svetlanskaya 22; tel. (4232) 22-35-70; fax (4232) 26-90-32; internet www.primorsky.ru/prim/duma/duma_new.html.

Chief Representative of Maritime (Primorskii) Krai in the Russian Federation: MIKHAIL N. MALGINOV; 123100 Moscow, pr. 1-i Krasnogvardeiskii 9/22/315; tel. (095) 255-82-14; fax (095) 255-82-13.

Head of the Vladivostok City Administration (Mayor): YURII M. KOPYLOV; 690600 Maritime Krai, Vladivostok, Okeanskii pr. 20; tel. (4232) 22-30-16; fax (4232) 22-68-40.

Stavropol Krai

Stavropol Krai is situated in the central Caucasus region and extends from the Caspian lowlands in the east to the foothills of the Greater Caucasus Mountains in the south-west. It is part of the Southern Federal Okrug and the North Caucasus Economic Area. Krasnodar Krai lies to the west, there is a short border with Rostov Oblast in the north-west of the Krai and it shares rather longer borders with Kalmykiya to the north-east and Dagestan to the east. Chechnya, Ingushetiya, North Osetiya (Ossetia)—Alaniya and Kabardino-Balkariya lie to the south, and Karachayevo-Cherkessiya to the south-west. The Krai's major rivers are the Kuban, the Kuma and the Yegorlyk. Much of its territory is steppe. Its total area is 66,500 sq km (25,670 sq miles), and it is divided into 26 administrative districts and 19 cities. The population of Stavropol Krai numbered 2,642,600 at 1 January 2002. The Krai's population density, therefore, was 39.7 per sq km. In 2001 some 55.1% of the population lived in urban areas. The Krai's administrative centre is at Stavropol, which had a population of 339,500 in 2001. Other major cities are Nevinnomyssk (131,800), Pyatigorsk (126,800) and Kislovodsk (111,900).

History

Stavropol city was founded in 1777 as part of the consolidation of Russian rule in the Caucasus. The territory was created on 13 February 1924, although it was originally known as South-Eastern Oblast and, subsequently, the North Caucasus Krai. It was named Ordzhonikidze Krai in 1937–43, before adopting its current title. The former Karachai and Cherkess Autonomous Oblasts, which were reconstituted as the Republic of Karachayevo-Cherkessiya upon the adoption of the 1992 Federation Treaty, previously formed part of the Krai.

In March 1994 elections were held to a new representative body, the State Duma. In June 1995 the town of Budennovsk, situated about 150 km north of the

Chechen border, was the scene of a massive hostage-taking operation by rebel Chechen forces; over 1,000 civilians were seized, but they were released after a few days. In the gubernatorial elections of November 1996 the Communist Party candidate, Aleksandr Chernogorov (a former State Duma deputy), defeated the government-supported incumbent, Petr Marchenko, winning 55% of the votes cast. In October 2000 four people died, and more than 100 people were wounded, as a result of three simultaneous bomb explosions in Pyatigorsk and Nevinomyssk. There was a series of further attacks, including bombings and the hijacking of a bus, in the Krai during 2001, which official sources attributed to Chechen separatists, and in which more than 20 people died. In an attempt to calm the disorder in the region, Chernogorov demanded that the Krai to be granted special territorial status, and demanded the implementation of stricter immigration controls within the Krai, although these appeals were rejected by the State Duma. Chernogorov was re-elected for a further term as Governor in a second round of voting in December 2000. Elections to the State Duma took place in December 2001. In June 2002 the regional legislature approved legislation, which, in contravention of federal requirements, sought to place restrictions on the number of immigrants permitted to settle in specific regions of the Krai.

Economy

In 1999 Stavropol Krai's gross regional product was 43,440.1m. roubles, or 16,148.1 roubles per head. Its main industrial centres are at Stavropol, Nevinnomyssk, Georgiyevsk and Budennovsk. In 2000 there were 944 km (587 miles) of railway lines and 7,497 km of paved roads on the Krai's territory. In September 1997 the federal Government announced that a new section of a petroleum pipeline from Baku, Azerbaijan, would cross Stavropol Krai, rather than run through Chechnya.

The Krai contains extremely fertile soil. Its agricultural production, which amounted to a value of 20,678m. roubles in 2000, consists mainly of grain, sunflower seeds, sugar beet and vegetables. Horticulture, viniculture and animal husbandry are also important. The sector employed 24.4% of the working population in 2000. The Krai's main industries are food-processing, mechanical engineering, production of building materials, chemicals and the production of natural gas, petroleum, non-ferrous metal ores and coal, and electrical energy. Around 15.9% of the labour force worked in industry in 2000, when total industrial output was worth 28,416m. roubles.

The economically active population in Stavropol Krai was 1,237,000 in 2000, when 13.8% of the region's labour force were unemployed, compared with 18.5% in the previous year. The average wage was 3,015.6 roubles per month in mid-2002. In 2000 there was a budgetary surplus of 387.1m. roubles. In that year the value of exports from the Krai amounted to US $271.6m., and imports were worth $97.3m. Foreign investment in the territory amounted to $34.2m. At 31 December 2000 there were 7,100 small businesses in operation.

Directory

Head of the Provincial Administration (Governor): ALEKSANDR L. CHERNO-GOROV; 355025 Stavropol, pl. Lenina 1; tel. (8652) 35-22-52; fax (8652) 35-06-60; e-mail stavadm@stavropol.net.

Chairman of the State Duma: ALEKSANDR A. SHIYANOV; tel. (8652) 34-82-55.

Representation of Stavropol Krai in the Russian Federation: 127025 Moscow, ul. Novyi Arbat 19/1713; tel. (095) 203-55-36; fax (095) 203-55-39.

Head of Stavropol City Administration (Mayor): MIKHAIL V. KUZMIN; 355000 Stavropol, pr. K. Marksa 95; tel. (8652) 26-03-10; fax (8652) 26-28-23; e-mail goradm@smtn.stavropol.ru; internet www.stavropol.net/stavropol.

OBLASTS (REGIONS)

Amur Oblast

Amur Oblast is situated in the south-east of the Russian Federation, to the west of Khabarovsk Krai. It forms part of the Far Eastern Federal Okrug and the Far Eastern Economic Area. The Jewish Autonomous Oblast lies to the south-east, Chita Oblast to the west and the Republic of Sakha (Yakutiya) to the north. Southwards it has an international border with the People's Republic of China. The Oblast's main river is the Amur, which is 2,900 km (1,800 miles) long. A large reservoir, the Zeya, is situated in the north of the region. A little under three-quarters of the Oblast's territory is forested. Its total area occupies 363,700 sq km (140,430 sq miles) and measures 750 km south to north and 1,150 km south-east to north-west. It is divided into 20 administrative districts and nine cities. The territory's inhabitants numbered some 982,200 at 1 January 2002 and the population density was, therefore, 2.7 per sq km. In 2001 most people (65.7%) lived in urban areas. Amur Oblast's administrative centre is at Blagoveshchensk, near the Chinese border, which had a population of 220,600 in 2001.

History

The Amur region was first discovered by European Russians in 1639 and came under Russian control in the late 1850s. Part of the pro-Bolshevik Far Eastern Republic (based in Chita) until its reintegration into Russia in 1922, Amur Oblast was formed on 20 October 1932.

In the first year of post-Soviet Russian independence there was a struggle for power in the territory, which the federal President, Boris Yeltsin, decided should be resolved by a gubernatorial election in December 1992. However, his appointed head of the administration was defeated. On 21 July 1993 Amur Oblast declared itself a republic, a measure that was condemned by the federal authorities. During the constitutional crisis of September–October, President Yeltsin was denounced by all the regional authorities. The Governor was, therefore, later dismissed and the Regional Soviet dissolved. Contention between executive and legislative organs resumed following the election of a new Regional Assembly in 1994. In January 1996 the Regional Administration brought action against the Regional Assembly for adopting a Charter, a republican constitution, some of the clauses of which ran counter to federal laws and presidential decrees. In the same month, in accordance with the Charter, the Assembly changed its name to the Council of People's Deputies. In elections to the Council of People's Deputies, held in March, Communist Party candidates won up to 40% of the votes cast. In response to these developments President Yeltsin again dismissed the Governor in June, and appointed Yurii Lyashko, formerly the chief executive of Blagoveshchensk city, in his place. A further gubernatorial election was held on 22 September. It was won by the communist-backed candidate, Anatolii Belonogov, by a narrow margin, but the results were subsequently annulled because of alleged irregularities. Belonogov, hitherto speaker of the regional legislature, and a communist, succeeded in securing a clear majority in the repeat election held in March 1997. In gubernatorial elections held in two rounds in March–April 2001 Belonogov was defeated by Leonid Korotkov, hitherto a deputy in the State Duma, and a member of the Communist Party until 1999.

Economy

Amur Oblast's gross regional product was 22,773.0m. roubles in 1999, equivalent to 22,534.1 roubles per head. Its main industrial centres are at Blagoveshchensk, Belogorsk, Raichikhinsk, Zeya, Shimanovsk and Svobodnyi. In 2000 there were 6,915 km of paved roads in the Oblast. There were 3,002 km of railway track, including sections of two major railways, the Trans-Siberian and the Far Eastern (Baikal–Amur). There are five river-ports, at Blagoveshchensk, Svobodnensk, Poyarkovsk, Amursk (all of which transport cargo to and from the People's Republic of China) and Zeisk. There is an international airport at Blagoveshchensk, which serves flights to Japan, the Democratic People's Republic of Korea (North Korea) and the Republic of Korea (South Korea), and (on a charter basis) to Turkey.

Agriculture in Amur Oblast, which employed 13.0% of its work-force in 2000, significantly less than in 1995, consists mainly of grain and vegetable production, animal husbandry and bee-keeping. The soil in the south of the region is particularly fertile—in 1998 Amur Oblast contained 57% of the arable land in the Russian Far East and produced 30% of its agricultural output. In 2000 agricultural output in Amur Oblast amounted to 6,637m. roubles. In 1998 timber reserves were estimated at 2,000m. cu m. The region is rich in mineral resources, but by the end of the 1990s it was estimated that only around 5% of these resources were being exploited. None the less, the mining sector produced around 15% of gross regional product in the late 1990s. In the late 1990s around 10–12 metric tons of gold were extracted annually, making the Oblast the third largest producer of gold in Russia. Other raw-material deposits in the Oblast include bituminous coal, lignite (brown coal) and kaolin. There are also substantial reserves of iron, titanium, silver and gold ores. Coal-mining is also important, as are mechanical engineering, electricity generation, electro-technical industry and the processing of agricultural and forestry products. In 2000 14.6% of the Oblast's work-force were employed in industry, and total output in the sector amounted to a value of 8,878m. roubles. The region contains the Amur Shipbuilding Plant. In 1997 the plant was contracted to build a 111-sq km steel platform for a foreign consortium, intended to exploit the petroleum and natural gas fields of Sakhalin Oblast. It has also proposed building nuclear-powered submarines for export to the People's Republic of China, in addition to those it continues producing for Russia, and a barge to contain nuclear waste. There is a hydroelectric power plant at Zeya, with a reservoir of 2,400 sq km. Another power-station was under construction at Bureya, the first part of which was expected to commence operations in 2003.

Amur's economically active population numbered 520,000 in 2000, when 13.4% of the region's labour force were unemployed. Those in employment earned, on average, 4,882.6 roubles per month in mid-2002. There was a budgetary deficit of 634m. roubles in 2000. In that year export trade amounted to a value of US $58.4m., and import trade totalled $17.1m. The Oblast's main trading partners were the People's Republic of China, Japan and North Korea. Foreign investment totalled $4.5m. in 2000. At 31 December 2000 there were 3,800 small businesses registered in the Oblast.

Directory

Head of the Regional Administration: LEONID V. KOROTKOV; 675023 Amur obl., Blagoveshchensk, ul. Lenina 135; tel. (4162) 44-03-22; fax (4162) 44-62-01; e-mail glava@amurobl.ru; internet www.amurobl.ru.

Chairman of the Regional Council of People's Deputies (Regional Council): STANISLAV I. GORYANSKII; 675023 Amur obl., Blagoveshchensk, ul. Lenina 135; tel. (4162) 44-38-53; fax (4162) 44-38-58.

Representation of Amur Oblast in the Russian Federation: 127006 Moscow, ul. M. Dmitrovka 3; tel. (095) 299-38-63; fax (095) 299-42-02.

Head of Blagoveshchensk City Administration (Mayor): ALEKSANDR M. KOLY-AGIN; 675023 Amur obl., Blagoveshchensk, ul. Lenina 133; tel. (4162) 42-49-85.

Archangel Oblast

Archangel (Arkhangelsk) Oblast is situated in the north of the Eastern European Plain. It lies on the White, Barents and Kara Seas (parts of the Arctic Ocean) and includes the northern archipelago of Zemlya Frantsa-Iosifa and the Novaya Zemlya islands. The Oblast forms part of the North-Western Federal Okrug and the Northern Economic Area. In the north-east the Nenets Autonomous Okrug, a constituent part of the Oblast, runs eastwards along the coast to end in a short border with the Yamal-Nenets AOk (part of Tyumen Oblast). The Republic of Komi lies to the south of the Nenets AOk and to the east of Archangel proper. Kirov and, mainly, Vologda Oblasts form the southern border and the Republic of Kareliya lies to the west. The Oblast contains several large rivers (the Severnaya Dvina, the Onega, the Mezen, the Pinega, the Vaga and the Pechora) and some 2,500 lakes. Some two-fifths of its entire area is forested—much of the north-west of the territory is taiga (forested marshland). The Oblast, including the autonomous okrug, occupies an area of 587,400 sq km (226,800 sq miles) and is divided into 20 administrative districts and 14 cities. It spans three climatic zones—arctic, sub-arctic and continental. The total population at 1 January 2002 was an estimated 1,428,900 and its population density, therefore, stood at 2.4 per sq km. In 2001 some 74.5% of the population lived in urban areas. Archangel Oblast's administrative centre is at Archangel (Arkhangelsk), which had 358,500 inhabitants in 2001. The Oblast's second city is Severodvinsk (232,800).

History

The city of Archangel was founded in the 16th century, to further Muscovite trade. It was the first Russian seaport and the country's main one until the building of St Petersburg in 1703. The port played a major role in the attack by the Entente fleet (British and French navies) against the Red Army in 1918, and was an important route for supplies from the Allied Powers during the Second World War. Archangel Oblast was founded on 23 September 1937.

On 13 October 1993 the Archangel Regional Soviet transferred its responsibilities to the Regional Administration. Communist candidates initially formed the largest single group elected to the legislative chamber of the Regional Deputies' Assembly, although supporters of the federal Government and liberal reformists also enjoyed respectable levels of support in the cities. In March 1996 the unpopular head of the regional administration, Pavel Pozdeyev, a federal appointee nominated only one month previously, was forced to leave his position. His predecessor, Pavel Balakshin, who was being investigated on charges of misuse of federal funds, initially refused to step down from the Federation Council, as his demotion required, and was subsequently elected as Mayor of Archangel City, a position he held until December 2000. Anatolii Yefremov's position as Governor was confirmed by his popular election to the post in December 1997, and by his re-election in December 2000.

Economy

All figures in this survey incorporate data for the Nenets AOk, which is also treated separately. Archangel Oblast's gross regional product totalled 38,994.1m. roubles in 1999, equivalent to 26,541.0 roubles per head. The Oblast's main industrial centres are at Archangel, Kotlas, Severodvinsk and Novodvinsk. In 2000 there were 1,764 km (1,096 miles) of railways and 7,118 km of paved roads on the Oblast's territory. Its main ports are Archangel, Onega, Mezen and Naryan Mar (sea- and river-ports).

The Oblast's agriculture, which employed just 5.8% of the labour force in 2000, consists mainly of grain and vegetable production, animal husbandry (livestock and reindeer) and hunting. Total agricultural output in the Oblast amounted to a value of 5,129m. roubles in 2000. Its industry, which employed 27.2% of the working population in that year, is based on timber and timber-processing (which accounted for 50.9% of industrial production in 2000), the extraction of minerals (in particular, bauxite), petroleum and natural gas, mechanical engineering and food-processing. Industrial output across the Oblast was worth 42,821m. roubles in 2000. In July 1998 it was announced that the federal Ministry of Finance was to allocate credit worth US $30m. for development of a diamond field in the Oblast, one of Russia's largest, run by Severoalmaz (Northern Diamonds) as part of a multinational consortium, although repeated licensing problems delayed progress.

The Oblast's economically active population amounted to 761,000 in 2000, when 12.2% of the region's labour force were unemployed. The average monthly wage was 5,094.2 roubles in mid-2002. In 2000 the Oblast recorded a budgetary surplus of 357.2m. roubles. External trade in that year amounted to US $873.6m., of which $769.6m. were exports, and $104.0m. were imports. Total foreign investment totalled $39.0m. in 2000. At 31 December 2000 there were 4,800 small businesses registered on the Oblast's territory.

Directory

Head of the Regional Administration (Governor): ANATOLII A. YEFREMOV; 163004 Archangel, pr. Troitskii 49; tel. (8182) 65-30-41; fax (8182) 64-65-11; internet www.dvinaland.ru.

Chairman of the Regional Deputies' Assembly: VITALII S. FORTYGIN; 163061 Archangel, pl. Lenina 1; tel. (8182) 64-66-81; fax (8182) 63-73-03.

Chief Representative of Archangel Oblast in the Russian Federation: BORIS A. GAGARIN; 127006 Moscow, ul. M. Dmitrovka 3/10; tel. (095) 299-44-12.

Head of Archangel City Administration: OLEG NILOV; 163061 Archangel, pl. Lenina 5; tel. (8182) 65-64-84; fax (8182) 65-20-71; e-mail webmaster@arhcity.ru; internet www.arhcity.ru.

Astrakhan Oblast

Astrakhan Oblast is situated in the Caspian lowlands and forms part of the Southern Federal Okrug and the Volga Economic Area. Lying between the Russian federal subject of Kalmykiya to the south and the former Soviet state of Kazakhstan to the east, Astrakhan is a long, relatively thin territory, which flanks the River Volga as it flows out of Volgograd Oblast in the north-west towards the Caspian Sea to the south-east, via a delta at Astrakhan. The delta is one of the largest in the world and occupies more than 24,000 sq km (9,260 sq miles) of the Caspian lowlands. It gives the Oblast some 200 km (over 120 miles) of coastline. It has one lake, the Baskunchak, measuring 115 sq km. Astrakhan occupies some 44,100 sq km (17,000 sq miles) and is divided into 11 administrative districts and six cities. At 1 January 2002 its total population was an estimated 1,008,700 and its population density, therefore, was 22.9 per sq km. In 2001 some 66.2% of the population lived in urban areas. The Oblast's administrative centre is at Astrakhan (formerly Khadzhi-Tarkhan), which had a population of 479,700 in January 2001. The city lies at 22 m (72 feet) below sea level and is protected from the waters of the Volga delta by 75 km of dykes. Other major cities are Akhtubinsk (47,200) and Znamensk (37,000).

History

The Khanate of Astrakhan, which was formed in 1446, following the dissolution of the Golden Horde, was conquered by the Russians in 1556. The region subsequently became an important centre for trading in timber, grain, fish and petroleum. Astrakhan Oblast was founded on 27 December 1943.

There was considerable hardship in the region with the dissolution of the USSR and the economic reforms of the early 1990s. Dissatisfaction was indicated by the relatively high level of support for the nationalist Liberal Democrats in the 1995 State Duma elections, and by the continued pre-eminence of the Communist Party in the Oblast. The Governor, Anatolii Guzhvin, initially a federal appointee, retained his post at elections in 1997, and was re-elected for a further term of office in December 2000, receiving 81% of the votes cast. In November 2001 an influx of Tajik refugees into the Oblast was reported, despite the temporary suspension of the railway link to the Tajik capital, Dushanbe, which prompted Guzhvin to request that the federal Government take measures to regulate illegal immigration.

Economy

Astrakhan Oblast's gross regional product was 18,942.9m. roubles in 1999, equivalent to 18,479.1 roubles per head. The Oblast's main industrial centres are at Astrakhan and Akhtubinsk. In 2000 there were 567 km of railways and 2,635 km of paved roads on the Oblast's territory. The rise in the level of the Caspian Sea (by some 2.6 m between the late 1970s and the late 1990s) and the resulting erosion of the Volga delta caused serious environmental problems in the region. These were exacerbated by the pollution of the water by petroleum products, copper, nitrates and other substances, which frequently contributed to the death of a significant proportion of fish reserves.

The Oblast remains a major producer of vegetables and cucurbits (gourds and melons). Grain production and animal husbandry are also important. Total agricultural production amounted to a value of 3,094m. roubles in 2000, when the sector employed 14.7% of the working population. The Oblast is rich in natural resources, including gas and gas condensate, sulphur, petroleum and salt. Its main industries are the production of petroleum and natural gas, food-processing, mechanical engineering, and electricity production. It was hoped that the former activity would improve the economic fortunes of the region, as the exploitation of Caspian hydrocarbons reserves increased. Industrial output in 2000 was worth 18,423m. roubles, and the sector employed 16.4% of the Oblast's labour force. Regional trade was also important to the economy of Astrakhan. The Lakor freight company established important shipping links with Iran, handling around 940,000 metric tons of cargo in 1996, and in early 2000 announced plans to develop a trade route with India. In September 1997 the company, with an Iranian group, Khazar Shipping, registered the Astrakhan–Nowshahr joint shipping line. Astrakhan's exports to Iran mainly comprised paper, metals, timber, mechanical equipment, fertilizers and chemical products.

Astrakhan Oblast's economically active population numbered 502,000 in 2000, when 11.5% of the region's labour force were unemployed. The average monthly wage was 3,708.2 roubles in mid-2002. In 2000 there was a budgetary surplus of 107.7m. roubles. In that year export trade totalled US $249.7m., and the value of imports amounted to $53.0m. Foreign investment in the territory amounted to

$0.4m., compared with $7.6m. in 1998. At 31 December 2000 there were 3,600 small businesses in operation.

Directory

Head of the Regional Administration (Governor): ANATOLII P. GUZHVIN; 414008 Astrakhan, ul. Sovetskaya 15; tel. (8512) 22-85-19; fax (8512) 22-95-14; e-mail ves@astrakhan.ru; internet www.adm.astranet.ru.

Chairman of the Representative Assembly: PAVEL P. ANISIMOV; 414000 Astrakhan, ul. Volodarskogo 15; tel. (8512) 22-96-44; fax (8512) 22-22-48; e-mail ootsops@astranet.ru.

Representation of Astrakhan Oblast in the Russian Federation: 125407 Moscow, ul. 3-aya Tveskaya-Yamskaya 58/5; tel. (095) 251-07-19; fax (095) 251-06-96.

Head of Astrakhan City Administration (Mayor): IGOR A. BEZRUKAVNIKOV; 414000 Astrakhan, ul. Chernyshevskogo 6; tel. (8512) 22-55-88; fax (8512) 24-71-76; e-mail munic@astranet.ru; internet astrakhan.astranet.ru/munic.htm.

Belgorod Oblast

Belgorod Oblast is situated in the south-west of the Central Russian Highlands. It forms part of the Central Federal Okrug and the Central Chernozem Economic Area. The Oblast lies on the international border with Ukraine, with the Oblasts of Kursk to the north and Voronezh to the east. Its main rivers are the Severnii Donets, the Vorskla and the Oskol. The territory occupies 27,100 sq km (10,460 sq miles) and measures around 260 km (160 miles) from west to east. It is divided into 21 administrative districts and 10 cities. It had an estimated population of 1,498,000 at 1 January 2002, giving a population density of 55.3 per sq km. In 2001 some 65.8% of the population inhabited urban areas. According to the 1989 census, 92.9% of the Oblast's inhabitants were ethnic Russians. The Oblast's administrative centre is at Belgorod, which had 342,000 inhabitants in 2001. A further major city is Staryi Oskol (215,200).

History

Belgorod was established as a bishopric during the early days of Orthodox Christianity. The region was part of Lithuania until 1503, when it was annexed by the Muscovite state. The new city of Belgorod was founded in 1593. Belgorod Oblast was formally established on 6 January 1954.

In the 1990s the region remained a resolutely conservative part of the 'red belt' of loyal communist support. In late 1993 President Boris Yeltsin dismissed the region's Governor and arranged for elections to a new Regional Duma to be held in 1994. The communists enjoyed a majority in this body, too, and there was constant conflict with the administration, the head of which, however, also enjoyed popular support. For this reason, the Oblast was one of only 12 areas in the Federation to be permitted gubernatorial elections in December 1995. The incumbent, Yevgenii Savchenko, a supporter of the federal Government, was duly elected, despite the continued strength of the Communist Party. Savchenko was re-elected in May 1999, with the leader of the Liberal Democratic Party of Russia, Vladimir Zhirinovskii, coming third in the poll, as part of his unsuccessful campaign to become a regional governor. In the elections to the Regional Duma of October 1997, the Communist Party secured 13 seats of the 35 in the Duma, becoming the only party to be represented in the parliament at that time.

Economy

In 1999 Belgorod Oblast's gross regional product amounted to 34,526.3m. roubles, or 23,097.6 roubles per head. The main industrial centres in the territory are situated at Belgorod, Shebekino and Alekseyevka. In 2000 there were 690 km of railway lines and 6,410 km of paved roads on the Oblast's territory.

Belgorod Oblast's principal crops are grain, sugar beet, sunflower seeds and essential-oil plants. Horticulture and animal husbandry are also important. In 2000 24.3% of the region's working population were engaged in the agricultural sector, which generated a total of 16,759m. roubles. There are substantial reserves of bauxite, iron ore and apatites. The Oblast's main industries are ore-mining (iron ores), the production of electricity, mechanical engineering, metal-working, chemicals, the manufacture of building materials and food-processing. Industry employed 21.5% of the work-force in 2000, and total industrial production was worth 41,426m. roubles.

The economically active population in Belgorod Oblast numbered 725,000 in 2000, when 5.8% of the region's labour force were unemployed. In mid-2002 the average monthly salary was 4,599.6 roubles. There was a budgetary surplus of 192.9m. in 2000. In that year export trade totalled US $536.4m., while import trade amounted to $576.8m. Foreign investment in the Oblast totalled $35.4m. in 2000, compared with $156.1m. in 1998. In 2000 there were 4,600 small businesses in the Oblast.

Directory

Head of the Regional Administration (Governor): YEVGENII S. SAVCHENKO; 308005 Belgorod, pl. Revolyutsii 4; tel. (0722) 22-42-47; fax (0722) 22-33-43; e-mail admin@regadm.bel.ru; internet beladm.bel.ru.

Chairman of the Regional Duma: ANATOLII YA. ZELIKOV; tel. (0722) 22-36-76; fax (0722) 32-24-37; e-mail duma@bel.ru; internet duma.bel.ru.

Chief Representative of Belgorod Oblast in the Russian Federation: ALEK-SANDR G. MATSEPURO; 113052 Moscow, Zagorodnoye shosse 5/21; tel. (095) 952-02-03; fax (095) 952-28-36; e-mail moscow@bel.ru.

Head of Belgorod City Administration: VASILII N. POTRYASAYEV; 308800 Belgorod, ul. Lenina 38; tel. (0722) 27-72-06.

Bryansk Oblast

Bryansk Oblast is situated in the central part of the Central Russian Highlands and is in the Central Federal Okrug and the Central Economic Area. It has international borders to the west (Belarus) and south (Ukraine), with Kursk and Orel Oblasts to the east, Kaluga to the north-east and Smolensk to the north-west. Bryansk's main river is the Desna, a tributary of the Dnepr (Dnieper), and just under one-third of its area is forested. The Oblast occupies 34,900 sq km (13,480 sq miles) of territory and measures 245 km (152 miles) from south to north and 270 km from west to east. It is divided into 27 administrative districts and 16 cities. At 1 January 2002 the region's estimated population was 1,410,300, giving a population density of 40.4 per sq km. In 2001 some 68.8% of the population inhabited urban areas. Bryansk, with a population of 450,600 at 1 January 2001, is the Oblast's administrative centre.

History

The ancient Russian city of Bryansk was part of the independent principality of Novgorod-Serversk until 1356. It was an early Orthodox Christian bishopric. The Muscovite state acquired the city from Lithuania in the 16th century. After the German invasion during the Second World War had been repelled, Bryansk Oblast was founded on 5 July 1944.

In the 1990s the region was considered part of the communist-dominated 'red belt'. Bryansk was one of the eight federal territories permitted gubernatorial elections in December 1992. The incumbent, a supporter of the federal President, Boris Yeltsin, was defeated by the communist-backed candidate, Yurii Lodkin. During the constitutional crisis of 1993 the regional authorities were, thus, united in condemning President Yeltsin's Decree 1,400, which dissolved the all-Russian parliament. Lodkin was then dismissed and the Soviet disbanded, being replaced

150

by a Regional Duma. The Communist Party secured about 35% of the votes cast in the region for the State Duma in December 1995. After a series of scandals involving successive, short-lived (and non-communist) governors, Lodkin returned to the post of governor, being elected to the position in December 1996. Relations with the federal centre improved after the signature of a power-sharing agreement in July 1997, although the Communist Party dominated the local elections held in the previous month and maintained its influence in the federal presidential election of March 2000. Lodkin was re-elected as Governor in December 2000, although he obtained only 29% of the votes cast.

Economy

Bryansk Oblast is one of the Russian Federation's major industrial regions. The territory's gross regional product was 18,554.3m. roubles in 1999, equivalent to 12,802.2 roubles per head. Its main industrial centres are at Bryansk and Klintsy. In 2000 there were 1,019 km of railway track on its territory, and 6,215 km of paved roads.

The Oblast's agriculture, which employed 19.1% of its work-force in 2000, consists mainly of grain and vegetable production and animal husbandry. Around one-half of its area is used for agricultural purposes. In 2000 total production in the sector was worth 10,256m. roubles. The Oblast's main industries are mechanical engineering, food-processing, electrical energy, the manufacture of building materials and timber-working. Industry employed 20.9% of the work-force in 2000 and generated 14,509m. roubles.

In 2000 the economically active population of Bryansk Oblast numbered 664,000, and some 13.1% of the region's labour force (more than in any other region in the Central Federal Okrug) were unemployed. In mid-2002 the average monthly wage was 2,641.7 roubles. There was a regional government budgetary surplus of 25.7m. roubles in 2000. In that year international trade comprised US $80.7m. of exports and $131.0m. of imports. Foreign investment amounted to $6.3m. At 31 December 2000 there were 3,800 small businesses registered in the region.

Directory

Head of the Regional Administration (Governor): YURII YE. LODKIN; 241002 Bryansk, pr. Lenina 33; tel. (0832) 36-26-11; fax (0832) 41-38-95; e-mail press@ admin.debryansk.ru; internet www.bryanskobl.ru

Chairman of the Regional Duma: STEPAN N. PONASOV; 241000 Bryansk, pl. K. Marksa 2; tel. (0832) 43-36-91; fax (0832) 74-31-95.

Chief Representative of Bryansk Oblast in the Russian Federation: NIKOLAI I. MOSKIN; 103025 Moscow, ul. Novyi Arbat 19; tel. and fax (095) 203-50-52.

Head of Bryansk City Administration (Mayor):VLADIMIR POLYAKOV; 241002 Bryansk, pr. Lenina 35; tel. (0832) 74-30-13; fax (0832) 74-47-30; e-mail postmaster@comimm@bryansk.su.

Chelyabinsk Oblast

Chelyabinsk Oblast is situated in the Southern Urals, in the Transural (Asian Russia). It forms part of the Urals Federal Okrug and the Urals Economic Area. Orenburg Oblast lies to the south, the Republic of Bashkortostan to the west, Sverdlovsk Oblast to the north and Kurgan Oblast to the east. There is an international border with Kazakhstan in the south-east. Much of the region lies on the eastern slopes of the southern Ural Mountains. The major rivers in the Oblast are the Ural and the Miass. It has over 1,000 lakes, the largest of which are the Uvildy and the Turgoyak. The Oblast covers an area of 87,900 sq km (34,940 sq miles) and is divided into 24 administrative districts and 30 cities. Chelyabinsk had an estimated population of 3,268,700 at 1 January 2002, giving a population density of 37.2 per sq km. In 2001 some 81.3% of the population inhabited urban areas. The Oblast's administrative centre is at Chelyabinsk, which had a population of 1,081,100 in 2001. Other major cities are Magnitogorsk (427,100), Zlatoust (195,900) and Miass (164,300).

History

Chelyabinsk city was established as a Russian frontier post in 1736, but was deep within Russian territory by the 19th century. The Oblast was created on 17 January 1934. The region was heavily industrialized during the Soviet period and was dominated by communist cadres well into the 1990s. In December 1992, at elections for the head of the regional administration, the incumbent Governor, a supporter of Boris Yeltsin, the Russian President, was defeated. President Yeltsin re-established his authority in late 1993 and required the election of a Duma during 1994. Both in this body, and in the local results of the general election of 1995, pro-Yeltsin and reformist forces also obtained significant levels of support. In the gubernatorial election of late 1996, however, Petr Sumin was returned to power. Sumin, a communist, had been removed as head of the regional administration following the attempted Soviet coup of 1991. Sumin's pro-communist movement also won an absolute majority of seats in the legislature in the local elections held in December 1997. Sumin was re-elected as Governor in December 2000.

Economy

In 1999 the gross regional product of the Oblast amounted to 84,579.6m. roubles, equivalent to 22,996.1 roubles per head. The region's major industrial centres are at Chelyabinsk, Magnitogorsk, Miass, Zlatoust and Kopeisk. Although output declined by one-half between 1989 and 1997, Magnitogorsk remains well-known as the city that produced the steel for over one-half of the tanks used by Soviet troops in the Second World War, and as the largest iron and steel production complex in the world. The Oblast is a major junction of the Trans-Siberian Railway. In 2000 there were 1,793 km (1,114 miles) of railway track in the Oblast and 8,065 km of paved roads.

The Oblast's agriculture, which employed 9.9% of the working population in 2000, consists mainly of animal husbandry, horticulture and the production of grain and vegetables. Total agricultural output in 2000 was worth 12,071m. roubles. The Oblast is one of the most polluted in the Federation; in particular, high rates of disease and environmental despoliation resulted from the Kyshtym nuclear accident of 1957, in the north of the territory, when up to three times the levels of radiation emitted at the Chornobyl (Chernobyl) disaster in Ukraine in 1986 were released into the surrounding area. Approximately 180 sq km of agricultural land remained out of use because of radioactivity, and water supplies in many parts of the region were also unsafe. Chelyabinsk Oblast became one of the most industrialized territories of the Russian Federation, following the reconstruction of plants moved there from further west during the Second World War. In 2000 industry employed some 30.9% of the economically active population. The Oblast's main industries are ferrous and non-ferrous metallurgy (which accounted for a total of 64.4% of industrial activity in 2000), ore-mining, mechanical engineering, metal-working, fuel and energy production, food-processing and the manufacture of building materials. In the north-west, the closed city of Ozersk (formerly Chelyabinsk-40) is a major plutonium-processing and -storage site, while in the west are centres for weapons manufacturing and space technology. The conversion of former military plants to civilian use in the 1990s meant that the former tank factory at Magnitogorsk began to produce tractors, and the Mayak nuclear armament plant (the location of the 1957 disaster) sought to become a recycling plant for foreign nuclear waste. In 2000 the industrial sector generated 146,116m. roubles.

The economically active population numbered 1,817,000 in 2000, when 8.1% of the labour force were unemployed. At mid-2002 those in employment earned an average wage of 3,953.7 roubles per month. The 2000 budget recorded a deficit of 422.3m. roubles. Export trade amounted to US $1,861.0m. in 2000, when imports were worth $586.9m. Attempts to attract foreign investment in the Oblast from the mid-1990s were largely successful: foreign capital amounted to $595.7m. by 2000, compared with $59.1m. in 1998. In 2000 there were some 119 enterprises with foreign capital in the Oblast. At 31 December 2000 there were 19,100 small businesses registered on the Oblast's territory.

Directory

Governor: PETR I. SUMIN; 454089 Chelyabinsk, ul. Tsvillinga 28; tel. (3512) 33-92-41; fax (3512) 33-12-83; internet www.ural-chel.ru.

Chairman of the Regional Duma: VIKTOR F. DAVIDOV; 454009 Chelyabinsk, ul. Kirova 114; tel. (3512) 61-41-54; fax (3512) 33-63-79.

Chief Representative of Chelyabinsk Oblast in the Russian Federation: OLEG N. ANDREYEV; 127422 Moscow, Dmitrovskii pr. 4A; tel. (095) 210-88-59; fax (095) 977-08-35.

Head of Chelyabinsk City Administration (Mayor): VYACHESLAV M. TARASOV; 454113 Chelyabinsk, pl. Revolyutsii 2; tel. (3512) 33-38-05; fax (3512) 33-38-55; internet www.chelyabinsk.ru/adm.

Chita Oblast

Chita Oblast is situated in Transbaikal, and forms part of the Siberian Federal Okrug and the East Siberian Economic Area. Buryatiya lies to the west, Irkutsk Oblast to the north, Sakha (Yakutiya) and Amur to the east. To the south there are international borders with the People's Republic of China and Mongolia. The Aga-Buryat Autonomous Okrug (AOk) lies within the Oblast, in the south. The western part of the region is situated in the Yablonovii Khrebet mountain range. Chita Oblast's major rivers are those in the Selenga, the Lena and the Amur basins. More than one-half of the Oblast's territory is forested. Excluding the AOk, the Oblast covers an area of 412,500 sq km (159,300 sq miles) and is divided into 28 districts and 10 cities. The population of the Oblast, excluding the AOk, was estimated at 1,157,600 at 1 January 2002, and its population density was 2.8 per sq km (less than one-third of the national average). In 2001 some 62.1% of the region's inhabitants lived in urban areas. The Oblast's administrative centre is at Chita, which had a population of 303,300 at that time. The region's other cities include Krasnokamensk (56,000) and Balei (renowned as the birthplace of Temujin—Chinghiz or Genghis Khan).

History

The city of Chita was established by the Cossacks in 1653, at the confluence of the Chita and Ingoda rivers. It was named Ingodinskoye Zirnove for a time. Chita was pronounced the capital of the independent, pro-Bolshevik Far Eastern Republic upon its establishment in April 1920. It united the regions of Irkutsk, Transbaikal, Amur and the Pacific coast (Maritime Krai, Khabarovsk Krai, Magadan and Kamchatka), but merged with Soviet Russia in November 1922. Chita Oblast was founded on 26 September 1937.

155

A new Regional Duma was elected in 1994. The communists and the nationalist liberal democrats were the most popular parties in the mid- and late 1990s. In a gubernatorial election held on 29 October 2001 the incumbent Governor, Ravil Genialutin, was re-elected with 57.4% of the votes cast.

Economy

All figures in this survey incorporate data for the Aga-Buryat AOk, which is also treated separately. Chita Oblast's gross regional product amounted to 22,160.9m. roubles in 1999, equivalent to 17,535.2 roubles per head. The region's main industrial centres are at Chita, Nerchinsk, Darasun, Olovyannaya and Tarbagatai. In 2000 there were some 2,399 km (1,490 miles) of railway track in the territory, including sections of the Trans-Siberian and the Far Eastern (Baikal–Amur) Railways. There were also 9,680 km of paved roads, and in 1998 there were 1,000 km of navigable waterways. The Chita–Khabarovsk highway (which was to form part of a direct route between Moscow and Vladivostok) was under construction in the late 1990s.

Chita Oblast's agriculture, which employed some 15.2% of its working population in 2000, consists mainly of animal husbandry (livestock- and reindeer-breeding) and fur-animal hunting. In that year total agricultural output amounted to a value of 6,062m. roubles. The region's major industries are non-ferrous metallurgy, electrical energy, mechanical engineering, fuel extraction (including uranium), processing of forestry and agricultural products, the manufacture of building materials and ore-mining. Industry employed some 14.4% of the work-force in 2000, when total industrial production was worth 9,316m. roubles. Coal-mining in the Oblast was centred around the Vostochnaya mine; gold- and tin-mining were based at Sherlovaya Govra; and lead- and zinc-ore mines are situated at Hapcheranga, 200 km south-east of Yakutsk. In 1992 it was revealed that thorium and uranium had been mined until the mid-1970s at locations just outside Balei. The resulting high levels of radiation had serious consequences among the town's population, with abnormally high incidences of miscarriages and congenital defects in children. The regional Government lacked sufficient funds to relocate Balei's inhabitants and reduce radiation in the area. In 1997, however, the Australian mining company, Armada Gold, announced that it planned to seal the abandoned mines and exploit the nearby gold deposits. A 'Chinese market' in Chita city reflects the importance of China as a major trading partner of the Oblast, in particular as a source of imports.

The territory had an economically active population of 565,000 in 2000, when 13.9% of the labour force were unemployed; the average monthly wage was 4,378.4 roubles in mid-2002. In 2000 the budget showed a deficit of 143.6m. roubles. In that year the Oblast's exports, largely comprising timber, metals and radioactive chemicals, amounted to US $103.6m., and imports amounted to $59.9m. For much of the 1990s foreign investment in the Oblast remained low, and it totalled just $414,000 in 2000. At 31 December 2000 a total of 3,100 small businesses were in operation in Chita Oblast.

Directory

Head of the Regional Administration (Governor): RAVIL F. GENIALUTIN; 672021 Chita, ul. Chaikovskogo 8; tel. (3022) 23-34-93; fax (3022) 23-02-22; internet www.adm.chita.ru.

Chairman of the Regional Duma: ALESKANDR F. EPOB; 67021 Chita, ul. Chaikov-skogo 8; tel. (3022) 23-58-59.

Representation of Chita Oblast in the Russian Federation: 127025 Moscow, ul. Novyi Arbat 19/2001; tel. (095) 203-33-28; fax (095) 203-45-39.

Head of Chita City Administration (Mayor): ALEKSANDR F. SEDIN; 672000 Chita, ul. Butina 39; tel. (3022) 23-21-01.

Irkutsk Oblast

Irkutsk Oblast is situated in eastern Siberia in the south-east of the Central Siberian Plateau. The Oblast forms part of the Siberian Federal Okrug and the East Siberian Economic Area. The Republic of Sakha (Yakutiya) lies to the north-east, Krasnoyarsk Krai (including the Evenk AOk) to the north-west and Tyva to the south-west. Most of the long south-eastern border is with Buryatiya and, in the east, Chita. Irkutsk Oblast includes the Ust-Orda Buryat Autonomous Okrug (AOk). Lake Baikal is the deepest in the world, possessing over 80% of Russia's, and 20% of the world's, freshwater resources. The Oblast's main rivers are the Angara (the only river to drain Lake Baikal), the Nizhnyaya Tunguska, the Lena, the Vitim and the Kirenga. More than four-fifths of the region's territory is covered with forest (mainly coniferous). The total area of the Oblast, excluding that of the AOk, is 745,500 sq km (287,838 sq miles) and stretches 1,400 km (850 miles) from south to north and 1,200 km west to east. The Oblast proper is divided into 27 administrative districts and 22 cities. The Oblast's estimated population, excluding the AOk, was 2,570,400 in January 2002, giving a population density of 3.4 per sq km. In 2001 some 79.3% of the total population lived in urban areas. The Oblast's administrative centre is at Irkutsk, which had a population of 587,200 in 2001. Other major cities in the region include Bratsk (278,800), Angarsk (264,000) and Ust-Ilimsk (106,600).

History

The city of Irkutsk was founded as an ostrog (military transit camp) in 1661, at the confluence of the Irkut and Angara rivers, 66 km to the west of Baikal. Irkutsk became one of the largest economic centres of eastern Siberia. After the collapse of the Russian Empire, the region was part of the independent, pro-Bolshevik Far Eastern Republic (based in Chita), which was established in April 1920 and merged with Soviet Russia in November 1922. On 26 September 1937 an Irkutsk Oblast was formed.

In late 1993, following the federal presidency's forcible dissolution of parliament, the executive branch of government secured the dissolution of the Regional Soviet, and in 1994 a Legislative Assembly was elected in its place. As a 'donor region' to the Russian Federation, central-regional relationships in Irkutsk Oblast were frequently strained. In May 1996 the regional and federal authorities signed a power-sharing agreement. The following year the Governor, Yurii Nozhikov, implemented a tax strike against Moscow in an attempt to compel the federal Government to pay greater attention to the Oblast's needs. Following Nozhikov's resignation in April 1997, the government-supported candidate, Boris Govorin (who also received Nozhikov's endorsement), was elected Governor, receiving 50.3% of the votes cast. At the gubernatorial election held in August 2001 Govorin was re-elected for a further term of office; however, the relatively high proportion of votes awarded to the Communist Party candidate, Sergei Levchenko, who received 45.4% (compared with the 47.5% received by Govorin), appeared to reflect increasing dissatisfaction with the economic situation in the region. In March 2002 the Chairman of the Legislative Assembly, Viktor Borovskii, who had been regarded as the leading opponent of Govorin in the region, was removed from office, and replaced by a loyalist, Sergei Shishkin. During the early 2000s proposals to unite the Ust-Orda Buryat AOk and Irkutsk Oblast became increasingly popular and appeared to be supported by the authorities in both the AOk and the Oblast; moreover, in September 2002 the Chairman of the Federation Council, Sergei Mironov, stated that the two federal subjects already satisfied the prerequisites for becoming a single unit.

Economy

Irkutsk Oblast is one of the most economically developed regions in Russia, largely owing to its significant fuel, energy and water resources, minerals and timber, and its location on the Trans-Siberian Railway. All figures in this survey incorporate data for the Usta-Orda Buryat AOk, which is also treated separately. In 1999 the Oblast's gross regional product totalled 85,889.1m. roubles, or 31,163.3 roubles per head. The region's main industrial centres are at Irkutsk, Bratsk, Ust-Ilimsk and Angarsk. The Oblast, which is traversed by the Trans-Siberian and the Far Eastern (Baikal–Amur) Railways, contained 2,479 km of railway track in 2000. There were almost 12,151 km of paved roads in the region, which carry some 40m. metric tons of freight annually in the late 1990s. The Oblast has two international airports, at Irkutsk and Bratsk, from which there are direct and connecting flights to Japan, the People's Republic of China, the Republic of Korea (South Korea), Mongolia and the USA. In the late 1990s approximately one-10th of the region's freight was transported by river—there are two major river-ports on the Lena river at Kirensk and Osetrovo (Ust-Kut). These are used to transport freight to Sakha (Yakutiya) and the northern seaport of Tiksi.

The Oblast's agriculture, which employed just 10.4% of its work-force in 2000, consists mainly of grain production, animal husbandry (fur-animal-, reindeer- and livestock-breeding), hunting and fishing. Total agricultural production in the territory generated 11,090m. roubles in 2000. The region contains the huge Kovyikinskoye oilfield, which was awaiting an international consortium with the resources to construct an export pipeline across the People's Republic of China. In the late 1990s more than 45% of the Oblast's fixed assets were in the industrial sector, which engaged some 24.7% of the working population in 2000. The main industries are non-ferrous metallurgy, the processing of forestry products, mining (coal, iron ore, gold, muscovite or mica, gypsum, talc and salt), mechanical engineering, metal-working, chemicals and petrochemicals, petroleum-refining, fuel extraction, electricity generation, and food-processing. In 2000 the total value of manufactured goods in the Oblast was 87,984m. roubles, of which the non-ferrous metallurgy industry contributed 27% and the timber and timber-processing industries 23%.

The economically active population in Irkutsk Oblast totalled 1,406,000 in 2000, when 11.4% of the labour force were unemployed. For those in employment, the average wage amounted to 4,966.2 roubles per month in mid-2002. In 2000 there was a budgetary deficit of 204.8m. roubles. In that year the value of exports from the territory amounted to some US $2,942.2m., while imports were worth $537.3m. Foreign investment in the territory was worth some $82.3m. At 31 December 2000 there were 13,800 small businesses registered in the Oblast.

Directory

Governor: BORIS A. GOVORIN; 664027 Irkutsk, ul. Lenina 1A; tel. (3952) 27-67-60; fax (3952) 24-33-40; internet www.admirk.ru.

Chairman of the Legislative Assembly: SERGEI I. SHISHKIN; 664027 Irkutsk, ul. Lenina 1A; tel. (3952) 24-17-60; fax (3952) 27-35-09; internet irk.gov.ru.

Chief Representative of Irkutsk Oblast in the Russian Federation: NIKOLAI V. YEROSHCHENKO; 109028 Moscow, per. Durasovskii 3/2; tel. (095) 916-17-08; fax (095) 915-70-58.

Head of Irkutsk City Administration (Mayor): VLADIMIR V. YAKUBOVSKII; tel. (3952) 27-56-90.

Ivanovo Oblast

Ivanovo Oblast is situated in the central part of the Eastern European Plain. It forms part of the Central Federal Okrug and the Central Economic Area. It is surrounded by the Oblasts of Kostroma (to the north), Nizhnii Novgorod (east), Vladimir (south) and Yaroslavl (north-west). Its main river is the Volga and one-half of its territory is forested. The Oblast covers a total area of 21,800 sq km (9,230 sq miles), and includes 21 administrative districts and 17 cities. Its estimated population at 1 January 2002 was 1,191,200, giving a population density of 54.6 per sq km. In 2001 some 82.4% of the population inhabited urban areas. Its administrative centre, Ivanovo, had a population of 452,100 in 2001.

History

The city of Ivanovo was founded in 1871 and was known as Ivanovo-Voznesensk until 1932. It was an important centre of anti-government activity during the strikes of 1883 and 1885 and in the 1905 Revolution. Ivanovo Oblast was founded on 20 July 1918.

In the post-Soviet era the region displayed support for political diversity and increasingly became associated with moderation. Although the Communist Party and Vladimir Zhirinovskii's nationalist Liberal Democrats both performed well in elections in 1994–95, moderates were successful in the gubernatorial and regional legislative elections held in 1996, and the elections to the State Duma in 1999. However, in the gubernatorial elections held in two rounds in December 2000, the Communist Party candidate, Vladimir Tikhonov, defeated the regional Prime Minister, Vladimir Golovkov. Legislative elections took place in the same month.

Economy

In 1999 Ivanovo Oblast's gross regional product totalled 12,760.9m. roubles, equivalent to 10,382.3 roubles per head. The region's main industrial centres are at Ivanovo (a major producer of textiles), Kineshma, Shuya, Vichuga, Furmanov, Teikovo and Rodniki. There are well-developed rail, road and river transport networks in the region and the largest international airport in central Russia. In 2000 there were 341 km (212 miles) of railways and 3,495 km of paved roads on the Oblast's territory.

Ivanovo Oblast was the historic centre of Russia's cotton-milling industry and was known as the 'Russian Manchester' at the beginning of the 20th century. Flax production was still an important agricultural activity in the region in the 1990s, as were grain and vegetable production and animal husbandry. However, agriculture employed just 9.6% of its work-force in 2000, and total agricultural production in that year amounted to a value of 4,421m. roubles. The region's main industries were light manufacturing (especially textiles), electrical energy, mechanical engineering, chemicals, food-processing, wood-working, handicrafts (especially lacquerware) and the production of building materials. Some 33.4% of its working population were engaged in the sector, which generated 14,374m. roubles in 2000.

The economically active population amounted to 600,000 in 2000, when 10.1% of the labour force were unemployed, compared with 18.6% in 1998. The average wage was 2,631.5 roubles per month in mid-2002. In 2000 the budget recorded a surplus of 162.4m. roubles. External trade was relatively low in that year, amounting to a value of US $65.7m. in exports and $198.4m. in imports. Although foreign investment amounted to only $120,000 in 1998, this figure had increased to $3.3m. by 2000. However, at that time there were only nine enterprises with foreign capital in the Oblast, fewer than in any other region of the Central Federal Okrug. At 31 December 2000 there were 5,100 small businesses registered in the region.

Directory

Head of the Regional Administration (Governor): VLADIMIR I. TIKHONOV; 153000 Ivanovo, ul. Baturina 5; tel. (0932) 41-77-05; fax (0932) 41-92-31; e-mail 001-07@adminet.ivanovo.ru; internet ivadm.ivanovo.ru.

Chairman of the Legislative Assembly: VALERII G. NIKOLOGORSKII; 153461 Ivanovo, ul. Pushkina 9; tel. and fax (0932) 41-60-68; e-mail zsio@gov.ivanovo.ru.

Representation of Ivanovo Oblast in the Russian Federation: 127025 Moscow, ul. Novyi Arbat 16/1714; tel. (095) 203-41-34; fax (095) 203-93-45.

Head of Ivanovo City Administration: ALEKSANDR V. GROSHEV; 153001 Ivanovo, pl. Revolyutsii 6; tel. (0932) 32-70-20; fax (0932) 41-25-12; e-mail office@ivgoradm.ivanovo.ru; internet ivgoradm.ivanovo.ru.

Kaliningrad Oblast

Kaliningrad Oblast forms the westernmost part of the Russian Federation, being an exclave separated from the rest of the country by Lithuania (which borders it to the north and east) and Belarus. Poland lies to the south. It falls within the North-Western Federal Okrug and is sometimes included in the North-Western Economic Area. The city of Kaliningrad (formerly Königsberg) is sited at the mouth of the River Pregolya (Pregel), where it flows into the Vistula Lagoon, an inlet of the Baltic Sea. The other main river is the Neman (Memel). The Oblast occupies 15,100 sq km (5,830 sq miles), of which only 13,300 sq km are dry land, the rest of its territory comprising the freshwater Kurshskaya Lagoon, in the north-west, and the Vistula Lagoon. The coastline is 140 km (87 miles) long. The Oblast is divided into 13 administrative districts and 22 cities. It had an estimated population of 943,200 at 1 January 2002 and its population density was, therefore, 62.5 per sq km. In 2001 some 76.7% of the population inhabited urban areas. The Oblast's administrative centre is at Kaliningrad, which had a population of 421,000 at 1 January 2001. Other cities in the Oblast are Chernyakhovsk (formerly Insterburg— 43,800) and Sovetsk (formerly Tilsit—43,700).

History

The city of Kaliningrad was founded in 1255, as Königsberg, during German expansion eastwards. The chief city of East Prussia, it was the original royal capital of the Hohenzollerns (from 1871 the German Emperors). After the Second World War it was annexed by the USSR and received its current name (1945). Most of the German population was deported and the city almost completely destroyed and rebuilt. On 7 April 1946 the region became an administrative-political entity within the Russian Federation.

In mid-1993 Kaliningrad Oblast requested the status of a republic, a petition refused by the federal authorities. On 15 October the Regional Soviet was disbanded by the head of the regional administration for failing to support the state presidency's struggle against the federal parliament. A new regional legislature, the Duma, was later formed. On 12 January 1996 Yurii Matochkin was one of the first oblast governors to sign a power-sharing agreement with the federal Government. Elections to the governorship were held in October, and were won by Leonid Gorbenko, an independent candidate.

Despite ambitions to transform the exclave into a free-trade zone, Kaliningrad was bedevilled by corruption and high levels of taxation. Moreover, on several occasions the federal authorities threatened to curtail the Oblast's special economic regulations, because of the competitive advantage given to Kaliningrad-based companies in the Russian market. Relations with the exclave's neighbours were also troubled at times. German groups in Russia (primarily those resident along the River Volga) and ultra-nationalists supported by the leader of the Liberal Democratic Party of Russia, Vladimir Zhirinovskii, made unsuccessful demands for increased German influence in the management of the Oblast. In July 1998 a proposal that the region be awarded the status of an autonomous Russian Baltic republic within Russia was submitted to the Federation Council. However, Governor Gorbenko opposed plans for greater autonomy, instead supporting the growth of closer ties with Belarus. In late 1998 the regional authorities declared a state of emergency as the population became dependent on food aid from Lithuania and Poland. In gubernatorial elections held in two rounds in November 2000, Gorbenko was defeated by Adm. Vladimir Yegorov, the former Commander of the Baltic Fleet. Yegorov was regarded as a pro-presidential candidate, and was elected largely on the basis of his anti-corruption campaign. In 2002, as the European Union (EU) prepared to admit several Eastern European countries, including Lithuania and Poland, in 2004, the status of Kaliningrad became an increasing source of contention; in particular, Russia objected to proposals that residents of Kaliningrad would require visas to travel to metropolitan Russia. In November 2002, at an EU-Russia summit meeting, held in Brussels, Belgium, Russia finally agreed to an EU proposal for simplified visa arrangements. According to the compromise accord, multiple-transit travel documentation would be made available to residents of the exclave travelling by motor vehicle. The EU also agreed to undertake a feasibility study on the possibility of allowing high-speed, sealed trains to operate between the exclave and the remainder of the Federation, thus negating the need for transit documents.

Economy

Kaliningrad Oblast is noted for containing more than 90% of the world's reserves of amber. Within Russia it is also noted for its reputedly flourishing parallel ('black') market, with federal officials suggesting in January 1999 that the region had become a major transhipment point for illegal drugs. In 1999 its gross regional product totalled 16,157.5m. roubles, or 17,006.1 roubles per head. Its main industrial centres are at Kaliningrad, Gusev and Sovetsk. There are rail services to Lithuania and Poland, and there were 639 km of railways on the Oblast's territory in 2000. In that year Kaliningrad Oblast's road network consisted of 4,577 km of paved roads. Its main ports are at Kaliningrad and Baltiisk.

Kaliningrad Oblast's agricultural sector, which employed 9.3% of its work-force in 2000, consists mainly of animal husbandry, vegetable growing and fishing. Total agricultural output was worth 3,628m. roubles in 2000. The Oblast has substantial reserves of petroleum (around 275m. metric tons), more than 2,500m. cu m in peat deposits and 50m. tons of coal. The industrial sector employed 19.4% of its working population and generated 14,410m. roubles in 2000. The region's main industries are the production of natural gas, mechanical engineering, electro-technical industry, the processing of agricultural and forestry products, light manu-facturing and the production and processing of amber. In 2000 some 749,000 tons of petroleum were extracted. The continuing strategic geopolitical situation of Kaliningrad Oblast meant that demilitarization proceeded at a much slower pace than it did elsewhere in the former USSR; in 1998 there were around 200,000 members of military units in the Oblast.

The economically active population numbered 489,000 in 2000, when some 15.4% of the labour force were unemployed, one of the highest levels in European Russia outside the North Caucasus. The average monthly wage was 3,832.1 roubles in mid-2002. The 2000 regional budget recorded a deficit of 22.6m. roubles, and the region is largely dependent on federal subsidies. Foreign investment totalled US $19.1m. in 2000, and there were hopes that the region would be favoured as an entry point to the Russian market. In 2000 export trade amounted to $441.6m, with the fishing industry representing a major source of exports; in that year imports were worth $809.0m. At 31 December 2000 there was a total of 7,600 small businesses registered in the region.

Directory

Head of the Regional Administration (Governor): VLADIMIR G. YEGOROV; 236007 Kaliningrad, ul. D. Donskogo 1; tel. (0112) 46-46-49; fax (0112) 46-38-62; e-mail egorov@kaliningrad.ru; internet www.gov.kaliningrad.ru.

Chairman of the Regional Duma: VLADIMIR A. NIKITIN; 236000 Kaliningrad, ul. Kirova 17; tel. (0112) 22-84-39; fax (0112) 22-84-82; e-mail nikitin@duma .kaliningrad.org; internet duma.kaliningrad.org.

Representation of Kaliningrad Oblast in the Russian Federation: 114049 Moscow, ul. Zhitnaya 14/3; tel. (095) 239-12-26.

Head of Kaliningrad City Administration (Mayor): YURII A. SAVENKO; 236040 Kaliningrad, ul. Pobedy 1; tel. (0112) 21-48-98; fax (0112) 21-16-77; e-mail mayor@klgd.ru; internet www.klgd.ru.

Kaluga Oblast

Kaluga Oblast is situated in the central part of the Eastern European Plain, its administrative centre, Kaluga, being 188 km (177 miles) south-west of Moscow. It forms part of the Central Federal Okrug and the Central Economic Area. Tula and Orel Oblasts lie to the south-east, Bryansk Oblast to the south-west, Moscow Oblast to the north-east and Smolensk Oblast to the north-west. Kaluga's main river is the Oka and some two-fifths of its territory is forested. It occupies 29,900 sq km (11,540 sq miles) and is divided into 24 administrative districts and 19 cities. The Oblast had a population of 1,058,900 in 2002 and a population density, therefore, of 35.4 per sq km. In 2001 some 74.3% of the population inhabited urban areas. Its administrative centre is at Kaluga, a river-port on the Oka river, which had a population of 335,300 in 2001. Other major cities in the Oblast include Obninsk (107,800), the site of the world's first nuclear power-station.

History

The city of Kaluga, first mentioned in the letters of a Lithuanian prince, Olgerd, in 1371, was founded as a Muscovite outpost. The region was the scene of an army mutiny in 1905 and was seized by Bolshevik troops at the end of 1917. Kaluga Oblast was founded on 5 July 1944.

Communist-affiliated managers of industrial and agricultural bodies dominated the new representative body, the Legislative Assembly, elected in March 1994. The Communist Party of the Russian Federation (CPRF) won over one-quarter of the region's votes in the 1995 elections to the State Duma. However, in elections to the Legislative Assembly in 1996 the CPRF failed to win any seats. Valerii Sudarenkov, the Governor from 1996, had previously been the Deputy Prime Minister of the Uzbek Soviet Socialist Republic (SSR—Uzbekistan). Sudarenkov did not stand for re-election in November 2000; his former deputy, Anatolii Artamonov, was elected to succeed him, with 57% of the votes cast.

Economy

In 1999 gross regional product in Kaluga Oblast totalled 17,300.8m. roubles, equivalent to 15,935.1 roubles per head. Apart from Kaluga, the region's main industrial centres are at Lyudinovo, Kirov, Maloyaroslavets and Sukhinichi. In 2000 there were 853 km of railway track in the Oblast, and 4,943 km of paved roads.

Certain areas of the Oblast contain fertile black earth (*chernozem*). Agriculture employed 11.7% of the work-force in 2000, comprising mainly animal husbandry and production of vegetables, grain and flax. Agricultural output amounted to a value of 6,478m. roubles in 2000. The Oblast's main industries are mechanical engineering, food-processing, wood-working, the production of building materials and electrical energy. The industrial sector employed 25.7% of the working population in 2000 and generated 22,148m. roubles.

The economically active population totalled 564,000 in 2000, when 8.2% of the labour force were unemployed. The average monthly wage in Kaluga Oblast was 3,503.4 roubles in mid-2002. In 2000 there was a budgetary surplus of 22.1m. roubles. In that year export trade amounted to a value of US $84.8m.; imports amounted to $127.7m. Total foreign investment totalled $80.7m. in 2000. At the end of 2000 there were 5,900 small businesses registered in the region.

Directory

Head of the Regional Administration (Governor): ANATOLII D. ARTAMONOV; 248661 Kaluga, pl. Staryi torg 2; tel. (0842) 56-23-57; fax (0842) 53-13-09; e-mail postmaster@admobl.kaluga.su; internet www.admobl.kaluga.ru.

Chairman of the Legislative Assembly: VALERII I. KRESTYANINOV; 248600 Kaluga, pl. Staryi torg 2; tel. (0842) 57-45-00; fax (08422) 4-63-81.

Representation of Kaluga Oblast in the Russian Federation: 125032 Moscow, ul. Tverskaya 9A/5A; tel. (095) 203-17-12; fax (095) 229-98-05; e-mail kaluga@orc.ru.

Head of Kaluga City Administration: VALERII G. BELOBROVSKII; 248600 Kaluga, ul. Lenina 93; tel. (0842) 56-26-46; fax (0842) 24-41-78; e-mail uprava@kaluga.ru; internet users.kaluga.ru/uprava.

Kamchatka Oblast

Kamchatka Oblast occupies the Kamchatka Peninsula in the easternmost part of Russia and is, therefore, part of the Far Eastern Federal Okrug and the Far Eastern Economic Area. The Peninsula, some 1,600 km (1,000 miles) in length and 130 km (80 miles) in width, separates the Sea of Okhotsk, in the west, from the Bering Sea, in the east. The Oblast also includes the Karaginskiye and Komandorskiye (Commander) Islands and the southernmost part of the Chukhotka Peninsula. In the latter area there are land borders with other Russian federal territories, the Chukchi Autonomous Okrug (AOk) to the north and Magadan Oblast to the west. This part of the Oblast, together with the northern section of the Kamchatka Peninsula, comprises the Koryak AOk. The region is dominated by the Sredinnii Khrebet mountain range, which is bounded to the west by a broad, poorly drained coastal plain, and to the east by the Kamchatka river valley. The territory's other main river is the Avacha. Two-thirds of its area is mountainous (including the highest point in the Russian Far East, Mt Klyuchevskaya, at 4,685 m—15,961 feet) and it contains many hot springs. Kamchatka Oblast covers an area of 472,300 sq km (182,350 sq miles), including the autonomous okrug, but only 170,800 sq km (65,946 sq miles), excluding the Koryak AOk. The Oblast, excluding the AOk, is divided into seven administrative districts and four cities. There is a high annual rate of precipitation in the region, sometimes as much as 2,000 mm, and temperatures vary considerably according to region. The average temperature for January is −16.4°C, while that for July is 13.0°C. At 1 January 2002 the estimated total population in the region proper was 351,700 and the population density, therefore, was 2.1 per sq km. In 2001 an estimated 81.1% of the region's population inhabited urban areas. The Oblast's administrative centre is at Petropav-lovsk-Kamchatskii, in the south-east, which was inhabited by 195,500 people.

History

The Kamchatka Peninsula was first sighted in 1697 and was annexed by Russia during the 18th century. Petropavlovsk came under Russian control in 1743. After the Soviet Revolution Kamchatka was part of the short-lived Far Eastern Republic. A distinct Kamchatka Oblast was formed on 20 October 1923, but as part of Khabarovsk Krai until 23 January 1956.

Following the dissolution of the USSR in 1991, Kamchatka tended to be supportive of the federal Government. In the general election of December 1995, however, the most successful party was the liberal, and usually anti-government, Yabloko, which obtained 20% of the votes cast in the Oblast (a higher proportion than the reformists obtained even in the great cities). This success was largely because the local candidate, Mikhail Zadornov, was a popular figure, who was subsequently appointed as the federal Minister of Finance in 1997. Yabloko repeated this success in the Oblast legislative elections of December 1997, in which it won nine seats, coming second only to the Communist Party, with 10. Persistent difficulties with fuel supplies led the federal Prime Minister, Sergei Stepashin, to threaten to implement federal rule over the region in July 1999. At the gubernatorial election held in December 2000, the communist candidate, Mikhail Mashkovtsev, was elected Governor; the incumbent, Vladimir Biryukov, had declined to stand.

Economy

The waters around Kamchatka Oblast (the Sea of Okhotsk, the Bering Sea and the Pacific Ocean) being extremely rich in marine life, make fishing, especially of crabs, the dominant sector of Kamchatka Oblast's economy, accounting for over 90% of its trade in the mid-1990s. The region's fish stocks comprise around one-half of Russia's total. All figures in this survey incorporate data for the Koryak AOk, which is also treated separately. In 1999 the Oblast's gross regional product (GRP) amounted to 15,462.2m. roubles, or 39,984.9 roubles per head. Petropavlovsk is one of two main industrial centres and ports in the territory, the other being Ust-Kamchatka. There is an international airport, Yelizovo, situated 30 km from Petropavlovsk-Kamchatskii. In 2000 there were 1,338 km of paved roads in the Oblast.

Apart from fishing, agriculture in Kamchatka Oblast consists of animal husbandry (livestock, reindeer, mostly in the Koryak AOk, and fur animals), poultry farming and hunting. Just 4.7% of the working population were employed in agriculture in 2000, when agricultural output amounted to 1,677m. roubles. There are deposits of gold, silver, natural gas, sulphur and other minerals in Kamchatka Oblast, which by the early 2000s had been explored and were in the process of development. The relatively limited industrial sector, which employed 26.8% of the work-force in 2000, is based on the processing of agricultural products and coal and electricity production. Total industrial output was worth 15,565m. roubles in 2000.

The economically active population of Kamchatka Oblast numbered 226,000 in 2000, when 16.0% of the labour force were unemployed. Those in employment earned an average of 8,177.6 roubles per month in mid-2002, a relatively high wage compared with the rest of the Russian Federation, but one balanced by the high cost of living in the Oblast. Moreover, wages arrears prompted municipal workers in Petropavlosk-Kamchatskii to observe a widespread strike from late November. There was a budgetary deficit of 267.5m. roubles in 2000. Foreign investment in the Oblast amounted to US $29.4m. in that year, although international trade was limited, amounting to just $122.5m. in exports and $29.6m. in imports. With trade dominated by the fishing industry, one of the Oblast's main foreign markets was Japan. At 31 December 2000 there were 2,000 small businesses registered in the region.

Directory

Governor: MIKHAIL B. MASHKOVTSEV; 683040 Kamchatka obl., Petropavlovsk-Kamchatskii, pl. Lenina 1; tel. (4152) 11-20-96; fax (41522) 7-38-43; e-mail kra@svyaz.kamchatka.su.

Chairman of the Legislative Assembly: LEV N. BOITSOV; 683040 Kamchatka obl., Petropavlovsk-Kamchatskii, pl. Lenina 1; tel. (4152) (4152) 11-28-95.

Chief Representative of Kamchatka Oblast in the Russian Federation: MIKHAIL M. SITNIKOV; 119002 Moscow, Denezhnyi per. 12/16; tel. (095) 241-03-13; fax (095) 241-35-46.

Head of Petropavlovsk-Kamchatskii City Administration: YURII I. GOLENISH-CHEV; 683040 Kamchatka obl., Petropavlovsk-Kamchatskii, ul. Leninskaya 14; tel. (41522) 2-49-13; e-mail citiadm@svyaz.kamchatka.su.

Kemerovo Oblast

Kemerovo Oblast, also known as the Kuzbass, is situated in southern central Russia and forms part of the Siberian Federal Okrug and the West Siberian Economic Area. It lies to the west of Krasnoyarsk Krai and the Republic of Khakasiya. Tomsk lies to the north, Novosibirsk to the west and the Altai Krai and the Republic of Altai to the south-west. The region lies in the Kuznetsk basin, the area surrounding its main river, the Tom. The territory of the Oblast occupies 95,500 sq km (36,870 sq miles) and is divided into 19 administrative districts and 20 cities. At 1 January 2002 the total population was 2,940,500 and the population density in the region was 30.8 per sq km. Some 86.7% of the population inhabited urban areas in 2001. The region's administrative centre is at Kemerovo, which had a population of 487,200 at that time. Other major cities are Novokuznetsk (564,500), Prokopevsk (231,200), Leninsk-Kúznetskii (111,600), Kiselevsk (108,200) and Mezhdurechensk (105,300).

History

Kemerovo (formerly Shcheglovsk) was founded in 1918 and became the administrative centre of the Oblast at its formation on 26 January 1943. The city is at the centre of Russia's principal coal-mining area. The region maintained its strong

171

communist tradition throughout the 1990s. In July 1997 the Governor, Mikhail Kislyuk, a former head of the Kuzbass coal workers, was dismissed by President Boris Yeltsin, as the result of a dispute over unpaid pensions arrears. Kislyuk had earned criticism, as had the federal authorities, for refusing to schedule elections to a new Duma (to replace the bicameral Regional Assembly—elected in March 1994, its activities were suspended in 1995).

In the December 1995 federal general election, the Communist Party won 48% of the regional votes cast, its second highest proportion in any constituent unit of the Federation. Much of this support was secured because of the popular leadership of Amangeldy Tuleyev, speaker of the suspended local assembly (and a candidate in the federal presidential election of mid-1996). Tuleyev contested the federal presidency in 1991, 1996 and 2000, and spent 11 months in 1996–97 as the Minister for Co-operation with Members of the CIS. Having been appointed Governor by Yeltsin, following the removal of Kislyuk, Tuleyev's position was confirmed by an overwhelming victory in popular elections to the post in October 1997. (He received 94.6% of the votes cast.) In April 1999 his electoral bloc went on to win 34 of the 35 seats available in elections to the regional council, and all 11 seats in the local legislative elections. These results were considered by many to reflect a desire for more paternalistic, economically interventionist policies, as social conditions in the region worsened. In May 1998 widespread industrial action by coal-miners over wage arrears threatened to bring the regional administration into direct confrontation with the federal Government. The workers blockaded a section of the Trans-Siberian Railway, seriously affecting rail transportation throughout the country, and the strike did not end until late July. At this time Tuleyev's administration signed a framework agreement with the federal Government on the delimitation of powers, and accompanied by 10 accords aimed at strengthening the economy of the region. None the less, during 1998 Kemerovo was regarded as the federal unit with the fourth-worst record on wage arrears, and its economy remained troubled. Despite the economic situation, Tuleyev was widely considered to be Russia's most popular regional leader and, when he stood for the presidency of the Russian Federation in March 2000, Tuleyev received 51.6% of the votes cast in Kemerovo Oblast, more than twice the number of votes cast there for Vladimir Putin. In January 2001 Tuleyev announced his resignation, thus bringing forward the gubernatorial election to April of that year, several months earlier than previously scheduled. His opponents criticized this decision as a tactic to ensure his re-election, as the Governor had widespread popular support at that time. In the election, held on 22 April, Tuleyev received 93.5% of the votes cast.

Economy

The economy of Kemerovo Oblast is based on industry. It is rich in mineral resources and contains the Kuzbass basin, one of the major coal reserves of the world. The region produced over 35% of Russia's coal in the late 1990s, but intensive mining in the Soviet period had resulted in severe environmental degradation. In 1999 Kemerovo's gross regional product amounted to 68,975.4m. roubles, equivalent to 23,011.0 roubles per head. The Oblast's main industrial centres are at Kemerovo, Novokuznetsk, Prokopevsk, Kiselevsk and Leninsk-Kuznetskii. In 2000 the region had 1,728 km (1,074 miles) of railway track and 5,635 km of paved roads on its territory.

Kemerovo Oblast's agriculture, which employed just 5.5% of the work-force in 2000, consists mainly of vegetable production, animal husbandry, bee-keeping and fur-animal hunting. The value of agricultural output in 2000 was 9,614m. roubles. In the mid-1990s reserves of coal to a depth of 1,800 m (5,900 feet) were estimated at 733,400m. metric tons. In the same period deposits of iron ore were estimated at 5,250m. tons. Production of complex ores, ferrous and non-ferrous metallurgy, chemicals, mechanical engineering, metal-working and food-processing are also important industries in the region. The industrial sector as a whole employed 31.7% of the working population in 2000 and generated 103,511m. roubles.

The economically active population numbered 1,475,000 in 2000, when 10.4% of the labour force were unemployed. The average monthly wage was 4,345.0 roubles in mid-2002. The 2000 regional budget registered a surplus of 401.9m. roubles. In that year export trade totalled US $1,854.7m., and imports were worth $169.0m. From the mid-1990s foreign investors showed some interest in exploiting the region's coal reserves. Total foreign investment in the Oblast in 2000 amounted to $5.1m. Economic reforms introduced after 1992 were fairly effective: by 1995 some 61% of employees were working in the private sector. In the late 1990s the regional Government aimed to promote small businesses, of which there were 11,700 registered at 31 December 2000.

Directory

Head of the Regional Administration (Governor): AMANGELDY M. TULEYEV; 650099 Kemerovo, pr. Sovetskii 62; tel. (3842) 36-34-09; fax (3842) 58-31-56; e-mail postmaster@ako.kemerovo.su; internet www.kemerovo.su.

Chairman of the Legislative Assembly: GENNADII T. DYUDYAYEV; 650099 Kemerovo, pr. Sovetskii 62; tel. (3842) 58-41-42; fax (3842) 58-54-51.

Chief Representative of Kemerovo Oblast in the Russian Federation: SERGEI V. SHATIROV; 115184 Moscow, ul. B. Tatarskaya 5/14/9; tel. and fax (095) 953-54-89.

Head of Kemerovo City Administration (Mayor): VLADIMIR V. MIKHAILOV; 650099 Kemerovo, pr. Sovetskii 54; tel. (3842) 36-46-10; fax (3842) 58-18-91; e-mail sityadm@kuzbass.net.

Kirov (Vyatka) Oblast

Kirov Oblast is situated in the east of the Eastern European Plain. It forms part of the Volga Federal Okrug and the Volga-Vyatka Economic Area. It is bordered by Archangel and Komi to the north, the Komi-Permyak AOk (part of Perm Oblast) and Udmurtiya to the east, Tatarstan and Marii-El to the south, and Nizhnii Novgorod, Kostroma and Vologda to the west. Its main rivers are the Kama and the Vyatka; in addition there are almost 20,000 rivers and more than 1,000 lakes on its territory. Kirov occupies a total area of 120,800 sq km (46,640 sq miles) and measures 570 km (354 miles) from south to north and 440 km from west to east. It is divided into 39 administrative districts and 18 cities. The total population at 1 January 2002 was 1,560,000 and the population density was 12.9 per sq km. Around 71.0% of the population inhabited urban areas in 2001. At the census of 1989 ethnic Russians comprised 90.4% of the population. The Oblast's administrative centre is at Vyatka (Kirov), a river-port, which had 466,300 inhabitants in 2001. Other major cities are Kirovo-Chepetsk (91,300) and Vyatskiye Polyany (42,200).

History

The city and its region were known as Kirov from the formation of the latter on 7 December 1934, but the city was renamed Vyatka in 1992. In September 1993 a draft constitution for Kirov Oblast was prepared, which referred to the Oblast as Vyatka Krai and provided for a universally elected governor and a new legislature, a provincial duma. On 18 October the Kirov Regional Soviet voted to disband itself. The federal authorities refused to acknowledge the area's redesignation as a krai and, during 1994, a Regional Duma was elected. The most popular party in the mid-1990s was that of the nationalist supporters of Vladimir Zhirinovskii, although members of the old communist establishment were well represented in its ranks. Election to the governorship of the Oblast was held in October 1996 and was won by the Communist Party candidate, Vladimir Sergeyenkov, by a narrow margin; he was re-elected, with 58% of the votes cast, on 26 March 2000. In October 1997 the Governor of the Oblast signed a power-sharing treaty with federal President Boris Yeltsin, with the specific hope that investment in the extraction of raw materials and health care would benefit the region.

Economy

In 1999 the Oblast's gross regional product (GRP) stood at 28,543.1m. roubles, equivalent to 17,886.4 roubles per head. Its main industrial centres are at Vyatka, Slobodskoi, Kotelnich, Omutninsk, Kirovo-Chepetsk and Vyatskiye Polyany. In 2000 there were 1,098 km of railway track in the region, 8,915 km of paved roads and over 2,000 km of navigable waterways on the Vyatka river. Owing to the density of rivers in the region its soil is high in mineral salts, reducing its fertility.

The Oblast's agriculture, which employed 17.3% of the working population in 2000, consists mainly of animal husbandry and the production of grain, flax and vegetables. Total output within the sector amounted to 11,752m. roubles in 2000. Kirov Oblast has significant deposits of peat, estimated at 435m. metric tons, and phosphorites, reserves of which amounted to some 2,000m. tons in the mid-1990s. Its main industries are mechanical engineering, the production of electrical energy, metal-working, ferrous and non-ferrous metallurgy, chemicals, the processing of agricultural and forestry products and light manufacturing. In March 1998 the regional administration signed a protocol with the federal ministries of defence and the economy on the restructuring of the Oblast's military-industrial complex, which was significantly underachieving (in 1997 the sector accounted for just one-10th of the Oblast's GRP, despite owning 58% of its main assets). The region was also renowned for the manufacturing of toys and wood products (especially skis). Industry employed 27.2% of the work-force in 2000 and generated 32,858m. roubles.

The economically active population numbered 844,000 in 2000, when 8.2% of the Oblast's labour force were unemployed, one of the lowest levels recorded in any federal subject. The average monthly wage was 3,105.2 roubles at mid-2002. In 2000 the Oblast recorded a budgetary deficit of 187m. roubles. In the late 1990s exports, the value of which amounted to US $387.8m. in 2000, largely comprised chemical and petrochemical goods, while imports (worth $31.6m. in 2000) were dominated by automobiles and equipment and food products. In 2000 foreign investment amounted to $14.7m. In late 2000 there were 3,900 small businesses registered in Kirov Oblast.

Directory

Head of the Regional Administration (Governor): VLADIMIR N. SERGEYENKOV; 610019 Kirov obl., Vyatka, ul. K. Libknekhta 69; tel. (8332) 62-95-64; fax (8332) 62-89-58; e-mail region@gov-vyatka.ru; internet gov-vyatka.ru.

Chairman of the Regional Duma: ALEKSANDR N. STRELNIKOV; 610019 Kirov obl., Vyatka, ul. K. Libknekhta 69; tel. (8332) 62-48-00; fax (8332) 38-17-50; e-mail assembly@gov-vyatka.ru.

Representation of Kirov (Vyatka) Oblast in the Russian Federation: Moscow.

Head of Vyatka (Kirov) City Administration: VASILII A. KISELEV; 610000 Kirov obl., Vyatka, ul. Vorovskogo 39; tel. (8332) 62-89-40; fax (8332) 67-69-91.

Kostroma Oblast

Kostroma Oblast is situated in the central part of the Eastern European Plain. It forms part of the Central Federal Okrug and the Central Economic Area. It is bordered by Vologda Oblast to the north, Kirov Oblast to the east, Nizhnii Novgorod and Ivanovo Oblasts to the south and Yaroslavl Oblast to the west. Its main rivers are the Volga, the Kostroma, the Unzha, the Vokhma and the Vetluga. It has two major lakes—the Galichskoye and the Chukhlomskoye. The total area of Kostroma Oblast is 60,100 sq km (23,200 sq miles), almost three-quarters of which is forested. It is divided into 24 administrative districts and 12 cities. The region had an estimated population of 776,400 at 1 January 2002, giving a population density of 12.9 per sq km. In 2001 some 66.1% of the population inhabited urban areas. The Oblast's administrative centre is at Kostroma, a river-port situated on both banks of the Volga, and a popular tourist resort as part of the 'Golden Ring', which had 287,000 inhabitants in 2001.

History

The city of Kostroma was founded in the 12th century. Kostroma Oblast was formed on 13 August 1944. The region remained loyal to the communist *nomenklatura* in the 1990s—its local council supported the federal parliament in its 1993 defiance of the Russian President, Boris Yeltsin, and was replaced by a new representative body in 1994. The Communist Party of the Russian Federation (CPRF) was the main party in the regional Duma, and the CPRF candidate, Viktor Shershunov, was successful in achieving election as Governor in December 1996 (although Yeltsin had been the preferred candidate in the presidential election of June of that year). Shershunov was re-elected to serve a further term of office in December 2000.

Economy

In 1999 gross regional product in Kostroma Oblast amounted to 14,286.9m. roubles, or 18,098.5 roubles per head. The Oblast's main industrial centres are at Kostroma, Sharya, Nerekhta, Galich, Bui, Manturovo and Krasnoye-on-Volga (Krasnoye-na-Volge). The region has major road and rail networks—in 2000 there were 640 km (398 miles) of railways in use on its territory and 5,507 km of paved roads. There were 985 km of navigable waterways in 1998.

Agriculture in Kostroma Oblast, which employed 10.4% of the work-force in 2000, consists mainly of production of grain, flax (the region is one of Russia's major producers of linen) and vegetables, and animal husbandry. Total agricultural output in 2000 was worth 5,437m. roubles. The region has an energy surplus, exporting some four-fifths of electrical energy produced. Electricity generation comprised 29.9% of total industrial production in Kostroma Oblast in 2000. The other main industries in the region are light manufacturing, wood-working, mechanical engineering, food- and timber-processing and handicrafts (especially jewellery). The territory is also an important military centre, with numerous rocket silos, of which 23 had been converted to agricultural use by early 1996, with plans to recultivate a further 20. Some 24.2% of the Oblast's working population was engaged in industry in 2000, when industrial production amounted to a value of 13,305m. roubles.

The economically active population numbered 387,000 in 2000, when 8.6% of the labour force of the region were unemployed. The average wage in the Oblast was 3,164.1 roubles per month in mid-2002. There was a budgetary deficit of some 36.2m. roubles in 2000. In that year external trade comprised US $69.8m. of exports and $19.3m. of imports, one of the lowest levels in the Central Federal Okrug. Foreign investment totalled $4.7m. At 31 December 2000 there were 3,200 small businesses registered in the Oblast.

Directory

Head of the Regional Administration (Governor): VIKTOR A. SHERSHUNOV; 156006 Kostroma, ul. Dzerzhinskogo 15; tel. (0942) 31-34-72; fax (0942) 31-33-95; e-mail shershunov@kos-obl.kmtn.ru; internet www.region.kostroma.net.

Chairman of the Regional Duma: ANDREI I. BYCHKOV; 156000 Kostroma, Sovetskaya pl. 2; tel. (0942) 57-62-52.

Chief Representative of Kostroma Oblast in the Russian Federation: GALINA M. PSHENITSYNA; 127025 Moscow, ul. Novyi Arbat 19/1811; tel. (095) 203-42-44; fax (095) 203-41-69.

Head of Kostroma City Administration: BORIS K. KOROBOV; 156000 Kostroma, pl. Sovetskaya 1; tel. (0942) 31-44-40; fax (0942) 31-39-32; internet www.boriskorobov.ru.

Kurgan Oblast

Kurgan Oblast is situated in the south of the Western Siberian Plain. It forms part of the Urals Federal District and the Urals Economic Area. Chelyabinsk Oblast lies to the west, Sverdlovsk Oblast to the north and Tyumen Oblast to the north-east. There is an international border with Kazakhstan to the south. The main rivers flowing through Kurgan Oblast are the Tobol and the Iset and there are numerous lakes (more than 2,500) in the south-east of the region. The Oblast occupies 71,000 sq km (27,400 sq miles) and measures 290 km (180 miles) from south to north and 430 km from east to west. It is divided into 24 administrative districts and nine cities, and had an estimated population of 1,074,400 at 1 January 2002, giving a population density of 15.1 per sq km. In 2001 some 55.3% of the population inhabited urban areas, the lowest urban population of any region in the Urals Economic Area. Its administrative centre is at Kurgan, which had a population of 359,700 in 2001.

History

The city of Kurgan was founded as a tax-exempt settlement in 1553, on the edge of Russian territory. By the Soviet period, when there was some industrialization, it was a firmly ethnically Russian area. Kurgan Oblast was formed on 6 February 1943. The Communist Party of the Russian Federation (CPRF) was the largest party in the Regional Duma elected on 12 December 1993, and remained the most popular party in the Oblast at elections to the State Duma in 1995, although on that occasion it was closely followed by the nationalist Liberal Democratic Party of Russia. In the gubernatorial election of late 1996 the CPRF candidate, Oleg Bogomolov, hitherto speaker of the Regional Duma, was voted into office, running unopposed in the second round of the election after his opponent stood down. Bogomolov was re-elected in December 2000.

Economy

Kurgan Oblast, with its fertile soil and warm, moist climate, is the agricultural base of the Urals area, producing around one-10th of the region's grain, meat and milk. In 1999 its gross regional product amounted to 15,424.2m. roubles, equivalent to 14,016.9 roubles per head. Its main industrial centres are at Kurgan, a river-port in the south-east of the region, and Shadrinsk. In 2000 there were 748 km of railways and 6,393 km of paved roads on the Oblast's territory. The Trans-Siberian Railway passes through the Oblast, as do several major petroleum and natural gas pipelines.

The Oblast's important agricultural sector employed 28.5% of the work-force in 2000 and consists mainly of grain production and animal husbandry. Total agricultural production in the region was worth 7,896m. roubles in 2000. Its main industries are mechanical engineering, metal-working, chemicals, electricity production, manufacturing of building materials, and food-processing. The industrial sector employed 18.9% of the working population and generated 14,774m. roubles in 2000.

The economically active population numbered 529,000 in 2000. The rate of unemployment increased from the late 1990s, reaching 13.2% of the labour force by 2000. Those in employment earned, on average, 3,030.1 roubles per month in mid-2002. There was a budgetary deficit of 142.7m. roubles in 2000, when foreign investment totalled US $582,000. In 2000 external trade amounted to a value of $183.9m., while imports totalled $68.1m. The economic situation of the region deteriorated markedly from the late 1990s, and in mid-2002 it was reported that up to 60% of the Oblast's budget comprised transfers from the federal Government, and that around 60% of the region's population lived in conditions of, or approaching, poverty. In late 2000 there were 2,900 small businesses registered in the Oblast.

Directory

Head of the Regional Administration (Governor): OLEG A. BOGOMOLOV; 640024 Kurgan, ul. Gogolya 56; tel. (3522) 41-70-30; fax (3522) 41-71-32; e-mail kurgan@admobl.kurgan.ru; internet www.admobl.kurgan.ru.

Chairman of the Regional Duma: VALERII Z. PONOMAREV; 640024 Kurgan, ul. Gogolya 56; tel. (3522) 41-72-17.

Chief Representative of Kurgan Oblast in the Russian Federation: OLEG YE. PANTELEYEV; 103798 Moscow, ul. M. Dmitrovka 3; tel. (095) 200-39-78; fax (095) 299-33-67.

Head of Kurgan City Administration (Mayor): ANATOLII F. YELCHANINOV; 640000 Kurgan, pl. Lenina; tel. (3522) 41-76-51; fax (3522) 46-51-64; internet www.munic.kurgan.ru.

Kursk Oblast

Kursk Oblast is situated within the Central Russian Highlands. It forms part of the Central Federal Okrug and the Central Chernozem Economic Area. An international boundary with Ukraine lies to the south-west, with neighbouring Russian federal territories consisting of Bryansk in the north-west, Orel and Lipetsk in the north, Voronezh in the east and Belgorod in the south. Its main river is the Seim. The Oblast measures 171 km (106 miles) from south to north and 305 km from west to east. It occupies 29,800 sq km (11,500 sq miles) and is divided into 28 administrative districts and 10 cities. It had a population of 1,284,500 in 2002, when its population density was 43.1 per sq km. In 2001 some 61.6% of the population inhabited urban areas. The Oblast's administrative centre is at Kursk, which had 437,400 inhabitants at 1 January 2001. The second largest city in the region is Zheleznogorsk (98,200).

History

The city of Kursk, one of the most ancient in Russia, was founded in 1032 and became famous for its nightingales and Antonovka apples. The region was the scene of an army mutiny in 1905 and, in 1943, of a decisive battle against German forces during the Second World War. Kursk Oblast was formed on 13 July 1934. The Communist Party of the Russian Federation (CPRF) dominated the regional assembly, a Duma, elected in 1994. In December 1995 the party's candidates to the federal State Duma secured 28% of the regional votes. The former Russian Vice-President, Aleksandr Rutskoi, was elected regional Governor on 20 October 1996. However, he was prevented from standing as a candidate in the election of 22 October 2000, one day before the election, owing to a legal technicality. In a second round of voting on 5 November, the CPRF candidate, Aleksandr Mikhailov, defeated the pro-Government, former Federal Security Service (FSB) General, Viktor Surzhikov. Immediately after being elected, Mikhailov provoked controversy by making a number of anti-Semitic remarks, prompting Rutskoi (who had a Jewish mother) to threaten to take legal action.

Economy

Kursk Oblast's gross regional product stood at 25,351.6m. roubles in 1999, equivalent to 19,182.5 roubles per head. Its main industrial centres are at Kursk and Zheleznogorsk. In 2000 there were 1,067 km of railway lines and 6,055 km of paved roads on the Oblast's territory.

The region's agriculture, which employed 24.6% of the working population in 2000, consists mainly of sugar beet and grain production, horticulture and animal husbandry. Total agricultural production in 2000 amounted to a value of 13,753m. roubles. The territory contains a major iron-ore basin, with significant deposits of Kursk magnetic anomaly. Kursk Oblast's main industries were the production of electricity, production and enrichment of iron ores, mechanical engineering, electro-technical products and chemicals, and timber- and food-processing. Some 21.2% of the work-force were engaged in industry in 2000, when the sector's output was worth 26,109m. roubles.

The economically active population in Kursk Oblast numbered 650,000 in 2000, when 10.4% of the labour force were unemployed, compared with 6.1% in 1995. The average monthly wage in the region was 2,719.0 roubles in mid-2002. In 2000 there was a budgetary deficit of 113.7m. roubles. From the mid-1990s the Oblast's main foreign trading partners were Poland and the Czech Republic, although it also had economic links with other European countries, North America, India and Turkey. Its principal exports comprised iron ore and concentrate, automobiles and machinery. In 2000 the total value of external trade was US $111.1m., of which imports accounted for $179.9m. Foreign investment in that year amounted to $7.5m. At 31 December 2000 some 2,800 small businesses were registered in the Oblast.

Directory

Head of the Regional Administration (Governor): ALEKSANDR N. MIKHAILOV; 305002 Kursk, Krasnaya pl., Dom Sovetov; tel. (07122) 2-62-62; fax (0712) 56-58-89; e-mail intercom@region.kursk.ru; internet www.kurskonline.ru.

Chairman of the Regional Duma: ALEKSANDR N. ANPILOV; 305001 Kursk, ul. S. Perovskoi 24; tel. (0712) 56-09-91; fax (0712) 56-20-06; e-mail oblduma@kursknet.ru; internet www.oblduma.kursknet.ru.

Representation of Kursk Oblast in the Russian Federation: Moscow; tel. (095) 917-08-69.

Head of Kursk City Administration: SERGEI I. MALTSEV; 305000 Kursk, ul. Lenina 1; tel. (07122) 2-63-63; fax (07122) 2-43-16; e-mail kursk@pub.sovest.ru; internet www.sovtest.ru/kursk.

Leningrad Oblast

Leningrad Oblast is situated in the north-west of the Eastern European Plain. It lies on the Gulf of Finland, an inlet of the Baltic Sea, and forms part of the North-Western Federal Okrug and the North-Western Economic Area. The Republic of Kareliya (Karelia) lies to the north and the oblasts of Volodga to the east and Novgorod and Pskov to the south. There is an international border with Estonia to the west and with Finland to the north-west. Two-thirds of the Oblast is forested and over one-10th is swampland. Its main rivers are the Neva, the Sayas, the Luga and the Vuoksa. Lake Ladoga, the largest lake in Europe, with a surface area of 17,800 sq km, forms a partial border with Kareliya, and the southern tip of Lake Onega (9,700 sq km) also lies within Leningrad Oblast. The Oblast, including St Petersburg city, occupies 85,900 sq km (33,166 sq miles) and is divided into 17 administrative districts and 31 cities. Its total population at 1 January 2002, excluding the St Petersburg city region, was 1,649,600, and in 2001 some 66.0% of the population of the Oblast inhabited urban areas. Its administrative centre is at St Petersburg, now a federal city in its own right. The largest cities within the Oblast proper are Gatchina (population 82,300) and Vyborg (79,200).

History

The city of St Petersburg (known as Petrograd in 1914–24 and Leningrad until 1991) was built in 1703. Leningrad Oblast, which was formed on 1 August 1927 out of the territories of five regions (Cherepovets, Leningrad, Murmansk, Novgorod and Pskov), was heavily industrialized during the Soviet period, particularly during

1926–40. The region did not change its name when the city reverted to the name of St Petersburg in October 1991.

In mid-1996 an agreement delimiting the division of powers between the federal and regional governments was signed. Later that year gubernatorial elections were held, which were won by an independent candidate, Vladimir Gustov. On 24 September 1998 the federal President, Boris Yeltsin, approved a proposal to merge the Oblast with the federal city of St Petersburg, although any immediate implementation seemed unlikely. Gustov resigned to take up the position of Deputy Prime Minister in September 1998, and his replacement, Valerii Serdyukov, confirmed his position on 5 September 1999, by securing 30% of the votes cast in an election contested by 16 candidates. The power-sharing agreement signed by the federal and regional authorities in 1996 was annulled in April 2002.

Economy

Leningrad Oblast's gross regional product amounted to 42,604.2m. roubles in 1999, equivalent to 23,395.9 roubles per head. Its main industrial centres are at St Petersburg, Vyborg (both major seaports), Sestroretsk and Kingisepp. A new port opened at Primorsk in December 2001, as part of the country's Baltic Pipeline System, to facilitate the transportation of petroleum. In 2000 the region contained 2,833 km (1,760 miles) of railway track, of which 1,352 km were electrified in 1999. In 2000 there were 10,498 km of paved roads.

The Oblast's agriculture, which employed 11.7% of the working population in 2000, consists mainly of animal husbandry and vegetable production. Total agricultural output was worth 14,857m. roubles in 2000. The region's timber reserves are estimated to cover 6.1m. ha (15m. acres). Its major industries are the processing of forestry and agricultural products, mechanical engineering, non-ferrous metallurgy, chemicals and petrochemicals, petroleum-refining, the production of electrical energy, the production of building materials, bauxites, slate and peat. Some 25.4% of the Oblast's work-force was engaged in industry in 2000, when industrial output amounted to a value of 56,951m. roubles.

The economically active population numbered 851,000 in 2000, when 9.7% of the labour force were unemployed—a relatively low figure compared with elsewhere in the Russian Federation, and a marked decrease compared with the figures recorded in 1998 and 1999, which had been in excess of 14%. The average monthly wage was 4,466.0 roubles in mid-2002. In 2000 the budget showed a surplus of 449.0m. roubles. The Oblast enjoys a relatively high level of external trade; in 2000 exports were worth US $2,098.6m., while imports amounted to $460.0m. Foreign investment amounted to $305.6m. in 2000, compared with $190.7m. in 1998. In 2002 the American Chamber of Commerce in Russia, which unites US business interests, named Leningrad Oblast its 'region of the year', and in the first half of that year the region recorded growth of 36.6%, compared with the national average of some 3%. At the end of 2000 there were 12,000 small businesses registered in Leningrad Oblast.

Directory

Head of the Regional Administration (Governor): VALERII P. SERDYUKOV; 193311 St Petersburg, Suvorovskii pr. 67; tel. (812) 274-35-63; fax (812) 271-56-27; internet www.lenobl.ru.

Chairman of the Regional Legislative Assembly: VITALII N. KLIMOV; 193311 St Petersburg, Suvorovskii pr. 67; tel. (812) 274-68-73; fax (812) 274-85-39; e-mail klimov@assemblylenobl.ru; internet www.assemblylenobl.ru.

Chief Representative of Leningrad Oblast in the Russian Federation: ALEKSEI I. AKULOV; 121019 Moscow, ul. Novyi Arbat 15/1/1604; tel. (095) 291-33-55; e-mail plorf@mail.ru.

Lipetsk Oblast

Lipetsk Oblast is situated within the Central Russian Highlands, some 508 km (315 m) south-east of Moscow. It forms part of the Central Federal Okrug and the Central Chernozem Economic Area. It is bordered by Voronezh and Kursk Oblasts to the south, Orel Oblast to the west, Tula Oblast to the north-west, Ryazan Oblast to the north and Tambov Oblast to the east. Its main rivers are the Don and the Voronezh. The Oblast occupies 24,100 sq km (9,300 sq miles) and is divided into 18 administrative districts and eight cities. It had an estimated population of 1,228,900 at 1 January 2002, when its population density was, therefore, 50.0 per sq km. In 2001 some 64.4% of the Oblast's population inhabited urban areas. Its administrative centre is at Lipetsk, which had a population of 519,200 in 2001. The Oblast's second largest city is Yelets (117,900).

History

Lipetsk was founded in the 13th century and was later famed for containing one of Russia's oldest mud-bath resorts and spas. In the late tsarist and Soviet period the region became increasingly industrialized. Lipetsk Oblast was formed on 6 January 1954. By the 1990s it was considered part of the 'red belt' of support for the Communist Party of the Russian Federation (CPRF) across central Russia. Thus, in December 1992, when Lipetsk was one of eight territorial units permitted to hold gubernatorial elections (in an attempt to resolve the dispute between the head of the administration and the regional assembly), the incumbent, a supporter of the federal Government, was defeated by the CPRF candidate. In September 1993 both the Regional Soviet and the Governor, therefore, denounced the Russian President's dissolution of the federal parliament. Subsequently, the territory was obliged to comply with the directives of the federal Government. Legislative elections were held in the region on 6 March 1994, but were invalidated, owing to a low level of attendance. Further elections were held later that year. Political apathy also contributed to a relatively low level of support for the CPRF, in comparison to other 'red belt' regions, in the election to the State Duma held in December 1995 (29%). However, in the election to the federal presidency of March 2000, Lipetsk Oblast awarded the CPRF candidate, Gennadii Zyuganov, a higher proportion of the votes (47.4%) than did any other federal subject. On 12 April 1998 the Chairman of the Regional Council of Deputies (legislature), Oleg Korolev, won an overwhelming victory (some 79% of the votes cast) in the gubernatorial election. He was supported primarily by the CPRF, but also by the local branch of Yabloko and other political movements. Korolev was re-elected on 14 April 2002, with 73% of the votes cast, after his principal rival withdrew his candidacy.

Economy

In 1999 Lipetsk Oblast's gross regional product totalled 31,923.6m. roubles, or 25,695.1 roubles per head. Its main industrial centres are at Lipetsk, Yelets, Dankov and Gryazi. In 2000 there were 752 km (467 miles) of railway lines and 5,157 km of paved roads on the Oblast's territory. Yelets and Gryazi contain the region's major railway junctions.

The region's agriculture consists mainly of animal husbandry, horticulture and the production of grain, sugar beet, makhorka tobacco and vegetables. Some 21.6% of the work-force was engaged in agriculture in 2000. Agricultural output in that year amounted to a value of 10,625m. roubles. The Oblast's main industries are ferrous metallurgy (which comprised 65% of the region's total industrial output in 2000), mechanical engineering, metal-working, electro-technical industry, food-processing and the production of electricity. Novolipetsk MetKom (New Lipetsk Metallurgical Group), based in the region, is one of the country's major industrial companies. In 2000 the industrial sector employed 24.2% of the region's working population and generated 61,245m. roubles.

The economically active population totalled 603,000 in 2000, when 8.5% of the labour force were unemployed. Those in employment earned, on average, 3,475.2 roubles per month in mid-2002. In 2000 the regional budget recorded a surplus of 901.4m. roubles. In that year exports amounted to US $1,053.6m. and imports were worth $161.0m. Foreign investment amounted to $1.4m. in that year. At 31 December 2000 there were around 4,300 small businesses registered in the territory.

Directory

Head of the Regional Administration (Governor): OLEG P. KOROLEV; 398014 Lipetsk, Sobornaya pl. 1; tel. (0742) 77-65-96; fax (0742) 72-24-26; e-mail office@admlr.lipetsk.ru; internet www.admlr.lipetsk.ru.

Chairman of the Regional Council of Deputies: ANATOLII I. SAVENKOV; 398014 Lipetsk, Sobornaya pl. 1; tel. (0742) 74-35-08.

Representation of Lipetsk Oblast in the Russian Federation: Moscow.

Head of Lipetsk City Administration (Mayor): ALEKSANDR S. KOROBEINIKOV; 398600 Lipetsk, ul. Sovetskaya 22; tel. (0742) 77-66-17; fax (0742) 77-44-30.

Magadan Oblast

Magadan Oblast is situated in the north-east of Russia and forms part of the Far Eastern Federal Okrug and the Far Eastern Economic Area. To the north-east, on the Chukotka Peninsula, lies the Chukot AOk, which, until 1992, formed part of Magadan Oblast. The rest of its border with territory on Chukotka is with the Koryak AOk (Kamchatka Oblast), which lies to the east. Magadan has a coastline on the Sea of Okhotsk in the south-east. Khabarovsk Krai lies to the south-west of the region and the Republic of Sakha (Yakutiya) to the north-west. Its main river is the Kolyma, which flows northwards and drains into the Arctic Ocean by way of Yakutiya. A considerable proportion of the territory of the region is mountainous, while the area around the Anadyr estuary is low marshland. Much of the Oblast is tundra or forest-tundra. The Oblast occupies a total area of 461,400 sq km (178,150 sq miles—much reduced from when it included the Chukot AOk). It is divided into six administrative districts and two cities. The climate in the region is severe, with winters lasting from six to over seven months. The average temperature in January is –29.4°C, while that in July is 14.4°C. The Oblast had an estimated population of 229,200 at 1 January 2002. It is one of the most sparsely populated regions, with a population density of just 0.5 per sq km. The majority of the population (91.1%) inhabited urban areas in 2001. Its administrative centre is at the only large city in the Oblast, Magadan, which had a population of 120,600 in 2001.

History
Russians first reached the Magadan region in the mid-17th century. At the beginning of the Soviet period it was in the Far Eastern Republic, which in 1922 was reintegrated into Russia. Magadan Oblast was formed on 3 December 1953, although it then included the Chukot AOk. The successful rejection of Magadan's jurisdiction over the Chukotka Peninsula (acknowledged by the federal authorities in 1992) massively reduced Magadan's territory and contributed to local feeling of remoteness and of neglect by the centre. Thus, in the elections to the State

188

Duma held in December 1995, candidates of the nationalist Liberal Democratic Party of Russia secured 22% of the votes cast in the region and remained relatively popular there during the late 1990s. Both the communists and the existing federal authorities were also identified with the political establishments. However, the Regional Duma (elected in 1994) was still dominated by the old *nomenklatura* class. The gubernatorial election of 3 November 1996 was won by Valentin Tsvetkov, a candidate backed by the communist-dominated Popular-Patriotic Union. In June 1999 a special economic zone was created in the Oblast, in the hope that investors would facilitate the exploitation of the region's rich natural resources. Tsvetkov was re-elected as Governor in November 2000; however in mid-October 2002 he was shot and killed, in an apparent contract killing. He was succeeded, on an acting basis, by Nikolai Dudov, hitherto First Vice-Governor of the Oblast. A gubernatorial election was scheduled to be held on 2 February 2003.

Economy

Magadan Oblast is Russia's principal gold-producing region. Its gross regional product in 1999 amounted to 11,328.6m. roubles, equivalent to 47,941.5 roubles per head. The Oblast's main industrial centres are at Magadan and Susuman. Magadan and Nagayevo are its most important ports. There are no railways in the territory, but there are 2,231 km (1,386 miles) of paved roads. There is an international airport at Magadan.

The region's primary economic activities are fishing, animal husbandry and hunting. These and other agricultural activities, which employed 4.1% of the region's work-force, generated just 373m. roubles in 2000. Ore-mining is important: apart from gold, the region contains considerable reserves of silver, tin and wolfram (tungsten). It is also rich in peat and timber. In early 1998 the regional Government hired a prospecting company to explore offshore petroleum deposits in the Sea of Okhotsk, in a zone thought to hold around 5,000m. metric tons of petroleum and natural gas. The Kolyma river is an important source of hydroelectric energy. In 1997 the Pan American Silver Corporation of Canada purchased a 70% stake in local company ZAO Dukat, to reopen a defunct silver mine in the Oblast, which contained an estimated 477m. troy ounces of silver and 1m. troy ounces of gold. However, licensing and other bureaucratic obstacles delayed operations. Other industry includes food-processing, mechanical engineering and metal-working. In 2000 22.7% of the working population were engaged in industry, and industrial output amounted to 10,728m. roubles. Construction is a significant source of employment, engaging 10.6% of the labour force in 2000.

The economically active population of the Oblast numbered 144,000 in 2000, when 10.8% of the labour force were unemployed, a reduction of almost one-half compared with the previous year. The average monthly wage was some 7,101.1 roubles in mid-2002, one of the highest figures in the Federation. In 2000 the budget recorded a deficit of 192.3m. roubles, and throughout the 1990s persistent deficit problems, not helped by high wages, led to continuing problems with payment arrears. The cost of living in the region is among the highest in the Russian Federation. The value of external trade was relatively low; in 2000 exports were worth only US $3.8m., while imports amounted to $41.3m. Foreign investment in the Oblast amounted to $27.7m. in 2000. At 31 December 2000 there were 2,900 small businesses registered in the Oblast.

Directory

Governor: NIKOLAI N. DUDOV (acting); 685000 Magadan, ul. Gorkogo 6; tel. (41322) 2-31-34; fax (41322) 7-89-01; e-mail info@magadan.ru; internet www .magadan.ru.

Chairman of the Regional Council of Deputies: SERGEI I. MAZHARIN; 685000 Magadan, ul. Gorkogo 6; tel. (41322) 2-31-00; fax (41322) 2-55-12.

Representation of Magadan Oblast in the Russian Federation: 103025 Moscow, ul. Novyi Arbat 19; tel. (095) 203-92-74.

Head of Magadan City Administration (Mayor): NIKOLAI B. KARPENKO; 685000 Magadan, pl. Gorkogo 1; tel. (41300) 2-50-47; fax (41322) 2-49-40; e-mail admin@cityadm.magadan.ru.

Moscow Oblast

Moscow Oblast is situated in the central part of the Eastern European Plain, at the Volga-Oka confluence. It forms part of the Central Federal Okrug and the Central Economic Area. Moscow is surrounded by seven other oblasts: Tver and Yaroslavl to the north, Vladimir and Ryazan to the east, Tula and Kaluga to the south-west and Smolensk to the west. Most of the region is forested and its main rivers are the Moskva and the Oka. The territory of the Oblast (including Moscow City) covers an area of 47,000 sq km (18,147 sq miles) and has 39 administrative districts and 75 cities. Its total population, excluding Moscow City, was estimated at 6,409,700 at 1 January 2002. Inhabitants of urban areas comprised around 80.2% of the region's total population in 2001. The Oblast's administrative centre is in Moscow City. Within the Oblast proper, there are several cities with a population of over 100,000 including (in order of size) Podolsk, Lyubertsy, Mytishchi, Kolomna, Elektrostal, Khimki and Korolyev.

History

The city of Moscow was established in the mid-12th century and became the centre of a burgeoning Muscovite state. The region soon became an important trade route between the Baltic Sea in the north and the Black and Caspian Seas in the south. It first became industrialized in the early 18th century, with the development of the textiles industry, in particular the production of wool and cotton. The region and the city of Moscow were captured by the troops of Emperor Napoleon I of France in 1812, but the invaders were forced to retreat later that year. German invaders reached the Moscow region (which had been formed as Moscow Oblast on 14 January 1929) in 1941, and the Soviet Government was removed from the city until 1943. Between late 1941 and early 1942 the German

191

forces were driven from the Oblast's territory. Otherwise, the region and the city have benefited from Moscow being the Soviet, and the Russian, capital.

As the seat of government, in the 1990s the federal executive could rely on a reasonable level of support in the Moscow region. Our Home is Russia, the party of Viktor Chernomyrdin, the federal Prime Minister, achieved 14% of the votes cast in the general election (not as high as in the city itself, and not as high as the Communist Party, with 22%) in 1995. In simultaneous local elections for a governor, the pro-Government incumbent won, but only after a second round of voting. The gubernatorial elections of December 1999–January 2000 were similarly closely fought, with Col-Gen. Boris Gromov, an ally of Moscow City Mayor Yurii Luzhkov, and a former State Duma deputy and Deputy Minister of Defence, emerging the victor. Relative prosperity kept discontent to a minimum and the region did not experience the problems of wage arrears to the same extent as elsewhere in the Federation—it was among the three regions with the best record for timely payment during 1998.

Economy

In 1999 Moscow Oblast's gross regional product (GRP) amounted to 160,034.6m. roubles, or 24,509.9 roubles per head. The main industrial centres are at Podolsk, Lyubertsy, Kolomna, Mytishchi, Odintsovo, Noginsk, Serpukhov, Orekhovo-Zuyevo, Shchelkovo and Sergiyev Posad (formerly Zagorsk). The latter city is an important centre of Russian Orthodoxy, containing Russia's foremost monastery and two medieval cathedrals. In 2000 there were 2,738 km (1,701 miles) of railways and 16,134 km of paved roads on the Oblast's territory.

Moscow Oblast's agriculture, which employed 8.6% of the region's work-force in 2000, consists mainly of animal husbandry and the production of vegetables and grain. Total agricultural production generated 25,326m. roubles in 2000. The Oblast's industry, in which some 24.3% of the working population were engaged in 2000, mainly comprised heavy industry. The region's major industries are mechanical engineering, radio electronics, chemicals, light manufacturing, textiles, ferrous and non-ferrous metallurgy, metal-working, the manufacture of building materials, wood-working and handicrafts (ceramics, painted and lacquered wooden ornaments). The region's military-industrial complex is also important. Industrial output was worth 137,537m. roubles in 2000.

The economically active population in the Oblast was 3,531,000 in 2000, when 7.4% of the labour force were unemployed. The average monthly wage was 4,741.7 roubles in mid-2002. In 2000 there was a regional budgetary surplus of 2,339.6m. roubles. The Oblast's external trade increased significantly during the late 1990s, and exports amounted to US $2,079.8m. in 2000, when imports were worth $2,109.3m. Total foreign investment in Moscow Oblast amounted to $290.6m. in 2000. In 1997 there was a total of 110 joint enterprises operating in the Oblast, of which 78 had foreign partners, particularly from Germany, Italy and the USA. In 2000 there were some 46,000 small businesses registered in the Oblast.

Directory

Governor: BORIS V. GROMOV; 103070 Moscow, pl. Staraya 6; tel. (095) 206-60-93; fax (095) 928-98-12; e-mail adm@obladm.msk.su; internet www.mosreg.ru.

Chairman of the Regional Duma: VIKTOR A. YEGEREV (acting); 103070 Moscow, pl. Staraya 6; tel. (095) 206-42-37; fax (095) 925-26-42.

Representation of Moscow Oblast in the Russian Federation: Moscow.

Murmansk Oblast

Murmansk Oblast occupies the Kola Peninsula, which neighbours the Barents Sea to the north and the White Sea to the east. It forms part of the North-Western Federal Okrug and the Northern Economic Area. It has international borders with Norway and Finland to the west and the Russian federal subject of Kareliya (Karelia) lies to the south. Much of its territory lies within the Arctic Circle. The major rivers in the Oblast are the Ponoi, the Varguza, the Umba, the Kola, the Niva and the Tulona. It has several major lakes, including the Imandra, Umbozero and Lovozero. The territory of the Oblast covers an area of 144,900 sq km (55,930 sq miles), extending some 400 km (250 miles) from south to north and 500 km from west to east. The climate in the Oblast is severe and changeable, influenced by cold fronts from the Arctic and warm, moist weather from the Atlantic. Its total population was estimated at 977,600 at 1 January 2002, when it had a population density of 6.7 per sq km. In 2001 some 91.7% of the population inhabited urban areas. Murmansk Oblast is divided into five administrative districts and 16 cities. Its administrative centre is at the only large city in the region, Murmansk, a major seaport and tourist centre, which had a population of 370,700 in 2001.

History

Murmansk city was founded in 1916, as a fishing port on the Barents Sea, and was known as Romanov-on-Murman (Romanov-na-Murmane) until the following year. After the Bolshevik Revolution of 1917 Murmansk region was a centre of anti-communist resistance until a peace treaty was signed with the Soviet Government on 13 March 1920. Murmansk Oblast was formed on 28 May 1938.

The development of industry in the region, particularly after the Second World War, resulted in a steady increase in population until the late 1950s. However, heavy industry, particularly the sulphurous emissions from the vast nickel-smelting works on the Kola Peninsula, were accused of causing major environmental damage by the neighbouring Nordic nations (agreement on the monitoring and limiting of this was achieved, to an extent, in mid-1996). The concentration of nuclear reactors on the Kola Peninsula, considered to be the world's most hazardous, is also a major source of concern—in July 2002 the European Union pledged considerable funds to improving atomic safety and environmental degradation in the region. In the 1990s political allegiances in the Oblast as a whole were fairly evenly balanced, with both the reformist Yabloko movement and the nationalist Liberal Democrats receiving over 10% of the votes cast overall in the 1995 and, more unusually, the 1999 general elections, although disparity by area was immense. A candidate favoured by Aleksandr Lebed, Yurii Yevdokimov, was elected in the Oblast's first ever direct poll to the governorship, held in November 1996, after a second round; he was re-elected, with 86% of the votes cast, on 26 March 2000. A power-sharing agreement was signed between the federal and regional authorities in November 1997. On 21 March 2002 elections to the regional legislature were held.

Economy

In 1999 Murmansk Oblast's gross regional product stood at 42,976.7m. roubles, or 43,332.0 roubles per head. The Oblast's principal industrial centres are at Murmansk, Monchegorsk, Kirovsk, Zapolyarnyi and Apatity. In 2000 there were 891 km of railway track in the region, with Murmansk, Apatity, Olenegorsk and Kandalaksha the main railway junctions, and 2,503 km of paved roads. The port at Murmansk is Russia's sole all-weather Northern port, through which some 12m. metric tons of cargo pass every year. This is also the base for the world's only nuclear ice-breaker fleet, the Northern Fleet, and the scene of the 'Kursk' submarine disaster in August 2000. There is an international airport at Murmansk, which operates flights to destinations in Finland, Norway and Sweden.

The Oblast's agricultural sector, which, owing to its extreme climate, employed just 2.0% of the work-force in 2000, consists mainly of fishing (the region produces 45% of the country's fish supplies) and animal husbandry. In 2000 agricultural production generated a total of 1,107m. roubles. The territory is rich in natural resources, including phosphates, iron ore and rare and non-ferrous metals. In 1985 the Shtokmanovsk gas-condensate deposit, the world's largest, was opened on the continental shelf of the Barents Sea. It was hoped that by 2005 the deposit would supply most of the north and north-west of the country. The region produces almost all of Russia's apatites, over 40% of its nickel, some 14% of its refined copper and about 11% of its concentrates of iron. Some 26.9% of the Oblast's working population were engaged in industry in 2000, when the industrial sector generated 48,585m. roubles. Its major industries are the production and enrichment of ores and ferrous metals, ore-mining, ferrous metallurgy, chemicals and petro-chemicals, the production of electricity and food-processing. In 1995 the United Nations Development Programme approved a project to strengthen the economy of the area and encourage sustainable development. In 1999 LUKoil, the domestic petroleum producer, signed an agreement with Governor Yevdokimov, which made Murmansk a base for exploration of the Barents Sea, in association with the natural-gas producer, Gazprom. LUKoil also agreed to accept payment in barter, in addition to money, for supplies of petroleum to the region. In late November 2002 LUKoil and three other large-scale domestic petroleum companies, Tyumen Oil Co (TNK), Siberian Oil Co (Sibneft) and Yukos, announced that they were to co-operate in the development of a deep-sea oil terminal in Murmansk, and connecting pipelines, at a projected cost of some US $4,500m., in an attempt to increase exports.

In 2000 the region's economically active population numbered some 583,000. Unemployment declined in the late 1990s, from 21.1% of the labour force in 1998, to 12.8% in 2000. In mid-2002 the average monthly wage in the Oblast was some 7,275.8 roubles, one of the highest in the Federation. The 2000 budget recorded a surplus of 104.6m. roubles. The Oblast's major exports are non-ferrous metals, fish products and apatite concentrate. In 2000 exports amounted to US $592.6m., and imports were worth $130.3m. Foreign investment totalled $44.0m. in 2000. The Kola Centre for Business Development, employing Russian and US specialists, opened in Murmansk in 1997. It holds annual conventions bringing together companies from across and outside the Barents Region. At 31 December 2000 there were 2,900 small businesses registered in the Oblast.

Directory

Head of the Regional Administration (Governor): YURII A. YEVDOKIMOV; 183006 Murmansk, pr. Lenina 75; tel. (8152) 48-62-01; fax (8152) 47-65-03; e-mail evdokimov@murman.ru; internet gov.murman.ru.

Chairman of the Regional Duma: PAVEL A. SAZHINOV; 183016 Murmansk, ul. S. Perovskoi 2; tel. (8152) 45-36-72; fax (8152) 45-97-79; e-mail murduma@com .mels.ru.

Chief Representative of Murmansk Oblast in the Russian Federation: PETR I. ZELENOV; 103851 Moscow, ul. B. Nikitskaya 12; tel. (095) 229-69-77; fax (095) 229-53-51.

Head of Murmansk City Administration: OLEG P. NAIDENOV; 183006 Murmansk, pr. Lenina 75; tel. (8152) 45-81-60.

Nizhnii Novgorod Oblast

Nizhnii Novgorod Oblast is situated on the middle reaches of the Volga river. It forms part of the Volga Federal Okrug and the Volga-Vyatka Economic Area. Mordoviya and Ryazan lie to the south, Vladimir and Ivanovo to the west, Kostroma to the north-west, Kirov to the north-east and Marii-El and Chuvashiya to the east. Its major rivers are the Volga, the Oka, the Sura and the Vetluga. The terrain in the north of the Oblast is mainly low lying, with numerous forests and extensive swampland. The southern part is characterized by fertile black soil (*chernozem*). The Oblast occupies a total area of 76,900 sq km (29,690 sq miles) and measures some 400 km (250 miles) from south to north and 300 km from east to west. It is divided into 48 administrative districts and 28 cities. At 1 January 2002 it had an estimated total population of 3,598,300 and a population density, therefore, of 46.8 per sq km. Some 78.2% of the Oblast's inhabitants resided in urban areas in 2001. Its administrative centre is at Nizhnii Novgorod (formerly Gorkii), which lies at the confluence of the Volga and Oka rivers. The city is Russia's fourth largest, with a population of 1,343,300 in 2001. Other major cities include Dzerzhinsk (formerly Chernorech—with an estimated population of 274,900 in 2001), Arzamas (109,600), Sarov (formerly Arzamas-16—84,900) and Pavlovo (69,600).

History

Nizhnii Novgorod city was founded in 1221 on the borders of the Russian principalities. With the decline of Tatar power the city was absorbed by the Muscovite state. The Sarov Monastery, one of Russian Orthodoxy's most sacred sites, was founded in the region. Industrialization took place in the late tsarist

197

period. In 1905 mass unrest occurred among peasants and workers in the region, which was one of the first areas of Russia to be seized by the Bolsheviks in late 1917. Nizhnii Novgorod Oblast was formed on 14 January 1929. In 1932–90 the city and region were named Gorkii, and for much of the time the city was 'closed', owing to the importance of the defence industry.

In 1991 the Russian President, Boris Yeltsin, appointed a leading local reformer, Boris Nemtsov, Head of the Regional Administration (Governor). Nemtsov instituted a wide-ranging programme of economic reform, which was widely praised by liberals and by the federal Government. Nemtsov secured popular election in December 1995, and was a prominent advocate of democratization and decentralization in the Federation. In June 1996 Nemtsov signed a treaty on the delimitation of powers with the federal Government, giving the Oblast greater budgetary independence and more control over its public property. In April 1997 Nemtsov was appointed to the federal Government; gubernatorial elections were subsequently held, in which the pro-Government candidate, Ivan Sklyarov (former Mayor of Nizhnii Novgorod), defeated Gennadii Khodyrev (who was supported both by the Communist Party of the Russian Federation—CPRF and the nationalist Liberal Democrats) after a 'run-off' vote in July. The Oblast's economic situation subsequently deteriorated somewhat, and the federal Government withheld funds for the continuing conversion of the Oblast's defence industry. At the second round of gubernatorial elections held in July 2001, Khodyrev, by this time a CPRF deputy in the State Duma, was elected Governor, obtaining almost 60% of the votes cast. Following his election, Khodyrev suspended his membership of the CPRF, apparently in response to allegations that the federal Government was to transfer the administrative centre of the Volga Federal Okrug to another city in the event of the election of a communist governor. In mid-September the regional Legislative Assembly voted in favour of a proposal made by Khodyrev that he act both as Governor and as Prime Minister of the Oblast. In 2001 the city of Nizhnii Novgorod became the first area in Russia to implement proposals that permitted objectors to compulsory military service to perform an alternative, civilian service; however, in early 2002 President Putin criticized these measures, and several of those undertaking civilian service were subsequently inducted into the military. Elections to the regional Legislative Assembly in March 2002 resulted in the formation of a centre-right majority in the new chamber, including many representatives of business interests in the Oblast, with Unity and Fatherland-United Russia becoming the single largest party grouping. In April the power-sharing treaty agreed in 1996 was annulled. Khodyrev finally resigned from the CPRF in May 2002, in protest at the expulsion of State Duma Chairman Gennadii Seleznev from the party.

Economy

In 1999 the Oblast's gross regional product amounted to 83,456.2m. roubles, or 22,741.4 roubles per head. Its principal industrial centres are at Nizhnii Novgorod, Dzerzhinsk and Arzamas. Nizhnii Novgorod contains a major river-port, from which it is possible to reach the Baltic, Black, White and Caspian Seas and the Sea of Azov. In 2000 there were 12,978 km of paved roads and 1,214 km of railway track in the region. In 1985 an underground railway system opened in Nizhnii Novgorod and in 1994 an international airport was opened, from which Lufthansa (of Germany) operates flights to the German city of Frankfurt. In late

1996 plans to extend the Second Trans-European Corridor to Nizhnii Novgorod were initiated by the Russian Government and the European Union.

Reform of the farming sector in the 1990s involved extensive privatization and investment in rural infrastructure. Agriculture in the region, which employed 7.7% of the working population in 2000, consists mainly of the production of grain, sugar beet, flax and onions and other vegetables, although the Oblast lacks many areas with the fertile black topsoil typical of the European Plain. Animal husbandry and poultry farming are also important. In 2000 total agricultural output was worth 15,212m. roubles. As one of the three most industrially developed regions in Russia, however, it was the Oblast's industry that provided some 80% of total production (industrial output generated 106,984m. roubles in 2000). The principal industries of the Oblast include the manufacture of automobiles, mechanical engineering, metal-working, ferrous metallurgy, chemicals, petrochemicals, the processing of agricultural and forestry products, the production of electricity and light manufacturing. The Italian automobile company, Fiat, announced a joint venture with the GAZ—Gorkii Automobile plant for the production, sale and servicing of three models of car in Nizhnii Novgorod by 2002. In 2000 some 30.3% of the working population was engaged in industry. During the Soviet period the region was developed as a major military-industrial centre, with the defence sector accounting for around three-quarters of the regional economy, and Gorkii became a 'closed' city. The Oblast also contains the secret city of Arzamas-16 (now Sarov), a centre of nuclear research. In the early 1990s much of Governor Nemtsov's reform programme was aimed at the conversion of as much of the industrial base to civilian use as possible, but this process was made increasingly difficult as federal funds became less readily available. Indeed, defence-industry production in the region increased by 130% in 1999 compared with the previous year, although, overall, the Oblast was among those that dealt most successfully with the transition from military to civilian industry.

The economically active population numbered 1,871,000 in 2000, when 7.5% of the labour force were unemployed. The average monthly wage in the Oblast was 3,403.5 roubles in mid-2002. The 2000 budget recorded a deficit of 1,267.6m. roubles. In 2000 external trade in the Oblast comprised US $861.8m. in exports and $321.2m. in imports. The Oblast exports principally to Belarus, Belgium, France, Kazakhstan, Switzerland and the United Kingdom, and imports goods from Austria, Belarus, the People's Republic of China, Germany, Kazakhstan, the Netherlands, Ukraine and the USA. In 1997 there were 1,153 joint-stock companies in the region, as well as 34 commercial banks and 35 insurance companies. Nizhnii Novgorod Oblast was the first Russian federal subject, other than the two federal cities, to have issued Eurobonds. In 2000 foreign investment in the region totalled $64.3m. Infrastructure for small-business development had resulted in the emergence of some 13,600 small businesses by the end of 2000.

Directory

Head of the Regional Administration (Governor and Prime Minister): GENNA-DII M. KHODYREV; 603082 Nizhnii Novgorod, Kreml, kor. 1; tel. (8312) 39-13-30; fax (8312) 39-06-29; e-mail official@kreml.nnov.ru.

Chairman of the Legislative Assembly: YEVGENII B. LYULIN; 603082 Nizhnii Novgorod, Kreml, kor. 2; tel. (8312) 30-91-36; fax (8312) 30-91-55; e-mail nnovg@duma.gov.ru.

Representation of Nizhnii Novgorod Oblast in the Russian Federation: Moscow; tel. (095) 203-77-41.

Head of Nizhnii Novgorod City Administration (Mayor): VADIM BULAVINOV; 603082 Nizhnii Novgorod, Kreml, kor. 5; tel. (8312) 39-15-06; fax (8312) 39-13-02; e-mail lebedev@admgor.nnov.ru; internet www.admcity.nnov.ru.

Novgorod Oblast

Novgorod Oblast is situated in the north-west of the Eastern European Plain, some 500 km (just over 300 miles) north-west of Moscow and 180 km south of St Petersburg. It forms part of the North-Western Federal Okrug and the North-Western Economic Area. Tver Oblast lies to the south-east, Pskov Oblast to the south-west and Leningrad and Vologda Oblasts to the north. The territory's major rivers are the Msta, the Lovat and the outlet of Lake Ilmen, the Volkhov. Just over two-fifths of its territory is forested (either taiga—forested marshland—or mixed forest). The region contains the Valdai state national park. Its territory covers an area of 55,300 sq km (21,350 sq miles) and extends 250 km from south to north and 385 km from west to east. It is divided into 21 administrative districts and 10 cities. At 1 January 2002 the population of the Oblast was estimated at 710,900 and its population density, therefore, was 12.9 per sq km. In 2001 the urban population was reckoned at 70.6% of the total. The region's administrative centre is at Great (Velikii) Novgorod, which lies on the River Volkhov, some 6 km from Lake Ilmen (it had a population of some 226,500 in 2001).

History

One of the oldest Russian cities, Great Novgorod remained a powerful principality after the dissolution of Kievan Rus, and even after the Mongol incursions further to the south-west. In 1478 Ivan III ('the Great'), prince of Muscovy and the first Tsar of All Russia, destroyed the Republic of Novgorod, a polity sometimes used as evidence for the rather spurious claim of a democratic tradition in Russia. Its wealth and importance, based on trade, declined after the foundation of St Petersburg. Novgorod Oblast was formed on 5 July 1944.

In the mid-1990s the region displayed a relatively high level of support for reformists and the centrist supporters of the federal Government of President Boris Yeltsin. The Oblast was permitted gubernatorial elections in December 1995, which were won by the pro-Yeltsin incumbent, Mikhail Prusak. Prusak's administration was characterized by his policy of pragmatic compromise with regard to the economy, spreading the region's economic benefits as widely as possible. Similar policies prevailed in the Duma, the members of which did not bear allegiance to any national political party. Prusak, whose policies were widely admired by national political leaders, including the federal President elected in 2000, Vladimir Putin, was re-elected for a further term of office on 5 September 1999, with approximately 90% of the votes cast. Prusak (who was appointed as Chairman of the Democratic Party of Russia in September 2001) combined demands for regional governors to be appointed rather than elected, and even for the end of direct elections to the federal presidency, with support for the purported (historical) 'Novgorod model' of federalism, property rights and subsidiarity.

Economy

In 1999 Novgorod Oblast's gross regional product amounted to 16,409.7m. roubles, equivalent to 22,417.7 roubles per head. The Oblast's major industrial centres are at Great Novgorod and Staraya Russa (a 19th century resort town famous for its mineral and radon springs and therapeutic mud). The major Moscow–St Petersburg road and rail routes pass through the region. In 2000 there were 1,147 km (713 miles) of railways on the Oblast's territory. The road system, comprising 8,644 km of paved roads in 2000, is its major transport network.

The region's agriculture, which employed 12.1% of the work-force in 2000, consists mainly of flax production and animal husbandry. Its major natural resource is timber: in the late 1990s some 2.5m. cu m were produced annually, but it was thought that there was potential for this amount to be expanded by four or five times. In 2000 total agricultural production amounted to a value of 4,314m. roubles. The region's major industries include mechanical engineering, chemicals, wood-working, the processing of forestry and agricultural products, ferrous metallurgy and electricity production. The industrial sector employed 24.6% of the working population in 2000, and generated 18,909m. roubles. Great Novgorod city is an important tourist destination, attracting around 1m. visitors annually.

The economically active population totalled 365,000 in 2000, when 7.8% of the labour force were unemployed. Those in employment in mid-2002 earned an average wage of 3,557.5 roubles per month. In 2000 the regional budget showed a surplus of 57.6m. roubles. In that year the external trade of the Oblast comprised US $271.6m. in exports and $64.4m. in imports. Legislative conditions for foreign investors in Novgorod Oblast were considered to be favourable in the 1990s, owing to a foreign company's exemption from all local taxes until its project returned a profit. The multinational company Cadbury's Schweppes invested $150m. in a chocolate factory in the region, which opened in 1996 and was the largest project the company had been involved in, outside the United Kingdom. In 2000 total foreign investment in the region amounted to $49.5m. At 31 December 2000 there were 3,000 small businesses registered in the region.

Directory

Head of the Regional Administration (Governor): MIKHAIL M. PRUSAK; 173005 Velikii Novgorod, Sofiiskaya pl. 1; tel. (8162) 13-12-02; internet region.adm.nov.ru.

Chairman of the Regional Duma: ANATOLII A. BOITSEV; 173005 Velikii Novgorod, Sofiiskaya pl. 1; tel. (81622) 7-54-60.

Chief Representative of Novogorod Oblast in the Russian Federation: VLADI-

MIR N. PODOPRIGORA; 127006 Moscow, ul. M. Dmitrovka 3/219–220; fax (095) 299-40-04.

Head of Great (Velikii) Novgorod City Administration (Mayor): NIKOLAI GRAZHDANKIN; 173007 Velikii Novgorod, ul. B. Vlasevskaya 4; tel. (81622) 7-30-58; fax (8162) 13-25-99; e-mail mayor@adm.nov.ru; internet www.adm.nov.ru.

Novosibirsk Oblast

Novosibirsk Oblast is situated in the south-east of the Western Siberian Plain, at the Ob-Irtysh confluence. The Oblast forms part of the Siberian Federal Okrug and the West Siberian Economic Area. Its south-western districts lie on the international border with Kazakhstan. The neighbouring federal territories are Omsk Oblast to the west, Tomsk Oblast to the north, Kemerovo Oblast to the east and Altai Krai to the south. The region's major rivers are the Ob and the Om. The Oblast has around 3,000 lakes, the four largest being Chany, Sartlan, Ubinskoye and Uryum. About one-third of its territory is swampland. It occupies a total area of 178,200 sq km (68,800 sq miles) and measures over 400 km (250 miles) from south to north and over 600 km from west to east. It is divided into 30 administrative districts and 14 cities. At 1 January 2002 the Oblast had an estimated population of 2,717,400, and a population density, therefore, of 15.2 per sq km. In 2001 some 73.9% of the population inhabited urban areas. There is a small German community in the Oblast, constituting 2.2% of its population in 1989. Just over one-half of the region's inhabitants live in its administrative centre, Novosibirsk, which had a population of 1,393,200 in 2001. Other major cities included Berdsk (87,100) and Iskitim (68,400).

History

The city of Novosibirsk (known as Novonikolayevsk until 1925) was founded in 1893, during the construction of the Trans-Siberian Railway. It became prosperous through its proximity to the Kuznetsk coal basin (Kuzbass). The Oblast, which was formed on 28 September 1937, increased in population throughout the Soviet period as it became heavily industrialized, and was a major centre of industrial production during the Second World War.

In October 1993 the Russian President, Boris Yeltsin, dismissed the head of the regional administration, Vitalii Mukha. In 1994 elections were held to a new representative body, which was dominated by the Communist Party of the Russian Federation (CPRF), following elections in 1994 and 1998. It was constantly in dispute with the regional administration, the head of which was a presidential appointment. In an effort to resolve this power struggle, the President permitted the Oblast a gubernatorial election in December 1995. It was the CPRF candidate, Mukha, who was returned to his former post by the electorate. Despite his support for the communists, Mukha failed publicly to endorse any federal presidential candidate prior to the June 1996 elections. He was involved in further disagreements, primarily over unpaid debts, with the federal authorities during the late 1990s. In January 2000 another politician regarded as a left-wing statist, despite his reported closeness to 'oligarch' Boris Berezovskii, was elected as the new regional Governor. Viktor Tolokonskii, who had previously served as Mayor of Novosibirsk City, defeated Ivan Starikov, the federal deputy economy minister, by a margin of just 2% in the second round of voting. Support for the CPRF declined somewhat in the regional legislative elections of December 2001, when the party and its ally, the Agrarian Party of Russia, secured just 18 of the 49 seats available, while the remainder were filled by independent candidates.

Economy

In 1999 Novosibirsk Oblast's gross regional product stood at 58,301.8m. roubles, or 21,217.6 roubles per head. Novosibirsk city is a port on the Ob river, and is also the region's principal industrial centre. In 2000 there were 1,530 km of railways and 9,506 km of paved roads on the Oblast's territory. There are four airports in the region, including Tolmachevo, an international airport.

The Oblast's agriculture employed 15.6% of its working population in 2000 and consists mainly of animal husbandry, fur-animal breeding and the production of grain, vegetables, potatoes and flax. Agriculture generated 21,678m. roubles in 2000, compared with a total of 36,487m. roubles contributed by the industrial sector. Extraction industries involved the production of coal, petroleum, natural gas, peat, marble, limestone and clay. Manufacturing industry includes non-ferrous metallurgy, mechanical engineering, metal-working, chemicals, electricity generation, food-processing, light manufacturing, timber production and the manufacture of building materials. Industry employed some 18.6% of the region's work-force in 2000. In the mid-1990s the region's defence industry was largely converted to civilian use—by 1999 only 15% of the output from the former military-industrial complex was for military purposes.

The Oblast's economically active population totalled 1,380,000 in 2000, when 13.4% of the labour force were unemployed. The average monthly wage in the region was 3,892.7 roubles in mid-2002. The 2000 budget showed a deficit of 798.7m. roubles. In 2000 the Oblast's external trade comprised US $463.8m. in exports and $262.2m. in imports. In the same year foreign investment in the Oblast totalled some $157.2m. roubles. At the end of the year there were some 23,700 small businesses registered in the region, one of the largest figures in any federal subject outside Moscow and St Petersburg.

Directory

Head of the Regional Administration (Governor): VIKTOR A. TOLOKONSKII; 630011 Novosibirsk, Krasnyi pr. 18; tel. (3832) 23-08-62; fax (3832) 23-57-00; internet www.adm.nso.ru

Chairman of the Regional Council of People's Deputies: VIKTOR V. LEONOV; 630011 Novosibirsk, ul. Kirova 3; tel. (3832) 23-62-52; fax (3832) 23-23-78.

Chief Representative of Novosibirsk Oblast in the Russian Federation: NINA M. PIRYAZEVA; Moscow; tel. (095) 203-27-20.

Head of Novosibirsk City Administration (Mayor): VLADIMIR F. GORODETSKII; 630099 Novosibirsk, Krasnyi pr. 34; tel. (3832) 22-49-32; fax (3832) 22-08-58; e-mail cic@admnsk.ru; internet novosibirsk.sol.ru.

Omsk Oblast

Omsk Oblast is situated in the south of the Western Siberian Plain on the middle reaches of the Irtysh river. Kazakhstan lies to the south. Other federal subjects that neighbour the Oblast are Tyumen to the north-west and Tomsk and Novosibirsk to the east. Omsk forms part of the Siberian Federal Okrug and the West Siberian Economic Area. Its major rivers are the Irtysh, the Ishim, the Om and the Tara. Much of its territory is marshland and about one-quarter is forested. The total area of Omsk Oblast covers some 139,700 sq km (53,920 sq miles). It measures some 600 km (370 miles) from south to north and 500 km from west to east and is divided into 32 administrative districts and six cities. At 1 January 2002 the region had a total population of 2,127,000 and a population density, therefore, of 15.2 per sq km. Of the Oblast's inhabitants, some 67.2% lived in urban areas in 2001. Its administrative centre is at Omsk, which lies at the confluence of the Ob and Irtysh rivers and had a population of 1,138,400 in 2001.

History

The city of Omsk was founded as a fortress in 1716. In 1918 it became the seat of Adm. Aleksandr Kolchak's 'all-Russian Government' (in which he was 'Supreme

207

Ruler'). However, Omsk fell to the Bolsheviks in 1919 and Kolchak 'abdicated' in January 1920. Omsk Oblast was formed on 7 December 1934.

In the 1990s the region was generally supportive of the Communist Party of the Russian Federation (CPRF), although the nationalist Liberal Democrats also enjoyed a significant level of popularity. The regional Governor, Leonid Polezhayev, although a supporter of the federal state President, Boris Yeltsin, was well respected locally and was re-elected in December 1995. In May 1996 the regional and federal administrations signed a treaty on the delimitation of powers. Legislative elections were held in the Oblast on 22 March 1998, in which the CPRF and other leftist candidates won 30 assembly seats and a majority of seats on Omsk city council. Polezhayev was re-elected in September 1999, defeating the regional leader of the CPRF, Aleksandr Kravets. Nevertheless, Omsk was one of four regions in which the CPRF candidate, Gennadii Zyuganov, received a larger proportion of the votes cast than Vladimir Putin in the federal presidential election of March 2000. The Oblast abolished its power-sharing treaty with the Federal Government in mid-2001. At elections to the Legislative Assembly on 24 March 2002 supporters of Polezhayev, including, notably, members of the Unity and Fatherland-United Russia party, retained control of the Assembly.

Economy

In 1999 Omsk Oblast's gross regional product amounted to 40,591.1m. roubles, equivalent to 18,702.1 roubles per head. Omsk is one of the highest-ranking cities in Russia in terms of industrial output. The region lies on the Trans-Siberian Railway and is a major transport junction. In 2000 it contained 775 km of railway track, 7,662 km of paved roads and over 1,250 km of navigable waterways. There were also some 580 km of pipeline on its territory, carrying petroleum and petroleum products. There are two airports—a third, international airport was under construction in the late 1990s.

The Oblast's soil is the fertile black earth (*chernozem*) characteristic of the region. Its agriculture, which generated a total of 15,827m. roubles in 2000, and employed some 19.0% of the work-force, consists mainly of the production of grain, flax, sunflower seeds and vegetables, and animal husbandry and hunting. The region's mineral reserves include clay, peat and lime. There are also deposits of petroleum and natural gas. Industry employed 18.5% of the work-force in 2000. The Oblast's main industries are electricity generation, fuel, chemical and petrochemical production, mechanical engineering, petroleum-refining and food-processing. Total industrial production amounted to a value of 28,494m. roubles in 2000. The Omsk petroleum refinery is one of Russia's largest and most modern and is part of Sibneft (Siberian Oil Co), one of the country's newer, vertically integrated petroleum companies. The region's exports primarily comprise chemical, petrochemical and petroleum products.

The economically active population numbered 1,040,000 in 2000, when 13.9% of the region's labour force were unemployed, almost twice the rate recorded in 1996. In mid-2002 the average wage in the Oblast was 3,464.0 roubles per month, although it was named as one of the worst regions in Russia for wages arrears. The 2000 budget recorded a surplus of 326.1m. roubles. In that year external trade comprised US $911.2m. in exports and $150.9m. in imports. The Oblast's main trading partners include the People's Republic of China, Cyprus, Germany, Kazakhstan, Spain, Switzerland and the United Kingdom. Foreign investment in the region in 2000 totalled some $791.8m., an increase of 75% compared with 1998. In that year there were some 74 enterprises in the Oblast with foreign capital. At 31 December 2000 there was a total of 10,900 small businesses registered in the region.

Directory

Head of the Regional Administration (Governor): LEONID K. POLEZHAYEV; 644002 Omsk, ul. Krasnyi Put 1; tel. (3812) 24-14-15; fax (3812) 24-23-72; e-mail webmaster@info.omskelecom.ru; internet region.omskelecom.ru.

Chairman of the Regional Legislative Assembly: VLADIMIR A. VARNAVSKII; 640002 Omsk, ul. Krasnyi Put 1; tel. (3812) 24-23-33; fax (3812) 23-24-66; e-mail root@topos.omsk.ru.

Representation of Omsk Oblast in the Russian Federation: 107078 Moscow, per. B. Kozlovskii 14–15/1; tel. (095) 921-65-54; fax (095) 921-21-57.

Head of Omsk City Administration (Mayor): YEVGENII I. BELOV; 644099 Omsk, ul. Gagarina 34; tel. (3812) 24-30-33; fax (3812) 24-49-34; e-mail grad@omsknet.ru; internet www.omsk.ru.

Orel Oblast

Orel Oblast is situated in the central part of the Eastern European Plain within the Central Russian Highlands. The Oblast forms part of the Central Federal Okrug and the Central Economic Area. It is surrounded by five other oblasts: Kursk (to the south), Bryansk (west), Kaluga (north-west), Tula (north-east) and Lipetsk (east). The Ukrainian border lies some 180 km (just over 100 miles) to the south-west. The Oblast's major river is the Oka, the source of which is found in the south-west. There are a total of around 2,000 rivers, with a combined length of 9,100 km, although none are navigable. Just over 7% of the Oblast's area is forested. The territory of Orel Oblast covers an area of 24,700 sq km (9,530 sq miles) and is divided, for administrative purposes, into 24 districts and seven cities. At 1 January 2002 the estimated population of the Oblast was 883,500 and the population density was 35.8 per sq km. Some 62.8% of the inhabitants of the region lived in urban areas in 2001. The Oblast's administrative centre is at Orel, which had 338,800 inhabitants in 2001. Other major cities are Livny (53,600) and Mtsensk (50,300).

History

Orel was founded as a fortress in 1566. In the 1860s it served as a place of exile for Polish insurgents and was later a detention centre for prisoners on their way to exile in Siberia. Orel Oblast was formed on 27 September 1937. In post-Soviet Russia it formed part of the political 'red belt'. The Communist Party candidate defeated the pro-Government incumbent in elections for a head of the regional administration in December 1992. The victor was eventually dismissed and the regional legislature dissolved by presidential decree, following its criticism of the federal Government during the constitutional crisis of 1993. A 50-seat Regional Duma, elected in March 1994, was dominated by the Communist Party of the Russian Federation (CPRF), which received 45% of the votes cast in the Oblast during the 1995 elections to the State Duma. Despite the loyalty to President Yeltsin shown by the head of the regional administration, Yegor Stroyev (a former cabinet member and the speaker of the upper house of the federal parliament, the Federation Council), the greatest show of support in the presidential election of 1996 was for Gennadii Zyuganov, the CPRF candidate. Although Orel Oblast was Zyuganov's home region, he received 44.6% of the regional votes cast in the federal presidential election of 26 March 2000, which was 1.2% fewer than the number of votes cast in support of Vladimir Putin. In the regional legislative elections of March 1998 just 11 CPRF deputies were elected, compared with the 37 seats won by candidates nominated by initiative groups. Stroyev was re-elected Governor, with more than 97% of the votes cast, in October 1997. He was one of the most consistent opponents of power-sharing agreements between regional and federal government, and in September 2000 he advocated closer co-operation with the People's Republic of China and other Asian countries. Following his re-election as Governor in October 2001, Stroyev resigned from the Federation Council in early December, in order to comply with legislation introduced by President Putin, which prevented regional governors from holding seats in the Council. In the regional legislative elections held in March 2002 the CPRF retained just three seats.

Economy
Orel Oblast's gross regional product amounted to 17,928.2m. roubles in 1999, equivalent to 19,884.8 roubles per head. The principal industrial centres in the region are at Orel, Livny and Mtsensk. Orel city lies on the Moscow–Simferopol (Crimea, Ukraine) highway and is an important railway junction. In 2000 there were 590 km of railway track in the Oblast and 4,032 km of paved roads.

Orel Oblast is an important agricultural trade centre. In 2000 around 21.6% of the economically active population were engaged in agriculture. Agricultural production consists mainly of grain, sugar beet, sunflower seeds, potatoes, vegetables, hemp and animal husbandry, and amounted to a value of 9,567m. roubles in 2000. There are some 17.5m. cu m of timber reserves in the Oblast and a major source of iron ore, at Novoyaltinskoye. However, this and reserves of other minerals in the region have generally not been exploited to their full potential. The industrial sector employed around 22.2% of the economically active population in 2000 and generated some 13,805m. roubles in that year. The Oblast's main industries are mechanical engineering, metallurgy, chemicals, light manufacturing, the production of building materials and food-processing. It produces around one-third of its electrical-energy requirements, the remainder being supplied by neighbouring Oblasts (Tula, Kursk and Lipetsk).

The region's economically active population numbered 445,000 in 2000, when 8.5% of the labour force were unemployed. In mid-2002 those in employment earned an average of 3,079.6 roubles per month. There was a budgetary surplus of 53.9m. roubles in 2000. In that year external trade amounted to a value of US $83.3m. in exports, and $121.4m. in imports. Total foreign investment in Orel Oblast amounted to $42.8m. At 31 December 2000 there were some 2,500 small businesses in operation in the region.

Directory
Head of the Regional Administration (Governor): YEGOR S. STROYEV; 302021 Orel, pl. Lenina 1; tel. (0862) 41-63-13; fax (0862) 41-25-30; e-mail post@adm .oryol.ru; internet www.adm.orel.ru.

Chairman of the Regional Duma: NIKOLAI A. VOLODIN; 302021 Orel, pl. Lenina 1; tel. (0862) 41-58-53; fax (0862) 41-60-22.

Chief Representative of Orel Oblast in the Russian Federation: MARINA G. ROGACHEVA; 109240 Moscow, ul. Goncharnaya 12/3; tel. (095) 915-85-51; fax (095) 915-86-14.

Head of Orel City Administration (Mayor): VASILII I. UVAROV; 302000 Orel, Proletarskaya gora 1; tel. (0862) 43-33-12; fax (08622) 6-39-44.

Orenburg Oblast

Orenburg Oblast is situated in the foothills of the Southern Urals. It forms part of the Volga Federal Okrug and the Urals Economic Area. Orenburg sprawls along the international border with Kazakhstan, which lies to the south and east. Samara Oblast lies to the west, and in the north-west of the territory there is a short border with the Republic of Tatarstan. The Republic of Bashkortostan and Chelyabinsk Oblast neighbour the north of the Oblast. Orenburg's major river is the Ural. The region occupies a total area of 124,000 sq km (47,860 sq miles) and is divided into 35 districts and 12 cities. At 1 January 2002 the total population of the Oblast was 2,199,400 and the population density was, therefore, 17.7 per sq km. In 2001 some 56.8% of the population lived in urban areas. The Oblast's administrative centre is at Orenburg, which had 516,600 inhabitants in 2001. Other major cities are Orsk (274,600) and Novotroitsk (109,600).

History

The city of Orenburg originated as a fortress in 1743. During the revolutionary period Orenburg was a headquarters of 'White' forces and possession of it was fiercely contested with the Bolsheviks. The city was also a centre of Kazakh (then erroneously known as Kyrgyz) nationalists and was the capital of the Kyrgyz ASSR in 1920–25. The region was then separated from the renamed Kazakh ASSR. Orenburg Oblast was formed on 7 December 1934.

The Communist Party of the Russian Federation (CPRF) remained the most popular party into the 1990s, winning 24% of the votes cast in the region at the general election of December 1995. Simultaneous elections to the post of governor, however, were won by the incumbent, Vladimir Yelagin, who was popular, despite expressing support for the Russian President, Boris Yeltsin. He was, however, defeated in the gubernatorial elections of December 1999 by the former chair of the State Duma Committee on Agrarian Issues, Aleksei Chernyshev. The region

213

was considered strategically important, owing to its proximity to Kazakhstan, a fact that led to the signature, on 30 January 1996, of an agreement between the regional administration and President Yeltsin. The accord defined the powers and areas of remit of the federal and local authorities. In regional legislative elections held at the end of March 1998 the CPRF maintained its relatively high level of support, but in the election of March 2002 the representation of left-wing deputies declined to just four seats. The power-sharing treaty signed in 1996 was annulled in April 2002.

Economy

The Oblast's gross regional product was 56,583.4m. roubles in 1999, or 25,411.3 roubles per head. In 2000 there were 1,652 km (1,027 miles) of railways and 13,032 km of paved roads on the Oblast's territory. Its principal industrial centres are at Orenburg, Orsk, Novotroisk, Mednogorsk, Buzuluk, and Buguruslan. Owing to the region's high degree of industrialization, and that of its neighbours, Chelyabinsk and Bashkortostan, there is a high level of pollution in the atmosphere. Around 1m. metric tons of harmful substances are emitted annually, including almost 700 tons of nickel and one ton of lead. In addition, the intensive exploitation of petroleum and gas deposits have caused serious damage to the land—around 60% of arable land is eroded or in danger of suffering erosion.

Agriculture in Orenburg Oblast, which employed 20.8% of the work-force in 2000, consisted mainly of grain, vegetable and sunflower production and animal husbandry. Agricultural output in the region in 2000 amounted to a value of 20,063m. roubles. The Oblast's major industries are ferrous and non-ferrous metallurgy, mechanical engineering, metal-working, natural gas production, electrical energy, chemicals, food-processing and the production of petroleum, ores, asbestos (the region produces around two-fifths of asbestos produced in Russia) and salt. In 2000 some 21.7% of the working population were engaged in industry, which generated a total of 63,704m. roubles.

The economically active population stood at 1,040,000 in 2000, when some 11.8% of the labour force were unemployed, more than twice the level recorded in 1996. The regional average monthly wage was 3,232.9 roubles in mid-2002. The Oblast's budget for 2000 showed a deficit of 2,716.6m. roubles, and in 2002 the region was named as one of the worst for wage arrears. In 2000 external trade comprised US $1,333.1m. in exports and $601.6m. in imports. Total foreign investment in the region in that year amounted to some $78.8m. At 31 December 2000 there were 7,600 small businesses registered in the Oblast.

Directory

Head of the Regional Administration (Governor): ANDREI A. CHERNYSHEV; 460015 Orenburg, Dom Sovetov; tel. (3532) 77-69-31; fax (3532) 77-38-02; e-mail office@gov.orb.ru; internet www.orb.ru.

Chairman of the Legislative Assembly: YURII V. TROFIMOV; 460015 Orenburg, Dom Sovetov; tel. (3532) 77-35-63; e-mail parlament@gov.orb.ru; internet www.parlament.orb.ru.

Chief Representative of Orenburg Oblast in the Russian Federation: VYACHESLAV S. RYABOV; 127025 Moscow, ul. Novyi Arbat 19/2014; tel. (095) 203-85-32; fax (095) 203-59-76.

Head of Orenburg City Administration (Mayor): YURII MISCHERYAKOV; 461300 Orenburg, ul. Sovetskaya 60; tel. (3532) 77-50-55; fax (3532) 77-60-58; e-mail glava@admin.orenburg.ru; internet www.orenburg.ru.

Penza Oblast

Penza Oblast is situated in the Volga Highlands (Privolzhskaya Vozvyshennost), to the south of the Republic of Mordoviya. It forms part of the Volga Federal Okrug and the Volga Economic Area and shares borders with Ulyanovsk Oblast to the east, Saratov Oblast to the south, Tambov Oblast to the south-west and touches Ryazan Oblast to the north-west. Penza's major river is the Sura, a tributary of the River Volga. Its territory covers an area of 43,200 sq km (16,750 sq miles) and is divided into 28 districts and 11 cities. At 1 January 2002 the population of the Oblast was estimated to be 1,504,100, giving a population density, therefore, of 34.8 per sq km. In 2001 some 64.4% of the population inhabited urban areas. Its administrative centre, Penza, had a population of 524,900 in 2001. The region's other major cities are Kuznetsk (97,500) and Zarechnyi (63,700).

History

The city of Penza was founded in 1663 as an outpost on the south-eastern border of the Russian Empire. The region was annexed by Bolshevik forces in late 1917 and remained under the control of the Red Army throughout the period of civil war. Penza Oblast was formed on 4 February 1939. Described as part of the 'red belt' of communist support in the 1990s, in 1992 the Communist Party candidate defeated the pro-Yeltsin Governor in elections to head the regional administration. The communists controlled the Legislative Assembly, elected in 1994 (although the federal presidency replaced the governor), and, almost exactly three years after the gubernatorial elections, obtained some 37% of the local vote in the federal general elections of December 1995. Although the presidentially appointed Governor, Anatolii Kovlyagin, was a member of the pro-Government movement, Our Home is Russia, he failed to give public support to the federal Government's reforms during the mid-1990s. On 12 April 1998 a new Governor, Vasilii Bochkarev, was elected. His campaign promoted effective management and pragmatism, and he contested the election as an independent. Bochkarev was re-elected on 14

April 2002, with the support of the pro-Government Unity and Fatherland-United Russia party.

Economy

In 1999 Penza's gross regional product was 19,686.5m. roubles, or 12,816.7 roubles per head. The Oblast's principal industrial centres are at Penza and Kuznetsk. In 2000 there were 827 km (514 miles) of railway track in the region, which included lines linking the territory to central and southern Russia as well as the Far East and Ukraine and Central Asia. Some 6,239 km of paved roads included several major highways.

Around three-quarters of the agricultural land in the Oblast consists of fertile black earth (*chernozem*). Agricultural activity, which employed 19.7% of the workforce in 2000, consists mainly of the production of grain, sugar beet, potatoes, sunflower seeds and hemp. Animal husbandry is also important. Total agricultural production amounted to a value of 7,883m. roubles in 2000. The main industries are mechanical engineering, the processing of timber and agricultural products, chemicals and the production of electricity. Industry employed some 23.1% of the working population in 2000, and generated 17,895m. roubles.

The economically active population in Penza Oblast numbered 768,000 in 2000, when 11.2% of the labour force were unemployed. Those in employment earned an average of 2,585.0 roubles per month in mid-2002. The 2000 regional budget showed a surplus of 122.8m. roubles. The external trade of the Oblast was relatively low, amounting to US $53.7m. in exports and $34.1m. in imports in 2000. Foreign investment in the Oblast in that year amounted to just $443,000. In 2000 there was a total of 6,100 small businesses registered in the Oblast.

Directory

Head of the Regional Administration (Governor): VASILII K. BOCHKAREV; 440025 Penza, ul. Moskovskaya 75; tel. (8412) 55-04-11; fax (8412) 63-35-75; e-mail pravobl@sura.com.ru; internet www.penza.ru.

Chairman of the Legislative Assembly: VIKTOR A. LAZUTKIN; 440025 Penza, ul. Moskovskaya 75; tel. (8412) 69-54-50; fax (8412) 55-25-95; e-mail zsobl@sura.ru.

Chief Representative of Penza Oblast in the Russian Federation: MELS U. NOSINOV; 127025 Moscow, ul. Novyi Arbat 19/1914; tel. (095) 203-10-75; fax (095) 203-48-93.

Head of Penza City Administration: ALEKSANDR S. KALASHNIKOV; 440064 Penza, Gorodskaya Duma, pl. Marshala Zhukova 4; tel. (8412) 66-29-85; fax (8412) 6-65-88.

Perm Oblast

Perm Oblast is situated on the western slopes of the Central and Northern Urals and the eastern edge of the Eastern European Plain. It forms part of the Volga Federal Okrug and the Urals Economic Area. The Komi-Permyak Autonomous Okrug (AOk) forms the north-western part of the Oblast, providing part of the northern border with the Republic of Komi and most of the western border with Kirov Oblast. The Republic of Udmurtiya also lies to the west, the Republic of Bashkortostan to the south and Sverdlovsk Oblast to the east. Apart from the Kama, its major rivers are the Chusovaya, the Kosva and the Vishera. The Kamsk reservoir lies in the centre of the region. Its territory, including that of the AOk, occupies an area of 160,600 sq km (61,990 sq miles) and extends some 600 km (370 miles) from south to north and 400 km from west to east. The Oblast, excluding the AOk, is divided into 29 districts and 24 cities. The region's total population at 1 January 2002 was estimated at 2,923,700, giving a population density of 18.2 per sq km. In 2001 some 75.1% of the population inhabited urban areas. The Oblast's administrative centre is at Perm, which had a population of 1,004,800 in 2001. Other major cities include Berezniki (with a population of 182,200) and Solikamsk (105,400).

History

Perm city was founded in 1723, with the construction of a copper foundry. Industrial development was such that by the latter part of the 20th century the city extended for some 80 km along the banks of the Kama. Perm Oblast was formed on 3 October 1938. The city was called Molotov in 1940–57 and entry was forbidden to foreigners until 1989. In December 1993 there were regional elections for a new parliament, the Legislative Assembly. On 31 May 1996 the regional administration signed a power-sharing treaty with the Russian President, Boris Yeltsin. In December the Governor, Genadii Igumnov, retained his post in direct elections, and pro-reform candidates loyal to Igumnov were successful in securing an absolute majority of seats in elections to the regional legislature in December 1997. Following the gubernatorial election held in December 2000, Igumnov was replaced as Governor by Yurii Trutnev, hitherto the Mayor of Perm City. Elections to a new Legislative Assembly were held in December 2001. In July 2002, following visits by the Chairman of the Federation Council, Sergei Mironov, and the Presidential Representative in the Volga Federal Okrug, Sergei Kiriyenko, to Perm and to Kudymkar, the administrative centre of the Komi-Permyak AOk, Trutnev announced that measures to merge the two federal subjects would be instigated in the near future.

Economy

All figures in this survey include data pertaining to the Komi-Permyak AOk, which is also treated separately. In 1999 Perm Oblast's gross regional product amounted to 94,893.9m. roubles, or 31,928.2 roubles per head. Its major industrial centres are at Perm, Berezniki, Solikamsk, Chusovoi and Krasnokamsk. In 2000 there were 1,494 km of railways and 10,143 km of paved roads on the Oblast's territory.

Agriculture in the Oblast, which in 2000 employed just 10.9% of the working population, consists mainly of grain and vegetable production and animal husbandry. In 2000 agricultural production was worth 14,977m. roubles, compared with a total in the industrial sector of 110,377m. roubles. The main industries are coal, petroleum, natural gas, potash and salt production, mechanical engineering, electro-technical industries, chemicals and petrochemicals, petroleum-refining, the processing of forestry and food products, ferrous and non-ferrous metallurgy, and printing. Some 25.6% of the working population were engaged in industry in 2000.

The economically active population numbered 1,466,000 in 2000, when 10.4% of the labour force were unemployed. The average wage was above the national average, amounting to 4,375.3 roubles per month in mid-2002. In 2000 there was a budgetary surplus of 323.2m. roubles. In that year external trade amounted to a value of US $2,341.8m. in exports and $265.6m. in imports. The region was named as the eighth-highest in Russia, in terms of investment potential, in late 1999, and in 2000 foreign investment amounted to $96.9m. At 31 December 2000 there were 8,200 small businesses registered in the region.

Directory

Governor: YURII P. TRUTNEV; 614006 Perm, ul. Kuibysheva 14; tel. (3422) 34-07-90; fax (3422) 34-89-52; internet www.trutnev.ru.

Chairman of the Legislative Assembly: NIKOLAI A. DEVYATKIN; 614006 Perm, ul. Lenina 51; tel. (3422) 58-75-55; fax (3422) 34-27-47; e-mail parliament @perm.ru; internet www.parliament.perm.ru.

Chief Representative of Perm Oblast in the Russian Federation: NIKOLAI P. ARTAMONOV; 103795 Moscow, ul. M. Dmitrovka 3; tel. (095) 299-48-36; fax (095) 209-08-97.

Head of Perm City Administration: ARKADII KAMENEV; 614000 Perm, ul. Lenina 15; tel. (3422) 12-44-01; fax (3422) 34-94-11; e-mail permduma@nevod.ru; internet www.gorodperm.ru.

Pskov Oblast

Pskov Oblast is situated on the Eastern European Plain. The Oblast forms part of the North-Western Federal Okrug and the North-Western Economic Area. It has international borders with Belarus to the south and Latvia and Estonia to the west. During the first half of the 1990s Estonia and Latvia questioned Russia's sovereignty of parts of Pskov Oblast and by the beginning of the 2000s there had still been no formal ratification of the now accepted border delimitations. Smolensk Oblast lies to the south-east, Tver and Novgorod Oblasts to the east and Leningrad Oblast to the north-east. Pskov's major river is the Velikaya and around two-fifths of its territory is forested. On its border with Estonia lie the Pskovskoye (Pihkva) and Chudskoye (Peipsi) lakes. Pskov Oblast covers an area of 55,300 sq km (21,350 sq miles) and measures 380 km (236 miles) from south to north and 260 km from west to east. It is divided into 24 administrative districts and 14 cities. The population at 1 January 2002 was estimated at 778,000 and the population density was, therefore, 14.1 per sq km. Around 94.3% of the territory's inhabitants were ethnic Russian in 1989, and 66.4% inhabited urban areas in 2001. The Oblast's administrative centre is at Pskov, which had a population of 200,100 in 2001. The second largest city is Velikiye Luki (115,000).

History

Pskov region was acquired by the Muscovite state in 1510. Previously, in 1242, it was the area in which Muscovite Prince Aleksandr Nevskii defeated an army of Teutonic knights, who sought to expand eastwards. The Oblast was created on 23 August 1944. Some territory to the south of Lake Pskov was transferred from Estonia to Pskov Oblast in 1945, remaining a cause for dispute between the newly independent Estonia and the Russian Federation in the 1990s. In 1995 Estonia formally renounced any territorial claim, but it remained eager to secure Russian acknowledgement of the 1920 Treaty of Tartu (by which Estonia had been awarded the disputed territory), which would render the Soviet occupation illegal. The Oblast was a traditional bastion of support for the extreme nationalist policies of Vladimir Zhirinovskii; a gubernatorial election was held on 21 October 1996, which was won by Yevgenii Mikhailov, a former Liberal Democrat deputy. The eastward expansion of the North Atlantic Treaty Organization (NATO) was a major issue in the election campaign, as were proposals that the regional Government receive a share of the customs revenue generated by trade with the Baltic States. As Governor, Mikhailov visited both the Chechen Republic of Ichkeriya (Chechnya) and the Serbian province of Kosovo and Metohija in the Federal Republic of Yugoslavia, reflecting the high levels of support for him among the military (accounting for approximately one-10th of the population of Pskov Oblast). Mikhailov was re-elected as Governor in November 2000.

Economy

In 1999 Pskov Oblast's gross regional product amounted to 11,548.8m. roubles, equivalent to 14,312.6 roubles per head. The Oblast's principal industrial centres are at Pskov and Velikiye Luki. In 2000 there were 1,092 km of railway track in the region and 9,954 km of paved roads. There is an airport at Pskov, which was upgraded to international status in the late 1990s.

In 1996–98 a federal programme for the socio-economic development of Pskov Oblast invested some 1,500,000m. old roubles in the improvement of agriculture in the region. Agricultural activity, which employed 21.4% of the work-force in 2000, consists mainly of animal husbandry and the production of grain, potatoes, vegetables and flax. Total output in the sector amounted to a value of 5,428m. roubles in 2000. The region's major industries are the production of electricity, manufacture of building materials, mechanical engineering, light manufacturing, food-processing and wood-working. Industry employed 18.9% of the working population in 2000, and generated 8,306m. roubles. According to local official sources, industry in the Oblast was completely privatized by 1995, although it was severely affected by the 1998 financial crisis, and the proportion of the working population employed in the sector declined by more than one-quarter in 1995–2000. Owing to its three international borders, there are two representatives of foreign consulates, Latvian and Estonian, operating in the region. Pskov's main trading partners are Estonia, Finland and Germany.

Pskov Oblast's economically active population numbered 377,000 in 2000, when 12.6% of the labour force were unemployed. In mid-2002 those in employment earned, on average, 2,954.6 roubles per month, reflecting Pskov's status as one of the poorer areas of the Russian Federation. There was a budgetary deficit of 158m. roubles in 2000. In that year external trade amounted to a value of US $108.2m. in exports and $77.6m. in imports, the lowest figures in the North-Western Federal

Okrug. In 2000 foreign investment in the region totalled $1.1m. At 31 December 2000 2,800 small businesses were registered in the Oblast.

Directory

Head of the Regional Administration (Governor): YEVGENII E. MIKHAILOV; 180001 Pskov, ul. Nekrasova 23; tel. (8122) 16-22-03; fax (8122) 16-03-90; e-mail glava@obladmin.pskov.ru; internet www.pskov.ru.

Chairman of the Regional Assembly: YURII A. SHCHMATOV; 180001 Pskov, ul. Nekrasova 23; tel. (8122) 16-24-44; fax (8122) 16-00-51.

Chief Representative of Pskov Oblast in the Russian Federation: IGOR P. NOVOSELOV; Moscow; tel. (095) 928-84-43; fax (095) 928-07-95.

Head of Pskov City Administration (Mayor): MIKHAIL YA. KHORONEN; 180000 Pskov, ul. Nekrasova 22; tel. (8122) 16-26-67.

Rostov Oblast

Rostov Oblast is situated in the south of the Eastern European Plain, in the Southern Federal Okrug and the North Caucasus Economic Area. It lies on the Taganrog Gulf of the Sea of Azov. Krasnodar and Stavropol Krais lie to the south and the Republic of Kalmykiya to the east. Volgograd Oblast lies to the north-east and Voronezh Oblast to the north-west. The region has an international border with Ukraine to the west. Its major rivers are the Don and the Severnyi Donets. The Volga–Don Canal runs through its territory. Rostov Oblast covers an area of 100,800 sq km (38,910 sq miles) and consists of 43 administrative districts and 23 cities. The region is relatively densely populated, having an estimated 4,286,200 inhabitants at 1 January 2002, giving it a population density of 42.5 per sq km. Some 67.5% of the region's inhabitants resided in urban areas in 2001. Its administrative centre is at Rostov-on-Don (Rostov-na-Donu), which had a population of 997,800 in 2001. Other major cities are Taganrog (with a population of 280,900), Shakhty (218,200), Novocherkassk (181,600), Volgodonsk (179,100) and Novoshakhtinsk (99,900).

History

Rostov-on-Don was established as a city in 1796. It became an important grain-exporting centre in the 19th century, and increased in economic importance after the completion of the Volga–Don Canal. Rostov Oblast was formed in September 1937. The region became heavily industrialized after 1946 and, therefore, considerably increased in population.

In the mid-1990s the liberal Yabloko bloc enjoyed its highest level of support outside the two federal cities and Kamchatka in Rostov, and it managed to obtain over 15% of the votes cast in some parts of the Oblast in elections to the State

Duma in December 1999. The regional Government signed a power-sharing treaty with the federal authorities in June 1996. The Oblast directly elected the incumbent, Vladimir Chub, as Governor in September of that year. Chub was re-elected for a further term of office on 23 September 2001, as the candidate of the pro-Government Unity, receiving 78% of the votes cast.

Economy

In 1999 Rostov Oblast's gross regional product stood at 68,975.9m. roubles, or 15,780.0 roubles per head. The Oblast's main industrial centres are at Rostov-on-Don, Taganrog, Novocherkassk, Shakhty, Kamensk-Shakhtinskii, Novoshakhtinsk and Volgodonsk. In 2000 there were 1,858 km (1,154 miles) of railways and 11,525 km of paved roads on the Oblast's territory. Its ports are Rostov-on-Don (connected by shipping routes to 16 countries) and Ust-Donetskii, both of which are river-ports.

The Oblast is one of the major grain-producing regions in Russia, with agricultural land comprising some 85% of its territory. The production of sunflower seeds, coriander, mustard, vegetables and cucurbits (gourds and melons) is also important, as are viniculture and horticulture. The sector employed some 19.2% of the working population in 2000, when total agricultural output amounted to a value of 27,882m. roubles. The Oblast is situated in the eastern Donbass coal-mining region and contains some 6,500m. metric tons of coal, as well as significant deposits of anthracite. It is also rich in natural gas, reserves of which are estimated at 54,000m. cu m. Its other principal industries are food-processing and mechanical engineering: Rostov-on-Don contained some 50 machine-building plants. In the early 1990s the industrial association, Rostselmash, produced 70% of all grain combines in Russia (although the quantity produced in 1999 was less than one-50th of that achieved 15 years earlier) and Krasnyi Aksai manufactured 50% of all tractor-mounted cultivators (although from 1997 it specialized in the assembly of automobiles for Daewoo of the Republic of Korea); in Novocherkassk, Krasnyi Kotelshchik produced 70% of Russia's electric locomotives, and is now a joint-stock company; and 60% of the country's steam boilers were made in Taganrog, where the largest industrial concern in the Oblast, Taganrog Metallurgical Plant (TagMet), is located. Light manufacturing, chemicals and ferrous and non-ferrous metallurgy are also major economic activities. In 2000 some 20.0% of the Oblast's working population were employed in industry, and industrial production was worth 57,372m. roubles.

The economically active population numbered 2,062,000 in 2000, when 14.9% of the labour force were unemployed. In mid-2002 those in employment earned an average monthly wage of 3,115.2 roubles. The 2000 budget showed a surplus of 95.4m. roubles. In the same year external trade amounted to a value of US $709.2m. in exports and $519.6m. in imports; total foreign investment in the region amounted to $91.1m. At 31 December 2000 there were some 25,000 small businesses registered in the Oblast.

Directory

Head of the Regional Administration (Governor): VLADIMIR F. CHUB; 344050 Rostov-on-Don, ul. Sotsialisticheskaya 112; tel. (8632) 44-18-10; fax (8632) 44-12-24; e-mail pressa_rra@donpac.ru; internet www.donland.ru.

Chairman of the Legislative Assembly: ALEKSANDR V. POPOV; 344050 Rostov-on-Don, ul. Sotsialisticheskaya 112; tel. (8632) 40-14-47; fax (8632) 40-55-82.

Representation of Rostov Oblast in the Russian Federation: 127025 Moscow, ul. Novyi Arbat 19/1909; tel. (095) 203-94-71; fax (095) 203-89-58.

Head of Rostov-on-Don City Administration (Mayor): MIKHAIL A. CHERNY-SHEV; 344007 Rostov-on-Don, ul. B. Sadovaya 47; tel. (8632) 44-13-23; fax (8632) 66-62-62; internet www.rostov-gorod.ru.

Ryazan Oblast

Ryazan Oblast is situated in the central part of the Eastern European Plain and forms part of the Central Federal Okrug and the Central Economic Area. Ryazan city lies some 192 km (just under 120 miles) south-east of Moscow. The other neighbouring regions are Vladimir (to the north), Nizhnii Novgorod (north-east), the Republic of Mordoviya (east), Penza (south-east), Tambov and Lipetsk (south), and Tula (west). There are some 2,800 lakes in the region (the largest being the Velikoye and the Dubovoye) and its major rivers are the Oka and the Don and their tributaries. The Oka extends 489 km (304 miles) along the borders with Moscow and Vladimir Oblasts. Its catchment area amounts to over 95% of the region's territory, which occupies an area of 39,600 sq km (15,290 sq miles) and is divided into 25 administrative districts and 12 cities. At 1 January 2002 its population was estimated at 1,255,000, giving a population density of 31.7 per sq km. In 2001 some 68.5% of the population inhabited urban areas. The Oblast's principal city is Ryazan, with a population of 523,400 at 1 January 2001.

History

Ryazan city was an early Orthodox Christian bishopric. The Oblast was formed on 26 September 1937. In the 1990s it was described as part of the 'red belt' of communist support in Russia. With 31% of the Oblast's participating electorate voting for the Communist Party of the Russian Federation (CPRF) in the general election of December 1995, this party was also able to dominate the Regional Duma. In October 1998 the incumbent Governor was removed by the federal Government; the acting Governor, Igor Ivlev, lost the subsequent election (held in December) to the CPRF candidate, Vyacheslav Lyubimov. The region co-operated in a federal experiment with jury trials from 1993, but they were abolished, apparently for financial reasons, in December 1998. In April 1999, at the time of the aerial bombardment of Serbia, the Federal Republic of Yugoslavia, by North Atlantic Treaty Organization (NATO) forces, Lyubimov was one of the leading

227

supporters in the Federation Council of the expansion of the Russia-Belarus Union to include Yugoslavia. Lyubimov was re-elected as Governor in December 2000.

Economy

In 1999 Ryazan Oblast's gross regional product amounted to 22,789.8m. roubles, or 17,666.5 roubles per head. The Oblast's industrial centres are at Ryazan, Skopin, Kasimov and Sasovo. In 2000 there were 942 km of railways and 6,596 km of paved roads in the region.

The Oblast's warm, moist climate is conducive to agriculture, which consists mainly of grain and vegetable production, horticulture and animal husbandry, and employed 18.1% of the work-force in 2000. Total agricultural production amounted to a value of 10,432m. roubles in that year. There are 162.8m. cu m of timber reserves in the region and substantial reserves of brown coal and peat, estimated at around 302m. metric tons and 222m. tons, respectively. Deposits of peat are concentrated in the north, the east and the south-west of the region. The Oblast's main industries are mechanical engineering, the generation of electrical energy, petroleum-processing, the production of building materials, light manufacturing and food-processing. In 2000 some 24.7% of the working population were engaged in industry, which generated a total of 22,781m. roubles.

The economically active population numbered 613,000 in 2000, when 9.5% of the labour force were unemployed. In mid-2002 those in employment earned, on average, 3,425.3 roubles per month. The 2000 budget showed a surplus of 75.2m. roubles, and foreign investment in the region totalled US $1.3m. in that year. In 2000 external trade amounted to a value of $788.0m. in exports and $64.5m. in imports. At 31 December 2000 there were 6,400 small businesses registered in the Oblast.

Directory

Head of the Regional Administration (Governor): VYACHESLAV N. LYUBIMOV; 390000 Ryazan, ul. Lenina 30; tel. (0912) 27-21-25; fax (0912) 44-25-68; e-mail korn@adm1.ryazan.su; internet www.gov.ryazan.ru.

Chairman of the Regional Duma: VLADIMIR N. FEDOTKIN; 390000 Ryazan, ul. Pochtovaya 50/57; tel. (0912) 77-48-82; fax (0912) 21-64-22; e-mail duma@org .etr.ru.

Representation of Ryazan Oblast in the Russian Federation: 127025 Moscow, ul. Novyi Arbat 19/2213; tel. (095) 203-61-78; fax (095) 203-61-85.

Head of Ryazan City Administration (Mayor): PAVEL D. MAMATOV; 390000 Ryazan, ul. Radishcheva 28; tel. (0912) 77-34-02; fax (0912) 24-05-70; e-mail glava@cityadmin.ryazan.ru.

Sakhalin Oblast

Sakhalin Oblast comprises the island of Sakhalin and the Kurile (Kuril) Islands in the Pacific Ocean. It forms part of the Far Eastern Federal Okrug and the Far Eastern Economic Area. The island of Sakhalin lies off the coast of Khabarovsk Krai, separated from the mainland by the Tatar Strait. Eastward lie the Kurile Islands (annexed by the USSR in 1945, but claimed by Japan), which are an archipelago of some 56 islands extending from the Kamchatka Peninsula in the north-east, to Hokkaido Island (Japan) in the south-west. Sakhalin Island is 942 km (just over 580 miles) in length and contains two parallel mountain ranges running north to south and separated by a central valley. The highest peaks on the island, both belonging to the eastern range of mountains, are Lopatin (1,609 m or 5,281 feet) and Nevelskogo (1,397 m). The north-west coast of the island is marshland, and much of its area is forested. The Kurile Islands are actively volcanic and contain many hot springs. There are some 60,000 rivers on Sakhalin Island, the major ones being the Poronai (350 km in length), the Tym (330 km), the Viakhtu (131 km) and the Lyutoga (130 km), all of which are frozen during the winter months, December–April/May. The Kurile Islands contain around 4,000 rivers and streams and the largest waterfall in the Russian Federation, Ilya Muromets. Sakhalin Oblast covers a total area of 87,100 sq km (33,620 sq miles) and is divided into 17 administrative districts and 18 cities. The estimated total population at 1 January 2002 was 584,700, the region's population density being 6.7 per sq km. Some 86.7% of the region's total population resided in urban areas in 2001. The population of the Oblast was reported to have declined by some 110,000, or 15%, between 1991 and 1998, largely reflecting migration from the region as a result of the decline of its industrial base. The Oblast's administrative centre is at Yuzhno-Sakhalinsk, which had 176,200 inhabitants in 2001. Other cities include Kholmsk (39,400) and Korsakov (37,900). All these settlements are on Sakhalin Island.

History

Sakhalin was traditionally known as a place of exile for political opponents to the tsars. It was originally inhabited by the indigenous Gilyak people; Russians first reached the island in 1644, although the region was assumed to be a peninsula until the early 19th century. The island was conquered by the Japanese at the end of the 18th century, but Russia established a military base at Korsakov in 1853. Joint control of the island followed until 1875, when it was granted to Russia in exchange for the Kurile Islands. Karafuto, the southern part of the island, was won by Japan during the Russo–Japanese War (1904–05), but the entire island was ceded to the USSR in 1945. The Kurile Islands, which were discovered for Europeans by the Dutch navigator, Martin de Vries, in 1634, were divided between Japan and Russia in the 18th century and ruled jointly until 1875. Russia occupied the islands in 1945 and assumed full control in 1947. The southern Kuriles remained disputed between Japan and the newly independent Russia. Sakhalin Oblast had been formed on 20 October 1932 as part of Khabarovsk Krai. It became a separate administrative unit in 1947, when the island was united with the Kuriles.

On 16 October 1993 the head of the regional administration disbanded the Regional Soviet; a Regional Duma was elected in its place. In May 1995 a major earthquake, one of the largest ever to occur in Russia, destroyed the town of Neftegorsk in the north of the region, and claimed an estimated 2,000 lives. In May 1996 the then Russian President, Boris Yeltsin, signed a power-sharing treaty with the regional Government. The gubernatorial elections of October 1996 and October 2000 were won by the incumbent, Igor Farkhutdinov. In 1998 Russia and Japan agreed to attempt to settle their territorial dispute by 2000. However, in September 2000 President Vladimir Putin rejected continuing Japanese demands for the sovereignty of four of the Southern Kuriles (known as the 'Northern Territory' to Japan), and the continuing dispute meant that the two countries had still to sign a peace treaty officially to mark the end of the Second World War. In December 1998 the Oblast authorities signed a friendship and economic co-operation accord with the Japanese province of Hokkaido, and a further agreement was signed in January 2000. A special economic zone in the Southern Kuriles was established in the late 1990s, in order to encourage foreign investment.

Economy

In 1999 Sakhalin Oblast's gross regional product amounted to 28,329.3m. roubles, or 46,980.5 roubles per head. The Oblast's principal industrial centres are at Yuzhno-Sakhalinsk, Kholmsk, Okha (the administrative centre of the petroleum-producing region), Nevelsk, Dolinsk and Poronaisk. In 2000 there were 957 km of railways and 1,820 km of paved roads in the Oblast. Its ports are Kholmsk (from where the Kholmsk-Vanino ferry connects Sakhalin Island with the mainland) and Korsakov. There are flights to Moscow, Khabarovsk, Vladivostok, Petropavlovsk-Kamchatskii and Novosibirsk, and international services to Alaska, the USA, the Republic of Korea (South Korea) and Japan.

Agriculture in the region is minimal, owing to its unfavourable climatic conditions—agricultural land occupies only 1% of its territory. It employed just 4.6%

of the working population in 2000, and consists mainly of potato and vegetable production, animal husbandry and fur farming. Total agricultural production amounted to a value of 1,865m. roubles in 2000. Annual catches of fish and other marine life amount to around 400,000 metric tons. Fishing and fish-processing is the major traditional industry, accounting for two-fifths of industrial production. The entire industrial sector employed some 24.9% of the region's work-force and generated 30,166m. roubles in 2000. There is some extraction of coal and, increasingly, petroleum and natural gas in, and to the north of, Sakhalin Island. Some petroleum is piped for refining to a plant in Komsomolsk-on-Amur (Khabarovsk Krai), although from 1994 the Oblast had its own refinery, with a capacity of some 200,000 tons per year. Coal was the region's primary source of energy, but in the late 1990s a gradual conversion to gas was initiated. The further development of Sakhalin's rich hydrocarbons reserves was the subject of negotiations between a number of Russian and foreign companies in the mid-1990s. By 1999 four major consortia had been formed. Sakhalin-1, a project to produce petroleum on the continental shelf of Sakhalin Island, comprised Rosneft (of which Sakhalinmornef-tegas is a local subsidiary and which had a 40% stake), Exxon (of the USA) and Sodeco (of Japan), both of which had a 30% stake. Sakhalin-2, two fields containing an estimated 1,000m. barrels of petroleum and 408,000m. cu m of natural gas, was run by Sakhalin Energy Investment, comprising Mitsui and Mitsubishi (of Japan), Marathon (of the USA) and the Anglo-Dutch company, Shell. Sakhalin-3, backed by Mobil and Texaco (of the USA), was seeking to develop what was potentially the largest field on the Sakhalin shelf, containing an estimated 320m. tons of recoverable reserves. It was hoped that the proceeds from the ongoing projects would help to alleviate the high level of poverty in the region. In July 1998 the federal premier, Sergei Kiriyenko, signed a resolution extending a federal programme on social and economic development of the Oblast, to be financed by proceeds from Sakhalin-1 and Sakhalin-2, until 2005. In 2001 Exxon Mobil was undertaking a project to examine the feasibility of constructing a pipeline to export petroleum and gas from Sakhalin to Japan. In July 2002 it was announced that Rosneft was to undertake the development of a further project, Sakhalin-5, in association with British Petroleum (United Kingdom). In addition, food-processing was a significant industrial sector in the Oblast, accounting for 27% of such activity in 2000.

Sakhalin Oblast's economically active population totalled 324,000 in 2000, when 13.0% of the labour force were unemployed, compared with 20.4% in the previous year. The average monthly wage in the region amounted to some 6,735.7 roubles in mid-2002. The 2000 budget showed a surplus of 147.9m. roubles In the same year exports from the Oblast were valued at US $425.3m. and imports to the Oblast were worth $85.1m.; total foreign investment in the region amounted to some $250.6m. At 31 December 2000 4,800 small businesses were registered in the Oblast.

Directory

Governor: IGOR P. FARKHUTDINOV; 693011 Sakhalin obl., Yuzhno-Sakhalinsk, Kommunisticheskii pr. 39; tel. (4242) 43-14-02; fax (4242) 23-60-81; e-mail webmaster@adm.sakhalin.ru; internet www.adm.sakhalin.ru.

Chairman of the Regional Duma: VLADIMIR YEFREMOV; 693000 Sakhalin obl., Yuzhno-Sakhalinsk, ul. Chekhova 37; tel. (4242) 42-14-89; fax (4242) 72-15-46; e-mail duma@duma.sakhalin.ru; internet www.duma.sakhalin.ru.

Representation of Sakhalin Oblast in the Russian Federation: Moscow; tel. (095) 973-19-95.

Head of Yuzhno-Sakhalinsk City Administration (Mayor): FEDOR I. SIDORENKO; 693023 Sakhalin obl., Yuzhno-Sakhalinsk, ul. Lenina 173; tel. (4242) 72-25-11; fax (4242) 23-00-06.

Samara Oblast

Samara Oblast is situated in the south-east of the Eastern European Plain on the middle reaches of the Volga river. It forms part of the Volga Federal Okrug and the Volga Economic Area. Its southernmost tip lies on the border with Kazakhstan. Saratov lies to the south-west, Ulyanovsk to the west, Tatarstan to the north and Orenburg to the east. The Volga snakes through the west of the territory. The Oblast's other major rivers are the Samara, the Sok, the Kunel, the Bolshoi Igruz and the Kondurcha. The region occupies an area of 53,600 sq km (20,690 sq miles). It is divided into 27 districts and 11 cities. Owing to its proximity to the Kazakh desert, the southernmost part of the Oblast is prone to drought. The region is densely populated, with an estimated population of 3,258,700 at 1 January 2002, and a population density, therefore, of 60.8 per sq km. In 2001 some 80.5% of the population inhabited urban areas. The majority of the population, 83.4%, was ethnic Russian. There were also significant communities of Mordovians, Chuvash, Tatars and Ukrainians. The administrative centre is at Samara (formerly Kuibyshev), which had 1,146,400 inhabitants in 2001. The region's other major towns are Tolyatti (724,300), Syzran (184,300) and Novokuibyshevsk (115,100).

History

Samara city was founded in 1586 as a fortress. It increased in prosperity after the construction of the railways in the late 19th century. Samara Oblast was founded on 14 May 1928, as the Middle Volga Oblast. In 1929 it was upgraded to the status of a krai, which was renamed Kuibyshev Krai in 1935. On 5 December 1936 Kuibyshev Krai became Kuibyshev Oblast. (The territory assumed its current name in 1991.) The city became the headquarters of the Soviet Government between 1941 and 1943, when Moscow was threatened by the German invasion.

The local legislature defied President Boris Yeltsin in the constitutional crisis of 1993, and was dissolved in October and replaced by a Regional Duma. There was more support in the region for the candidacy of Boris Yeltsin in the presidential election of mid-1996 than for his communist rival, Gennadii Zyuganov, owing to the strong leadership of the Governor, Konstantin Titov. In the election held in December Titov was returned to the post of Governor. Titov, who was reportedly offered a senior cabinet post by President Yeltsin and who expressed a willingness to take a senior post under President Vladimir Putin, was an ambitious economic reformer. As the informal head of the 'Great Volga' inter-regional association, Titov sought to protect the power and relative independence of governors from the central authorities. He also strongly urged the Regional Duma to approve legislation on land ownership, which was achieved in June 1998. Titov attempted to gain a higher profile in national politics by standing for the presidency of the Russian Federation at the elections of March 2000. However, his performance, even in Samara Oblast, where he obtained only 20% of the votes cast and came third, was disappointing. Consequently, he resigned from the post of Governor in April, but stood as a candidate for re-election in July, in an attempt to confirm his legitimacy; he was re-elected with 53% of the votes cast.

Economy

In 1999 Samara Oblast's gross regional product amounted to 21,328.4m. roubles, or 36,736.1 roubles per head. The Oblast's major industrial centres are at Samara, Tolyatti, Syzran and Novokuibyshevsk. In 2000 there were 1,382 km (859 miles) of railways and 7,350 km of paved roads in the region.

Agriculture in the Oblast, which employed just 8.7% of the working population in 2000, consists mainly of animal husbandry and the production of grain, sugar beet and sunflower seeds. Total agricultural production in 2000 was worth 16,520m. roubles. There are some reserves of petroleum and natural gas in the region. Its main industries are mechanical engineering, metal-working, petroleum production and refining, food-processing and petrochemicals. The Oblast's principal company is AvtoVAZ (Volga Automobile Plane) JSC, manufacturer of the Lada automobile, accounting for over 40% of industrial output in the region, and the largest automobile manufacturer in Russia. In 2002, as part of a joint venture with the US corporation, General Motors, AvtoVAZ also began to manufacture Chevrolet Niva automobiles and sports-utility vehicles. In 2000 some 28.7% of the region's work-force were engaged in industry, which generated 161,001m. roubles.

The economically active population of Samara Oblast numbered 1,692,000 in 2000, when 10.3% of the labour force were unemployed. In mid-2002 those in employment earned an average wage of 4,317.7 roubles per month, well above the national average. In 2000 the regional budget showed a surplus of 557.4m.

roubles. In December 2001, however, the Oblast's Governor, Konstantin Titov, issued a decree introducing state control over the finances of Samara city and two rural districts of the Oblast, the debts of which exceeded 10% of their total consolidated budgets. In 2000 total foreign investment in the region amounted to US $236.3m. By August 1998 some 300 foreign companies, including some of the world's largest, such as Coca-Cola and General Motors of the USA and Nestlé of Switzerland, had invested in the region, attracted by its technologically advanced industrial base, reputation for creditworthiness and well-educated, urbanized labour force. In 2000 the external trade of the region amounted to some $3,514.6m. in exports and $626.2m. in imports, representing one of the highest levels of trade in any federal subject. At 31 December 2000 there were some 27,600 small businesses in operation.

Directory

Governor: KONSTANTIN A. TITOV; 443006 Samara, ul. Molodogvardeiskaya 210; tel. (8462) 32-22-68; fax (8462) 32-13-40; e-mail governor@samara.ru; internet www.adm.samara.ru.

Chairman of the Regional Duma: VIKTOR F. SAZANOV; 443110 Samara, ul. Molodogvardeiskaya 187; tel. (8462) 32-75-06; fax (8462) 33-33-96; e-mail samgd@duma.sam-reg.ru; internet www.duma.sam-reg.ru.

Representative of Samara Oblast in the Russian Federation: GENNADII V. GENDIN; 127030 Moscow, per. Veskovskii 2; tel. (095) 973-19-95; fax (095) 973-05-54; e-mail tradoc@samarapostpred.ru.

Head of Samara City Administration (Mayor): GEORGII S. LIMANSKII; 443010 Samara, ul. Kuibysheva 135/137; tel. (8462) 32-20-68; fax (8462) 33-67-41; e-mail city@vis.infotel.ru.

Saratov Oblast

Saratov Oblast is situated in the south-east of the Eastern European Plain. It forms part of the Volga Federal Okrug and the Volga Economic Area. On the border with Kazakhstan (to the south-east), the federal territories adjacent to Saratov are Volgograd (south), Voronezh and Tambov (west), and Penza, Ulyanovsk and Samara (north). Its main river is the Volga. The west of the Oblast (beyond the left bank of the Volga) is mountainous, the east low-lying. The region's territory occupies an area of 100,200 sq km (38,680 sq miles). It comprises 38 districts and 18 cities. At 1 January 2002 it had an estimated total of 2,676,400 inhabitants, and a population density of 26.7 per sq km. In 2001 some 73.0% of the Oblast's population inhabited urban areas. Its administrative centre is at Saratov, a major river-port on the Volga, with a population of 864,400 in 2001. Other major cities were Balakovo (207,500) and Engels (190,600).

History

Saratov city was founded in 1590 as a fortress city, to protect against nomad raids on the Volga trade route. Strategically placed on the Trans-Siberian Railway, it was seized by Bolshevik forces in late 1917 and remained under communist control, despite attacks by the 'White' forces under Adm. Aleksandr Kolchak in 1918–19. The Oblast was formed in 1936, having been part of a Saratov Krai from 1934. The region became heavily industrialized in the Soviet period, before the Second World War.

Saratov remained an important centre for the military and for communist support into the 1990s. However, in September 1996 Dmitrii Ayatskov, a presidential appointment, retained his post heading the regional administration, having secured 81.4% of the popular vote to become the first popularly elected regional leader in Russia. He was re-elected for a further term in April 2000, amid accusations of electoral manipulation, which removed all other serious candidates from the contest, and press censorship. As Governor, Ayatskov carried out extensive reform

236

to the region's agro-industrial sector, which culminated, in November 1997, in the passing in the Oblast of the first law in Russia to provide for the purchase and sale of agricultural land. The law greatly diminished the power base of communists and nationalists in the region, and by April 1998 land sales had already generated 3m. roubles for the regional economy. A series of bilateral trade agreements signed with the Mayor of Moscow, Yurii Luzhkov, in August 1996, also benefited the economy of Saratov Oblast.

Economy

In 1999 Saratov Oblast's gross regional product totalled 48,595.4m. roubles, equivalent to 17,888.3 roubles per head. The region's major industrial centres are at Saratov, Engels and Balakovo. In 2000 there were 2,298 km (1,428 miles) of railways and 10,169 km of paved roads on the Oblast's territory. It was the major Soviet/Russian arsenal for chemical weapons, provoking some local concern. In January 1996 it was announced that chemical weapons stored near the village of Gornyi would be destroyed, in accordance with international agreements. A new chemicals-weapons processing plant was scheduled to commence operations in December 2002.

Its agriculture, which employed some 19.7% of the working population in 2000, consists primarily of animal husbandry and the production of grain (the Oblast is one of Russia's major producers of wheat), sunflower seeds and sugar beet. In 2000 total agricultural production amounted to a value of 19,733m. roubles. The Oblast's main industries are mechanical engineering, the production of electricity, petroleum-refining, chemicals, the manufacture of building materials, food-processing and the production of petroleum and natural gas. In the late 1990s the region produced over 30% of the cement and 20% of the mineral fertilizer produced in the Volga Economic Area. Total industrial production was worth 41,878m. roubles in 2000, and some 20.3% of the work-force was engaged in industry at that time.

The region's economically active population numbered 1,321,000 in 2000, when 9.5% of the labour force were unemployed. In mid-2002 the average wage in the Oblast was 2,796.3 roubles per month. The regional budget for 2000 showed a deficit of 101.2m. roubles. In that year the value of external trade amounted to US $511.3m. in exports and $147.2m. in imports. Foreign investment amounted to $5.5m. in 2000, when 48 joint enterprises were registered in the region; of these, 10 involved partners from Cyprus, and nine involved partners from Germany. At 31 December 2000 there were 10,800 small businesses registered in the region.

Directory

Head of the Regional Administration (Governor): DMITRII F. AYATSKOV; 410042 Saratov, ul. Moskovskaya 72; tel. (8452) 72-20-86; fax (8452) 72-52-54; e-mail governor@gov.saratov.ru; internet www.gov.saratov.ru.

Chairman of the Regional Duma: SERGEI A. SHUVALOV; 411031 Saratov, ul. Radishcheva 24A; tel. (8452) 73-28-84; fax (8452) 72-23-31; e-mail post@srd.ru; internet www.srd.ru.

Representation of Saratov Oblast in the Russian Federation: 109028 Moscow, per. Podkopayevskii 7/3; tel. and fax (095) 917-05-19.

Head of Saratov City Administration (Mayor): YURII N. AKSENENKO; 410600 Saratov, ul. Pervomaiskaya 78; tel. (8452) 24-02-49; fax (8452) 24-84-44; e-mail mayor@admsaratov.ru; internet www.admsaratov.ru.

Smolensk Oblast

Smolensk Oblast is situated in the central part of the Eastern European Plain on the upper reaches of the Dnepr (Dnieper). It forms part of the Central Federal Okrug and the Central Economic Area. An international boundary with Belarus lies to the south-west, while Pskov and Tver Oblasts lie to the north, Moscow to the north-east and Kaluga and Bryansk to the south-east. The Oblast covers an area of 49,800 sq km (19,220 sq miles) and extends for some 280 km (175 miles) from south to north and 250 km from west to east. It is divided into 25 administrative districts and 15 cities. The estimated population was 1,098,300 at 1 January 2002, and the population density 22.1 per sq km. Some 70.5% of the region's inhabitants lived in urban areas in 2001. Its administrative centre is at Smolensk, a river-port on the Dnepr, with 347,600 inhabitants in 2001.

History

Smolensk city was first documented in 863, as the chief settlement of the Krivichi, a Slavic tribe. It became an Orthodox Christian bishopric in 1128. It achieved prosperity during the 14th and 15th centuries as it was situated on one of the Hanseatic trade routes. Smolensk was the site of a major battle in 1812, between the Russian imperial army and the forces of Emperor Napoleon I of France, who subsequently went on to occupy the city of Moscow for a time. It was seized by the Bolsheviks in late 1917 and remained under their control for the duration of the civil war. Smolensk Oblast was formed on 27 September 1937.

The communist establishment remained in control of the region in the early years of Russia's restored independence. The Communist Party of the Russian Federation (CPRF) won the most seats in the Regional Duma elected in 1994 and secured the highest proportion of the votes of any party in elections to the State

Duma in both 1995 and 1999. In the gubernatorial election of April–May 1998, after a second round of voting, the CPRF candidate and Mayor of Smolensk, Aleksandr Prokhorov, defeated the incumbent. However, support for the CPRF declined significantly in the regional legislative elections held in May 2002. In the same month Viktor Maslov, a general in the Federal Security Service (FSB) was elected as the new Governor of Smolensk Oblast, receiving 41% of the votes cast, compared with the 34% received by Prokhorov. Maslov's campaign had concentrated on issues of law and order, and concern about, in particular, organized crime, which was subsequently heightened, following the assassination of Vladimir Prokhorov, the First Deputy Governor and Maslov's campaign manager, in early August.

Economy

In 1999 Smolensk Oblast's gross regional product amounted to 21,729.0m. roubles, or 19,057.2 roubles per head. Its major industrial centres are at Smolensk, Roslavl, Safonovo, Vyazma, and Yartsevo. In 2000 there were 1,258 km of railway lines and 8,862 km of paved roads in the Oblast.

Agriculture in Smolensk Oblast, which employed 17.3% of the work-force in 2000, mainly consists of animal husbandry and the production of grain, sugar beet and sunflower seeds. Total agricultural output was worth 6,273m. roubles in 2000. Its main industries are textiles, mechanical engineering, chemicals, light manufacturing, food-processing, electrical-energy production and the production of building materials. In 2000 23.7% of the work-force were engaged in industry. Total industrial production in that year amounted to a value of 27,037m. roubles.

The region's economically active population numbered 565,000 in 2000, when 12.2% of the labour force were unemployed. The average wage in the Oblast stood at 3,305.6 roubles per month in mid-2002. The 2000 budget showed a deficit of 9.4m. roubles. In 2000 the value of external trade amounted to US $412.3m. in exports and $107.3m. in imports. Total foreign investment in the region amounted to $10.9m. in that year. At 31 December 2000 there were 2,600 small businesses in operation.

Directory

Head of the Regional Administration (Governor): VIKTOR N. MASLOV; 214008 Smolensk, pl. Lenina 1; tel. (08100) 3-66-11; fax (08100) 3-68-51; e-mail maslov@ admin.smolensk.ru; internet admin.smolensk.ru.

Chairman of the Regional Duma: VLADIMIR I. ANISIMOV; 214008 Smolensk, pl. Lenina 1; tel. (08122) 3-67-00; fax (08122) 3-71-85; e-mail duma@admin .smolensk.ru; internet admin.smolensk.ru/~duma.

Representation of Smolensk Oblast in the Russian Federation: Moscow.

Head of Smolensk City Administration: IVAN A. AVERCHENKOV; 214000 Smolensk, ul. Oktyabrskoi Revolyutsii 1/2; tel. and fax (08100) 3-11-81; e-mail smol@admin.smolensk.ru; internet admin.smolensk.ru/~smol.

Sverdlovsk Oblast

Sverdlovsk Oblast is situated on the eastern, and partly on the western, slopes of the Central and Northern Urals and in the Western Siberian Plain. It forms part of the Urals Federal Okrug and the Urals Economic Area. Tyumen Oblast lies to the east (with its constituent Khanty-Mansii AOk to the north-west), there is a short border with the Republic of Komi in the north-west and Perm Oblast lies to the west. To the south are Bashkortostan, Chelyabinsk and Kurgan. The region's major rivers are those of the Ob and Kama basins. The west of the region is mountainous, while much of the eastern part is taiga (forested marshland). The territory of the Oblast covers an area of 194,800 sq km (75,190 sq miles) and is divided into 30 administrative districts and 47 cities. At 1 January 2001 the estimated population totalled 4,572,800, and the population density was 23.5 per sq km. As many as 87.5% of the region's inhabitants lived in urban areas in 2001. The Oblast's administrative centre is at Yekaterinburg (formerly Sverdlovsk), which had a population of 1,256,900 in 2001. Other major cities are Nizhnii Tagil (386,900), Kamensk-Uralskii (188,300) and Pervouralsk (135,000).

History

Yekaterinburg city was founded in 1821 as a military stronghold and trading centre. Like the Oblast (formed on 17 January 1934) it was named Sverdlovsk in 1924 but, unlike the Oblast, reverted to the name of Yekaterinburg in 1991. The city was infamous as the location where the last Tsar, Nicholas II, and his family were assassinated in 1918. The region became a major industrial centre after the Second World War.

Following the disintegration of the USSR, Sverdlovsk Oblast was among the most forthright in demanding regional rights from the centre. In September 1993 the Regional Soviet adopted a draft constitution for a 'Ural Republic', which was officially proclaimed on 27 October by the Regional Soviet and the head of the regional administration. The 'Ural Republic' was dissolved by presidential decree, however, and Eduard Rossel, the head of the regional administration, was dismissed on 9 November. In 1994 elections were held to a Regional Duma. In August 1995 Rossel was reinstated as Governor, having won the direct election to head the regional administration. His popularity enabled him to establish an independent 'Transformation of the Urals Movement' that eclipsed support for the national parties in the region in the federal elections of December 1995.

As Governor, Rossel continued to strive for more autonomy for the Oblast, one of the most powerful and potentially most prosperous regions in the Federation. In January 1996 Rossel signed an agreement on the division of powers and spheres of competence between federal and regional institutions. This accord was the first of its kind to be signed with a federal territory that did not have republican status. In April elections were held to the Regional Duma. Less than one-third of the electorate participated, but some 35% voted for Rossel's Transformation bloc. Subsequently, however, the Governor's popularity began to decline: in April 1998 the Transformation bloc won just 9.3% of the votes to the regional legislature and claimed just two seats in the lower house; it had previously held the majority there. Rossel was re-elected as Governor of Sverdlovsk Oblast on 12 September 1999. It was believed that Urals Federal Okrug, formed in mid-2000 by President Vladimir Putin, incorporated several regions traditionally regarded as part of Siberia, so as to inhibit any revival of an appeal for a 'Ural Republic'.

Economy

Sverdlovsk Oblast is a leading territory of the Russian Federation in terms of industry; the concentration of industry in the Oblast is around four times the average for a federal unit. In 1999 the territory's gross regional product amounted to 123,408.9m. roubles, equivalent to 26,674.9 roubles per head. Its most important industrial centres are at Yekaterinburg, Nizhnii Tagil, Pervouralsk, Krasno-uralsk, Serov, Alapayevsk and Kamensk-Uralskii. In 2000 there were 3,569 km (2,218 miles) of railway lines and 10,457 km of paved roads on the Oblast's territory. There is an international airport, Koltsovo.

The Oblast's agriculture, which employed just 6.6% of its work-force in 2000, consists of grain production and animal husbandry. Total agricultural output in 2000 was worth 16,857m. roubles. There is some extraction of gold and platinum in the Oblast. Its main industries are ferrous and non-ferrous metallurgy, the production of electrical energy, mechanical engineering (the most important plant being the Yekaterinburg-based Uralmash), food-processing and the production of copper and other ores, bauxite, asbestos, petroleum, peat and coal. Industry employed some 32.2% of the working population in 2000 and generated 168,220m. roubles. The services sector was also of increasing significance in the regional economy; the Oblast was given approval to issue US $500m.-worth of Eurobonds.

Sverdlovsk's economically active population numbered 2,328,000 in 2000, when 10.0% of the labour force were unemployed. The average monthly wage in the region was 4,731.5 roubles in mid-2002. The 2000 budget showed a surplus of 756.0m. roubles, and total foreign investment in that year was US $163.1m.; international trade amounted to some $2,779.6m. in exports and $578.7m. in imports. At 31 December 2000 there were 21,600 small businesses registered in the region.

Directory

Governor: EDUARD E. ROSSEL; 620031 Sverdlovsk obl., Yekaterinburg, pl. Oktyabrskaya 1; tel. (3432) 51-13-65; fax (3432) 70-54-72; e-mail press-center@ midural.ru; internet www.rossel.ru.

Chairman of the Government: ALEKSEI P. VOROBEV; 620031 Sverdlovsk obl., Yekaterinburg, pl. Oktyabrskaya 1; tel. (3432) 51-29-20; fax (3432) 77-17-00.

Legislative Assembly: 620031 Sverdlovsk obl., Yekaterinburg, pl. Oktyabrskaya 1; tel. (3432) 78-91-08; fax (3432) 71-80-48; e-mail duma@midural.ru; internet www.duma.midural.ru.

  Chairman of the House of Representatives: VIKTOR V. YAKIMOV; tel. (3432) 71-86-60; fax (3432) 78-91-02; e-mail presspalata@duma.midural.ru.

  Chairman of the Regional Duma: YEVGENII N. PORUNOV; tel. (3432) 71-74-53; fax (3432) 78-92-79.

Chief Representative of Sverdlovsk Oblast in the Russian Federation: VLADIMIR S. MELENTIYEV; 121019 Moscow, ul. Novyi Arbat 21; tel. and fax (095) 291-90-72.

Head of Yekaterinburg City Administration (Mayor): ARKADII M. CHERNETSKII; 620014 Sverdlovsk obl., Yekaterinburg, pr. Lenina 24; tel. (3432) 56-29-90; fax (3432) 71-79-26; e-mail glava@sov.mplik.ru; internet www.sov.mplik.ru.

Tambov Oblast

Tambov Oblast is situated in the central part of the Oka-Don plain. It forms part of the Central Federal Okrug and the Central Chernozem Economic Area. Penza and Saratov Oblasts lie to the east, Voronezh to the south, Lipetsk to the west and Ryazan to the north. Tambov city lies 480 km (298 miles) south-east of Moscow. Its major rivers are the Tsna and the Vorona. Its territory occupies 34,300 sq km (13,240 sq miles) and measures around 250 km from south to north and 200 km from west to east. The Oblast is divided into 23 administrative districts and eight cities. At 1 January 2002 its population was estimated at 1,240,700, giving a population density of 36.2 per sq km. In 2001 some 58.0% of the population inhabited urban areas. The administrative centre is at Tambov, which had a population of 308,000 in 2001. The second largest city in the Oblast is Michurinsk (116,800).

History

Tambov city was founded in 1636 as a fort to defend Moscow. The region was the scene of an army mutiny during the anti-tsarist uprising of 1905, and came under Bolshevik control immediately following the October Revolution in 1917. The Oblast, which was formed on 27 September 1937, was considered part of the 'red belt' of committed Communist Party adherence in the 1990s. The dissolution of the local council in October 1993, and its replacement by a Regional Duma, did not ease the tension between the communist-led assembly with the regional administration. Having appointed Oleg Betin, a locally respected Governor, President Boris Yeltsin permitted a gubernatorial election in Tambov in December

1995. However, Betin lost to the Communist Party of the Russian Federation candidate, Aleksandr Ryabov, and was, instead, appointed as presidential representative to the region. Betin, thus, remained visible in the political life of the Oblast prior to his election as governor in December 1999, with the support of two centrist movements, Fatherland and Unity, in December 1999. In elections held to the Regional Duma in March 1998 (at which the rate of participation was just over 25%), the greatest number of seats was won by a local pro-market Party, comprised largely of young directors of firms and enterprises. New elections to the Regional Duma were held in December 2001; the rate of voter participation was unexpectedly high, at some 40%.

Economy

In 1999 Tambov Oblast's gross regional product amounted to 17,878.8m. roubles, equivalent to 14,016.0 roubles per head. The region's industrial centres are at Tambov, Michurinsk, Morshansk, Kotovsk and Rasskazovo. It is situated on the ancient trading routes from the centre of Russia to the lower Volga and Central Asia and contains several major road and rail routes. In 2000 there were 746 km of railway lines and 5,284 km of paved roads in the region.

The Oblast's agriculture, which employed a relatively high proportion of the work-force (some 28.8% in 2000) consists mainly of the production of grain, sugar beet, sunflower seeds and vegetables. Animal husbandry and horticulture are also important. Total agricultural output was worth 9,658m. roubles in 2000. The principal industries in the Oblast are mechanical engineering, metal-working, chemicals and petrochemicals, the production of electrical energy, light manufacturing and food-processing. In 2000 17.9% of the working population was engaged in industry. Total industrial production in that year amounted to a value of 12,557m. roubles.

The economically active population stood at 583,000 in 2000, when 8.2% of the labour force were unemployed. In mid-2002 the average monthly wage in the Oblast was 3,305.6 roubles. There was a budgetary surplus of 105.3m. roubles in 2000. In that year the value of external trade amounted to only US $32.8m. in exports and $45.4m. in imports; foreign investment in the Oblast stood at $9.5m. At 31 December 2000 3,600 small businesses were registered in the region.

Directory

Head of the Regional Administration (Governor): OLEG I. BETIN; 392017 Tambov, ul. Internatsionalnaya 14; tel. (0752) 72-25-18; fax (0752) 71-51-27; e-mail post@regadm.tambov.ru; internet www.regadm.tambov.ru.

Chairman of the Regional Duma: VLADIMIR N. KAREV; 392017 Tambov, ul. Internatsionalnaya 14; tel. (0752) 71-23-70; fax (0752) 71-07-72.

Representation of Tambov Oblast in the Russian Federation: Moscow.

Head of Tambov City Administration (Mayor): ALEKSEI YU. ILYIN; 392000 Tambov, ul. Kommunalnaya 6; tel. (0752) 72-20-30; fax (0752) 72-47-71; e-mail cvc_t@rambler.ru; internet www.cityadm.tambov.ru.

Tomsk Oblast

Tomsk Oblast is situated in the south-east of the Western Siberian Plain. It forms part of the Siberian Federal Okrug and the West Siberian Economic Area. Kemerovo and Novosibirsk Oblast lie to the south, Omsk to the south-west, the Khanty-Mansii AOk (part of Tyumen Oblast) to the north-west and Krasnoyarsk Krai to the east. Its major rivers are the Ob, the Tom, the Chulym, the Ket, the Tym and the Vasyugan. The Ob flows for about 1,000 km (almost 400 miles) from the south-east to the north-west of the territory. Its largest lake is the Mirnoye. Almost all the Oblast's territory taiga (forested marshland), and over one-half of its total area is forested. It occupies 316,900 sq km (122,320 sq miles) and is divided into 16 administrative districts and six cities. At 1 January 2002 its total population was 1,060,800, giving a population density of only 3.3 per sq km. In 2001 67.2% of the population inhabited urban areas. Around 88.2% of the population were ethnically Russian at this time, 2.6% were Ukrainian and 2.1% Tatar. The administrative centre of the Oblast is at Tomsk, which had a population of 483,100 in 2001. The other major city in the region is Seversk (119,500).

History

Tomsk city was founded as a fortress in 1604. It was a major trading centre until the 1890s, when the construction of the Trans-Siberian Railway promoted other centres. Tomsk Oblast was formed on 13 August 1944. In 1993 the Regional Soviet was initially critical of President Boris Yeltsin's forcible dissolution of the federal parliament. It too, therefore, was disbanded and replaced (in elections in December) by a Regional Duma. The Communist Party of the Russian Federation remained the most popular party in the region, securing 19% of the votes cast in elections to the State Duma in 1995. However, in a simultaneous gubernatorial election for the Oblast, the pro-Yeltsin incumbent, Viktor Kress, won the popular mandate to head the regional administration. In elections to the regional legislature in January 1998, independent candidates fared well, with the business lobby winning 30 of the 42 seats. Kress, the Chairman of the inter-regional association 'Siberian

Accord', and a member of Our Home is Russia, was re-elected with a clear majority at the gubernatorial election of 5 September 1999.

Economy

In 1999 the gross regional product of Tomsk Oblast amounted to 31,166.3m. roubles, equivalent to 29,135.5 roubles per head. The industrial sector plays a dominant role in the economy of the Oblast. Its major industrial centres are at Tomsk, Kopashevo, Asino and Strezhevoi. In 2000 there were 346 km of railways and 3,512 km of paved roads on the Oblast's territory.

The Oblast's agricultural sector, which generated 5,719m. roubles in 2000, consists mainly of animal husbandry, the production of grain, vegetables and flax, fishing, hunting and fur farming. Some 10.7% of the Oblast's working population was engaged in agriculture in 2000. Around 1.4m. ha (3.4m. acres) of the Oblast's territory was used for agricultural purposes, of which one-half was arable land. The Oblast has substantial reserves of coal as well as of petroleum and natural gas (estimated at 333.7m. metric tons and 300,000m. cu m, respectively). Its other main industries are mechanical engineering, metal-working, the electro-technical industry, the processing of agricultural products and chemicals. Industry employed 21.5% of the working population in 2000, and industrial output amounted to a value of 24,393m. roubles in that year.

The economically active population of Tomsk Oblast numbered 532,000 in 2000, when 12.2% of the labour force were unemployed. The average monthly wage was 5,508.4 roubles in mid-2002. There was a budgetary deficit of 108.8m. roubles in 2000. The Oblast's most significant partners in international trade are the USA and the Republic of Korea, with the chemical industry accounting for the majority of this activity. In 2000 the value of external trade amounted to US $719.1m. in exports and $50.8m. in imports. In that year total foreign investment amounted to $25.1m. At 31 December 2000 6,900 small businesses were registered in the region.

Directory

Head of the Regional Administration (Governor): VIKTOR M. KRESS; 634050 Tomsk, pl. Lenina 6; tel. (3822) 51-05-05; fax (3822) 51-03-23; e-mail ato@ tomsk.gov.ru; internet www.tomsk.gov.ru.

Chairman of the Legislative Assembly (Regional Duma): BORIS A. MALTSEV; 634050 Tomsk, pl. Lenina 6; tel. (3822) 51-04-24; fax (3822) 51-06-02; e-mail duma@tomsk.gov.ru; internet duma.tomsk.gov.ru.

Representation of Tomsk Oblast in in the Russian Federation: Moscow; tel. (095) 200-39-80.

Head of Tomsk City Administration (Mayor): ALEKSANDR S. MAKAROV; 634050 Tomsk, pr. Lenina 73; tel. (3822) 52-68-99; fax (3822) 52-68-60; e-mail pmayor@admin.tomsk.ru; internet admin.tomsk.ru.

Tula Oblast

Tula Oblast is situated in the central part of the Eastern European Plain in the northern section of the Central Russian Highlands. It forms part of the Central Federal Okrug and the Central Economic Area. Tula Oblast is bordered by the Oblasts of Ryazan to the east, Lipetsk to the south-east, Orel to the south-west, Kaluga to the north-west and Moscow to the north. Tula city is 193 km (about 120 miles) south of Moscow City. The region's major rivers are the Oka, the Upa, the Don and the Osetr. The territory of the Oblast covers an area of 25,700 sq km (9,920 sq miles) and extends for 230 km from south to north and 200 km from west to east. It is divided into 23 administrative districts and 21 cities. It is a highly populated area, with a total population of 1,690,000 at the beginning of 2002, and a population density of 65.8 per sq km. At 1 January 2001 some 81.5% of the Oblast's population inhabited urban areas. The Oblast's administrative centre is at Tula, a military town, which had a population of 495,500 in 2001. Other major cities include Novomoskovsk (with 135,300 inhabitants).

History

The city of Tula was founded in the 12th century. It became an important economic centre in 1712, with the construction of the Imperial Small Arms Factory. Tula Oblast was founded on 26 September 1937. Tula's armaments industry meant that it was closed to foreigners for most of the Soviet period.

On 7 October 1993 the Tula Regional Soviet refused to disband itself, but was subsequently dissolved and its functions transferred to the Regional Administration. A new representative body, the 48-seat Regional Duma, was later elected and remained dominated by members of the former communist *nomenklatura*. The

Communist Party of the Russian Federation (CPRF) remained the most widely supported party in the Oblast throughout the 1990s, receiving the largest proportion of the votes cast for any party in the State Duma elections of both 1995 and 1999. The Oblast also had a high-profile CPRF Governor, following the election of Vasilii Starodubtsev in March 1997. He had previously been known nationally as a participant in the coup organized against the Soviet leader, Mikhail Gorbachev, in August 1991, in an attempt to prevent the fragmentation of the USSR. Starodubtsev's continuing reputation as a radical communist was reflected in his standing as the sole 'red belt' governor to support the candidacy of Gennadii Zyuganov in the presidential election of 26 March 2000. Starodubtsev was also elected as a CPRF member of the State Duma in the legislative election of December 1999, but he refused to take his seat as, to do so, he would have been required to relinquish his position as Oblast Governor. Like his predecessor, Nikolai Sevryugin (who was subsequently detained on charges of bribe-taking and theft), Starodubtsev was accused of corruption, in regard to alleged tax evasion worth US $5m. during his tenure at a collective farm, prior to his election as Governor. Starodubtsev also implemented controversial policies as Governor; within seven months of taking office his generous support for the agrarian sector, in particular, had added $68m. to the Oblast's existing debts of $10m. Gubernatorial elections, held in two rounds in April 2001, aroused widespread controversy. One day before the first round of the elections a meeting of the electoral commission, which reportedly had been convened to consider withdrawing the right of one candidate, Andrei Samoshin, to participate in the election, was attacked by a group of men, and fighting ensued; the commission had previously accused Samoshin of misusing electoral funds and violating campaign procedures. In the event, Samoshin was permitted to participate, coming in second place, with 21.0% of the votes cast, behind Starodubtsev, with 49.4%, less than the 50% of the votes required for an outright victory. However, Samoshin withdrew his candidacy on 19 April, three days before the 'run-off' election was due to take place, citing his dissatisfaction with the conduct of the electoral commission. Despite his reluctance to participate, the commission ruled that the third-placed candidate, Viktor Sokolovskii, was to stand against Starodubtsev in the 'run-off' election. On 22 April Starodubtsev received over 71% of the votes cast in the second round of voting, for which Sokolovskii had refused to campaign.

Economy

In 1999 Tula Oblast's gross regional product amounted to 30,286.0m. roubles, or 17,232.4 roubles per head. Its important industrial centres are at Tula, Novomoskovsk, Shchekino, Aleksin, Uzlovaya and Yefremov. In 2000 there were 1,103 km of railway lines and 5,162 km of paved roads in the Oblast.

Around 73.7% of the Oblast's territory is used for agricultural purposes. Agricultural activity, in which some 11.4% of the working population were engaged in 2000, consists primarily of animal husbandry and production of grain, potatoes and sugar beet. Agricultural production was worth 10,449m. roubles in 2000. The Oblast's main industries are mechanical engineering, metal-working, chemicals, ferrous metallurgy, food-processing, the production of brown coal (lignite) and the generation of electricity. Industry employed approximately 28.0% of the working population in 2000, and total industrial production amounted to a value of 45,032m. roubles. Ferrous metallurgy, mechanical engineering and metal-working dominated exports in the region. A tourism sector is encouraged by the city's history and the Yasnaya Polyana country estate of Count Leo Tolstoy (1828–1910), the writer.

The economically active population in the Oblast numbered 831,000 in 2000, when 9.7% of the labour force were unemployed. In mid-2002 those in employment earned an average monthly wage of 3,368.1 roubles; the region was named as one of the worst for wage arrears in that year. The 2000 budget showed a surplus of 233.9m. roubles. The main foreign trading partners of the Oblast are Germany, Italy, the Republic of Korea (South Korea), Switzerland and the USA. In 2000 external trade comprised US $651.5m. of exports and $139.9m. of imports. Total foreign investment amounted to $81.6m. in that year. At 31 December 2000 6,300 small businesses were registered in Tula Oblast.

Directory

Head of the Regional Administration (Governor): VASILII A. STARODUBTSEV; 300600 Tula, pl. Lenina 2; tel. (0872) 27-84-36; fax (0872) 20-63-26; e-mail michel@michel.tula.adm.tula.ru; internet www.starodubtsev.tula.ru.

Chairman of the Regional Duma: OLEG D. LUKICHEV; 300600 Tula, pl. Lenina 2; tel. (0872) 20-50-24; fax (0872) 36-47-66; e-mail oblduma@duma.tula.ru.

Representation of Tula Oblast in the Russian Federation: 127030 Moscow, Veskovskii per. 2; tel. (095) 978-14-56; fax (095) 978-06-43.

Head of Tula City Administration (Mayor): SERGEI I. KAZAKOV; Tula; tel. (0872) 27-80-85.

Tver Oblast

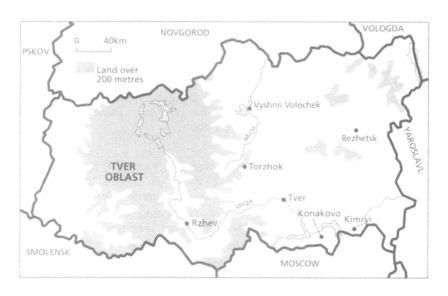

Tver Oblast (known as Kalinin from 1931 to 1990) is situated in the central part of the Eastern European Plain. It forms part of the Central Federal Okrug and the Central Economic Area. Moscow and Smolensk Oblasts lie to the south, Pskov to the west, Novgorod and Vologda to the north and Yaroslavl to the east. Its westernmost point lies some 50 km (just over 30 miles) from the border with Belarus. The major rivers in the region are the Volga, which rises within its territory, the Mologa and the Tvertsa. The Zapadnaya Dvina and the Msta rivers also have their sources in the Oblast. It has more than 500 lakes, the largest of which is the Seliger, and contains nine reservoirs. The western part of the territory is mountainous, containing the Valdai Highlands. About one-third of the territory of the Oblast is forested. It occupies 84,100 sq km (32,460 sq miles) and is divided into 36 administrative districts and 23 cities. At 1 January 2001 the region had 1,575,000 inhabitants, and a population density, therefore, of 18.7 per sq km. In 2001 some 73.6% of the population inhabited urban areas. The administrative centre is at Tver (formerly Kalinin), a river-port, which at the beginning of January 2001 had a population of 447,100.

History

The city of Tver was founded as a fort in the 12th century. The Oblast was formed in January 1935. In the 1990s the region's relations with the federal Government, led by President Boris Yeltsin, were not always cordial. Having criticized Yeltsin for his policy towards the federal parliament, in October 1993 the Tver Regional Soviet refused to disband itself. It was subsequently obliged to comply with the directives of the federal authorities and a new body, the Legislative Assembly, was elected the following year. This, too, was dominated by members of the Communist Party of the Russian Federation (CPRF) and was obstructive of executive action. President Yeltsin appointed a respected local figure to head the regional administration and decided to permit a gubernatorial election in December 1995. The incumbent was defeated by Vladimir Platov, then a member of the CPRF; in the simultaneous election to the State Duma, the CPRF secured 27% of the regional vote, compared with only 8% for the pro-Yeltsin bloc. The federal Government attempted to placate local opinion, therefore, and in June 1996 the regional authorities were granted greater autonomy with the signing of a power-sharing treaty. Platov, by then one of the founders of the pro-Vladimir Putin Unity electoral bloc, won a second term in office in the second round of voting at the gubernatorial election held in January 2000, narrowly defeating the CPRF candidate and promising reform and improved living standards. Unity also obtained the largest number of votes cast for any party in elections to the State Duma in the Oblast in the previous month.

Economy

In 1999 Tver Oblast's gross regional product amounted to 27,887.7m. roubles, equivalent to 17,307.6 roubles per head. Industry is the dominant branch of the Oblast's economy. The principal industrial centres are Tver, Vyshnii Volochek, Rzhev, Torzhok and Kimryi. The region is crossed by road and rail routes between Moscow and Rīga, Latvia, and a highway between Moscow and St Petersburg. In 2000 the total length of railway track in the Oblast was 1,811 km, and the network of paved roads was 14,959 km long. There were 924 km of navigable waterways in the region in 1998, mainly on the Volga. There is an international airport at Tver.

Around 2.4m. ha (5.9m. acres) of the Oblast's territory is used for agricultural purposes, of which two-thirds is arable land. Agriculture in Tver Oblast, which employed around 14.8% of the work-force in 2000, consists mainly of animal husbandry and the production of vegetables, potatoes and flax (the region grows around one-quarter of flax produced in Russia). Total agricultural output amounted to a value of 9,238m. roubles in 2000. The region contains deposits of peat, lime and coal, and is famous for its mineral-water reserves. Its major industries are mechanical engineering, metal-working, electricity generation, light manufacturing, chemicals, wood-working, the processing of forestry and agricultural products, printing and glass-, china- and faience-making. In 2000 some 28.0% of the Oblast's working population were engaged in industry, and total industrial production was worth 28,539m. roubles. In 1998 there were 20 commercial banks and 100 insurance companies and branches in operation on the Oblast's territory.

The region's economically active population numbered 778,000 in 2000, when 9.4% of the labour force were unemployed. The average wage amounted to 3,413.9 roubles per month in mid-2002. The 2000 regional budget showed a deficit of 51.3m. roubles. Tver's main trading partners in the late 1990s were the People's Republic of China, Germany, Switzerland, Turkey and the USA. In 2000 external trade amounted to a value of US $105.0m. in exports and $174.2m. in imports. In 1998 a social and cultural development programme for Tver Oblast (for 1998–2005) was adopted by the federal Government, which gave tax incentives to foreign investors. Total foreign investment in the Oblast amounted to $7.9m. in 2000. In that year 3,600 small businesses were operating in the region, employing 38,000 people.

Directory

Head of the Regional Administration (Governor): VLADIMIR I. PLATOV; 170000 Tver, ul. Sovetskaya 44; tel. (0822) 33-10-51; fax (0822) 42-55-08; e-mail tradm@tversa.ru; internet www.region.tver.ru.

Chairman of the Legislative Assembly: VYACHESLAV A. MIRONOV; 170000 Tver, ul. Sovetskaya 33; tel. (0822) 33-10-11; fax (0822) 33-29-60; e-mail zsto@tversu.ru.

Representation of Tver Oblast in the Russian Federation: 103246 Moscow, ul. B. Dmitrovka 26; tel. (095) 926-65-19; fax (095) 292-14-85.

Head of Tver City Administration (Mayor): ALEKSANDR P. BELOUSOV; 170640 Tver, ul. Sovetskaya 11; tel. (0822) 33-01-31; fax (0822) 42-59-39; e-mail info@www.tver.ru; internet www.tver.ru.

Tyumen Oblast

Tyumen Oblast is situated in the Western Siberian Plain, extending from the Kara Sea in the north to the border with Kazakhstan in the south. It forms part of the Urals Federal Okrug and the West Siberian Economic Area. Much of its territory comprises the Khanty-Mansii and Yamal-Nenets Autonomous Okrugs (AOks). To the west (going south to north) lie Kurgan, Sverdlovsk, Komi and the Nenets AOk—part of Archangel Oblast; to the east lie Omsk, Tomsk and Krasnoyarsk—in the far north the border is with Krasnoyarsk's Taimyr AOk. The region has numerous rivers, its major ones being the Ob, the Taz, the Pur and the Nadym. Much of its territory is taiga (forested marshland). The territory of the Oblast, including that of the AOks, occupies an area of 1,435,200 sq km (554,130 sq miles) and is divided into 38 administrative districts and 28 cities. The Oblast, in particular that section within the AOks, is a sparsely populated region: the estimated total population at 1 January 2002 was 3,272,200 and the population density was 2.3 per sq km. When the area of the AOks is excluded, the area of the Oblast is 161,800 sq km, and the population of this area was 1,339,500 in 2002, giving a population density of 8.3 per sq km. The Oblast, excluding the AOks, is divided into 22 administrative districts and five cities. In 2001 some 76.6% of the entire Oblast's inhabitants lived in urban areas. The Oblast's administrative centre is at Tyumen, which then had a population of 500,200. Other major cities outside the AOks are Tobolsk (96,800) and Ishim (60,200).

History

Tyumen city was founded in 1585 on the site of a Tatar settlement. It subsequently became an important centre for trade with the Chinese Empire. Tyumen Oblast was formed on 14 August 1944. The region became industrialized after the Second World War. On 21 October 1993 the Regional Soviet in Tyumen Oblast repealed its earlier condemnation of government action against the federal parliament but refused to disband itself. Legislative elections were held in the Oblast in March

1994, but the results in several constituencies were declared invalid, owing to a low level of participation. Eventually a new assembly, the Regional Duma, was elected. It remained communist-led, but the pro-Government faction was well represented. This position was confirmed by regional results in the general election of 1995. During the mid-1990s the exact nature of the relationship between Tyumen Oblast proper and the two AOks, which wished to retain a greater share of the income from their wealth of natural resources, became a source of intra-élite contention, despite the establishment of a co-ordinating administrative council between the three entities in 1995. In 1997 the two AOks (which between them accounted for over 90% of the output and profits in the oblast) had boycotted the gubernatorial elections for the Oblast, while a subsequent Constitutional Court ruling failed to clarify the status of the AOks in relation to the Oblast. However, the AOks did participate in elections to the Regional Duma later in 1997. In 1998 Sergei Korepanov, the former Chairman of the Yamal-Nenets legislature, was elected Chairman of that of Tyumen. This was widely considered to form part of a plan by representatives of the AOks (who together constituted a majority of seats in the oblast legislature) to remove the Governor of Tyumen, Leonid Roketskii. At the gubernatorial election held on 14 January 2001, Sergei Sobyanin, a former speaker in the legislature of the Khanty-Mansii AOk and the first deputy presidential representative in the Urals Federal Okrug, defeated Roketskii, obtaining more than 51% of the votes cast.

Economy

All figures in this survey include data for the two AOks, which are also treated separately. In the mid-1990s Tyumen Oblast was considered to have great economic potential, owing to its vast hydrocarbons and timber reserves (mainly located in the Khanty-Mansii and Taimyr AOks). In 1999 its gross regional product amounted to 356,139.0m. roubles, equivalent to 110,475.2 roubles per head (by far the highest figure in the Russian Federation). Its main industrial centres are at Tyumen, Tobolsk, Surgut, Nizhnevartovsk and Nadym. In 2000 there were 2,451 km (1,523 miles) of railway lines and 9,361 km of paved roads on the Oblast's territory.

The Oblast's agriculture, which employed just 6.1% of its work-force in 2000, consists mainly of animal husbandry (livestock- and reindeer-breeding), fishing, the production of grain, flax and vegetables, fur farming and hunting. In 2000 agricultural production was worth 12,310m. roubles. In the late 1990s the Oblast's reserves of petroleum, natural gas and peat were estimated at 60%, 90% and 36%, respectively, of Russia's total supply. The Tyumen Oil Company (TNK), formed in 1995 from nine other companies, is among the largest petroleum companies in Russia and produced 156m. barrels of crude petroleum in 1996. From 1997, when the state's share in the company was reduced to less than one-half, TNK became increasingly market-driven and dismissed around one-quarter of its work-force by 1999, as one of its largest subsidiaries, Nizhnevartovskneftegaz (NNG) became subject to bankruptcy procedures. Overall petroleum output in the region totalled 213m. metric tons in 2000. The Oblast's other major industries are the production of electrical energy, mechanical engineering and metal-working. Industry employed some 18.2% of the Oblast's working population in 2000 and generated a total of 469,374m. roubles, by far the highest level of any federal subject.

The economically active population totalled 1,687,000 in 2000, when 10.3% of the work-force were unemployed, compared with 14.0% in 1998. The average monthly wage was 12,400.9 roubles in mid-2002, among the highest wages in the Federation. The budget for 2000 showed a surplus of 6,323.2m. roubles. Trade figures for 2000 showed the Oblast to have generated some US $15,821.4m. in exports (of which some 92% were destined for non-member countries of the Commonwealth of Independent States) and to have purchased $807.0m. of imports. Total foreign investment in the Oblast amounted to $1,842.6m. in that year. At the end of 2000 12,500 small businesses were registered in the region.

Directory

Governor: SERGEI S. SOBYANIN; 625004 Tyumen, ul. Volodarskogo 45; tel. (3452) 46-77-20; fax (3452) 46-55-42; internet www.adm.tyumen.ru.

Chairman of the Regional Duma: SERGEI YE. KOREPANOV; 625018 Tyumen, ul. Respubliki 52, Dom Sovetov; tel. (3452) 45-50-81; e-mail tyumduma@sbtx.tmn.ru: internet www.tmn.ru/~tyumduma.

Representative of Tyumen Oblast in the Russian Federation: GEORGII V. GLYBIN; 119017 Moscow, ul. Pyatnitskaya 47/2; tel. and fax (095) 953-03-24.

Head of Tyumen City Administration: STEPAN M. KIRICHUK; 625036 Tyumen, ul. Pervomaiskaya 20; tel. (3452) 24-67-42; fax 46-42-72; e-mail ves@tyumen -city.ru; internet www.tyumen-city.ru.

Ulyanovsk Oblast

Ulyanovsk Oblast is situated in the Volga Highlands. It forms part of the Volga Federal Okrug and the Volga Economic Area. The Republics of Mordoviya and of Chuvashiya and Tatarstan lie to the north-west and to the north, respectively. There are also borders with Samara Oblast in the south-east, Saratov Oblast in the south and Penza Oblast in the south-west. The region's major river is the Volga. The region occupies an area of 37,300 sq km (14,400 sq miles) and is divided into 21 administrative districts and six cities. The estimated total population of the Oblast was 1,439,600 in January 2002, when the population density, therefore, was 38.6 per sq km. In 2001 some 73.2% of the population inhabited urban areas. The administrative centre at Ulyanovsk (formerly Simbirsk) had a population of 662,100 in 2001. The other major city in the region is Dimitrovgrad (136,400).

History

Simbirsk city was founded in 1648. Lenin (Vladimir Ulyanov) was born there in 1870, and it was his home until 1887. The city assumed his family name following his death in 1924. Ulyanovsk Oblast, which was formed on 19 January 1943, formed part of the 'red belt' of communist support in post-Soviet Russia. Thus, it refused to revert to its old name and also gave the Communist Party of the Russian Federation (CPRF) 37% of the regional votes cast in the 1995 elections to the federal State Duma. In December 1996 the CPRF-backed candidate, Yurii Goryachev, won the election to the governorship of the Oblast. Goryachev, whose support came largely from the Oblast's rural community, banned local privatization and collective-farm reforms, imposed restrictions on imports and exports, and subsidized bread prices until early 1997. Goryachev was defeated in the gubernatorial elections held in December 2000, and replaced by Gen. Vladimir Shamanov. In June 2002 the national power company, Unified Energy Systems (RAO EES Rossii), announced its intention to appeal to the federal authorities for the direct imposition of federal rule over Ulyanovsk Oblast, owing to the region's debts to that company.

Economy

In 1999 Ulyanovsk Oblast's gross regional product amounted to 26,050.1m. roubles, or 17,693.5 roubles per head. The Oblast's major industrial centres are at Ulyanovsk and Melekess. In 2000 there were 716 km (445 miles) of railway lines and 4,621 km of paved roads on the Oblast's territory.

Around 1.5m. ha of its territory is used for agricultural purposes, of which over four-fifths is arable land. Agriculture in the region, which employed some 15.8% of the working population in 2000, consists primarily of animal husbandry and the production of grain, sunflower seeds and sugar beet. Total agricultural production amounted to a value of 7,092m. roubles in 2000. The Oblast's main industries are mechanical engineering and metal-working, food-processing, electrical energy and fuel production, and the manufacture of building materials. The region's major companies included the UAZ automobile plant and the Aviastar-SP aeroplane manufacturer (both of which were working at 50% capacity in the late 1990s). Industry employed 28.8% of the working population in 2000, and generated some 28,961m. roubles.

The economically active population numbered 684,000 in 2000, when only 6.4% of the labour force were unemployed, the lowest level in any federal subject other than the two federal cities and the remote Evenk and Taimyr AOks. Those in employment earned an average of 2,907.5 roubles per month in mid-2002. There was a budgetary deficit of 383.1m. roubles in 2000. In that year external trade constituted US $173.1m. in exports and $52.9m. in imports; total foreign investment in the Oblast amounted to $1.5m. At 31 December 2000 5,000 small businesses were registered in the region.

Directory

Head of the Regional Administration (Governor): Gen. VLADIMIR A. SHAM-ANOV; 432970 Ulyanovsk, pl. Lenina 1; tel. (8422) 41-20-78; fax (8422) 32-52-44; e-mail admobl@mv.ru; internet obladm.ulntc.ru.

Chairman of the Legislative Assembly: BORIS I. ZOTOV; 432700 Ulyanovsk, ul. Radishcheva 1; tel. (8422) 41-34-52; fax (8422) 41-20-74; internet zsuo.ru.

Representative of Ulyanovsk Oblast in the Russian Federation: GENNADII V. SAVINOV; 119002 Moscow, per. Denezhnyi 12; tel. (095) 241-31-42; fax (095) 241-38-99.

Head of Ulyanovsk City Administration (Mayor): PAVEL ROMANENKO; 432700 Ulyanovsk, ul. Kuznetsova 7; tel. (8422) 41-20-78; fax (8422) 31-90-64.

Vladimir Oblast

Vladimir Oblast is situated in the central part of the Eastern European Plain. It forms part of the Central Federal Okrug and the Central Economic Area. It shares borders with Ryazan and Moscow to the south-west, Yaroslavl and Ivanovo to the north and Nizhnii Novgorod to the east. The Oblast's main rivers are the Oka and its tributary, the Klyazma. Over one-half of its territory is forested. It occupies a total of 29,000 sq km (11,200 sq miles) and measures around 170 km (106 miles) from south to north and 280 km from west to east. The Oblast is divided into 16 administrative districts and 23 cities. It had an estimated population of 1,573,900 at 1 January 2002, giving a population density of 54.3 per sq km. In 2001 some 80.4% of the population inhabited urban areas. The Oblast's administrative centre is at Vladimir, which had a population of 331,700 in 2001. Other major cities are Kovrov (159,300), Murom (139,500), Gus-Khrustalnyi (71,500) and Aleksandrov (65,000).

History

Founded in 1108 as a frontier fortress by Prince Vladimir Monomakh, after the disintegration of Kievan Rus, Vladimir city was the seat of the principality of Vladimir-Suzdal and an early Orthodox Christian bishopric. Vladimir fell under the rule of Muscovy in 1364 and was supplanted by Moscow as the seat of the Russian Orthodox patriarch, although Vladimir was chosen for the coronations of several Muscovite princes. It declined in importance from the 15th century. Vladimir Oblast was formed on 14 August 1944.

In the 1990s it awarded a respectable level of support to all the main national parties. In the December 1995 parliamentary election, the Communist Party of the Russian Federation (CPRF), the nationalist Liberal Democrats, and the pro-Government Our Home is Russia all obtained more than 10% of the votes cast, while in the December 1999 election the CPRF obtained only a slightly higher share of the votes cast than the recently formed pro-Government party, Unity. The

CPRF, however, secured the election of Nikolai Vinogradov, former Chairman of the Legislative Assembly, to the post of Governor in late 1996. Vinogradov was re-elected as Governor in December 2000, with some 66% of the votes cast, defeating Yurii Glasov, who had held the post in 1991–96.

Economy

Vladimir Oblast's gross regional product in 1999 totalled 25,577.0m. roubles, or 15,828.3 roubles per head. The Oblast's main industrial centres are at Vladimir, Kovrov, Murom, Aleksandrov, Kolchugino, Vyazniki and Gus-Khrustalnyi. In 2000 there were 929 km of railway track and 5,530 km of paved roads on its territory.

Agriculture in the region, which employed 9.9% of its work-force in 2000, consists mainly of animal husbandry, vegetable production and horticulture. Total agricultural output stood at 7,892m. roubles in 2000. Vladimir is rich in peat deposits and timber reserves, but relies on imports for around 70% of its energy supplies. The Oblast's main industries are mechanical engineering, metal-working, food-processing, the production of electrical energy, light manufacturing, chemicals, glass-making and handicrafts. Industrial output in 2000 was worth 36,010m. roubles. In that year a total of 33.8% of the working population were engaged in industry. Vladimir city's largest employer is the Vladimir Tractor Plant, which struggled to adapt to the new economic conditions from the 1990s.

The economically active population numbered 810,000 in 2000, when 12.2% of the labour force were unemployed. The average monthly wage in the Oblast was 3,128.2 roubles in mid-2002. In 2000 there was a regional surplus of 158.3m. roubles. In that year external trade constituted US \$101.1m. in exports and \$147.3m. in imports; total foreign investment amounted to some \$21.3m. At 31 December 2000 6,900 small businesses were registered in the region.

Directory

Head of the Regional Administration (Governor): NIKOLAI V. VINOGRADOV; 600000 Vladimir, pr. Oktyabrskii 21; tel. (0922) 33-15-52; fax (0922) 35-34-45; e-mail post@obladm.vladimir.ru; internet avo.ru.

Chairman of the Legislative Assembly: VITALII YA. KOTOV; 600000 Vladimir, Oktyabrskaya pr. 21; tel. (0922) 22-64-42; fax (0922) 22-60-13.

Representative of Vladimir Oblast in the Russian Federation: ANDREI V. YARIN; Moscow; tel. (095) 299-66-49.

Head of Vladimir City Administration: IGOR V. SHAMOV; 600000 Vladimir, ul. Gorkogo 36; tel. (0922) 23-28-17; fax (0922) 23-85-54; e-mail mayor@ cityadmin.vladimir.su; internet www.cityadm.vladimir.su.

Volgograd Oblast

Volgograd Oblast is situated in the south-east of the Eastern European Plain. It forms part of the Southern Federal Okrug and the Volga Economic Area. The Oblast has an international border with Kazakhstan to its east. The federal subjects of Astrakhan and Kalmykiya lie to the south-east, Rostov to the south-west, Voronezh to the north-west and Saratov to the north. The Oblast's main rivers are the Volga and the Don. Its terrain varies from fertile black earth (*chernozem*) to semi-desert. Volgograd city is the eastern terminus of the Volga–Don Canal. The region occupies an area of 113,900 sq km (43,980 sq miles) and is divided into 33 administrative districts and 19 cities. At 1 January 2002 it had an estimated total of 2,636,500 inhabitants, and a population density of 23.1 per sq km. In 2001 some 73.9% of the population lived in urban areas. In 1989 around 89% of the population were ethnic Russians, while 3% were Ukrainians, 2% were Kazakhs and 1% were Tatars. In the early 1990s there was an influx of immigrants to the Oblast from more unstable areas of the Caucasus. The Oblast's administrative centre is at Volgograd, which had a population of 982,900 in 2001. Other major cities are Volzhskii (281,700) and Kamyshin (124,100).

History

The city of Volgograd (known as Tsaritsyn until 1925 and Stalingrad from 1925 until 1961) was founded in the 16th century, to protect the Volga trade route. It was built on the River Volga, at the point where it flows nearest to the Don (the two river systems were later connected by a canal). The Oblast was formed on 10 January 1934. In 1942–43 the city was the scene of a decisive battle between the forces of the USSR and Nazi Germany.

In October 1993 the Regional Soviet in Volgograd Oblast eventually agreed to a reform of the system of government in the Oblast. It decided to hold elections to a new 30-seat Regional Duma, which took place the following year. The Communist Party of the Russian Federation (CPRF) was the largest single party. The continued pre-eminence of the old ruling élite was confirmed by the 27% share of the regional poll secured by the CPRF list in the 1995 election to the State Duma. Furthermore, the December 1996 gubernatorial election was won by Nikolai Maksyuta, a communist and a former Chairman of the regional assembly. In December 1998 CPRF candidates won some 23 of the 32 seats in the regional legislative elections. On 24 September the Regional Duma had voted for the principle of restoring the Oblast's previous name of Stalingrad, and this notion remained popular. Maksyuta was re-elected for a second term as Governor on 19 December 1999.

Economy

In 1999 Volgograd Oblast's gross regional product amounted to 49,974.2m. roubles, or 18,602.7 roubles per head. Its main industrial centres are at Volgograd, Bolzshkii and Kamyshyn. In 2000 there were 1,619 km (1,006 miles)of railways and 8,701 km of paved roads. In 1996 construction of a road bridge across the Volga river into Volgograd began.

The region's principal agricultural products are grain, sunflower seeds, fruit, vegetables, mustard and cucurbits (gourds and melons). Horticulture and animal husbandry are also important. In 2000 18.8% of the Oblast's work-force were engaged in agriculture. Total agricultural production amounted to a value of 16,724m. roubles in that year. The Oblast's mineral reserves include petroleum, natural gas and phosphorites. The main industries in the Oblast are petroleum-refining, chemicals and petrochemicals, mechanical engineering, metal-working, ferrous and non-ferrous metallurgy, the production of electricity, the manufacture of building materials, light manufacturing, food-processing and the production of petroleum and natural gas. Industry employed 23.7% of the working population in 2000, when total industrial production was worth 56,995m. roubles.

The economically active population of the Oblast numbered 1,295,000 in 2000, when 9.7% of the labour force were unemployed. The average monthly wage was 3,312.7 roubles in mid-2002. In 2000 there was a budgetary deficit of 695.7m. roubles. In that year external trade constituted US $869.8m. in exports and $252.7m. in imports; total foreign investment amounted to $139.5m. In 2000 there were some 94 joint foreign enterprises in the region, including 10 with investment from Cyprus and eight with investment from the United Kingdom. At the end of 2000 13,000 small businesses were registered in the region.

Directory

Head of the Regional Administration (Governor): NIKOLAI K. MAKSYUTA; 400098 Volgograd, pr. Lenina 9; tel. (8442) 33-66-88; fax (8442) 93-62-12; e-mail glava@volganet.ru; internet www.volganet.ru.

Chairman of the Regional Duma: SERGEI MIKHAILOV; 400098 Volgograd, pr. Lenina 9; tel. (8442) 36-54-25; fax (8422) 36-44-03.

Representation of Volgograd Oblast in the Russian Federation: Moscow; tel. (095) 229-96-73.

Head of Volgograd City Administration (Mayor): YURII V. CHEKHOV; 400131 Volgograd, ul. Volodarskogo 5; tel. (8442) 33-50-10; internet www.volgadmin.ru.

Vologda Oblast

Vologda Oblast is situated in the north-west of the Eastern European Plain. It forms part of the North-Western Federal Okrug and the Northern Economic Area. It has a short border, in the north-west, with the Republic of Kareliya, which includes the southern tip of Lake Onega (Onezhskoye). Onega also forms the northern end of a border with Leningrad Oblast, which lies to the west of Vologda. Novgorod Oblast lies to the south-west and Tver, Yaroslavl and Kostroma Oblasts to the south. Kirov Oblast forms an eastern border and Archangel Oblast lies to the north. The region's main rivers are the Sukhona, the Yug, the Sheksna and the Mologa. There are three major lakes, in addition to Lake Onega—Beloye, Bozhe and Kubenskoye. Vologda Oblast occupies 145,700 sq km (56,250 sq miles) and extends for 385 km (240 miles) from south to north and 650 km from west to east. It is divided into 26 administrative districts and 15 cities. The Oblast's population at the beginning of 2002 was estimated at 1,301,100 and the population density was, therefore, 8.9 per sq km. Some 68.3% of the total population inhabited urban areas in 2001. The Oblast's administrative centre is at Vologda, which had a population of 298,200 in 2001. Its other major city is Cherepovets (323,300).

History

Vologda province was annexed by the state of Muscovy in the 14th century. The city was, for a time, the intended capital of Tsar Ivan IV ('the Terrible', 1533–84). Until the Bolshevik Revolution of 1917 the province was administered by governors appointed by the Tsar. Vologda Oblast was formed on 23 September 1937.

In 1991 the newly elected Russian President, Boris Yeltsin, appointed a new head of administration of Vologda Oblast. In mid-1993 the Vologda Oblast declared itself a republic, but failed to be acknowledged as such by the federal authorities. On 13 October the Regional Soviet transferred its responsibilities to the Regional Administration and elections were later held to a Legislative Assembly. In 1995 ballots implemented the Statutes of Vologda Oblast, according to which the region's

Governor would lead the executive. There was a high level of support for the nationalist Liberal Democrats, particularly in the countryside, for much of the 1990s. In June 1996 Boris Yeltsin dismissed the local Governor, who was subsequently arrested and imprisoned on charges of corruption. His successor, Vyacheslav Pozgalev, won 80% of the votes cast in a direct election in late 1996, and was re-elected for a further term of office on 19 December 1999, with 83% of the votes cast.

Economy

In 1999 Vologda Oblast's gross regional product amounted to 47,279.0m. roubles, equivalent to 35,591.0 roubles per head. Its main industrial centres are at Vologda, Cherepovets, Velikii Ustyug and Sokol. In 2000 there were 768 km of railway track in general use on its territory, as well as 11,766 km of paved roads. There are some 1,800 km of navigable waterways, including part of the Volga–Baltic route network.

Agriculture in Vologda Oblast, which employed 11.7% of the work-force in 2000, consists mainly of animal husbandry and production of flax and vegetables. The region is famous for its butter. In 2000 total agricultural output was worth 9,878m. roubles. The territory imports around one-half of its electrical energy from other Oblasts (Kostroma, Kirov, Leningrad, Tver and Yaroslavl). Its main industries are ferrous metallurgy (the region produces some 20% of Russia's iron, 19% of its rolled stock and 18% of its steel), chemicals (around 11% of the country's mineral fertilizers are manufactured in Vologda Oblast), the processing of forestry products, mechanical engineering, pharmaceuticals, glass-making, food-processing and handicrafts, such as lace-making. In 2000 29.1% of the region's working population were engaged in industry. The industrial sector generated a total of 87,603m. roubles.

The Oblast's economically active population numbered 673,000 in 2000, when the rate of unemployment was 8.0%. Those in employment in mid-2002 earned, on average, 4,525.8 roubles per month. The 2000 budget showed a surplus of 308.3m. roubles. In 2000 export trade constituted US $1,518.2m. in exports and $126.8m. in imports; total foreign investment in the Oblast in that year amounted to $19.9m. In December 2000 6,000 small businesses were registered in the region.

Directory

Governor: VYACHESLAV YE. POZGALEV; 160035 Vologda, ul. Gertsena 2; tel. (8172) 72-07-64; fax (8172) 25-15-54; e-mail governor@vologda-oblast.ru; internet www.vologda-oblast.ru.

Chairman of the Legislative Assembly: NIKOLAI V. TIKHOMIROV; 160035 Vologda, ul. Pushkinskaya 25; tel. (8172) 72-02-60; fax (8172) 25-11-33; e-mail zsvo@vologda.ru.

Chief Representative of Vologda Oblast in the Russian Federation: VLADIMIR S. SMIRNOV; Moscow; tel. (095) 201-73-03; fax (095) 201-55-24.

Head of Vologda City Administration: ALEKSEI S. YAKUNICHEV; 160035 Vologda, ul. Kamennyi most 4; tel. (8172) 72-00-42; fax (8172) 72-25-59.

Voronezh Oblast

Voronezh Oblast is situated in the centre of the Eastern European Plain on the middle reaches of the Volga. It forms part of the Central Federal Okrug and the Central Chernozem Economic Area. There is a short border with Ukraine in the south. Of the neighbouring Russian federal territories, Belgorod and Kursk lie to the west, Lipetsk and Tambov to the north, a short border with Saratov to the north-east, Volgograd to the east and Rostov to the south-east. The west of the territory is situated within the Central Russian Highlands and the east in the Oka-Don Lowlands. Its main rivers are the Don, the Khoper and the Bityug. The Voronezh region occupies an area of 52,400 sq km (20,230 sq miles) and is divided into 32 administrative districts and 15 cities. The Oblast's estimated population at 1 January 2002 was 2,414,700, and its population density was, therefore, 46.1 per sq km. In 2001 some 62.1% of the population lived in urban areas. The region's administrative centre is at Voronezh, which had a population of 901,800 in 2001.

History

Voronezh city was founded in 1586 as a fortress. The centre of a fertile region, the city began to industrialize in the tsarist period. Voronezh Oblast was formed in June 1934. In the immediate post-Soviet years the region remained committed to the Communist Party of the Russian Federation (CPRF), which controlled the Regional Duma. The region also largely supported the CPRF leader, Gennadii Zyuganov, in the presidential election of June 1996, although this level of support was not repeated in the election of March 2000. A CPRF member and former speaker of the Oblast assembly, Ivan Shabonov, was elected Governor in December 1996. At the gubernatorial election held in December 2000 Shabonov received only 15% of the votes cast, and was defeated by Federal Security Service (FSB) Gen. Vladimir Kulakov, who obtained some 60% of the votes. Subsequently, at the regional legislative election held in March 2001 the CPRF reduced its level of representation from 23 seats to just five.

Economy

In 1999 Voronezh Oblast's gross regional product amounted to 40,710.1m. roubles, equivalent to 16,503.2 roubles per head. The important industrial centres in the Oblast are at Voronezh, Borisoglebsk, Georgii u-Dezh, Rossosh and Kalach. In 2000 the territory contained some 1,189 km (739 miles) of railway track (of which 60.2% are electrified) and 9,102 km of paved roads. The road network includes sections of major routes, such as the Moscow–Rostov, Moscow–Astrakhan and Kursk–Saratov highways. There are some 640 km of navigable waterways.

Around 4.7m. ha (11.6m. acres—90% of the total) of Voronezh's territory is used for agricultural purposes, of which 3.1m. ha is arable land. In 2000 24.3% of the Oblast's working population were employed in the agricultural sector. The Oblast's agriculture consists mainly of the production of grain, sugar beet, sunflower seeds, fruit and vegetables. Animal husbandry was also important. Total agricultural production amounted to a value of 19,134m. roubles in 2000. Its main industries are mechanical engineering, metal-working, chemicals and petrochemicals, the production of electricity, the manufacture of building materials and food-processing. In 2000 some 19.8% of the work-force were engaged in industry, the output of which was valued at a total of 33,131m. roubles.

The Oblast's economically active population numbered 1,179,000 in 2000, when 10.0% of the labour force were unemployed. In mid-2002 the Oblast's average wage was 2.817.3 roubles per month. There was a budgetary deficit of 275.6m. roubles in 2000. In that year the value of external trade amounted to US $182.4m. in exports and $168.2m. in imports. Foreign investment in the region increased dramatically from the mid-1990s, and in 2000 it amounted to $20.9m., compared with $4.0m. in 1998. In 2000 there were 53 joint- or foreign enterprises, established primarily with funds from Belarus, Cyprus, Germany, the United Kingdom and the USA. At 31 December 2000 there were 11,000 small businesses registered in the region.

Directory

Head of the Regional Administration: VLADIMIR G. KULAKOV; 394018 Voronezh, pl. Lenina 1; tel. (0732) 55-27-37; fax (0732) 55-38-78; internet admin.vrn.ru.

Chairman of the Regional Duma: ALEKSEI M. NAKVASIN; 394018 Voronezh, ul. Kirova 2; tel. (0732) 55-06-88; fax (0732) 52-09-22; e-mail voblduma@inbox.ru.

Representative of Voronezh Oblast in the Russian Federation: ALEKSANDR I. FIRSOV; 127006 Moscow, ul. M. Dmitrovka 3/10/501; tel. (095) 250-98-55; fax (095) 299-90-27.

Head of Voronezh City Administration (Mayor): ALEKSANDR KOVALEV; 394067 Voronezh, ul. Plekhanovskaya 10; tel. (0732) 55-34-20; fax (0732) 55-47-16; e-mail admin@city.vrn.ru; internet www.city.vrn.ru.

Yaroslavl Oblast

Yaroslavl Oblast is situated in the central part of the Eastern European Plain. It forms part of the Central Federal Okrug and the Central Economic Area. Ivanovo Oblast lies to the south-east, Vladimir and Moscow Oblasts to the south, Tver Oblast to the west, Vologda Oblast to the north and Kostroma Oblast to the east. Yaroslavl city, which lies on the Volga, is 282 km (175 miles) north-east of Moscow. The region has 2,500 rivers and lakes, the two principal lakes being Nero and Pleshcheyevo, and there is a large reservoir at Rybinsk. The Volga river flows for 340 km through the region. Its territory, just over two-fifths of which is forested, covers a total area of 36,400 sq km (14,050 sq miles) and is divided into 17 administrative districts and 11 cities. The estimated total population in the Oblast at the beginning of 2002 was 1,386,300, giving a population density of 38.1 per sq km. In 2001 some 80.4% of the population inhabited urban areas. The Oblast's administrative centre is at Yaroslavl, which had a population of 608,800 in 2001. Other major cities are Rybinsk (238,300), Tutayev (45,400) and Pereslavl-Zalesskii (44,500).

History

Yaroslavl city is reputed to be the oldest town on the River Volga, having been founded *circa* 1024. The region was acquired by the Muscovite state during the reign of Ivan III (1462–1505). Yaroslavl Oblast was formed in March 1936. In the 1990s the region developed a liberal and diverse political climate. A range of interests was represented in the new, 23-seat Regional Duma elected in February

1994. Thus, in December 1995 the federal President, Boris Yeltsin, permitted his appointed Governor, Anatolii Listisyn, to contest a direct election for the post, which he won. He was re-elected for a further term on 19 December 1999, obtaining around 65% of the votes cast.

Economy

In 1999 Yaroslavl Oblast's gross regional product amounted to 37,749.3m. roubles, equivalent to 26,580.3 roubles per head. The major industrial centres in the region are at Yaroslavl itself, Rybinsk, Tutayev, Uglich and Pereslavl-Zalesskii. There are river-ports at Yaroslavl, Rybinsk and Uglich. Its total length of railway track amounted to 650 km in 2000. The Oblast lies on the main Moscow–Yaroslavl–Archangel and Yaroslavl–Kostroma highways. In 2000 the total length of paved roads in the territory was 6,270 km. There are also around 789 km of navigable waterways.

The climate and soil quality in the region is not favourable to agriculture. Agricultural activity, which employed just 10.1% of the working population in 2000, consists primarily of animal husbandry and the production of vegetables, flax and grain. Total agricultural output was worth 7,361m. roubles in 2000. The main industries are mechanical engineering (Rybinsk Motors is Russia's largest manufacturer of aircraft engines), chemicals and petrochemicals, petroleum-refining, peat production, the production of electricity and the processing of agricultural products. In 2000 industrial output in the region amounted to a value of 45,534m. roubles and industry employed some 31.1% of the work-force.

The economically active population numbered 747,000 in 2000, when the region had one of the lowest rates of unemployment (7.3%) in the Federation. The average wage was 3,908.4 roubles per month in mid-2002. In 2000 there was a regional budgetary surplus of 240.8m. roubles. In that year total foreign investment in the region amounted to US $7.7m., and external trade amounted to a value of $869.5m. in exports and $191.9m. in imports. At 31 December 2000 there were 7,300 small businesses registered in the Oblast.

Directory

Governor: ANATOLII I. LISITSYN; 150000 Yarovslavl, pl. Sovetskaya 3; tel. (0852) 72-81-28; fax (0852) 32-84-14; internet www.adm.yar.ru.

Chairman of the Regional Duma: ANDREI G. KRUTIKOV; 150000 Yaroslavl, pl. Sovetskaya 5; tel. (0852) 30-50-83; fax (0852) 72-76-45; e-mail duma@adm.yar.ru.

Representation of Yaroslavl Oblast in the Russian Federation: Moscow; tel. (095) 253-45-18.

Head of Yaroslavl City Administration (Mayor): VIKTOR V. VOLONCHUNAS; 150000 Yaroslavl, ul. Andropova 6; tel. (0852) 30-46-41; fax (0852) 30-52-79; e-mail ird@gw.city.yar.ru; internet www.city.yar.ru.

FEDERAL CITIES

Moscow

Moscow (Moskva) is located in the west of European Russia, on the River Moskva, which crosses the city from the north-west to the south-east. It is connected to the Volga river system by the Moscow–Volga Canal. Moscow is included in the Central Federal Okrug and the Central Economic Area. The city's total area is 994 sq km (384 sq miles). Moscow is the largest city in the Russian Federation and had an estimated total population of 8.5m. at 1 January 2002; the population of the city declined by some 460,000 in 1990–2002. In 1999 around 89.7% of the city's population were ethnic Russians, 2.9% were Ukrainians and 2.0% were Jews.

History

Moscow city was founded in about 1147. In 1325 it became the seat of the Eastern Orthodox Metropolitan of Russia (from 1589–1721 and after 1917 the Patriarch of the Russian Orthodox Church) and the steadily expanding Muscovite state became the foundation for the Russian Empire. The centre of tsarist government was moved to St Petersburg in 1712, but Moscow was restored as the Russian and Soviet capital in March 1918.

In the 1980s and 1990s, while reformists enjoyed considerable support in the city, there were also powerful forces of conservatism. On 12 June 1991 the first mayoral elections were held in the city. They were won by the democrat Gavriril Popov, but he resigned in 1992 after the economic situation of the city deteriorated to such an extent that food-rationing was introduced, and Yurii Luzhkov, head of the City Government, was appointed by federal President Boris Yeltsin in his place. On 7 October 1993 the powers of the City Soviet were suspended by presidential decree. Elections to a new 35-member Municipal Duma were held on 12 December. The Duma held its first session on 10 January 1994.

In a mayoral election held simultaneously with the federal presidential election on 16 June 1996, the reformist, generally pro-Government incumbent, Yurii Luzhkov, was re-elected by a large majority (88.7%). Thereafter Luzhkov became an increasingly high-profile political figure nation-wide. In February 1998 the Russian Constitutional Court ruled Moscow City's strict controls over residence permits to be illegal and the Supreme Court outlawed such permits (*propiski*, a legacy of the Soviet era) that July. However, Luzhkov opposed or ignored his critics, and even the ruling of the Constitutional Court. Indeed, following a number of bomb attacks in the city in late 1999, which killed over 200 people, the city's unconstitutional laws were implemented yet more firmly, with non-permanent residents of the city compelled to re-register immediately or be deported. In 1997 Luzhkov also attempted to intervene in international affairs, claiming the city of Sevastopol in Crimea (administered by Ukraine since 1954) as Russian territory. The Mayor also created a considerable power base in the capital city, and by the end of 1998 the Moscow City Government owned controlling stakes in a television station, a bank, and a range of other businesses; moreover, Luzhkov concluded a number of trade agreements with other regions. In June 1998 Luzhkov signed a power-sharing treaty with the federal authorities, following a protracted period of negotiation that resulted in the city receiving taxation and budget privileges. None the less, in municipal elections held in December 1997 the majority of seats were won by the pro-reform Democratic Choice bloc. In 1998 Luzhkov founded a nation-wide political movement, Fatherland, which subsequently joined with St Petersburg Mayor Vladimir Yakovlev's All Russia, to contest the December 1999 State Duma elections as a centrist, anti-Kremlin electoral bloc. Luzhkov had also been expected to stand as a candidate in the 2000 election for the federal presidency. Although Luzhkov was re-elected as Mayor by a clear majority on 19 December 1999, in the simultaneous nation-wide elections to the State Duma Fatherland— All Russia came third, behind the Communist Party of the Russian Federation and the newly formed pro-Government bloc, Unity. Many of Luzhkov's supporters in the regions backed the candidacy of Vladimir Putin in the presidential campaign, and, after a period of neutrality, Luzhkov and the Fatherland movement also gave their backing to Putin. (Indeed, in 2001 Fatherland—All Russia merged with Unity to form a new bloc, Unity and Fatherland-United Russia) In elections to the Municipal Duma held in December 2001 Fatherland and Unity parties each secured seven seats, followed by the pro-market Union of Rightist Forces with six seats, and the liberal Yabloko with four seats.

Economy

In 1999 the city of Moscow's gross regional product amounted to 677,372.2m. roubles, equivalent to 78,487.7 roubles per head (the second highest rate in the Russian Federation after the petroleum-producing Tyumen Oblast). There are nine railway termini in the city and 11 electrified radial lines. The metro system includes 11 lines and 164 stations and extends for 266 km (165 miles). Its trolleybus and tram routes are 1,700 km long, its bus routes 5,700 km. The public-transport system carries around 6.5m. passengers per day. Moscow's waterways connect with the Baltic, White, Caspian and Black Seas and the Sea of Azov. There are also four airports on the city's territory.

Moscow's industry consists primarily of mechanical engineering, electricity production, production of chemicals, petroleum-refining and food-processing. Industry employed around 13.3% of the city's working population in 2000 (in contrast to the 0.2% engaged in agriculture) and generated 224,765m. roubles, a figure surpassed in the Russian Federation only by Tyumen Oblast, which has the majority of gas and petroleum deposits in the Federation. The Moskvich Inc. Automobile Plant, in which the City Government held a controlling stake from 1998, is one of Moscow's principal companies. In 2000 some 15.4% of the working population of Moscow City were engaged in the construction sector. The services sector was also significant in the city economy, with the city authorities having successfully consolidated its leading position within Russia during the reform period of the 1990s: in 2000 some 18.9% of the working population of the city were employed in the services sector. Although the financial crisis of August 1998 led to a restructuring of the banking and financial sector, the city was sufficiently resourced to recover. As the Russian capital, the city was the site of a large number of government offices, as well as the centre for major business and financial companies. Tourism was another important service industry.

The economic problems of the 1990s were less accentuated in Moscow than in the rest of Russia. In 2000 the proportion of the labour force that was unemployed in Moscow City, at 3.8%, was lower than. elsewhere in the Russian Federation, with the exception of the remote Evenk Autonomous Okrug. (In 2000 the economically active population of the city stood at 4.28m.) In mid-2002 those in employment earned, on average, 6,845.2 roubles per month, one of the highest rates in the Federation. The 2000 budget showed a substantial surplus, of 22,634.6m. roubles, but the city finances, while undoubtedly healthy, are notoriously lacking in transparency. In 2000 international trade amounted to a value of US $24,593.1m. in exports and $10,882.8m. in imports, by far the highest level of any federal subject. Capital investment in the city represents around one-10th of that in Russia as a whole. In 2000 some 47% of Russian enterprises and organizations involving foreign capital were situated in Moscow City and the surrounding Moscow Oblast; in 2000 there were some 5,849 such enterprises and organizations in the region, of which 632 were joint ventures with partners from the USA, 587 had Cypriot partners, 535 had Chinese, and 512 German. Total foreign investment in the city amounted to $4,037.1m. in 2000. In September 1997 Moscow became the first city in Russia to enter the international capital market and place a Eurobonds issue. Local companies also flourished, in one of the few regions of Russia that could claim significant economic growth during the 1990s. At the end of 2000 there were 180,000 small companies registered in the city.

Directory

Mayor and Prime Minister of the Government of Moscow Federal City: YURII M. LUZHKOV; 103032 Moscow, ul. Tverskaya 13; tel. (095) 229-48-87; internet www.mos.ru.

Chairman of the Municipal Duma: VLADIMIR M. PLATONOV; 101498 Moscow, ul. Petrovka 22; tel. (095) 923-50-80; fax (095) 209-69-76; e-maild29@mcd.mos.ru; internet duma.mos.ru.

Representation of Moscow Federal City in the Russian Federation: Moscow.

St Petersburg

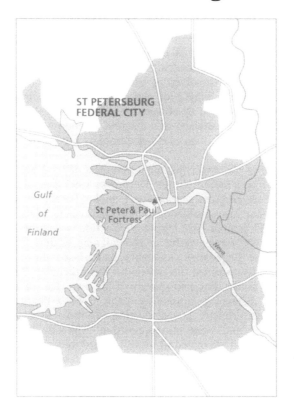

St Petersburg (Sankt Peterburg) is a seaport at the mouth of the River Neva, which drains into the easternmost part of the Gulf of Finland (part of the Baltic Sea). St Petersburg is included in the North-Western Federal Okrug and the North-Western Economic Area. The city's territory, including a total of 42 islands in the Neva delta, occupies an area of 570 sq km (220 sq miles—making it the smallest of the Russia's federal subjects), of which its waterways comprise around 10%. There are more than 580 bridges in the city and surrounding area, including 20 drawbridges. The population of the city was an estimated 4.60m. at 1 January 2002, making it Russia's second largest city.

History

St Petersburg was founded by the Tsar, Peter (Petr) I ('the Great') in 1703, as a 'window on the West', and was the Russian capital from 1712 to 1918. At the beginning of the First World War, in 1914, the city was renamed Petrograd. Following the fall of the Tsar and the Bolshevik Revolution in 1917, the Russian capital was moved back to Moscow. In 1924 the city was renamed Leningrad. During the Second World War it was besieged by German troops for 870 days, between November 1941 and January 1944. In June 1991 the citizens of Leningrad voted to restore the old name of St Petersburg and their decision was effected in October. On 24 September 1998 the federal President, Boris Yeltsin, approved the administrative merger of the city with Leningrad Oblast, although actual implementation required a number of other stages, including a referendum; there was no indication when, or if, the unification would actually occur.

During the federal constitutional crisis of 1993 the city legislature variously opposed and complied with the demands of the Russian President, Boris Yeltsin. The city Soviet was finally dissolved by presidential decree on 22 December. On 24 April 1996 the liberal Mayor of the city, Anatolii Sobchak, approved a draft treaty on the delimitation of powers between St Petersburg and the federal Government. Sobchak was defeated in a mayoral election held in May by another liberal, Vladimir Yakovlev, who soon acquired a reputation for autocracy in government.

The city was one of just two constituent members of the Federation to give the reformist Yabloko bloc a majority in the December 1995 general election. A series of corruption scandals damaged support for Yabloko, because it was the dominant party in the city, but also disillusioned potential voters (thus, a low level of participation in the December 1998 legislative election was to the cost of Yabloko). In addition, the Mayor was powerful in campaigning against the movement. On 14 January 1998 the Legislative Assembly had passed the controversial City Charter, which greatly restricted the powers of the executive. Yakovlev not only challenged it in the courts, but also sponsored his own 'list' of candidates in the legislative election, distancing himself from the Moscow-based political parties. Following a poor performance at the election, Yabloko subsequently distanced itself from Yakovlev and went into opposition. The city legislature attracted controversy in 1999, as it attempted to bring forward the date of the gubernatorial election. However, the Supreme Court ruled that attempts to hold the election earlier than originally scheduled, believed to be of benefit to the incumbent Governor, Yakovlev, were invalid. None the less, Yakovlev won the election, which was finally held in May 2000, obtaining around 73% of the votes cast and securing the support of the Communist Party of the Russian Federation and nationalist elements. At the regional legislative election held in December 2002 the majority of the incumbent deputies were re-elected to the regional assembly.

Economy

In 1999 St Petersburg's gross regional product amounted to 161,748.5m. roubles, or 34,333.5 roubles per head, less than one-half of the figure recorded in Moscow.

Industry in St Petersburg, which employed around 20.2% of its work-force in 2000 (compared with the 0.8% engaged in agriculture), consists mainly of mechanical engineering, ferrous and non-ferrous metallurgy, electricity generation, manufacture of chemicals and petrochemicals, rubber production, light manufacturing, the manufacture of building materials, food- and timber-processing, and printing. Total industrial production in the city amounted to a value of 126,234m. roubles in 2000. The city is also an important centre for service industries, such as tourism, financial services and leisure activities; in 2000 the services sector employed some 20.2% of the city's work-force.

The economically active population in St Petersburg amounted to 2.42m. in 2000, when 6.3% of the work-force were unemployed, one of the lowest rates in Russia. In mid-2002 the average wage in St Petersburg was 5,350.0 roubles, somewhat higher than the national average. The 2000 city budget showed a surplus of 1,637.0m. roubles. The city is an important centre of trade: in 2000 external trade comprised some US \$2,544.4m. in exports and \$2,598.6m. in imports; although this figure was relatively high compared with the majority of federal subjects, it comprised only around 14% of the value of Muscovite trade in that year. In the late 1990s around 30% of Russia's imports and 20% of its exports passed through St Petersburg. In 2000 foreign investment in St Petersburg amounted to \$1,159.9m., compared with \$413.3m. in 1998. However, by 2002 it was not a strong commercial capital—the number of Western companies it had attracted and the extent of its property development failed to rival those of Moscow. The re-nationalization of the famous Lomonosov Porcelain Factory, which took place following a court ruling in St Petersburg in October 1999, annulled its privatization six years earlier, and caused some concern to foreign investors. In 2000 there were some 1,943 joint enterprises in St Petersburg and the surrounding Leningrad Oblast, some 378 of which had Finnish partners, mainly in the Vyborg area, while 253 firms had US partners and 225 had German partners. In 2000 there were some 109,200 small businesses registered in St Petersburg City.

Directory

Mayor (Governor and Premier of the City Government): VLADIMIR A. YAKOVLEV; 193060 St Petersburg, Smolnyi dvorets; tel. (812) 278-59-24; fax (812) 278-18-27; e-mail gov@gov.spb.ru; internet www.government.spb.ru.

Chairman of the Legislative Assembly: SERGEI B. TARASOV; 190107 St Petersburg, Isaakievskaya pl. 6; tel. (812) 319-99-31; e-mail starasov@assembly.spb.ru; internet www.assembly.spb.ru.

Representation of St Petersburg Federal City in the Russian Federation: 123001 Moscow, ul. Spiridonovka 20/1; tel. (095) 290-43-64; fax (095) 203-50-60.

AUTONOMOUS OBLAST

Jewish Autonomous Oblast

The Jewish Autonomous Oblast (Yevreiskaya AOb—Birobidzhan) is part of the Amur river basin, and is included in Russia's Far Eastern Federal Okrug and Far Eastern Economic Area. It is situated to the south-west of Khabarovsk Krai (of which it formed a part until 1991), on the international border with the People's Republic of China. There is a border with Amur Oblast in the north-west. Apart from the River Amur, which is frozen for around five months of the year, the region's major river is the Tungusk. Forest, which is particularly concentrated in the north-west, covers more than one-third of its territory. Around one-half is mountainous, with the south and east occupying the western edge of the Central Amur Lowlands. It occupies 36,000 sq km (13,900 sq miles) and has five administrative districts and two cities. The Jewish AOb had a population of 195,600 in January 2001, and a population density, therefore, of 5.4 per sq km. Around 67.1% of its population inhabited urban areas in 2001. The census of 1989 found that ethnic Russians accounted for some 83.2% of the AOb's population and ethnic Jews for 4.2% (although this figure can be expected to have decreased subsequently; in the early 1950s the Jews had constituted around one-quarter of the population of the Oblast). Indeed, in 1990 alone, around 1,000 of the 9,000 Jews resident in the Oblast the previous year emigrated to Israel. The regional capital is at Birobidzhan, which had a population of 78,400 in January 2001.

History

The majority of Russian Jews came under Russian control following the Partitions of Poland in 1772–95. The Soviet regime established an autonomous Jewish province at Birobidzhan in 1928, but it never became the centre of Soviet (or Russian) Jewry, largely because of its remote location and the absence of any prior Jewish settlement there. (In Imperial Russia between 1835 and 1917, Jews were required to receive special permission to live outside the 'Pale of Settlement' to the south-west of the Empire, which constituted territories largely in present-day Belarus, Lithuania, Poland and Ukraine.) This province was renamed the Jewish AOb on 7 May 1934 and formed part of Khabarovsk Krai until 25 March 1991. In the early post-Soviet period the region remained a redoubt of communist support. Despite the advice of the Russian President, Boris Yeltsin, at a session on 14 October 1993 the Regional Soviet announced that it would not disband itself. Subsequently, however, the council was replaced by a new body, the Legislative Assembly, elections to which confirmed Communist Party domination. A gubernatorial election held on 20 October 1996 was won by the incumbent, Nikolai Volkov; he was re-elected with 57% of the votes cast on 26 March 2000.

Economy

In 1999 the Jewish AOb's gross regional product stood at 2,443.5m. roubles, equivalent to 12,156.7 roubles per head. Birobidzhan is the region's main industrial centre. In 2000 there were 309 km (192 miles) of railway track, including a section of the Trans-Siberian Railway, and 1,609 km of paved roads on the AOb's territory. In February 2000 the opening of a bridge across the Amur river provided improved road and rail links with the city of Khabarovsk and the People's Republic of China. There are around 600 km of navigable waterways in the south of the Jewish AOb.

Agriculture, which employed 13.6% of the region's work-force in 2000, and generated a total of 906m. roubles in that year, consists mainly of grain, soybean, vegetable and potato production, animal husbandry, bee-keeping, hunting and fishing. There are major deposits of coal, peat, iron ore, manganese, tin, gold, graphite, magnesite and zeolite, although they are largely unexploited. The main industries are mechanical engineering, the manufacture of building materials, the production of electricity, wood-working, light manufacturing and food-processing. Industry employed around 15.3% of the AOb's working population and generated a total of 1,172m. roubles in 2000. In the mid-1990s the region's foreign economic activity was largely concentrated in the Far East, including the People's Republic of China and Japan.

In 2000 the AOb's economically active population numbered 94,000. Although more than one-quarter of the labour force were unemployed in 1997, by 2000 the unemployment rate had declined to 15.2%. In mid-2002 the average monthly wage in the AOb was 4,254.2 roubles. The 2000 budget showed a surplus of 35.3m. roubles. In that year external trade amounted to a value of US $12.1m. in exports and $4.6m. in imports. In 2000 foreign investment amounted to just $58,000; five of the seven foreign- or jointly-owned enterprises operating in the territory had Chinese partners. On 31 December 2000 500 small businesses were registered in the region.

Directory

Head of the Regional Administration: NIKOLAI M. VOLKOV; 682200 Jewish AOb, Birobidzhan, pr. 60-letiya SSSR 18; tel. (42622) 6-02-42; fax (42622) 4-07-25; e-mail gov1@eao.ru; internet www.eao.ru.

Chairman of the Legislative Assembly: ANATOLII F. TIKHOMIROV; 682200 Jewish AOb, Birobidzhan, pr. 60-letiya SSSR 18; tel. (42622) 6-04-72; fax (42622) 6-04-78; e-mail press-zs@eao.ru; internet www.eao.ru/law.

Representation of the Jewish Autonomous Oblast in the Russian Federation: Moscow.

Head of Birobidzhan City Administration: (vacant); Jewish AOb, 682200 Birobidzhan, ul. Lenina 29; tel. (42622) 6-22-02; fax (42622) 4-04-93.

AUTONOMOUS OKRUGS (DISTRICTS)

Aga-Buryat Autonomous Okrug

The Aga-Buryat Autonomus Okrug (AOk) is situated in the south-east of Transbaikal, in the southern part of Chita Oblast. It forms part of the Siberian Federal Okrug and the East Siberian Economic Area. Its major rivers are the Onon and the Ingoda, and about one-third of its territory is forested. Aga settlement is about 550 km (just under 350 miles) to the east of Ulan-Ude, the capital of Buryatiya (which lies to the west of Chita Oblast). The AOk contains varied terrain, ranging from desert to forest-steppe. The Aga-Buryat AOk occupies a total of 19,000 sq km (7,340 sq miles) and extends for about 250 km from south to north and 150 km from west to east. It has three administrative districts and four 'urban-type settlements' (towns). Its climate is severe and annual precipitation is as little as 250mm–380 mm (about 100 inches–150 inches) per year. Its population at 1 January 2002 was estimated at 79,600, giving a population density, therefore, of 4.2 per sq km. In 2001 just 32.3% of the population inhabited urban areas. In 1989 ethnic Buryats were found to make up some 54.9% of the population, and ethnic Russians 40.8%. The Buryats inhabiting the district are Transbaikal Buryats, who are more closely related to their Mongol ancestors than their western counterparts, the Irkutsk Buryats. The administrative centre is at Aginskoye settlement, which had a population of just 9,500 in January 2001.

History

The Aga-Buryat-Mongol AOk was created on 26 September 1937, as part of Stalin—Iosif Dzhugashvili's policy of dispersing the Buryat population, whom he perceived as a threat because of their ethnic and cultural links with the Mongolian People's Republic (Mongolia). Its formation occurred as part of the division of the East Siberian Oblast into Chita and Irkutsk Oblasts (the former of which it became a part). It assumed its current name on 16 September 1958.

Under the Federation Treaty of March 1992, the AOk was recognized as one of the constituent units of the Russian Federation. The area attracted some notoriety in 1997, when Iosif Kobzon, a popular singer frequently referred to as the 'Russian Frank Sinatra', won a by-election for a seat representing the AOk in the State Duma, obtaining 84% of the votes cast. Kobzon attracted controversy, owing to his reputedly close connections with organized crime both within Russia and in the USA. (Kobzon subsequently suspended his membership of the Duma, in order to protest against anti-Semitic declarations by deputies of the Communist Party of the Russian Federation.) The incumbent Head of the Okrug Administration, Bair Zhamsuyev, was re-elected in October 2000, obtaining more than 89% of the votes cast.

Economy

The Autonomous Okrug's transport infrastructure is relatively unsophisticated—in 2000 there were only 71 km of railway track and 900 km of paved roads. The economy of the Aga-Buryat AOk is based on agriculture, which consists mainly of animal husbandry (particularly sheep-rearing), fur-animal farming and grain production. Agricultural production amounted to a value of 605m. roubles in 2000 and employed some 36.9% of the Okrug's work-force. The territory is rich in reserves of wolfram (tungsten) and tantalum. Its main industries are non-ferrous metallurgy, ore-mining, the manufacture of building materials and the processing of agricultural products. Industry employed just 6.5% of the Okrug's work-force in 2000, and produced output worth 127m. roubles. The district's main foreign trading partners are the People's Republic of China and Mongolia. The transport, trade and services sectors were fully privatized by 1995. The Aga-Buryat AOk is one of the most under-developed federal territories in terms of its health and social-security provision and educational establishments.

In 2000 the economically active population of the AOk numbered 32,000, and from the mid-1990s, when separate figures for the AOk began to become available, the district was consistently among those federal subjects with the highest levels of unemployment. In 1998 some 35.2% of the labour force were unemployed, although by 2000 the rate had declined to 25.6%. The average monthly wage was just 2,524.6 roubles in mid-2002. The 2000 district budget showed a surplus of 35.1m. roubles. Some 400 small businesses were registered in the territory at late 2000.

Directory

Head of the District Administration: BAIR B. ZHAMSUYEV; 674460 Chita obl., Aga- Buryat AOk, pos. Aginskoye, ul. Bazara Rinchino 92; tel. (30239) 3-41-52; fax (30239) 3-49-84.

Chairman of the District Duma: DASHI TS. DUGAROV; 674460 Chita obl., Aga-Buryat AOk, pos. Aginskoye, ul. Bazara Rinchino 92; tel (30239) 3-44-81; fax (30239) 3-49-59.

Representation of the Aga-Buryat Autonomous Окrug in Chita Oblast: Chita.

Chief Representative of the Aga-Buryat Autonomous Okrug in the Russian Federation: VLADIMIR D. SHOIZHILZHAPOV; 103025 Moscow, ul. Novyi Arbat 19; tel. (095) 203-95-09; fax (095) 203-80-14.

Chukot Autonomous Okrug

The Chukot Autonomous Okrug (AOk—Chukotka) is situated on the Chukotka Peninsula and an adjacent section of the mainland. The Okrug forms part of the Far Eastern Federal Okrug and the Far Eastern Economic Area. It is the easternmost part of Russia and faces the East Siberian Sea (Arctic Ocean) to the north and the Bering Sea to the south; the Anadyr Gulf, part of the Bering Sea, cuts into the territory from the south-east. The USA (Alaska) lies eastwards across the Bering Straits. The western end of the district borders the Republic of Sakha (Yakutiya) to the west, and Magadan Oblast (of which Chukotka formed a part until 1992) to the south. Also to the south lies the Koryak AOk (part of Kamchatka Oblast). The district's major river is the Anadyr. The Chukot AOk occupies an area of 737,700 sq km (284,830 sq miles), of which approximately one-half lies within the Arctic Circle, and is divided into eight administrative districts and three cities. Its climate is severe; the average temperature in January is -29.2°C, and in July it is 9.4°C. The AOk is a sparsely populated area, with an estimated total of 73,800 inhabitants at 1 January 2002, and a population density of 0.1 per sq km. Approximately 68.3% of the territory's population inhabited urban areas in 2001. Around 80,000 people left the AOk between 1991 and 2002, reducing the population by about one-half. According to the census of 1989, ethnic Russians represented 66.1% of the region's total population, while only 7.3% were Chukchi. The Chukchi speak the Chukotic language as their native tongue, which belongs to the Paleo-Asiatic linguistic family. Until the 20th century the Chukchi (who call themselves the Lyg Oravetlyan, and are also known as the Luoravetlan, Chukcha and Chukot) could be subdivided into several distinct tribal groups. Traditionally they were also divided into two economic groups, the nomadic and semi-nomadic reindeer herders (the Chavchu or Chavchuven), and the coastal dwellers (known as the An Kalyn). The district's administrative centre is at Anadyr, which had a population of 12,000 in 2001, compared with 17,000 in 1989.

History

Russian settlers first arrived in the territories inhabited by Chukchi tribes in the mid-17th century. Commercial traders, fur trappers and hunters subsequently established contact with the Chukchi and many were forcibly converted to Orthodox Christianity and enserfed. Economic co-operation continued to expand and reached its height in 1905, with the construction of the Trans-Siberian Railway. A Chukot Okrug was created as part of Magadan Oblast by the Soviet Government on 10 December 1930, as part of its policy to incorporate the peoples of the north of Russia into the social, political and economic body of the USSR. It later acquired autonomous status. Simultaneously, collectivization was introduced into the district. Throughout the 1950s and 1960s eastern Siberia was rapidly industrialized, resulting in extensive migration of ethnic Russians to the area and a drastic reduction of the territory available to the Chukchi for herding reindeer. Many abandoned their traditional way of life to work in industry.

After 1985 the Chukchi, in common with the rest of the Soviet population, experienced more political freedom. On 31 March 1990 the Chukchi participated in the creation of the Association of the Peoples of the North. They also campaigned for the ratification of two international conventions, which would affirm their right to the ownership and possession of the lands they traditionally inhabited. In the early 1990s the Chukchis began to demand real political autonomy: in February 1991 the legislature of the Chukot AOk seceded from Magadan Oblast and declared the territory the Chukot Soviet Autonomous Republic (the word 'Soviet' was dropped from the district's title following the disintegration of the USSR in December). This measure failed to be recognized by the federal Government, although the district was acknowledged as a constituent member of the Federation by the Treaty of March 1992 and, subsequently, as free from the jurisdiction of Magadan Oblast. At the gubernatorial election held in December 2000, the incumbent Governor, Aleksandr Nazarov, withdrew his candidacy. Roman Abramovich, an 'oligarch' associated with the petroleum company Sibneft (Siberian Oil Co), was elected in his place, receiving 91% of the votes cast.

Economy

Alone among the autonomous okrugs, Chukotka is no longer included in a larger territory and there has been, therefore, fuller coverage of it in official statistics. In 1999 the AOk's gross regional product amounted to 3,212.1m. roubles, equivalent to 43,173.5 roubles per head. Although relatively high, this level of regional wealth was highly dependent on federal transfers. In 2000 the territory had 1,279 km (795 miles) of paved roads and a relatively undeveloped infrastructure. Anadyr is one of the district's major ports, the others being Pevek, Providenya, Egvekinot and Beringovskii.

The AOk's agricultural sector, which employed 8.6% of its work-force in 2000, consists mainly of fishing, animal husbandry (especially reindeer-breeding) and hunting. Total agricultural production was worth 86m. roubles in 2000. In 1992 it was estimated that some 500,000 reindeers were raised in state-controlled breeding areas. The region contains reserves of coal and brown coal (lignite), petroleum and natural gas, as well as gold, tin, wolfram (tungsten), copper and other minerals. It is self-sufficient in energy, containing two coal-mines, six producers of electricity and one nuclear power-station. Its main industries are ore-mining and food-processing. Industry employed some 19.3% of the AOk's working population in 2000 and generated 2,332m. roubles.

The AOk's economically active population numbered 48,000 in 2000. The rate of unemployment has been relatively low, compared with other regions in the Far East of Russia; in 2000 10.0% of the labour force were unemployed. Those in employment in mid-2002 earned an average of 12,195.5 roubles per month, well above the national average, although this was counterbalanced by some of the highest living costs in the Federation; in November 1999 a typical 'consumer basket' cost about three times as much in Anadyr as the national average and, indeed, considerably more than elsewhere in the Russian Far East. The 2000 district government budget showed a deficit of 3.0m. roubles, representing a considerable improvement on earlier records; in 1994 and 1995 the deficit had exceeded the entire gross output of the district. The external trade of the district is minimal, and in 2000 exports amounted to only US $0.3m. and imports to $1.9m. At 31 December 2000 there were 100 small businesses registered in the AOk; an extra-budgetary fund was created for the support and development of small business during 1996 and 1997, although little success was evident.

Directory

Head of the District Administration (Governor): ROMAN A. ABRAMOVICH; 689000 Chukot AOk, Anadyr, ul. Beringa 20; tel. (42722) 2-42-62; fax (42722) 2-27-25; internet www.chukotka.org.

Chairman of the District Duma: VASILII N. NAZARENKO; 686710 Chukot AOk, Anadyr, ul. Otke 29; tel. (42722) 2-25-24; fax (42722) 2-44-70.

Chief Representative of the Chukot Autonomous Okrug in the Russian Federation: VLADIMIR S. VILDIAAIKIN; 101000 Moscow, ul. Myasnitskaya 26/2; tel. (095) 925-95-13; fax (095) 925-82-27.

Head of Anadyr City Administration: VIKTOR A. KHVAN; 689000 Chukot AOk, Anadyr, ul. Beringa 45; tel. (41361) 4-45-33; fax (41361) 4-22-16.

Evenk Autonomous Okrug

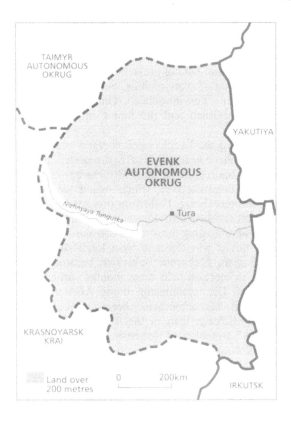

The Evenk Autonomous Okrug (AOk) is a land-locked territory situated on the Central Siberian Plateau. It is part of the Siberian Federal Okrug and the East Siberian Economic Area. The district forms the central-eastern part of Krasnoyarsk Krai, with the core territories of the province lying to the west and south and the other autonomous okrug, the Taimyr (Dolgan-Nenets) AOk, to the north. Sakha (Yakutiya) adjoins to the east, and Irkutsk to the south-east. It has numerous rivers, the largest being the Nizhnyaya Tunguska and the Podkammenaya Tunguska, both tributaries of the Yenisei. The Evenk AOk occupies a total area of 767,600 sq km (296,370 sq miles), of which almost three-quarters is forested, and comprises three administrative districts and one 'urban-type settlement' (town). At 1 January 2002 the population was estimated at 18,200. Its population density, of 0.02 per sq km, was the lowest in the Federation. In 2001 some 28.6% of the population inhabited urban areas. According to the 1989 census, ethnic Russians comprised some 67.5% of the district's population and ethnic Evenks 14.0%. The Evenks' native tongue is part of the Tungusic group of the Tungusic-Manuchu division of the Uralo-Altaic language family. The region's administrative centre is at Tura settlement, which had just 5,300 inhabitants on 1 January 2001.

History

The Evenks, who are thought to be descended from a mixture of Tungus and Yukagir culture, were first identified as a distinct group in the 14th century. Their first contact with Russians occurred in the early 17th century, as Russian Cossacks and fur trappers advanced eastwards through Siberia. By the mid-1620s many Evenks were forced to pay fur taxes to the Russian state. The Evenks' right to land, pasture, and hunting and fishing preserves was officially guaranteed in 1919 by the Soviet Commissariat of Nationalities, but in 1929 forced collectivization of their economic activities was introduced. On 10 December 1930 the Evenk National Okrug was established and the first Congress of Evenk Soviets was convened.

Nationalist feeling among the Evenks later emerged as a result of environmental damage sustained from the construction of hydroelectric projects and extensive mineral development in the region. In the 1980s there were plans to build a dam across the Nizhnyaya Tunguska river, which would have flooded much of the territory of the Autonomous Okrug. Following protests by the Evenks, and by the Association of the Peoples of the North (formed in 1990), the project was abandoned. In the post-Soviet period, following the forcible dissolution of the federal parliament in 1993, the District Soviet was replaced by a Legislative Assembly or Suglan. The speaker of the Suglan, Aleksandr Bokivkov, became Governor of the AOk in March 1997, after an election held three months earlier was annulled, owing to various irregularities. The relationship of the AOk to Krasnoyarsk Krai, of which it also forms a part, has, on occasion, been a source of difficulties, although to a considerably lesser extent than in the Taimyr (Dolgan-Nenets) AOk (see below). From June 1997 a number of agreements were signed between the Evenk AOk and Krasnoyarsk Krai, regulating specific economic issues and stating that the residents of the Okrug would participate fully in all gubernatorial and legislative elections in the Krai. Subsequently, proposals that envisaged a merger of the Krai with both of its constituent AOks gained in popularity, particularly following the appointment of the hitherto Taimyr (Dolgan-Nenets) Governor, Aleksandr Khlopanin, as Governor of Krasnoyarsk Krai in October 2002. On 8 April 2001 Boris Zolotarev, a director of the petroleum company, Yukos, was elected Governor of the AOk, receiving 51.8% of the popular vote.

Economy

Despite its size and, indeed, its potential wealth, the Evenk AOk remains an undeveloped and economically insignificant producer. In 2000 13.6% of its working population were occupied in agriculture, producing total output worth 54m. roubles. The AOk's agriculture consists mainly of fishing, hunting, reindeer-breeding and fur farming. The estimated combined hydroelectric potential of the district's two major rivers is 81,300m. kWh. Its main industries otherwise are the production of petroleum, natural gas, graphite and Iceland spar, and food-processing. In 2000 industry employed 15.3% of the Okrug's work-force, and generated 112m. roubles.

The economically active population of the Okrug numbered 11,000 in 2000, when the rate of unemployment, at 3.2%, was the lowest of any territory in the Russian Federation. The average monthly wage was some 7,898.1 roubles in mid-2002. The 2000 budget showed a deficit of 137.0m. roubles. At 31 December 2000 no small businesses were registered in the AOk.

Directory

Head of the District Administration: BORIS N. ZOLOTAREV; 663370 Krasnoyarsk Krai, Evenk AOk, pos. Tura, ul. Sovetskaya 2; tel. (39113) 2-26-57; fax (39113) 2-26-55; e-mail sokolovamr@krasn.evenkya.ru; internet www.evenkya.ru.

Chairman of the District Legislative Assembly (Suglan): ANATOLII YE. AMOSOV; 663370 Krasnoyarsk Krai, Evenk AOk, pos. Tura, ul. Sovetskaya 2; tel. and fax (39113) 2-29-02.

Representation of the Evenk Autonomous Okrug in Krasnoyarsk Krai: 660097 Krasnoyarsk, pr. Mira 36/719; tel. and fax (3912) 26-34-55.

Chief Representative of the Evenk Autonomous Okrug in the Russian Federation: GALINA F. SEMENOVA; 127025 Moscow, ul. Novyi Arbat 19/1531; tel. and fax (095) 203-77-87.

Khanty-Mansii Autonomous Okrug

The Khanty-Mansii Autonomous Okrug (AOk) is situated in the Western Siberian Plain and the Ob-Irtysh river basin. The district forms part of the Urals Federal Okrug and the West Siberian Economic Area, and lies within the territory of Tyumen Oblast. The other autonomous okrug within Tyumen Oblast, the Yamal-Nenets AOk, lies to the north, while to the south of the district's centre lies the region of Tyumen proper. Komi is to the west and Sverdlovsk to the south-west; to the south-east lies Tomsk and to the east Krasnoyarsk. Apart from the Ob and the Irtysh, the district's other major rivers are the Konda, the Sosva, the Vakh, the Agan and the Bolshoi Yugan. It has numerous lakes, and much of its territory is Arctic tundra (frozen steppe) and taiga (forested marshland). More than one-third of the territory of the Khanty-Mansii district is forested. It occupies a total of 523,100 sq km (201,970 sq miles) and measures about 900 km (560 miles) from south to north and 1,400 km from east to west. There are nine administrative districts in the AOk and 16 cities. Its estimated total number of inhabitants was 1,423,800 at 1 January 2002, giving a population density of 2.7 per sq km. In 2001 as many as 91.3% of the population lived in urban areas. Ethnic Khants and Mansi, collectively known as Ob-Ugrian peoples, are greatly outnumbered by ethnic Russians in the district: the census of 1989 found that some 66.3% of total inhabitants were Russians, 11.6% Ukrainians, 7.6% Tatars, 2.4% Bashirs and 2.2% Belarusians, compared with just 0.9% Khants and 0.5% Mansi. The Khanty and the Mansii languages are grouped together as an Ob-Ugrian sub-division of the Ugrian division of the Finno-Ugrian group. The AOk's administrative centre is at the town of Khanty-Mansiisk, which had 39,700 inhabitants at 1 January 2001. Other major, and larger, cities in the Okrug are Surgut (278,900), Nizhnevartovsk (238,100) and Nefteyugansk (99,700).

History

The Khanty-Mansii region, known as the Yugra region in the 11th–15th centuries, came under Russian control in the late 16th and early 17th centuries as Russian fur traders established themselves in western Siberia. Attempts were made to assimilate the Khants and Mansi into Russian culture, and many were forcibly converted to Orthodox Christianity. The territory was created in December 1930, as the East Vogul (Ostyako-Vogulskii) National Autonomous Okrug (adopting its current name in 1940).

From about the time of the Second World War the district became heavily industrialized, causing widespread damage to fish catches and reindeer pastures. Consequently, during the period of *glasnost* (openness) in the late 1980s, many of the indigenous inhabitants of the area began to demand more cautious development policies that would guarantee the survival of their livelihood and cultures. In the mid-1990s the okrug authorities sought to establish local control over natural resources. In 1996 they appealed to the Constitutional Court against Tyumen Oblast's attempt to legislate for district petroleum and natural gas reserves, and a protracted dispute ensued. As in the neighbouring Yamal-Nenets AOk, the exact nature of the constitutional relationship between Khanty-Mansii and Tyumen Oblast remained obscure. Even the exact geographical delineation of the Okrug remained uncertain, with disputes over which jurisdiction had the authority to develop oilfields in the regions. This dispute partly reflected the domination of different interest groups in the two administrations—the district authorities favoured the federal Government and the energy industry, while the Communist Party of the Russian Federation still had strong support in Tyumen Oblast generally. Aleksandr Filipenko, the moderate head of the district administration, was returned to power in the gubernatorial election held in late 1996. He was re-elected, with 91% of the votes cast, in an election held simultaneously with the federal presidential election of 26 March 2000, in which he was a vocal supporter of Vladimir Putin's candidacy.

Economy

The AOk's economy is based on industry, particularly on the extraction and refining of petroleum. In the late 1990s it produced around 5% of Russia's entire industrial output and over 50% of its petroleum. Its main industrial centre is at the petroleum-producing town of Surgut. Its major river-port is at Nizhnevartovsk. In 2000 there were 1,073 km of railway track in the district and 1,698 km of paved roads, many of which were constructed during the 1990s. In September 2000 a long-awaited road bridge across the River Ob was opened.

Agriculture in the Khanty-Mansii AOk, which employed just 1.4% of the work-force in 2000, consists mainly of fishing, reindeer-breeding, fur farming, hunting and vegetable production. Total agricultural output in that year was worth 1,756m. roubles, while industrial production amounted to a value of some 375,665m. roubles. Industry, which employed some 19.4% of the work-force in 2000, is based on the extraction of petroleum and natural gas and the production of electricity. Khanty-Mansiisk Oil Company (KMOC) was formed in 1997 by the merger of Khanty-Mansiiskneftegazgeologiya (KMNGG)—a petroleum exploration company in possession of oilfields containing up to 3,000m. barrels of petroleum—and UPC (of Delaware, USA). KMOC is one of Russia's largest independent exploration companies. Surgutneftegaz (SNG) Oil Co, also based in the region, and founded in 1993, is also a significant producer of petroleum and natural gas, with some 84,500 employees in the early 2000s.

The economically active population of the Okrug numbered 771,000 in 2000, when 11.2% of the labour force were unemployed. The average monthly wage was some 15,183.9 roubles in mid-2002. In 2000 the local budget recorded a surplus of 6,274.3m. roubles. There was considerable foreign investment in the Okrug from the late 1990s, and it totalled US $61.3m. in 2000. Data for external trade, although substantial, are included within the aggregate figures for Tyumen Oblast (q.v.). On 31 December 2000 4,900 small businesses were registered in the Khanty-Mansii AOk.

Directory

Governor: ALEKSANDR V. FILIPENKO; 628001 Tyumen obl., Khanty-Mansii AOk, Khanty-Mansiisk, ul. Mira 5; tel. (34671) 3-20-95; fax (34671) 3-34-60; e-mail kominf@hmansy.wsnet.ru; internet www.hmao.wsnet.ru.

Chairman of the District Duma: VASILII S. SONDYKOV; 628011 Tyumen obl., Khanty-Mansii AOk, Khanty-Mansiisk, ul. Mira 5; tel. (34671) 9-28-28; fax (34671) 9-28-29; e-mail dumahmao@hmansy.swnet.ru.

Chief Representative of the Khanty-Mansii Autonomous Okrug in Tyumen Oblast: NIKOLAI M. DOBRYNIN; 626002 Tyumen, ul. Komsomolskaya 37; tel. (3452) 46-67-79; fax (3452) 46-00-91; e-mail hmaoda@tmn.ru.

Chief Representative of the Khanty-Mansii Autonomous Okrug in the Russian Federation: VLADIMIR A. KHARITON; 119002 Moscow, Starokonyushennyi per. 10/10/2; tel. (095) 920-42-38; fax (095) 291-17-62; e-mail ugra_msk@dial.cnt.ru.

Head of Khanty-Mansiisk City Administration: VLADIMIR G. YAKOVLEV; 626200 Tyumen obl., Khanty-Mansii AOk, Khanty-Mansiisk, ul. Dzerzhinskogo 6; tel. (34671) 3-23-80; fax (34671) 3-21-74.

Komi-Permyak Autonomous Okrug

The Komi-Permyak Autonomous Okrug (AOk) is situated in the Urals area on the upper reaches of the Kama river and forms the north-western part of Perm Oblast. The region is part of the Volga Federal Okrug and the Urals Economic Area. The other neighbouring federal territories are Komi to the north and north-west and Kirov to the west. A largely forested territory, it occupies an area of 32,900 sq km (12,700 sq miles) and comprises six administrative districts and one city. The region's population was estimated at 147,800 at 1 January 2002, and the population density was 4.5 per sq km. In 2001 26.1% of the population inhabited urban areas. According to the 1989 census, of the district's total population, some 60.2% were Komi Permyak and 36.1% ethnic Russian. The Komi Permyaks speak two dialects of the Finnic division of the Uralo-Altaic linguistic family. The district's administrative centre is at Kudymkar, which had a population of 34,300 at 1 January 2001.

History

The Komi Permyaks became a group distinct from the Komis in around 500, when some Komi (Zyryans) migrated from the upper Kama river region to the Vychegda basin, while the Komi Permyaks remained. The Komi-Permyak AOk was established on 26 February 1925. The area frequently perceived the central authorities to be neglectful of their interests, and the harsh economic conditions of the late 1990s doubtless contributed to the dissatisfaction that had earlier produced a significant level of support for the nationalist Liberal Democratic Party. In May 1996 the AOk's administration signed a treaty with the federal Government on the delimitation of powers between the two bodies. An August presidential decree permitted a gubernatorial election to be held in November; the post was retained by the incumbent, Nikolai Poluyanov. Poluyanov was defeated by the deputy president of the audit chamber of Perm Oblast, Gennadii Savelyev, in the gubernatorial election held in December 2000. Elections to the 15-member regional Legislative Assembly took place in December 2001.

Economy

In 2000 there were 1,488 km (925 miles) of paved roads in the AOk. The agriculture of the Komi Permyak AOk consists mainly of grain production, animal husbandry and hunting. In 2000 it occupied 31.7% of the work-force and produced output to the value of 1,277m. roubles. Its timber reserves are estimated at 322m. cu m. There are significant peat deposits and approximately 12.1m. metric tons of petroleum reserves. Its industry is based on the processing of forestry and agricultural products; the sector generated 693m. roubles in 2000 and employed 15.7% of the Okrug's work-force.

The economically active population numbered 66,000 in 2000, when 8.0% of the labour force were unemployed. The average monthly wage was just 2,535.9 roubles in mid-2002, and the Okrug is one of the most underdeveloped and deprived European regions of Russia. The district budget showed a deficit of 54.3m. roubles in 2000. Figures on the foreign investment in, and external trade with, the Okrug were unavailable, being included with those for the Perm Oblast as a whole, but in late 2000 there were approximately 100 small businesses registered in the Okrug.

Directory

Head of the District Administration: GENNADII P. SAVELYEV; 619000 Perm obl., Komi-Permyak AOk, Kudymkar, ul. 50 let Oktyabrya 33; tel. (34260) 2-09-03; fax (34260) 2-12-74.

Chairman of the Legislative Assembly: VALERII A. VANKOV; 619000 Perm obl., Komi-Permyak AOk, Kudymkar, ul. 50 let Oktyabrya 33; tel. and fax (32460) 4-12-97.

Representation of the Komi-Permyak Autonomous Okrug in Perm Oblast: Perm.

Chief Representative of Komi-Permyak Autonomous Okrug in the Russian Federation: TAMARA A. SYSTEROVA; Moscow; tel. (095) 203-94-08.

Head of Kudymkar City Administration: ALEKSANDR A. KLIMOVICH; 617420 Perm obl., Komi-Permyak AOk, Kudymkar, ul. Gorkogo 3; tel. (34260) 2-00-47.

Koryak Autonomous Okrug

The Koryak Autonomous Okrug (AOk) comprises the northern part of the Kamchatka Peninsula and the adjacent area of mainland. It forms part of the Far Eastern Federal Okrug, the Far Eastern Economic Area, and Kamchatka Oblast. Its eastern coastline lies on the Bering Sea, and its western shores face the Shelekhov Gulf (Sea of Okhotsk). South of the district lies the rest of Kamchatka Oblast. In the north it is bordered by the Chukchi AOk and Magadan Oblast, to the north and to the west, respectively. The Koryak AOk occupies 301,500 sq km (116,410 sq miles) and is divided, for administrative purposes, into four districts and two 'urban-type settlements' (towns). At 1 January 2002 its estimated total population was 28,500, and its population density, therefore, stood at just 0.1 per sq km. In 2001 just 25.8% of the population inhabited urban areas. The 1989 census showed that 62.0% of its population were ethnically Russian, 7.2% Ukrainian, 16.4% Koryak, 3.6% Chukchi and 3.0% Itelmeni. The administrative centre of the district is at Palana settlement, which had a population of just 4,100 on 1 January 2001.

History

The area was established as a territorial unit on 10 December 1930. Like the Chukchi, the Koryaks have always been divided into nomadic and semi-nomadic hunters and more sedentary coastal dwellers. They first encountered ethnic Russians in the 1640s, when Cossacks, commercial traders and fur trappers arrived in the district. The Soviet Government attempted to collectivize the Koryaks' economic activity, beginning with the fishing industry in 1929, and continuing with reindeer hunting in 1932, a measure that was violently opposed by the Koryak community. After the Second World War large numbers of ethnic Russians moved to the area, which was becoming increasingly industrialized. The resultant threat to the Koryaks' traditional way of life, and environmental deterioration, became a source of contention between the local community and the federal Government during the period of *glasnost* (openness) in the late 1980s. In the first years of independence, however, the local élite were sufficiently placated to be generally supportive of both the federal Government and, indeed, of the reformists. An independent candidate, Valentina Bronevich, was elected Governor in late 1996, the first woman to head the administration of a territorial unit in the Russian Federation. On 5 May 1999 Bronevich signed a co-operation agreement with the Governor of Kamchatka Oblast, Vladimir Biryukov. On 3 December 2000 a local businessman, Vladimir Loginov, defeated Bronevich in a single round of voting in the gubernatorial election, receiving 51% of the votes cast.

Economy

Much economic data on the Koryak AOk is incorporated into the figures for Kamchatka Oblast, although certain indicators are available. Fishing is the most important economic activity in the district, contributing 60% of total industrial output.

The AOk's agriculture, which employed 10.8% of the work-force in 2000, consists mainly of reindeer-breeding, fur farming and hunting. Total agricultural output was worth 61m. roubles in that year. The main industries are the production of non-ferrous metals (primarily palladium and platinum), food-processing, the production of electrical energy and the extraction of brown coal (lignite). Industry employed 21.7% of the work-force and generated a total of 2,939m. roubles in 2000.

The economically active population numbered 17,000 in 2000, when 12.5% of the labour force were unemployed. The average monthly wage was some 8,223.9 roubles in mid-2002. The budget recorded a deficit of 361.9m. roubles in 2000. By the early 2000s the Okrug remained impoverished and dependent on federal subsidies; in 1999 it had been named as being among the federal subjects with the highest rates of inflation and the least promising opportunities for investment, and in 2002 was named as one of the worst regions for wage arrears. In 2000 the region attracted foreign investment worth US $300,000, compared with $7.1m. in 1998. At the end of 2000 100 small businesses were registered in the territory.

Directory

Governor of the Koryak Autonomous Okrug: VLADIMIR A. LOGINOV; 683000 Kamchatka obl., Petropavlovsk-Kamchatskii, ul. Lenina 1; tel. (41522) 12-51-76; fax (41522) 11-26-95.

Chairman of the District Duma: VLADIMIR N. MIZININ; 684720 Kamchatka obl., Koryak AOk, pos. Palana, ul. Porotova 22; tel. (41543) 3-11-36.

Representation of the Koryak Autonomous Okrug in Kamchatka Oblast: Kamchatka obl., Petropavlovsk-Kamchatskii.

Chief Representative of the Koryak Autonomous Okrug in the Russian Federation: IRINA V. YEVDOKIMOVA; Moscow; tel. (095) 921-90-96.

Nenets Autonomous Okrug

The Nenets Autonomous Okrug (AOk) is part of Archangel (Arkhangelsk) Oblast and, hence, the North-Western Federal Okrug and the Northern Economic Area. It is situated in the north-east of European Russia, its coastline lying, from west to east, on the White, Barents and Kara Seas, parts of the Arctic Ocean. Most of the territory lies within the Arctic Circle. Archangel proper lies to the south-west, but most of the Nenets southern border is with the Republic of Komi. At its eastern extremity the district touches the Yamal-Nenets AOk (part of Tyumen Oblast) and, to the north-east, the Novaya Zemlya peninsula, which forms a part of Archangel Oblast proper. The major river is the Pechora, which drains into the Pechora Gulf of the Barents Sea just north of Naryan-Mar. The territory occupies an area of 176,700 sq km (68,200 sq miles) and extends some 300 km (190 miles) from south to north and 1,000 km from west to east. For administrative purposes it is divided into one city and two 'urban-type settlements' (towns). At 1 January 2002 the estimated total population of the Nenets AOk was 44,900 and its population density was 0.3 per sq km. Around 60.4% of the population inhabited urban areas in 2001. At 1 January 1997 estimated figures showed some 70.0% of the region's population were ethnic Russian, while 15.6% were Nenets and 9.5% Komi. The language spoken by the Nenets belongs to the Samoyedic group of Uralian languages, which is part of the Uralo-Altaic linguistic group. In 1997 a Norwegian anthropologist claimed to have discovered a forgotten tribe of nomads in the AOk, the Nentser, hitherto unrecognized by the Russian authorities. The Nentser inhabit a vast area south of the Novaya Zemlya islands and comprise around 200 reindeer herders. The district capital is at Naryan-Mar, the only city, which had a population of 18,200 at 1 January 2001.

History

The Nenets were traditionally concerned with herding and breeding reindeer. A Samoyedic people, they are believed to have broken away from other Finno-Ugrian groups in around 3000 BC and migrated east where, in around 200 BC, they began to mix with Turkish-Altaic people. By the early 17th century their territory had come entirely under the control of the Muscovite state. The Russians established forts in the region, from which they collected fur tax.

The Nenets AOk was formed on 15 July 1929. During the Soviet period, collectivization of the Nenets' economic activity, and the exploitation of petroleum and natural gas, which resulted in mass migration of ethnic Russians to the region, posed an increasing threat to the traditional way of life of the indigenous population and to the environment. In the early 1990s the Nenets organized public demonstrations against the federal Government's development projects.

On 11 March 1994 the federal President, Boris Yeltsin, suspended a resolution by the District Administration ordering a referendum to be held on the territory of the AOk. Participants in the referendum were to vote on the status of the district within the Russian Federation. Despite the President's move, however, the district maintained its style of the 'Nenets Republic'. A district Deputies' Assembly replaced the old legislature, and election results in the mid-1990s indicated continued disaffection with federal policies—there was strong support for the nationalist Liberal Democratic Party of Russia, led by Vladimir Zhirinovskii. The December 1996 election to head the district administration was won by an independent candidate and businessman, Vladimir Butov, who was re-elected on 14 January 2001, with some 68% of the votes cast. In June 2002 a warrant was issued for the arrest of Butov on charges of abuse of office, in particular with regard to his dismissal of three successive district prosecutors. Although the warrant was subsequently cancelled, concern was expressed that Butov had been absent from the region for several months.

Economy

As part of Archangel Oblast, the Nenets AOk is usually subsumed into the region's overall statistics, so few separate details are available. In 2000 the AOk contained 150 km (93 miles) of paved roads. The AOk's major ports are Naryan-Mar and Amderma.

Its agriculture, which employed 11.7% of the work-force and produced goods to a value of 158m. roubles in 2000, consists mainly of reindeer-breeding (around two-thirds of its territory is reindeer pasture), fishing, hunting and fur farming. There are substantial reserves of petroleum, natural gas and gas condensate, which have yet to be fully exploited. In 1997 Exxon Arkhangelsk Ltd, an affiliate of Exxon (of the USA), purchased a 50% stake in the development of oilfields in Timan-Pechora, although it was forced to withdraw after problems with tender arrangements. In 1998 Governor Bukov gave support to plans for the construction of a petroleum transportation terminal on the Barents Sea coast, allowing the Okrug to benefit from the potential wealth to be generated by the exploitation of the Timan-Pechora oilfields. These plans met with hostility from various sources, including the former federal Prime Minister, Viktor Chernomyrdin, but more particularly from the administration of the neighbouring Komi Republic, which lies on the route of the existing Kharyaga–Usinsk pipeline. Although Bukov's relations with the major fuel companies Gazprom and LUKoil were reported to be strained during the late 1990s, and petroleum deposits in the region were developed only slowly, a new sea terminal for petroleum transportation was opened at Varandey in August 2000. The annual capacity of this terminal, which was constructed by LUKoil and which was to be served by its fleet of ice-breaking tankers, was over 1m. metric tons, although this was expected to expand. Other sectors of the district's industry included the processing of agricultural products and the generation of electricity. Industry employed 12.6% of the Okrug's work-force in 2000, and produced output worth 6,612m. roubles in that year.

The economically active population numbered 24,000 in 2000, when 10.9% of the labour force were unemployed, compared with 20.0% in 1999. In mid-2002 the average monthly wage of 12,830.1 roubles was among the highest in the Russian Federation. The Nenets government budget recorded a surplus of 256.4m. roubles in 2000. In the late 1990s the Okrug was successful in attracting foreign investment, which totalled US $346.0m. in 1999. In December 2000 there were approximately 200 small businesses registered in the district.

Directory

Head of the District Administration: VLADIMIR YA. BUTOV; 166000 Archangel obl., Nenets AOk, Naryan-Mar, ul. Smidovicha 20; tel. (47833) 0-80-17; fax (81853) 4-22-69.

Chairman of the Deputies' Assembly: VITALINA F. GLAZUNOVA; 166000 Arch-angel obl., Nenets AOk, Naryan-Mar, ul. Smidovicha 20; tel. (81853) 4-21-59; fax (81853) 4-20-11; e-mail pred@atnet.ru.

Representation of the Nenets Autonomous Okrug in Archangel Oblast: Arch-angel.

Chief Representative of the Nenets Autonomous Okrug in the Russian Federa-tion: TATYANA A. MALYSHEVA; 127025 Moscow, ul. Novyi Arbat 19/1120; tel. (095) 203-90-39; fax (095) 203-91-74; e-mail neninter@atnet.ru.

Head of Naryan-Mar City Administration: GRIGORII B. KOVALENKO; 164700 Archangel obl., Nenets AOk, Naryan-Mar, ul. Lenina 12; tel. (81853) 2-21-53; fax (095) 253-51-00.

Taimyr (Dolgan-Nenets) Autonomous Okrug

Taimyr (Dolgan-Nenets) Autonomous Okrug (AOk) is situated on the Taimyr Peninsula, which abuts into the Arctic Ocean, separating the Kara and Laptev Seas. The district comprises the northern end of Krasnoyarsk Krai and, in common with its south-eastern neighbour, the Evenk AOk, forms part of the Siberian Federal Okrug and the East Siberian Economic Area. The Yamal-Nenets AOk, in Tyumen Oblast, lies to the west and the Republic of Sakha (Yakutiya) is located to the south-east. The Taimyr district's major rivers are the Yenisei (which drains into the Kara Sea in the west of the region), the Pyasina and the Khatanga. The district is mountainous in the south and in the extreme north and just under one-half of it is forested. It has numerous lakes, the largest being Lake Taimyr. The territory occupies a total area of 862,100 sq km (332,860 sq miles), which is divided into three administrative districts and one city. There are 262 km (163 miles) of paved roads. The climate in the AOk is severe, with snow for an average of 280 days per year. The Taimyr AOk had an estimated population of 44,300 at 1 January 2002. Its population density, therefore, was 0.05 per sq km, one of the lowest of any federal unit. Some 63.6% of the total population inhabited urban areas in

2001. In 1989 some 67.1% of the district's inhabitants were ethnic Russians, 8.8% Dolgans, 8.6% Ukrainians and 4.4% Nenets. The AOk's administrative centre is at Dudinka, its only city, which had a population of 26,700 in 2001.

History

The territory of the Taimyr district was first exploited by Russian settlers in the 17th century. An autonomous okrug was founded on 10 December 1930, as part of Krasnoyarsk Krai. In 1993, following Russian President Boris Yeltsin's forcible dissolution of the Russian parliament and his advice to the federal units, on 18 October the Taimyr District Soviet voted to disband itself and a District Duma was subsequently elected as the legislature. The administration was generally supportive of the federal regime of Boris Yeltsin, but there was also significant popular support for the nationalist Liberal Democratic Party. Tensions arose between Taimyr and Krasnoyarsk Krai, within which it is contained, in addition to being a federal subject in its own right. In October 1997 federal President Boris Yeltsin and first deputy premier Boris Nemtsov signed a power-sharing treaty with the leaders of the Taimyr AOk, Krasnoyarsk Krai and the other autonomous okrug within the Krai, the Evenk AOk. The first of its kind, this treaty clearly delineated authority between the national, krai and okrug authorities, and ensured that some of the wealth generated by the local company Norilsk Nickel, the world's largest producer of nickel, went to pay salaries and other benefits within the Okrug. None the less, the attitudes of Taimyr leaders towards the Krai were variable; the Okrug did not participate in elections to the Krai legislature in 1997 or 2000, although it did participate in the gubernatorial election of the Krai in April 1998. The victor in that election, Aleksandr Lebed, unilaterally cancelled the previous power-sharing agreement in October 1999, fuelling suspicions that he wished the Krai to reimpose greater control over the Okrug. At the gubernatorial election held in the AOk on 28 January 2001, Aleksandr Khloponin, hitherto the General Director of Norilsk Nickel, was elected as Governor, with some 63% of the votes cast, defeating the incumbent Governor, Gennadii Nedelin. Following Khlopanin's election as Governor of Krasnoyarsk Krai (q.v.) in September 2002, he was obliged to resign as Governor of the AOk; elections to this post were scheduled to be held in January 2003.

Economy

As with most of the autonomous okrugs, separate economic data on the Taimyr (Dolgan-Nenets) AOk are scarce, the district being part of Krasnoyarsk Krai. The major ports in the. AOk are Dudinka, Dikson and Khatanga. There is limited transport—only the Dudinka–Norilsk railway line (89 km, or 55 miles, long) operates throughout the year. The district's roads, which total 262 km in length, are concentrated in its more populous areas.

Agricultural production was valued at just 17m. roubles in 2000, mainly provided by fishing, animal husbandry (livestock- and reindeer-breeding) and fur-animal hunting. In that year agriculture employed just 4.5% of the AOk's work-force. There are extensive mineral reserves, however, including those of petroleum and natural gas. The main industries are ore-mining (coal, copper and nickel) and food-processing. In 2000 industry provided employment to some 21.2% of the work-force and produced an output equivalent to 170m. roubles. Norilsk Nickel accounted for some 20% of the world's, and 80% of Russia's, nickel output in the mid-

1990s. The plant also produced 19% of the world's cobalt (70% of Russia's), 42% of the world's platinum (100% of Russia's) and 5% of the world's copper (40% of Russia's). Its activity, however, caused vast environmental damage to its surroundings, in the form of sulphur pollution.

The economically active population numbered 27,000 in 2000, when only 5.7% of the labour force were unemployed. The average monthly wage in the region was some 10,736.2 roubles in mid-2002. The district administrative budget for 2000 showed a surplus of 405.0m. roubles. At the end of 2000 there were no small businesses registered in the Okrug.

Directory

Head of the District Administration (Governor): (vacant); 663210 Krasnoyarsk Krai, Taimyr (Dolgano-Nenets) AOk, Dudinka, ul. Sovetskaya 35; tel. (39111) 2-11-60; fax (39111) 2-52-74.

Chairman of the District Duma: VIKTOR V. SITNOV; 663210 Krasnoyarsk Krai, Taimyr (Dolgano-Nenets) AOk, Dudinka, ul. Sovetskaya 35; tel. (39111) 2-37-37; fax (39111) 2-54-38; e-mail maild@dumatao.krasnoyarsk.su.

Representation of the Taimyr (Dolgan-Nenets) Autonomous Okrug in Krasnoyarsk Krai: Krasnoyarsk.

Chief Representative of the Taimyr (Dolgan-Nenets) Autonomous Okrug in the Russian Federation: OLEG YE. MORGUNOV; Moscow; tel. (095) 120-45-36.

Head of Dudinka City Administration: SERGEI M. MOSHKIN; 663210 Krasnoyarsk Krai, Taimyr (Dolgano-Nenets) AOk, Dudinka, ul. Sovetskaya 35; tel. (39111) 2-13-30; fax (39111) 2-55-52.

Ust-Orda Buryat Autonomous Okrug

The Ust-Orda Buryat Autonomous Okrug (AOk) is situated in the southern part of the Lena-Angara plateau. The district forms part of Irkutsk Oblast and, hence, the Siberian Federal Okrug and the East Siberian Economic Area. It lies to the north of Irkutsk city, west of Lake Baikal. Its major rivers are the Angara and its tributaries, the Osa, the Ida and the Kuda. Most of its terrain is forest-steppe. It occupies an area of 22,400 sq km (8,650 sq miles) and comprises six administrative districts. At 1 January 2002 the estimated population was 142,500 and the population density stood at 6.4 per sq km. In 1992, the last year for which comprehensive demographic statistics were available, just 18.3% of the population of the AOk lived in urban areas. According to the 1989 census, some 56.5% of the population were ethnic Russians and 36.3% were western or Irkutsk Buryats. The capital is at Ust-Ordynskii settlement, which had a population of 13,600 in 2001.

History

The Buryat-Mongol Autonomous Soviet Socialist Republic (BMASSR), created in 1923, was restructured by Stalin (Iosif Dzhugashvili) on 26 September 1937. Anxious to discourage nationalism and links with Mongolia, Stalin had resolved to divide the Buryat peoples administratively. The Ust-Orda Buryat AOk, which represented the four western counties of the BMASSR, was established on the territory of Irkutsk Oblast. The Communist Party of the Russian Federation remained the most popular party in the Legislative Assembly (which replaced the District Soviet in 1994), although the federal Government also had important local supporters. In 1996 the federal President, Boris Yeltsin, had signed an agreement with the AOk's administration on the delimitation of powers between the federal and district authorities. Later that year an independent candidate, Valerii Maleyev, was elected Governor. In October 1999 the Governor of Irkutsk Oblast, Boris Govorin, stated that the AOk (70% of the budget of which consisted of federal transfers) should be re-incorporated into the Oblast proper, as the Oblast provided fuel and other resources to the AOk and there were concerns that Buryat nationalists might seek to unite the three nominally Buryat federal subjects. Maleyev was re-elected Governor in November 2000. In April 2001 Leonid Khutanov, the Chairman of the District Duma since 1994, was elected as the representative of the AOk to the Federation Council, the upper chamber of the federal parliament. During the early 2000s proposals to unite the Ust-Orda Buryat AOk and Irkutsk Oblast became increasingly popular and appeared to be supported by the authorities in both the AOk and the Oblast; moreover, in September 2002 the Chairman of the Federation Council, Sergei Mironov, stated that the two federal subjects already possessed the necessary preconditions for becoming a single unit.

Economy

Statistical information for Irkutsk Oblast generally includes data on the Ust-Orda Buryat AOk, so separate figures are limited. In 2000 there were 2,189 km (1,360 miles) of paved roads on the AOk's territory.

The district's agriculture consists mainly of grain production and animal husbandry. In 2000 some 56.5% of the AOk's working population was engaged in agriculture (by far the highest proportion of any federal subject), and production in that year was valued at 2,337m. roubles. Its main industries are the processing of agricultural and forestry products, the production of coal and gypsum, machine-building, metal-working, and the manufacture of building materials. Industry generated 281m. roubles in 2000 and employed just 5.9% of the work-force.

The economically active population numbered 67,000 in 2000, when 8.9% of the labour force were unemployed. In mid-2002 the average monthly wage was just 2,336.7 roubles. There was a budgetary surplus of 24.6m. roubles in 2000. In that year there were around 100 small businesses registered in the Okrug.

Directory

Head of the District Administration: VALERII G. MALEYEV; 666110 Irkutsk obl., Ust-Orda Buryat AOk, pos. Ust-Ordynskii, ul. Lenina 18; tel. (39541) 2-10-62; fax (39541) 2-25-93.

Chairman of the District Duma: ALEKSEI KHORINOYEV; 666110 Irkutsk obl., Ust-Orda Buryat AOk, pos. Ust-Ordynskii, ul. Lenina 18; tel. (39541) 2-16-87; fax (39541) 2-26-71.

Chief Representative of the Ust-Orda Buryat Autonomous Okrug in Irkutsk Oblast: NIKOLAI M. DOBRYNIN; 626002 Tyumen, ul. Komsomolskaya 37; tel. (3452) 46-67-79; fax (3452) 46-00-91; e-mail hmaoda@tmn.ru.

Chief Representative of the Ust-Orda Buryat Autonomous Okrug in the Russian Federation: OLEG B. BATOROV; 127025 Moscow, ul. Novyi Arbat 19; tel. and fax (095) 203-64-04.

Yamal-Nenets Autonomous Okrug

The Yamal-Nenets Autonomous Okrug (AOk) is situated on the Western Siberian Plain on the lower reaches of the Ob river. It forms part of Tyumen Oblast and, therefore, the Urals Federal Okrug and the West Siberian Economic Area. The territory lies on the Asian side of the Ural Mountains and has a deeply indented northern coastline, the western section, the Yamal Peninsula, being separated from the eastern section by the Ob bay. The rest of Tyumen Oblast, including the Khanty-Mansii AOk, lies to the south. To the west lie the Nenets AOk (part of Archangel Oblast) and the Republic of Komi, to the east Krasnoyarsk Krai (including the Taimyr AOk in the north-west). Apart from the Ob, the Yamal-Nenets district's major rivers are the Nadym, the Taz and the Pur. Around one-10th of its area is forested. The territory of the Yamal-Nenets AOk occupies 750,300 sq km (289,690 sq miles). It comprises seven administrative districts and seven cities. It had an estimated total population (at 1 January 2002) of 508,900 inhabitants, and a population density of 0.7 per sq km. In 2001 some 82.6% of the population inhabited urban areas. In the 1989 census, ethnic Russians represented some 59.3% of the population, Ukrainians 17.2% and Tatars 5.3%, while Nenets represented just 4.2%, although the proportion of Nenets was thought to have increased subsequently. The district administrative centre is at Salekhard, which had a population of 34,100 in January 2001. Its other major cities are Noyabrsk (97,800) and Novyi Urengoi (91,600).

History

The Nenets were traditionally a nomadic people, who were totally dominated by Russia from the early 17th century. The Yamal-Nenets AOk was formed on 10

December 1930. Environmental concerns provoked protests in the 1980s and 1990s, and prompted the local authorities (consisting of an administration and, from 1994, an elected Duma) to seek greater control over natural resources and their exploitation. The main dispute was with the central Tyumen Oblast authorities (more pro-communist than the AOk's own), and the AOk's rejection of oblast legislation on petroleum and natural gas exploitation first reached the Constitutional Court during 1996. Constitutional tensions between the two AOks contained within Tyumen Oblast, and the authorities of the Oblast proper, continued throughout the 1990s. The economic importance of the fuel industry in Yamal-Nenets was reflected in the AOk's political situation. Viktor Chernomyrdin, the leader of Our Home Is Russia and the former Chairman of the federal Government, was elected to the State Duma as a representative of Yamal-Nenets in 1998, and he retained his seat until his appointment as Russia's ambassador to Ukraine in May 2001. He had previously been head of the domestic gas monopoly, Gazprom, the largest employer in the AOk, and in the Duma became head of an inter-factionary group of deputies, Energiya (Energy). Moreover, in early 2000 the Governor of the AOk, Yurii Neyelov, was considered for a directorship at Gazprom; he retained his post in the gubernatorial election of 26 March 2000, securing some 90% of the votes cast.

Economy

Few statistical indicators are available as distinct from those for Tyumen Oblast in general. Agriculture, which in 2000 employed just 1.4% of the work-force in the Yamal-Nenets AOk consists mainly of fishing, reindeer-breeding (reindeer pasture occupies just under one-third of its territory), fur-farming and fur-animal hunting. Total agricultural production amounted to a value of just 244m. roubles in 2000. The AOk's main industries are the production of natural gas and petroleum and the production of electricity. In 2000 the industrial sector employed 21.8% of the work-force and generated a total of some 75,784m. roubles, a considerably larger amount than that generated by many oblasts or republics in the Russian Federation. The potential wealth of the district generated foreign interest. In January 1997 a loan of US $2,500m. to Gazprom was agreed by the Dresdner Bank group (of Germany), to support construction of the 4,200-km (2,610-mile) Jagal pipeline from the Autonomous Okrug to Frankfurt-an-der-Oder on the German border with Poland. This was to be the world's largest gas-transport project and was expected to be fully operational by 2005.

The economically active population numbered 303,000 in 2000, when 7.9% of the labour force were unemployed. In 2000 the district government budget showed a deficit of 384.7m. roubles. These statistics, like the high average monthly wage of 15,374.2 roubles (the highest in the Russian Federation) in mid-2002, have far more in common with those of the Khanty-Mansii AOk than those of the Tyumen Oblast as a whole. The Okrug has also been successful in attracting foreign investment, receiving US $102.9m. in 2000. No separate details for external trade are available, although it was believed to be substantial. At 31 December 2000 there were 2,600 small businesses registered in the Yamal-Nenets Autonomous Okrug.

Directory

Governor: YURII V. NEYELOV; 626608 Tyumen obl., Yamal-Nenets AOk, Salek-hard, ul. Respubliki 72; tel. (34922) 4-46-02; fax (34922) 4-52-89; internet www .yamal.ru.

Chairman of the District Duma: SERGEI N. KHARYUCHI; 629000 Tyumen obl., Yamal-Nenets AOk, Salekhard, ul. Respublika 72; tel. and fax (34591) 4-51-51.

Representation of the Yamal-Nenets Autonomous Okrug in Tyumen Oblast: Tyumen.

Chief Representative of Yamal-Nenets Autonomous Okrug in the Russian Federation: NIKOLAI A. BORODULIN; 101000 Moscow, per. Arkhangelskii 15/3; tel. (095) 924-67-89; fax (095) 925-83-38

Head of Salekhard City Administration: ALEKSANDR M. SPIRIN; 629000 Tyumen obl., Yamal-Nenets AOk, Salekhard, ul. Respubliki 72; tel. (34922) 4-50-67; fax (34922) 4-01-82; e-mail press@ytc.ru.

KRASNOYARSK KRAI

ARCHANGEL OBLAST

TYUMEN OBLAST

PART THREE
Select Bibliography

Select Bibliography

Alekseev, M. A., (Ed.). *Centre–Periphery Conflict in Post-Soviet Russia: A Federation Imperilled*. Basingstoke, Macmillan, 1999.

Bahry, D. *Outside Moscow: Power, Politics and Budgetary Policy in the Soviet Republics*. New York, NY, Columbia University Press, 1987.

Bassin, M. *Imperial Visions: Nationalist Imagination and Geographical Expansion in the Russian Far East*. Cambridge, Cambridge University Press, 1999.

Baxendale, J., Dewar, S., and Gowan, D. *The EU and Kaliningrad: Kaliningrad and the Impact of EU Enlargement*. London, Kogan Page, 2000.

Blum, D., (Ed.). *Russia's Future: Consolidation of Disintegration*. Oxford, Westview, 1994.

Bradshaw, M. J. *Regional Patterns of Foreign Investment in Russia*. London, Royal Institute of International Affairs, 1995.

   The Russian Far East. London, Royal Institute of International Affairs, 1999.

Bradshaw, M. J., (Ed.). *The Soviet Union: A New Regional Geography?* London, Belhaven Press, 1991.

   The Russian Far East and Pacific Asia. Richmond, Curzon Press, 2001.

Bukharayev, Ravil. *The Model of Tatarstan: Under Mintimer Shaimiyev*. Richmond, Curzon Press, 2001.

Centre for Co-operation with Non-members. *A Regional Approach to Industrial Restructuring in the Tomsk Region*. Paris, Organisation for Economic Co-operation and Development, 1998.

Chenciner, R., (Ed.). *Daghestan: Tradition and Survival*. London, Caucasus World, 1997.

Colton, T. *Moscow: Governing the Socialist Metropolis*. Cambridge, MA, Harvard University Press, 1995.

Dellenbrant, J. A. *The Soviet Regional Dilemma: Planning, People and Natural Resources*. London, M. E. Sharpe, 1986.

Dolkinskaya, I. *Transition and Regional Inequality in Russia: Reorganization or Procrastination?* Washington, DC, IMF, 2002.

Easter, G. M. *Reconstructing the State: Personal Networks and Elite Identity in Soviet Russia*. Cambridge, Cambridge University Press, 2000.

Fairlie, L. D., and Sergounin, A. *Are Borders Barriers? EU Enlargement and the Russian Region of Kaliningrad*. Helsinki, Finnish Institute of International Affairs, 2001.

Forsyth, J. *A History of the Peoples of Siberia*. Cambridge, Cambridge University Press, 1994.

Fowkes, B. *Russia and Chechnia: The Permanent Crisis*. Basingstoke, Macmillan, 1998.

Freinkman, L. *Subnational Budgeting in Russia*. Washington, DC, World Bank, 2000.

Friedgut, T. H., and Hahn, J. W., (Eds). *Local Power and Post-Soviet Politics*. Armonk, NY, M. E. Sharpe, 1995.

Gall, C., and de Waal, T. *Chechnya: Calamity in the Caucasus.* New York, NY, New York University Press, 1998.

Gibson, J., and Hanson, P., (Eds). *Transformation from Below: Local Power and the Political Economy of Post-Communist Transitions.* Cheltenham, Edward Elgar, 1996.

Glatter, P. *Tyumen: The West Siberian Oil and Gas Province.* London, Royal Institute of International Affairs, 1997.

Grant, B., and Pika, A., (Ed.). *Neotraditionalism in the Russian North.* Washington, DC, University of Washington Press, 1999.

Hahn, J., (Ed.). *Democratization in Russia: The Development of Legislative Institutions.* Armonk, NY, M. E. Sharpe, 1996.

   Regional Russia in Transformation. Washington, DC, Woodrow Wilson Center Press, 2001.

Hanson, P. *Regions, Local Power and Economic Change in Russia.* London, Royal Institute of International Affairs, 1994.

Hanson, P., and Bradshaw, M. J., (Eds). *Regional Economic Change in Russia.* Cheltenham, Edward Elgar, 2000.

Hill, F. *Russia's Tinderbox: Conflict in the North Caucasus and its Implications for the Future of the Russian Federation.* Cambridge, MA, Harvard University Press, 1995.

Human Rights Watch. *Russia, the Ingush–Ossetian Conflict in the Prigordnyi Region.* New York, NY, Human Rights Watch, 1996.

Huskey, E. *Presidential Power in Russia.* Armonk, NY, M. E. Sharpe, 1999.

Jacobs, E. M., (Ed.). *Soviet Local Politics and Government.* London, HarperCollins, 1983.

Jaimoukha, A. *The Circassians.* London, Caucasus World, 2001.

Joenniemi, P., and Prawitz, J. *Kaliningrad: The European Amber Region.* Aldershot, Ashgate, 1998.

Kirkow, P. *Russia's Provinces: Authoritarian Transformation versus Local Autonomy.* London, Macmillan, and New York, NY, St Martin's Press, 1998.

Kondrashev, S. *Nationalism and the Drive for Sovereignty in Tatarstan, 1988–92: Origins and Development (Studies in Diplomacy).* New York, NY, St Martin's Press, 1999.

Koropeckyi, I. S., and Schroeder, G. E., (Eds). *Economics of Soviet Regions.* New York, NY, Praeger, 1981.

Kotkin, S., and Wolff, D., (Eds). *Rediscovering Russia in Asia: Siberia and the Russian Far East.* New York, NY, M. E. Sharpe, 1995.

Krickus, R. J. *The Kaliningrad Question.* Lanham, MD, Rowman and Littlefield, 2002.

Lapidus, G. W., (Ed.). *The New Russia: Troubled Transformation.* Boulder, CO, Westview, 1995.

Lavrov, A. M., Makushkin, A. G., *et al. The Fiscal Structure of the Russian Federation: Financial Flows between the Centre and the Regions.* Armonk, NY, M. E. Sharpe, 2001.

Lieven, A. *Chechnya: Tombstone of Russian Power.* New Haven, CT, Yale University Press, 1998.

Lincoln, W. B. *The Conquest of a Continent: Siberia and the Russians.* New York, NY, Random House, 1994.

McAuley, M. *Russia's Politics of Uncertainty.* Cambridge, Cambridge University Press, 1997.

Mandelstam Balzer, M. *The Tenacity of Ethnicity.* Princeton, NJ, Princeton University Press, 1999.

Manezhev, S. A. *Russian Far East.* London, Royal Institute of International Affairs, 1993.

Melvin, N. *Regional Foreign Policies in the Russian Federation.* London, Royal Institute of International Affairs, 1995.

Minakir, P. A., and Freeze, G. L., (Eds). *The Russian Far East: An Economic Handbook.* Armonk, NY, M. E. Sharpe, 1994.

Moses, J. C. *Regional Party Leadership and Policy-Making in the USSR.* London, Praeger, 1974.

Mote, V. L. *Siberia.* Boulder, CO, Westview, 1998.

Murray, W. E., and Bradshaw, M. J. *Rising Tensions in the Natural Resource Market of Pacific Asia and the Role of the Russian Far East.* Birmingham, University of Birmingham, 1997.

Orttung, R. *From Leningrad to St Petersburg: Democratization in a Russian City.* New York, NY, St Martin's Press, 1995.

Orttung, R., (Ed.). *The Republics and Regions of the Russian Federation.* Armonk, NY, M. E. Sharpe, 2000.

Rigby, T. H. *Political Elites in the USSR: Central Leaders and Local Cadres from Lenin to Gorbachev.* Aldershot, Edward Elgar, 1990.

Rorlich, A.-A. *The Volga Tatars: A Profile in National Resilience.* Stanford, CA, Hoover Institution Press, 1986.

Ross, C. *Local Government in the Soviet Union: Problems of Implementation and Control.* London, Croom Helm, 1987.

Ruble, B. *Leningrad: Shaping a City.* Berkeley, CA, University of California Press, 1990.

Rutland, P. *The Politics of Economic Stagnation in the Soviet Union: The Role of Local Party Organs in Economic Management.* Cambridge, Cambridge University Press, 1993.

Scalapino, R. A., and Akaha, T., (Ed.). *Politics and Economics in the Russian Far East.* London, Routledge, 1997.

Schiffer, J. R. *Soviet Regional Economic Policy: The East–West Debate over Pacific Siberian Development.* London, Macmillan, 1989

Seely, R. *The Russo-Chechen Conflict 1800–2000.* London, Frank Cass, 2001.

Segbers, K. *Explaining Post-Soviet Patchworks Vol. 3: The Political Economy of Regions, Regimes and Republics.* Aldershot, Ashgate, 2001.

Smith, G., (Ed.). *The Nationalities Question in the Soviet Union,* 2nd edn. London, Longman, 1996.

Smith, S. *Allah's Mountains: The Battle for Chechnya.* London, I. B. Tauris, 2000.

Stephan, J. J. *The Russian Far East: A History.* Stanford, CA, Stanford University Press, 1996.

Stavrakis, P. J., de Bardeleben, J., and Black, L., (Eds). *Beyond the Monolith: The Emergence of Regionalism in Post-Soviet Russia.* Washington, DC, Woodrow Wilson Press Centre and John Hopkins Press, 1997.

Stoner-Weiss, K. *Local Heroes: The Political Economy of Russian Regional Governance.* Princeton, NJ, Princeton University Press, 1997.

Thornton, J., (Ed.) *Russia's Far East: A Region at Risk.* Seattle, WA, University of Washington Press, 2002.

Thubron, C. *In Siberia.* London, Penguin, 2000.

Tichotsky, J. *Russia's Diamond Colony.* Reading, Gordon & Breach, 2000.

Valencia, M. *The Russian Far East in Transition: Opportunities for Regional Economic Co-operation.* Boulder, CO, Westview, 1995.

Wallich, C. I., (Ed.). *Russia and the Challenge of Fiscal Federalism.* Washington, DC, World Bank, 1994.

Weinberg, R. *Stalin's Forgotten Zion: Birobidzhan and the Making of a Soviet Jewish Homeland.* Berkeley, CA, University of California Press, 1998.

Wood, A, and French, R. A., (Eds). *The Development of Siberia: People and Resources.* London, Macmillan, 1989.

Zelkina, A. *The Chechens.* London, Caucasus World, 2001.

PART FOUR
Indexes

Alphabetic List of Territories

(including a gazetteer of alternative names)

45	Adygeya	*Republic*
	Aga-Buryat AOk	*see Chita*
	Alaniya	*see North Osetiya*
121	Altai	Krai
48	Altai	Republic
139	Amur	Oblast
142	Archangel	Oblast
295	Nenets AOk (Nenets Republic)	Autonomous Okrug
145	Astrakhan	Oblast
	Balkariya	*see Kabardino-Balkariya*
	Bashkiriya	*see Bashkortostan*
52	Bashkortostan	Autonomous Republic
148	Belgorod	Oblast
	Birobidzhan	*see Khabarovsk (Jewish AO)*
150	Bryansk	Oblast
56	Buryatiya	Autonomous Republic
	Chechen Republic	*see Chechnya (Chechen Republic of Ichkeriya)*
	Chechen-Ingush ASSR	*see Chechnya (Chechen Republic of Ichkeriya) or Ingushetiya*
60	Chechnya (Chechen Republic of Ichkeriya)	Autonomous Republic
152	Chelyabinsk	Oblast
	Cherkessiya	*see Stavropol (Karachayevo-Cherkessiya)*
155	Chita	Oblast
279	Aga-Buryat AOk	Autonomous Okrug
	Chkalov	*see Orenburg*
282	Chukchi AOk	*see Chukot*
	Chukot (Chukotka) AOk	Autonomous Okrug
66	Chuvash Republic (Chuvashiya)	Autonomous Republic
	Circassia (Cherkessiya)	*see Stavropol (Karachayevo-Cherkessiya)*
69	Dagestan	Autonomous Republic
	Dolgan-Nenets AOk	*see Krasnoyarsk (Taimyr AOk)*
	East Vogul AOk	*see Tyumen (Khanty-Mansii AOk)*
	Evenk AOk	*see Krasnoyarsk*
	Far Eastern Republic	*see Chita Oblast, etc.*
	Gorkii	*see Nizhnii Novgorod*
	Gorno-Altai AO	*see Altai (Republic)*
	Gorskaya People's Republic	*see Kabardino-Balkariya, etc.*
	Ichkeriya	*see Chechnya*
	Ingodinskoye Zirnove	*see Chita*
73	Ingushetiya	Autonomous Republic
158	Irkutsk	Oblast
301	Ust-Orda Buryat AOk	Autonomous Okrug
161	Ivanovo	Oblast
276	Jewish AO (Birobidzhan)	Autonomous Oblast
77	Kabardino-Balkar (Kabardino-Balkariya) . .	Autonomous Republic
	Kabardiya	*see Kabardino-Balkariya*
	Kalinin	*see Tver*
163	Kaliningrad	Oblast
81	Kalmykiya	Autonomous Republic
166	Kaluga	Oblast
168	Kamchatka	Oblast
293	Koryak AOk	Autonomous Okrug

Federal Okrugs

Economic Areas

Central

Bryansk Oblast	150
Ivanovo Oblast	161
Kaluga Oblast	166
Kostroma Oblast	177
Moscow City	269
Moscow Oblast	191
Orel Oblast	210
Ryazan Oblast	227
Smolensk Oblast	238
Tula Oblast	247
Tver Oblast	250
Vladimir Oblast	258
Yaroslavl Oblast	267

Central Chernozem

Belgorod Oblast	148
Kursk Oblast	181
Lipetsk Oblast	186
Tambov Oblast	243
Voronezh Oblast	265

East Siberia

Buryatiya (Republic)	56
Chita Oblast	155
Aga-Buryat AOk	279
Irkutsk Oblast	158
Ust-Orda Buryat AOk	301
Khakasiya (Republic)	91
Krasnoyarsk Krai	130
Evenk AOk	285
Taimyr (Dolgan-Nenets) AOk . .	298
Tyva (Republic)	115

Far East

Amur Oblast	139
Chukot AOk	282
Jewish (Birobidzhan) AO . . .	276
Kamchatka Oblast	168
Koryak AOk	293
Khabarovsk Krai	124
Magadan Oblast	188
Maritime (Primorskii) Krai . .	133
Sakha—Yakutiya (Republic) . .	107
Sakhalin Oblast	229

North Caucasus

Adygeya (Republic)	45
Chechnya (Republic)—Chechen	
Republic of Ichkeriya . . .	60
Dagestan (Republic)	69
Ingushetiya (Republic) . . .	73
Kabardino-Balkar Republic	
(Kabardino-Balkariya) . . .	77
Karachayevo-Cherkessiya (Republic)	85
Krasnodar Krai	127

North Osetiya (Republic) . . . 103

North Osetiya (Republic) . . .	103
Rostov Oblast	224
Stavropol Krai	136

North

Archangel Oblast	142
Nenets AOk	295
Kareliya (Republic)	88
Komi (Republic)	94
Murmansk Oblast	194
Vologda Oblast	263

North-West

Leningrad Oblast	183
Novgorod Oblast	201
Pskov Oblast	221
St Petersburg Federal City . . .	273
and (usually) Kaliningrad Oblast . .	163

Urals

Bashkortostan (Republic) . . .	52
Chelyabinsk Oblast	152
Kurgan Oblast	179
Orenburg Oblast	213
Perm Oblast	218
Komi-Permyak AOk	291
Sverdlovsk Oblast	240
Udmurt Republic (Udmurtiya) . .	118

Volga

Astrakhan Oblast	145
Kalmykiya (Republic)	81
Penza Oblast	216
Samara Oblast	233
Saratov Oblast	236
Tatarstan (Republic)	111
Ulyanovsk Oblast	256
Volgograd Oblast	260

Volga-Vyatka

Chuvash Republic (Chuvashiya) . .	66
Kirov (Vyatka) Oblast	174
Marii-El (Republic)	97
Mordoviya (Republic)	100
Nizhnii Novgorod Oblast . . .	197

West Siberia

Altai Krai	121
Altai (Republic)	48
Kemerovo Oblast	171
Novosibirsk Oblast	204
Omsk Oblast	207
Tomsk Oblast	245
Tyumen Oblast	253
Khanty-Mansii AOk	288
Yamal-Nenets AOk	303

*For Product Safety Concerns and Information please contact
our EU representative GPSR@taylorandfrancis.com Taylor & Francis
Verlag GmbH, Kaufingerstraße 24, 80331 München, Germany*

T - #0015 - 270225 - C0 - 234/156/18 [20] - CB - 9781857431919 - Gloss Lamination